BUILDING A HEAVEN
ON EARTH

BUILDING A HEAVEN ON EARTH

Religion, Activism, and Protest
in Japanese-Occupied Korea

Albert L. Park

University of Hawai'i Press

HONOLULU

© 2015 University of Hawai'i Press
All rights reserved
Printed in the United States of America

20 19 18 17 16 15   6 5 4 3 2 1

Library of Congress Cataloging-in-Publication Data

Park, Albert L., author.
    Building a heaven on earth : religion, activism, and protest in
Japanese occupied Korea / Albert L. Park.
          pages cm
    Includes bibliographical references and index.
    ISBN 978-0-8248-3965-9
    1. Religion and sociology—Korea—History—20th century.
    2. Peasants—Religious life—Korea—History—20th century.
    3. Korea—History—Japanese occupation, 1910–1945.   I. Title.
    BL2233.P37 2014
    261.809519'09041—dc23

                                                              2014014763

University of Hawai'i Press books are printed on acid-free
paper and meet the guidelines for permanence and
durability of the Council on Library Resources.

Designed by Erika Arroyo

Printed by Sheridan Books, Inc.

In Memory of Andrew Park (1995–2012)

CONTENTS

ACKNOWLEDGMENTS

ᠵᢈᢦ

For me, writing a book has been a long, arduous, and challenging process that has been sustained only through the support and encouragement of mentors, colleagues, friends, and family. The germination of this book project occurred at the University of Chicago, where my faculty advisers helped me every step of the way on how to become a passionate and imaginative historian. I cannot thank Bruce Cumings enough for being such a compassionate mentor who taught me to study history with conviction and as a means to solve serious problems in the present world. Since the time he supervised my undergraduate thesis at Northwestern University, his scholarship has been a continuous source of intellectual inspiration. Above all, his friendship has helped me negotiate the complex world of academia and face any issues with confidence. I also especially want to thank Tetsuo Najita and James Ketelaar for teaching me the value of intellectual history and the power of ideas to cause social change. I am grateful to William H. Sewell Jr. for introducing me to critical theory and explaining difficult concepts in simple ways.

My cohorts at the University of Chicago have been an invaluable source of support, the best sounding board to test ideas, and the push behind my intellectual growth. Kornel Chang, Chong-Myong Im, and Mikael Wolfe have been warm sources of encouragement who helped me make sense of my rambling ideas. Michael Shin's intellectual rigor and work ethic have been valuable models for my own scholarship, and I am extremely grateful to him for supporting my academic career from its earliest stages. Suzy Kim deserves special thanks because she has been a caring friend who not only has given invaluable comments on almost all my work in the midst of her busy life but has also continuously encouraged me to think boldly. Namhee Lee's advice and help have made me into a better thinker and enhanced my scholarship, while Charles Armstrong, Robert Oppenheimer, and Theodore Jun Yoo have been tremendous in providing valuable advice and resources.

I am fortunate to have supportive colleagues at the Claremont Colleges. Angelina Chin, Arash Khazeni, and Samuel Yamashita at Pomona College have always helped me refine my ideas through reading groups and discussions over coffee and meals. Gaston Espinoza (Claremont McKenna College) helped me articulate the key points of my study and generously came up with the title of this book. The Department of History at Claremont McKenna College is a collection of outstanding and caring scholars and teachers. I especially want to thank Gary Hamburg, Nita Kumar, Arthur Rosenbaum, and Diana Selig for reading parts of my book manuscript and Jonathan Petropoulos for his wise counsel as I searched for a publisher for this book. David K. Yoo, who was my department mentor at Claremont McKenna and is now the director of Asian-American Studies at UCLA, has been an outstanding role model and friend. I am extremely fortunate to have learned from him how to stay steady and optimistic as an academic.

This book benefited tremendously from the insights and advice of various scholars. John Duncan, Tak Fujitani, Serk-bae Suh, and Ken Wells read the entire book manuscript or key chapters, and their suggestions vastly improved the book's arguments and their presentation. The book went in new and exciting directions after Emily Anderson kindly shared her work on Japanese Christian missionaries in colonial Korea, and George Kallander helped me avoid any serious misinterpretations of Tonghak thought through our informative conversations. I also want to thank Paul Chang, Lisa Kim Davis, Ken Kawashima, Gene Park, Ann Sherif, and Len Smith for showing me different ways to study history and sharing their belief in the book project.

Scholars in Korea have played pivotal roles both in helping me obtain invaluable historical resources and in providing critical feedback on my work. Not only has Kim Dong-no's work pushed the boundaries of my own work, but he has always generously arranged space for me to work at Yonsei University, especially providing me with an extremely comfortable office in the Institute for State Governance Studies in 2010–2011. Both Hong Song-chan and the late Pang Kie-chung introduced me to an exciting way of studying Korean history and have shared their wisdom over meals and classroom discussions. I was very fortunate to have received feedback on the book during its early stages from Professor Pang before he passed away. Finally, Chung Kyu-sik, Chang Shin, Pak Hyon, and Park Yun-jae went out of their way to share valuable resources with me.

I have been extremely fortunate to have the opportunity to present my work and receive feedback at several institutions: Chonnam University, Cornell University, Robinson College at Cambridge University, Seoul National University, UCLA, the University of California–Berkeley, the University of Michigan–Ann Arbor, and the University of Southern California (especially the Rising Star Workshop 2010). This book project has been generously supported by the Dean of Faculty Office at Claremont McKenna College, Fulbright Hays (Doctoral Dissertation Research Abroad) and Fulbright Hays

(Faculty Research Abroad), the Henry Luce Foundation, and the Korea Foundation.

I am especially grateful to my editor, Masako Ikeda, for her help. She has been a firm believer in my work since I first presented her my book. Not only has she efficiently overseen my coedited book, but she has also diligently and swiftly guided this book through the complex review and editing process. This book would not have come to fruition without her work and support. I also want to thank Hannah Lim for carefully going over the romanization of Korean words.

My family has been the biggest supporter of my work. I want to thank my family in South Korea, especially Injung, for always taking care of me and later my wife and daughter when visiting Korea. Words cannot express how much I appreciate the love and support from my mother and father. From early on, when they cultivated my love for history by buying history books and cards for me, to their financial support for undergraduate, graduate, and language work, they have always believed in me and have had confidence that I will succeed in everything. This book is a result of their love and unending help. I especially want to thank my nephew, Andrew Park, who sadly passed away before the publication of this book after a heroic fight against cancer. Andrew was a quiet teenager who showed me how to endure and persevere through the toughest challenges and enjoy every moment of daily life. For me, his love and care for others, even when he was extremely ill, have been models for living each day. Andrew, I miss you dearly.

My greatest thanks go to my daughter, Margot, and my partner and wife, Jennifer. Margot's unconditional love, infectious smile, and wonderful imagination have sustained me over the past three years of writing this book. I especially want to thank her for being such a great sleeper, which allowed me to write a great deal of this book in the evening. Jennifer has been my biggest supporter since we first met at the University of Chicago. She not only has patiently read and commented on the entire manuscript but has also been a wonderful therapist who has kept me sane throughout writing this book. Her love for me has given me the power and freedom to think and act boldly with confidence. She has been the loving, compassionate, and wise anchor in my life, and I therefore dedicate this book to her.

Introduction

When John H. Reisner, an expert on agriculture from Nanking University who conducted an extensive survey of the Korean agricultural economy in 1926, asked a "very respected and careful Korean thinker" what the present economic situation in colonial Korea was, the intellectual spoke of "economic difficulties" that had resulted from rupturing changes between the past and present:

> Before the coming of Japan, Korean society was divided into four principal groups, the scholar, the farmer, the artisan and the merchant. Life was lived simply and each group had definite sources of livelihood. In recent years the scholar has been displaced from the schools he used to teach and from the official positions to which scholarly attainments led. The farmer is suffering because he is being forced to let go of his land under conditions over which he has no control or knows not how to control. The artisan is unable to compete with modern industrial enterprises and the merchants are likewise unable to compete with the modern developments.[1]

These readjustments in the lives of Koreans, according to Reisner, were "much to their disadvantage and loss" and were spurred on by "Japanese competition" and Japanese colonialism in Korea (1910–1945). All aspects of society underwent significant economic transformation, but Reisner's report stressed that Koreans believed that the most distressing issues facing their country were issues centered on land or the vast problems in the agrarian economy.[2]

What caused Reisner and many Koreans to become worried over the state of affairs in rural Korea was the impact of capitalist development on rural conditions and peasant life. Under its design for a model political economy, the Japanese colonial government had pushed forward numerous reforms, such as the cadastral land survey (1910–1918) and programs to increase agricultural production, like the Thirty-Year Plan in 1920, which fundamentally reshaped the

1

agricultural and overall market economy in Korea and caused vast dislocations and conflicts in the countryside. The transforming capitalist economy had reconfigured the setting for work and life as it introduced challenges that led to new forms of poverty and eroded valuable customs and institutions that had long governed social relationships and anchored localities. Refusing to be idle in the face of such changes, a significant number of peasants fought to create new spaces of stability. This led to a series of conflicts with Korean landlords that jeopardized any hope for a united front against Japanese colonialism. Nationalist groups recognized that because most of the population lived in the countryside, it was imperative for them to settle rural problems through movements in order to materialize their visions of a modern nation-state. Resolving the land issue and combating peasant poverty quickly became leading issues in these movements.

At the same time rural Korea was undergoing significant transformation, an article in the July 1926 issue of *Sinin'gan* declared that an antireligion movement had erupted throughout the world and was now "starting to emerge in Chosŏn" (Korea).[3] Although religions had been celebrated as a source of relief and comfort during the decline of the Chosŏn state in the late nineteenth century and the first decade of colonial rule, criticisms of religion and calls for its destruction appeared widely in newspapers and magazines by the middle of the 1920s. The expression of antireligious messages quickly transitioned from discourse to concrete movements where men and women, mostly young, organized to attack and discredit religion and limit its influence in Koreans' everyday lives. To break the hold religion had on the consciousness of Koreans, protesters frequently voiced their opposition both inside and outside religious institutions. In fact, Protestant Christian leaders reported that "sometimes a youth will rise during a preaching service and, interrupting the sermon, launch out in a tirade against the 'Faith.'"[4] Although protests through print and movements on the ground diminished somewhat in the late 1920s, they continued into the 1930s to the extent that in 1932, Han Yong-un, a leading Buddhist monk, declared that the antireligion movement had become a serious social problem.[5]

More than a coincidence, the transformation of rural society and the rise of an antireligion movement were connected. Although antireligion protests were dismissed by numerous religious leaders as the rants of those controlled by leftist ideology, they were the result of Koreans' attempts to find appropriate language that described and made sense of the vast ideological, material, and structural transformations caused by forces in society, particularly capitalist development, that ruptured lives inside and outside rural Korea from 1920 to 1937. The unrest against religion stemmed from the belief that religious organizations cared only about spiritual matters and paid no attention to the economic, social, and cultural problems that were causing poverty in lives and instability in communities despite their influence and power in society. This book studies the religious community's response to these vast material and ideological developments in colonial society through an examination of the origins of faith-based social movements in Japanese-occupied Korea (1910–1945) in institutions that used religion as a vehicle to question the established norms of modernity, pursue social change, and promote the achievement of political, economic, and social justice. Exploring the dynamic relationship among religion, modernity, and colonialism, this study, in particular, focuses on the pursuit by the rural movements of the Young Men's Christian Association (YMCA), the Presbyterian Church, and Ch'ŏndogyo to create a heavenly kingdom on earth anchored in religion, agriculture, and a pastoral life. This book shows that in designing and carrying out spiritually based social movements in response to modernization under colonialism, these three institutions established discursive and material frameworks that afforded new forms of agency,[6] social organization, and the nation, which served as the basis of an alternative vision of modernity. In so doing, this book explains how these three rural movements laid down a path to modernity that promoted social activism, tested the boundaries of colonialism, and established the foundation for religious social movements in South Korea.

As a form of intellectual history, *Building a Heaven on Earth* grounds the rise of faith-based social movements during the colonial period in two categories: modern (modernity) and modernization. To help readers understand how these categories are used in this study, this introduction carefully lays out the meaning of the terms "modern" and "modernization" and discusses the relationship between this study and the field of colonial modernity in Korean studies. As a category for analyzing events, developments, and trends from 1910 to 1945 in Korea, colonial modernity has helped problematize "modern" and "modernization" and has introduced a nuanced way to examine the colonial period. But despite enabling deep and broad forms of analysis, colonial modernity has certain limitations that prevent a full representation of the complex experiences of life shaped by rupturing political, economic, and social forces. The inattentive focus on the political economy of the colonial period and the narrow definition of "modern" in the field of colonial modernity, in particular, have led to erroneous characterizations of groups, movements, and trends, including the interpretation of the YMCA, Presbyterian, and Ch'ŏndogyo rural campaigns as movements against modernity. By linking modernity to religion and agriculture, this study seeks to expand the category of colonial modernity and clarify the relationship between religion and modernization.

Modern

The YMCA, Presbyterian, and Ch'ŏndogyo rural movements formed in response to the rise of the modern period in Korea. Since the late nineteenth
century, defining the modern and locating its origins have been contentious
processes. On the one hand, theory-based modernization studies have argued
that reforms carried out by Japanese colonialism produced fundamental
changes that enabled Korea to become modern.[7] Known as the "modernizing
camp," these studies point out, for example, that capitalism in Korea originated
under colonial rule and that Western-style educational and health programs,
which had been introduced by the Japanese, contributed to the advancement
of Korean lives.[8] Stopping short of condoning colonialism, these studies nevertheless emphasize that Korea could not have reformed on its own and point
to the Japanese as bringing progress to Koreans. On the other hand, studies
written mostly by Korean scholars—known as "nationalist" studies—have argued that colonialism exploited the resources of Korea for the benefit of the
Japanese empire.[9] According to these studies, late Chosŏn society had shown
signs of becoming modern. Japanese colonialism, however, suppressed and delayed Korea's inherent process of becoming modern through policies and reforms that caused violent economic and social contradictions.

Resolving this debate between the modernizing and nationalist camps over
the origins and significance of the modern in Korean history has been extremely challenging because both sides give "modern" normative meaning and
value. This trend by scholars of Korean history to deploy "modern" as a normative category of analysis has a long history. "Modern" appeared at first "as a term
more or less synonymous with 'now' in the late sixteenth century, and in any
case [was] used to mark the period off from medieval *and* ancient times."[10]
More specifically, "modern" represented a chronological term that denoted a
new historical period starting in the middle of the fifteenth century in Europe. Several institutional features and forces collectively became dominant
elements that organized people's daily lives in new and powerful ways, thus
setting the modern period in Europe apart from previous historical periods.
In particular, the nation-state, capitalism, nationalism, secularization, and
urbanization significantly reshaped political and economic systems, culture,
and social relationships in Europe.[11]

"Modern," however, lost its meaning as a chronological term that simply
denoted a new historical period when it became intertwined with various
ideology-based processes that turned it into a normative category. Historical
totalities, such as Hegelian thought, Marxism, social Darwinism, and Rankian history, have played significant roles in turning "modern" into a normative category through which to measure the historical development and evo-

lution of all societies. These totalities envisioned a linear progression of time with various stages of history through which the goals of the respective totalities were played out. They stressed the necessity of reaching the modern period as a prerequisite to moving on to the highest stages of historical development and ultimately achieving the supreme form of humanity and society.[12] Equally important, they abstracted the modern period from its particular historical origins and claimed it as a universal stage of history that could and should be achieved by all in order to experience the highest state of humanity. With this new conception, "modern" began to shed its original identity as a simple marker of a historical period.

In stressing that the modern period was a universal stage of history that began in the West, these totalities of history started the process of "staging" the modern as "singular, original, present, and authoritative," according to Timothy Mitchell.[13] That is, because Westerners believed that the modern period originated nowhere else but in the West, they presented the view that they alone had the right to determine the constitutive nature and meaning of the modern, which included speaking of it as a phenomenon that all societies, irrespective of culture and history, needed to experience. Staging the modern as Western and universal, these historical totalities conceived the entire world as sharing the same evolutionary track that led to the modern period. For them, "History is the story of civilization, culture, or people whose diverse lives are imagined to share a singular epoch and to progress as a unit from one contemporaneous moment to the next."[14] Under this conception of history, attaining the modern period required non-Western societies to share the same temporality and space as the West and to follow and mimic it.

Framed as "truth" and what "ought" to be and backed by the political and military power of Western imperialism, these theories of history forced people in Asia to organize knowledge in a particular way and to adopt a particular ideological orientation and political, economic, and social development. In the production of knowledge, there are a number of examples of Japanese and Chinese scholars in the late nineteenth century who used Hegel's theory to dig into the past and identify which institutions and elements to eliminate or cultivate for the purpose of becoming modern.[15] As for ideology, many people in Asia during the late nineteenth and early twentieth centuries were guided by the belief that the modern period was the highest stage of humanity and a universal phenomenon that began in the West. Therefore, in order to start the linear development toward reaching the modern period in which one stage of development led to another and ultimately ended with them catching up with the West, they recognized that it was necessary to reject existing customs and institutions and adopt "the civilized and enlightened" ideas, practices, and institutions popular in the West that allowed it to enjoy "endless progress."

Government officials and nationalist leaders, in particular, advocated rationality and attacked religions such as Buddhism and shamanism for being systems of belief that promoted superstitions and thus uncivilized lives that were wasteful and full of disorder. The Meiji government in Japan, for example, early on persecuted Buddhism and tried to control it strictly as the government pursued the creation of an enlightened, rational government and society.[16] After the 1919 May Fourth Movement in China, nationalists and intellectuals waged brutal antireligion campaigns because they saw popular religion "as a principal obstacle to the establishment of a 'disenchanted' world of reason and plenty."[17] Although Christianity was heavily criticized and attacked, it was the only religion that enjoyed some protection because people respected and embraced it since they saw it as the ideology that had allowed the West to experience the modern period before anyone else. The development of industrial capitalism also was believed to be an essential piece of enabling a society to reach the modern period. This belief motivated countless people in East Asia to reject their agrarian heritage and a pastoral life and pursue industrial production. Finally, particularly for the growing youth population in China and Japan, achieving the modern stage of history also required urbanization because the environment in cities and overall urban life were considered incubators of the features of the modern period.[18]

After the Treaty of Kanghwa in 1876 that led to Korea's incorporation into the Western-controlled nation-state international system, Koreans articulated new ways for their country to become modern. Underlying the ideologies and discourses on modern development in the late nineteenth century, such as "civilization and enlightenment" (munmyŏng kaehwa), was the belief that carrying out Western-style political, economic, educational, social, and cultural reforms would enable Korean society to reach the modern stage of history and become better and more advanced than any society had been during the Chosŏn period.[19] After the 1919 March First Movement, prominent Korean leftists and bourgeois nationalists criticized certain traditions of Confucianism, envisioned Korea moving away from its agrarian roots, and argued for programs centered on industrialization and urbanization in order to create the ideal modern subject, such as the bourgeois and the proletariat.[20] Like their counterparts in the late nineteenth century, these leaders stressed that becoming modern required adoption of the very characteristics that had apparently enabled the West to experience progress and positive developments.

This book understands modern as a chronological category that became staged or imagined through ideological processes as a universal period of history that had its origins in the West and was considered the crucial step toward achieving progress and the highest state of being. The features of the modern period that had distinguished it from earlier periods became the chief elements of a model of development that many Koreans and non-Westerners believed they needed to adopt in order to reach the modern stage of history. For many Koreans during the colonial period, the process of becoming or achieving the state of being modern required the adoption and cultivation of particular features, especially capitalism, industrialization, urbanization, and secularization. This normative view of the modern or modernity became dominant throughout the colonial period. Consequently, the various alternative visions of modernity that arose during the 1920s and 1930s were designed and implemented to contest and supplant this prevailing view of modernity.

Modernization

From 1910 to 1945, the colonial government carried out a series of reforms that had been inspired by the "universal" model of modern development. The government spoke of these reforms as means to move Koreans away from their traditional, premodern lives toward civilized and modern lives, but it ultimately sought to transform Korea in order to ensure Korea's colonized status as a supplier of goods and resources to Japan and the empire. The colonial government envisioned its ruling apparatus as molding Koreans into disciplined, modern subjects who would exhibit proper thought and industrious conduct that would aid the mission of Japanese colonialism. Colonized subjects were expected to perform their duties through the rapidly changing capitalist system, which was being reshaped under the supervision of the colonial government. It tied the agrarian economy to market principles through economic reforms such as the cadastral land survey (1910–1918), created an elaborate transportation system of rail, roadways, and port cities that connected rural areas to cities in Korea and spaces outside Korea, and restructured the financial system. Finally, starting in the early 1930s as the Japanese empire expanded the responsibilities of its colonies, the colonial government oversaw the expansion of industrial production in the peninsula.[21]

These various political, social, and economic reforms served as tools to represent and materialize the modern and to condition Koreans to believe that Japan would lead them to the next stage of history. To stress further Japan's role in bringing the modern to Korea, the colonial government spent countless resources on building up cities in the peninsula. Redesigning cities to look like urban centers in the West was imperative because cities were regarded as the centers of modern development. The government carried out urban reform projects in 1912, 1919, and 1934. Besides infrastructural development of cities, government-organized industrial exhibitions further presented the city as the place to experience and cultivate the modern. The 1915 Chosŏn Industrial Exhibition in Seoul, for example, featured over seventeen exhibition halls related to industrial development and technology, and an outdoor theater played movies on various topics, including "conditions of the industrial work force." An ideological agenda grounded the 1915 exhibition in that the colonial government wanted Koreans to "realize that the principle of strengthening and enriching the country lies in improving and developing industries" and that the colonial government would help them achieve industrialization and thus become modern.[22] Staging industrial exhibitions only in urban centers, the colonial government not only required Koreans to travel to the city to learn about and experience the modern but also connected industrial development to the city. Urbanization grew during the late 1920s and 1930s as people from the country migrated to cities for the new opportunities in work and new settings for living.[23] Cities became places where Koreans yearned for and encountered "modern" experiences of consumption and entertainment through Western-style department stores, cafés, restaurants, bars, and movie theaters.

In colonial Korea and elsewhere,[24] reforms, projects, movements, and campaigns based on the principles of the Western, norm-based model of modern development were reshaping political, economic, social, and cultural landscapes; central states were expanding their powers to discipline the lives of their citizens in order to enhance and protect the nation-state; industrialization was destroying old environments and building up new ones while speeding "up the whole tempo of life"; "immense demographic upheavals" were occurring in ways that involved "severing millions of people from their ancestral habitats, hurling them halfway across the world into new lives"; and urbanization was causing "rapid and often cataclysmic" growth in cities. Most important, people experienced severe changes and dislocations because of the "ever-expanding, drastically fluctuating" capitalist market. Marshall Berman groups these developments and effects together as the "maelstrom of modern life."[25] Ruptures, changes, and transformations resulting from modern development fundamentally challenged and heavily influenced existing ideas, practices, institutions, and systems, creating a turbulent environment. Local cultures and built environments led to diverse ways in which people encountered modern development and experienced the maelstrom of modern life, but immense change and transformation were features shared by all undergoing the process of modernization.

This book characterizes "modernization" as the social processes that not only sought to materialize the normative understanding of "modern" but also brought the maelstrom of modern life into existence. In colonial Korea, the colonial government controlled the overall process of modernization. Yet far from being subjects without any forms of agency, Koreans participated in determining how modernization would take shape and form in the peninsula through their struggles against Japanese colonialism and their drives to build a new nation-state by means of economic, social, and cultural reforms and campaigns. The actions of the colonial government and Koreans unleashed changes through which colonial society experienced mass transformations on every level. Change had always been part of life in Korea, but observers of colonial society believed that the pace and magnitude of change were different under modernization. Multiple changes rapidly started to detach Korean society and people from the past through the erosion of several key traditions and customs that had anchored and guided people's lives. Economic and social forces played direct roles in the erosion of traditions, but in their pursuit of modernization, many Koreans swiftly rejected traditions and their role of instructing and setting the standards for the present and future.

Koreans during the 1920s and 1930s also viewed modernization as producing a process of change that appeared to be overpowering and uncontrollable. Koreans characterized modernization and its impact on society in the same manner as Anthony Giddens, who used the juggernaut as a metaphor for modernization: "the juggernaut—a runaway engine of enormous power which, collectively as human beings, we can drive to some extent but which also threatens to rush out of our control and which could rend itself asunder."[26] Giddens points out that because of the juggernaut, "feelings of ontological security and existential anxiety will coexist in ambivalence."[27] Like the juggernaut, modernization in 1920s and 1930s colonial Korea presented contradictions in that it produced changes that not only afforded new forms of consciousness, identity, and autonomy but also upset economic, social, and cultural standards, especially in the countryside, in ways that threatened people's ideological, material, and ontological well-being.

Religion, the Pastoral Life, and Colonial Modernity in Korea

Under modernization, Koreans faced a process of change that opened new opportunities and expanded life's possibilities, as well as creating instability, fragmentation, and disunities. Modernization in colonial Korea, particularly because it was undergirded by capitalism, demonstrated that becoming modern was a complex process that did not just "generate smooth or steadily 'progressive' historical changes; rather, it produce[d] temporal patterns that [were] contradictory, conflictual, cyclical, and chronically crisis-prone."[28] Modernization configured the present as an open and dynamic temporality full of material and ideological ruptures and transformations that produced feelings and experiences of exhilaration and disquiet. This process thus showed that colonization referred to the establishment of Japanese imperialism and "the spread of a political order that inscribes in the social world a new conception of space, new forms of personhood, and a new means of manufacturing the experience of the real."[29]

Material, intellectual, and structural changes and the diverse experiences that resulted from modernization from 1920 to 1937 caused many Koreans to develop ideologies and systems of belief that could resolve the vast contradictions in society in ways that afforded a dynamic personhood and a healthy and vibrant national body that could contest colonial rule. In pointing out methods to make sense of and deal with the process of modernization, leftists called for destructive forces to be swept away, including forms of capitalism that caused poverty and inequality. Leftists especially attacked religion as a tradition that was antimodern and called for a secular society. Echoing the rhetoric in campaigns against religion throughout the world in the 1920s, the antireligion language of Korean leftists expressed how religion constrained individuals by tying them to a larger cosmic scheme that determined their choices and values. As an irrational force that led people to be concerned only with issues of spirituality, religion not only prevented people from properly interpreting how the world operated, but also influenced them to do nothing to change and advance society. Many Koreans, including bourgeois nationalists, joined leftists in publicly questioning the value of religion and carrying out antireligion campaigns because they found that religious languages were limiting and oppressed true consciousness since these languages could not explain the meaning of the material and ideological changes occurring in the peninsula or help people concretely deal with the transforming environment.

This unpopular status of religion stood in sharp contrast to its popular reception before 1920. In particular, by the early 1900s, the Presbyterian Church and the YMCA became two of the most respected religious institutions in Korea, while Tonghak, the precursor to Ch'ŏndogyo, which blended Chinese Daoism, Buddhism, and Confucianism, was the leading religion in the countryside. Tonghak and Protestant Christianity became two of the most popular rhetorical and symbolic structures that promoted personal salvation and spiritual cultivation at a time when Koreans were subject to the vicissitudes of imperialism. In response to the contradictions of modernization and the antireligion campaigns, leaders from Ch'ŏndogyo, the Presbyterian Church, and the YMCA rearticulated conventional religious languages and transformed religion into a vehicle to question the norms of modernity, pursue social change in response to modernization, and achieve political, economic, and social justice. Their new, socially oriented religious systems of belief grounded their respective rural reconstruction movements, which represented the first institution-led religious social movements in modern Korean history.

Religious institutions were active in society and carried out social movements from the late nineteenth century to 1919 that introduced many reforms, especially in the areas of medicine and education.[30] Protestant institutions, such as the Presbyterian North Church and the Methodist North Church, constructed Western-style schools and hospitals, while Ch'ŏndogyo under the leadership of Son Pyŏng-hŭi after 1905 encouraged Western-style social, political, and economic reforms. Protestant missionaries and Ch'ŏndogyo leaders introduced these reforms in society because they valued them as means for Koreans to become civilized and enlightened, achieve the modern stage of history, and consequently attain the ultimate goal of a complete and vibrant spiritual life. Many religious institutions and leaders before 1919, in short, supported and carried out the process of modernization. Under this process, religious institutions exhorted followers to focus more on cultivating their individual spiritual lives than on questioning and dealing with the problems in society caused by modernization, such as social and economic inequality and poverty. Many Protestant missionaries and Korean Christian leaders, in particular, stressed that their followers should rely on God to take care of these worldly concerns. Although there were a number of Korean Christian followers who organized nationalist campaigns outside the purview of Christian institutions, their movements featured reforms that embodied the norms of modernity, especially the unquestioned belief of capitalism as "unselfish in spirit" and faith in its power to bring forth changes that only improved society and people's moral and ethical lives.[31] Faith-based social activism and social movements led by institutions, which criticized the norms of modernization and responded to its contradictions and problems by designing and implementing an alternative version of modernity, were rare before 1919.

By neglecting any discussion of the relationship between religion and modernization, the historiography on religion during the colonial period conspicuously glosses over the efforts of Christians, Buddhists, and followers of various new religions to address and combat the economic, social, and cultural problems resulting from modernization.[32] In particular, it overlooks the push by YMCA, Presbyterian, and Ch'ŏndogyo leaders to overcome the contradictions of modernization and create a new nation-state through the reconstruction of society into a paradise anchored by religion, agriculture, and pastoral living. As the first and largest social movements led by religious institutions, their reconstruction drives originated with the reconceptualization of traditional conventional language and practices in the Protestant Christian and Ch'ŏndogyo faiths—a process driven by the question of how Koreans should value and approach a present that was filled with changes, fragmentation, and contradictions caused by modernization. Yi Ton-hwa (Ch'ŏndogyo), Hong Pyŏng-sŏn (YMCA), and Pae Min-su (Presbyterian), in particular, became the leading voices in their respective organizations to design and offer new systems of belief that emphasized and valued the present as a temporality of possibilities. To them, the present with all its changes afforded new opportunities and means to reconstruct and enhance further everyday lives, social relationships, and the national community, and therefore Koreans should not fear the present as a temporality of destabilizing and destructive transformations. Despite the criticisms that religion was antimodern, they stressed that religion itself was rooted in the present and valued society because religious experiences were grounded in the everyday; religion was a critical mechanism in the present period because it was a source of meaning and permanence under capitalism, promoted morals and ethics, and inspired social activism and the creation of a just and peaceful world.

Yi, Hong, and Pae's efforts to reconceptualize religious language and reorient religious institutions in order to resituate religion's place under modernization distinguish them from other religious figures at that time. Whereas most leaders in all religions simply rejected the claims made by those criticizing religions, they fostered new religious ideas to help people make "cognitive maps" of the fragmented society, therefore helping people encounter the world as a comprehensible, mappable totality in order to enable a new consciousness and social practices.[33] Besides overcoming the static nature of religion through a linguistic turn, they published texts, spoke in public, and organized movements to lay out material frameworks through which Koreans could discover meaning, direction, and security within the shifting present.

In particular, Yi, Hong, and Pae's religious ideas informed the rural movements of their respective organizations. In order for Koreans to enjoy vibrant spiritual lives rooted in the present, the YMCA, Presbyterian, and Ch'ŏndogyo rural movements from 1925 to 1937 pursued the reconstruction of rural Korea into a heavenly kingdom on earth. Collectively becoming one of the largest and most powerful rural campaigns in Korean history, which covered almost every part of the peninsula, the three rural movements championed a pastoral life based on farming for several reasons, including the following: (1) farm work ensured a robust life of virtue and provided the means to manage capitalism; (2) the rural landscape was seen as a source of spiritual therapy in which people experienced the sacred in their daily interactions with nature; and (3) agriculture, a pastoral life, and the rural had anchored and constituted society and people's identity from the past to the present. The three movements were confident that they could further develop the present living and working conditions in the countryside for peasants and build a spiritual, agrarian paradise through the adoption of contemporary agrarian reforms from Denmark, where a successful model of modernity based on religion and agriculture had been created. Inspired by this model, the three Korean rural movements adopted a cooperative system to pool peasant labor and resources in order to create communities based on love and the Folk School program to turn rural youth into the vanguard of rural reconstruction. Through the incorporation of contemporary reforms into their process of modifying peasant and rural life in ways that would lead to new measures and models of modern living, the three rural movements featured a vision of modernity based on religion and agriculture.

In showing that the YMCA, Presbyterian, and Ch'ŏndogyo rural movements pursued their own form of modernity that emphasized religion, agriculture, and a pastoral life, this book engages the concept of colonial modernity. First outlined in *Colonial Modernity in Korea* (1999), colonial modernity represents an analytic concept to overcome the "modernizing" versus "nationalist" arguments concerning the relationship between Japanese colonialism and the origins of the modern period in Korea.[34] Japanese colonialism in Korea, according to Michael Robinson, "speeded the process of change in unique ways and created a form of modernization in which the process may be usefully termed 'colonial modernization' and the state of being 'colonial modernity.'" Colonial modernity includes the chief features of the modern, but "in a highly skewed form" that distinguishes the modern in Korea from that of the West and Japan. The primary feature of this skewed form of modernity was that the Japanese dominated the "modern sector."[35] Recognizing modernization in Korea as a process filtered and controlled by colonial power, colonial modernity stresses the everyday lives and identities of Koreans as influenced and shaped not only by the nation but also by such forces as class, culture, gender, and religion. Studies of colonial modernity carefully distinguish the many layers of life that emerged from diverse forms of behavior, practice, and thought to develop multifaceted and nuanced conceptions of reality that complicate the dichotomous modes of analysis of modernization versus exploitation.[36] Introducing concepts such as "hybridity," "translation," and "border crossing," colonial modernity has advanced the field of Korean studies on many levels because it has provided complex portraits and analysis of everyday life during the colonial period that, according to Cha Seung Ki (Ch'a Sŭng-ki), "identify the unique phenomena of modernity and the rupture points that existed in the daily life of colonies."[37]

Although recognizing the value of the concept of colonial modernity, this study also criticizes it on two levels. First, the field of colonial modernity has deemphasized the study of the political economy of the colonial period.[38] Following the trends in cultural studies, studies of colonial modernity in Korea have applied cultural theories to reveal the diverse dimensions of colonial life and the application of biopolitics and disciplinary power to redraw identities and experiences in daily life.[39] Although these studies supply excellent interpretations of micropolitics, they leave out any forms of analysis that examine macro developments, especially the changing of the economy and the rise of capitalism, and thus provide an incomplete picture of the relationship between language / discourse and social processes or the relationship between micro and macro processes. Second, and more important, studies of colonial modernity have configured modernity only as a linear form of development that emphasizes the secular, bourgeois / proletariat, urban spaces and industrial capitalism. These studies stress that Koreans during the colonial period defined the goal of modernity as the necessity to ascend to a new stage of history through adopting the features of the normative model of the modern. This strict interpretation of modernity causes anything outside this path of development to be characterized as antimodern. The only studies that investigate agrarian movements, including those of the YMCA and Ch'ŏndogyo, thus characterize them all as antimodern on the basis of colonial modernity's developmental model.[40] This narrow definition of modernity ties colonial modernity to traditional methodologies espoused by the modernization and exploitation camps.

This study argues that the YMCA, Presbyterian, and Ch'ŏndogyo rural movements negotiated modernization by furnishing new paradigms of what it meant to be modern through their religious beliefs and rural campaigns. In particular, an attitude and mode of living that were rooted in the present grounded their visions of modernity. Modernity has long been equated with the present,[41] and Charles Baudelaire has been recognized as a leading figure who carefully articulated the connection between them. Baudelaire stressed that as society underwent fundamental changes from the forces of modernization, everyday life in the present was now in flux, with changes and developments that led to the "transient," "fleeting," and "contingent" nature of modernity. But he believed that instead of fearing and rejecting the present that appeared to be unstable because of changes, people should be attentive to the new happenings and developments around them so that these events could be corralled in ways that would lead to innovations in human thought and practice. This position on the present stemmed from Baudelaire's rejection of the idea that the old or the past setting the "measures and models of human excellence that each new age must seek to emulate under altered conditions without ever hoping to surpass it."[42] To him, merely relying on the past for guidance, standards, and models of living, and ontological security prevented a person from fully focusing on and embracing what was happening in the present and thus caused that person to "throw away the value and privileges afforded by circumstances."[43] Baudelaire characterized modernity as an attitude of being mindful of, questioning, and valuing the present in order to be creative and innovative.

Fredric Jameson's characterization of modernity as a new "feeling" echoes Baudelaire's ideas in that "modernity . . . describe[s] the way 'modern' people feel about themselves. . . . This modern feeling now seems to consist in the conviction that we ourselves are somehow new, that a new age is beginning, that everything is possible and nothing can ever be the same again."[44] Baudelaire's and Jameson's conceptions of modernity deemphasize it as a state that arrives through the achievement of a certain stage of history or following the precepts of the normative understanding of the modern. Instead, it means cultivating a form of existence that is entrenched in the present by embracing it as a temporality full of marvelous and diverse opportunities that will contribute to the further development of individuals and societies.

The ideas and practices of the YMCA, Presbyterian, and Ch'ŏndogyo rural movements embodied and expressed Baudelaire's and Jameson's characterizations of modernity. Instead of privileging the past and allowing only it to determine and mediate wholly the state of the present and the future, the three movements emphasized the importance of a state of mind and life that was rooted in the present in order to create new religious, social, economic, and cultural paths for Koreans. Modernity, to them, was articulating solutions to problems in society and coming up with new ways to enhance life suited to present conditions. Yet, unlike Jameson and many other modernists, leaders of the three movements rejected the idea of getting "rid of all those old objects, values, mentalities, and ways of doing things."[45] Put differently, they refused to expel the past totally from the present for the sake of building an entirely new future—a path of development called for by many modern ideologies of the early twentieth century. The leaders of the three movements not only believed that the past still carried certain valuable elements for further cultivating and safeguarding lives, but also recognized that totally extinguishing the past would lead only to instability and more harm to people's lives. Through their concepts, then, the movements introduced an alternative vision of modernity that contested the normative meaning of the modern in ways that made allowance for the histories and legacies of Korea.

This study highlights the contingent and contested process of redefining the meaning of "modern" and negotiating modernization by the YMCA, Presbyterian, and Ch'ŏndogyo rural movements and considers why and how their leaders constructed multiple means, especially religious and economic, for the development of modernity. These means were a consequence of what can be characterized as the principle of reclamation—a process of development that involves taking what already exists and integrating it with present-day elements to create something that has richer value and meaning.[46] Guided by this principle, the movements introduced contemporary reforms that were compatible with religion and local customs, conditions, and history to enhance the agrarian heritage of peasants. Agrarian reforms were expected to value place, or that which existed; reconcile the past with the present; and encourage an organic process that fostered innovative diversity and a sound national community that would be able to negotiate the challenges of modernization, in particular capitalism. Outlining this process of development, this book demonstrates that the three movements offered an alternative to "high modernist" projects in colonial Korea, which called for destabilizing reforms that disregarded place for the sake of achieving the future, as well as an alternative to traditionalist movements whose temporal emphasis was the past.[47] Indeed, the three movements challenged both conservative agrarian campaigns that sought protection from changes through the restoration of traditions and modernist agrarian drives that aimed to prepare rural Korea for a new future based on industrialization and urbanization—two elements that the three movements believed would further unsettle society.

The three movements designed and carried out an alternative vision of modernity that featured the formation of temporal and spatial conditions appropriate to Korean society. The creation of this new temporality and space from 1925 to 1937 occurred specifically through a "negotiation between the local and received cultural habits—the culture of reference—and the requirements of the new global processes of capitalist expansion." Negotiation between "the new demands of capitalism and the market and the force of received forms of history and culture" was a worldwide experience in both the West and the supposed non-West.[48] The experiences resulting from these negotiations were similarly shared, but they also differed according to specific histories, cultures, and processes of these places. The emergence of similar and different experiences across places, and even within places, reflected the existence of multiple temporalities and spaces under modernity. This book shows that the three movements' vision of modernity was not centered on achieving "true time" or aligning Korea with the single temporality that had been staged by Western historical totalities as the authoritative path to becoming modern, but instead was "an inflection of a larger global process that constituted what might be called co-existing or co-eval modernity."[49]

Modernization, the Secular, and Religion

Since the advent of modernity in the West, intellectuals, social scientists, and individuals have described secularism as one of the "pillars of modernity" and have predicted that religion's influence, power, and significance would wane and ultimately disappear under modernization.[50] Secularization narratives of modernity have argued that creating a "new moral basis for social order" and envisioning and achieving social progress cannot be done without being liberated from religion because it is an "illusory solution to problems that could be met in modernity by more realistic and efficacious methods."[51] Realistic and efficacious methods would be anchored in reason or rational and scientific thought. But rather than receding, many religions have flourished under modernization, and thus numerous studies over the past decade have attempted to understand this development by reinterpreting the relationship between the secular and religion under modernity. Talal Asad has shed considerable light on this relationship because his most notable works try "to problematize 'the religion' and 'the secular' as clear-cut categories but also to search out for the conditions in which *they were* clear-cut and were sustained as such."[52] For example, Asad argues that religion is not a "transhistorical constant" and instead should be studied always in relation to social forces.[53] Asad stresses that "this is necessary . . . because religion cannot be consigned *a priori* to a sphere apart from the realm of power."[54] Through his framework for studying religion, it becomes apparent that religions, far from being static, have been continuously reconstituted to produce new modes of enchantment, agency, and living that people have relied on to negotiate the contradictions of modernization.[55]

Recent studies in anthropology have expanded the approach to understanding the reconstitution and endurance of religion under modernization by examining religion's part in the process of valuation.[56] Under this process, according to Courtney Bender and Ann Taves, "changing discourses around religion and secularity . . . create possibilities for marking, creating, and experiencing things of value, whether in the contemporary moment or in the past." Driven by the question "How do the historically contingent formulations of the religious and secular inform people's efforts to identify or create things of value, as well as their abilities to apprehend, experience, or create such things?" anthropological studies have shown that religions have produced new categories and languages as a result of their interactions with the forces of modernization and that these developments have given way to fresh forms of value that have given meaning to new experiences.[57] These studies have demonstrated that religions, in relation to modernization and secularization, have undergone a process of producing new forms of value that people find meaningful and that inform their consciousness, behavior, and lived relationships.[58]

This study contributes to the scholarship on the nature of religion under modernity by showing why and how the three rural movements partook in a process of valuation through reclamation. Their reclamation of traditional religious languages led to categories, such as agency, everyday life, labor, economy, and society, acquiring new meaning and value. These categories became popular means for explaining changes to participants in the movements and guiding people's daily lives under modernization. In particular, the categories that reclaimed society as a sacred space informed new visions of a modern Korea that inspired Koreans to address poverty and social inequality through the construction of a heavenly kingdom on earth. As reclaimed categories introduced new types of value and each of the movements pursued the realization of an alternative vision of modernity based on these values, this process of valuation became a powerful medium through which (1) religious language was transformed, (2) new material practices were envisioned, and (3) managing and guiding social processes toward the achievement of the ideal were legitimized and encouraged. Through reclamation, the three movements revalued religion as a legitimate method of knowing and solving problems stemming from modernization, which gave it a new significance and status in colonial society.

Scope of This Book

This book argues that the rise of faith-based social activism in modern Korea took place between 1920 and 1937 as YMCA, Presbyterian, and Ch'ŏndogyo rural leaders responded to the contradictions and changes caused by modernization by creating new religious languages, practices, and institutions that embodied and promoted alternative visions of modernity. Despite their different backgrounds, traditions, and histories, the three organizations shared a vision of religion as a system of ideas and practices that gave new value to society and everyday experiences and urged followers to build a "heaven on earth" by reconstructing social structures, especially economic ones, in order to achieve material stability and thus spiritual fulfillment. Equally important, they held a common vision of modernity that valued the present, religion, agriculture, and a pastoral way of life. These three groups found common ground not only in their concerns about the nature and impact of modernization on society but also in their creative ways of adapting traditional religious language and practices to changing conditions and building an alternative model of modern development. Compared with other religious and nationalist organizations, the rural campaign of these three organizations collectively became one of the largest nationalist movements in colonial Korea. Other religious groups spoke out against the norms of modernity, but few groups organized movements to contest modernization, and none of them were as large as the YMCA, Presbyterian, and Ch'ŏndogyo movements

Like all nationalist campaigns, all three movements soon ended after the colonial government began to mobilize Koreans for the war against China after 1937. At that time, all three movements had collectively touched almost every area of the Korean peninsula and had even reached parts of Manchuria. Each of the three movements had directly introduced new ideas, practices, and institutions to a large segment of the peasant population. The three movements also spread their ideas through the numerous journals and newspapers that they published and distributed throughout the country. Dismissing these movements because their achievements and results cannot be measured quantitatively overlooks how they established a discursive framework that challenged powerful modes of thought and practice and visions of the nation. Institutions and practices that embodied and spread their ideas enabled their concepts of religion, modernity, and the nation to become concrete and lived out in people's daily lives. Far from being free-floating concepts that were simply invented and consumed by a few individuals, their ideas contested popular and large-scale trends and widely served as seeds for the sprouting of alternative forms of consciousness and behavior and modes of living in the present and the future— potentialities that cannot be easily quantified in numbers. The three movements unleashed a dialectical process of change between the preexisting and the new that prevented the simple eradication of their ideas even after they ended. In fact, their ideas became sources for constructing the discourse on faith-based social movements in postliberation South Korea, which helped religious figures negotiate the contradictions of modernization. Widening the historiography of colonial Korea and postcolonial South Korea demands a full study of the YMCA, Presbyterian, and Ch'ŏndogyo rural movements.

This book does not exclusively study peasants and their everyday responses to modernization.[59] Instead, it is a form of intellectual history that focuses on why and how leaders of the movements transformed the discursive framework on religion, agrarian living, and modernity in colonial Korea and seeks to expand the meaning of modernity within the context of modern Korean history. Part I covers the transformation of religious ideas and practices in relation to colonial Korea's changing political economy. Specifically, Chapter 1 examines the origins of Tonghak and Protestant Christianity in Korea. In particular, it not only shows the institutional strength and influence of these two religions in Korean society but also argues that social activist language and practices that criticized modernization were not promoted by Tonghak and Protestant Christian institutions. Chapter 2 outlines the transforming capitalist economy in rural Korea and discusses how various nationalists and intellectuals responded to the agrarian crisis and saw rural Korea fitting into their visions of the ideal nation-state. This discursive description of the impact of capitalism on rural culture and society provides context for understanding why YMCA, Presbyterian, and Ch'ŏndogyo leaders created new faith-based social activist language and why the movements chose to focus their reconstruction efforts on the countryside. Chapter 3 shows how the changed reality due to capitalism and developments such as new colonial policies and antireligious movements led Yi Ton-hwa, Hong Pyŏng-sŏn, and Pae Min-su to reconceptualize ideas of time, space, and religious experience in order to help people negotiate modernity. Their reinterpretation of religious experience as being rooted in the present and everyday life and calls for religious institutions to build "heavenly kingdoms" furnished new ideas of agency and community and provided the rationale for the YMCA, Presbyterian, and Ch'ŏndogyo rural movements.

Part II looks at the YMCA, Presbyterian, and Ch'ŏndogyo drives to materialize their visions of a new spiritual nation. Chapter 4 outlines the organization of the three rural movements and especially introduces Chosŏn nongminsa, which was the main arm of Ch'ŏndogyo to design and carry out its rural campaign. This chapter also analyzes the three organizations' criticisms of urbanization and industrial capitalism and their support for a pastoral life, which they believed promised the cultivation of personality, social harmony, authentic wealth, a lasting national identity, and a sacred life.

Chapter 5 shows why all three movements turned to Denmark for practical solutions on how to reconstruct rural Korea. It focuses on the three movements' attempts to develop an ethical form of capitalism and a spiritual, moral economy by setting up a Danish-style cooperative system that promoted a communal form of labor, which encouraged the cultivation of personality and mutual love. Finally, Chapter 6 looks at the three movements' educational campaigns to help peasants imagine new spiritual communities, visualize and anticipate an agrarian modernism, and acquire the skills and knowledge to ensure the growth of rural Korea.

Part I

RELIGION, REVOLT, AND REIMAGINING
A MODERN KOREA, 1860–1937

1

Origins of Protestantism and Tonghak in Late Chosŏn Korea

Before being executed in 1864, Ch'oe Che-u, the founder of Tonghak, described the state of people's affairs in Korea by declaring that "people's minds were all confused and they did not know what to do."[1] Many Koreans at that time attributed their "confused" conditions to the weakening of the Confucian political order. In large part, the breakdown of the Confucian order stemmed from the gradual decline of the Chosŏn state (1392–1910) during the nineteenth century, a period when the government showed signs of failing to live up to its role as the benevolent Confucian leader that provided for the security and welfare of its people. As scholars of Chosŏn Korea have pointed out, state and society were fairly stable before 1800 through the government's upkeep of infrastructure, such as reservoirs and irrigation canals, and its maintenance of grain storage facilities for famine relief and price stability.[2] However, when crop failures and famines beset rural life in the late 1700s, the state was unable to supply the forms of welfare necessary to ease peasant hardship.[3] The inability to offer assistance resulted largely from the state's lack of money because questionable tax exemptions and corruption, in particular, caused a decline in tax revenues.[4] Without sufficient resources, the state could no longer continuously maintain dams and the irrigation system, which contributed to flooding, and the vast amount of granaries that had supplied essential grains and foodstuffs during times of famine. The weakening of the state led to periods of hardship during the nineteenth century for peasants—hardships that were further compounded by cholera outbreaks.[5]

For many peasants, the state's inability to safeguard individual lives showed how it was failing to carry out its Confucian-based mandate to protect the people. Peasants responded to these developments by staging popular uprisings against the state. The types of peasant uprisings ranged from regional conflicts, such as the Hong Kyŏngnae Rebellion of 1812, to national movements, such as the Tonghak Revolution in 1894.[6] Religious groups became the leading organizers behind several uprisings, including the Hong Kyŏngnae Rebellion, and grew in popularity as the breakdown of Confucian statecraft left several voids in society. People turned to religions, both new and established, in order to find forms of representation that could capture, explain, and give meaning to their new experiences. New religions, such as Namhak, which promised a new heaven on earth that would stamp out chaos and contradictions, and Chŭngsan, which predicted that changes would lead to the establishment of a utopian kingdom in Korea, emerged and quickly gained followers.[7] Established religions, such as various folk religions and shamanism, also became a source of meaning and direction for many Koreans.[8] Especially after the state formally dismantled the Confucian political order through the Kabo Reforms (1894–1895) and was unable to protect Korea from Japanese and Western imperialism, these religions flourished as they tried to express the experiences of Koreans in an understandable religious language that would give meaning and direction to their lives.[9]

Tonghak, the precursor of Ch'ŏndogyo, and Protestant Christianity arose in this new space to become significant and influential forces that reshaped the religious, social, and cultural spheres of late Chosŏn Korea. Examining the origins of these two religious groups, this chapter focuses on how Tonghak and Protestant Christianity emerged as two of the largest and most popular religious groups during the late nineteenth century and at the start of the twentieth century that reordered the world for their followers and supplied meaning and significance to the ongoing political transformations. In particular, this chapter analyzes how Tonghak and Protestant Christianity became influential religions, that is, how Tonghak and Protestant Christian leaders institutionalized their beliefs through the production and dissemination of ideas and practices that came to be recognized as Tonghak and Protestant Christianity. Combining primary materials written by Tonghak leaders, missionaries, and Korean Christian leaders with theories drawn from anthropology and religion, this chapter lays out the infrastructure through which Tonghak and Protestant Christian leaders spread their religious principles. In so doing, it shows how both Tonghak and Protestant Christian leaders and institutions did not promote any type of faith-based social activism before 1919.

Origins of Tonghak

Tonghak has a special place in modern Korean history because of its connection to one of the largest peasant uprisings, known as the Tonghak Revolution (1894).[10] Because the revolution has been interpreted as a people-centered movement that spoke out against Japanese imperialism, Tonghak has long been mythologized as an indigenous religious organization that protected and advanced the Korean nation. Before the revolution, however, Tonghak became a significant force in Chosŏn society because it was one of the few new religions to organize on a larger scale beyond its original circle of followers. Initiatives by its leaders, such as publishing writings, and its organizational structure made Tonghak's divine message on personal identity, morals, and ethics widely available for Koreans who were seeking ways to make sense of the changing world. Renamed Ch'ŏndogyo in 1905, Tonghak continued to prove itself as an influential force in society as it set up multiple social, economic, educational, and cultural institutions that shaped intellectual and popular thoughts and trends from 1920 to 1937.

Tonghak originated from what many people perceived as the strange thought and behavior of Ch'oe Che-u (1824–1864). Although his father was a Confucian scholar, his mother's background as an unmarried widow made Ch'oe ineligible for the civil service exam. Unable to perform other kinds of work, Ch'oe failed to maintain a stable standard of living for himself and his family. The combination of his own problems and the changes erupting throughout society, especially the threat of foreigners coming to Korea, appeared to cause Ch'oe to be without direction and full of anxiety and confusion.[11] Confucianism, for Ch'oe, no longer helped him understand his personal problems or the problems in Chosŏn society.[12] Feeling distressed and disoriented, Ch'oe had an experience one day in April 1860 that fundamentally changed his life. According to Ch'oe, he heard a voice that was difficult to describe saying, "Do not be afraid. I am known as *Sangje* [the Daoist ruler of heaven] among humanity. Do you not know me?"[13] Sangje told Ch'oe that he had no material form and that Ch'oe needed to teach humankind about the way (*pŏp*) and "relieve humanity from sickness."[14] To do so, Sangje gave Ch'oe a symbol that was an "elixir of life" and told him to teach it to others. Sangje promised Ch'oe a fulfilling immortal life if he performed this mission. Ch'oe took the symbol, wrote it on a piece of paper, and consumed it. Immediately, Ch'oe wrote that he grew healthier and stronger and that his "illness" disappeared. Moreover, he felt and experienced the feeling of immortality.[15] Applying the cure to others, he noticed other people's illnesses improving.

Through this experience in which Ch'oe met Sangje, consumed the "elixir of life," and felt immortal, stronger, and healthier, Ch'oe said that he entered into a new inner state in which he was able to overcome his fears, lifelessness, and anxieties.[16] For Ch'oe, the act of taking the symbol, writing it down, and consuming it provided the conscious means to work through the unknown and rediscover stability in his life. Through this process, he, in a sense, was able to improve his mental state in order to function in his everyday life. Indeed, when he said that his illness disappeared after consuming the piece of paper with the symbol, Ch'oe most likely was referring to his internal, mental condition. Yet more than just performing a function, Ch'oe's religious experience seemed to have brought him to a new state in which he felt connected to a larger being and the infinite universe. Thus Ch'oe believed that he was released from the problem of death and the other problems he faced. In other words, after meeting Sangje and eating the symbol on the paper, Ch'oe overcame concerns that plagued him, such as anxieties about death and the meaning of life, and saw the everyday world in a clear and different way while gaining a new perspective on the purpose of his life. Instead of struggling with fears of poverty and the future, Ch'oe understood that his role in the world was to articulate the divine message given to him and to spread it to others.

Using his experience with Sangje as a source of inspiration and direction, Ch'oe spent the following months articulating and defining the tenets of his new religious message, especially the meanings and roles of Sangje and Chigi (Ultimate Energy). Ch'oe eventually named his new religion Tonghak (Eastern Learning) in 1861 and often stated that it was a mixture of many religions in that it melded together tenets from other systems of knowledge, such as Catholicism and Confucianism, to produce a religion that truly addressed the needs of the people. According to Ch'oe, "Tonghak is like Confucianism, but it is not. . . . It is like Buddhism, but it is not. . . . It is like Daoism, but it is not."[17] From Buddhism, he adopted the ideas of benevolence, and he borrowed ideas about God from the Catholic meaning of God (Ch'ŏnju). From Confucianism and Daoism, respectively, he appropriated the idea of ideal human relations and ethical principles and the concept of changing the internal spirit in order to cleanse oneself from negative elements.[18] Ch'oe found each of these religions by itself conservative and unable to address the spiritual and material needs of people who were searching for direction and order in a time of instability. Ch'oe adopted the "moral bricolage" approach outlined by Claude Lévi-Strauss in that he constructed a new religion by piecing together parts from other religions and adopting signs and symbols from existing belief systems.[19] For Ch'oe, taking varying religious ideas and forming a new belief system was made easier by the facts that Buddhism, Catholicism, Confucianism, Daoism, and shamanism already existed on the peninsula and that their ideas were commonly known to many people. By using the moral bricolage approach, Ch'oe not only established a religion with which others could easily identify because of its familiarity, but also created a more powerful, appealing religion that could theoretically overcome the inability of the other religions to address the needs and desires of Koreans at that time.

Among the most important elements of the Tonghak religion that Ch'oe created and developed was the concept that humans can connect to and become part of Ultimate Reality. Throughout his writings, Ch'oe encountered difficulties writing about his various religious experiences.[20] In trying to name and describe Ultimate Reality, Ch'oe clearly showed the difficulty in describing his religious experiences and ideas. In his early works, Ch'oe writes that the

highest being whom he encountered and felt was Sangje, which was a tradi-
tional word used by Chinese and Koreans to describe God in heaven above.[21]
At other times, Ch'oe and other Tonghak leaders employed the widely used
Catholic word Ch'ŏnju (God) to describe the main being in heaven.[22] In
"Nonhakmun" Ch'oe took the characteristics found in Sangje and Ch'ŏnju and
attributed them to the word Chigi, which meant Ultimate Energy.[23] After
Ch'oe's death, later Tonghak writings replaced both Sangje and Ch'ŏnju with
Hanŭllim, which meant "the honorable Heaven."

In each use of Sangje, Ch'ŏnju, Hanŭllim, or Chigi, Ch'oe understood
them as a force or being that was the creative source out of which all objects
and forms of life emerge and in which all things are preserved. Moreover,
Ch'oe considered them as a force that was without limit and universal.[24] Describing Chigi, Ch'oe wrote, "*Chi* is the limitless or the infinite. *Chigi* is the being
who is immanent in all things and directs all. It has no form and therefore difficult to describe. Though it can be heard at times, it is an unseen force. It is the
Ultimate Energy of the universe."[25] Using this definition as a base, Ch'oe believed that Chigi was the force that created, unified, and moved all in the universe. Because it was the main force in the universe, Ch'oe also understood it
be to timeless and pervading all space.

When using Sangje, Ch'ŏnju, and Hanŭllim, Ch'oe in effect used the
words in the same way in which he used Chigi. On the basis of David Tracy's
thoughts on religion, then, Sangje, Ch'ŏnju, Hanŭllim, and Chigi essentially
can all be grouped under the term "Ultimate Reality," which Tracy describes
as the force that was the "origin and end of all Reality" and "from which all
comes and toward which all moves."[26] As the creator and mover of all existence,
Ultimate Reality is the creative and preserving force that exists in all objects
and beings in the universe and the everyday world. Sangje, Ch'ŏnju, Hanŭllim,
and Chigi could therefore signify Ultimate Reality.

Because Ultimate Reality was a force immanent and residing in all, Ch'oe
concluded that all individuals possessed the power to become part of and one
with Ultimate Reality. Unlike the Christian concept of God as a distant and
transcendent being who possessed only divine nature, Ch'oe believed that
Ultimate Reality resided within humans, who thereby could connect with this
divine force. Throughout his various religious experiences, Ch'oe often heard
Ultimate Reality reaffirming the fact that as the main force in the universe, it
resided in humans. In one experience, Ch'oe felt the divine power with him
and internally heard Ultimate Reality saying, "My soul is your soul."[27]

To a large extent, Ch'oe's idea of the immanence of Ultimate Reality in
humans is quite similar to transcendental beliefs popularized by Ralph Waldo
Emerson in early nineteenth-century America and to Hinduism in that both
postulated that a higher being resided in the human soul and that individuals

were harmoniously and naturally connected to the higher being.[28] For transcendentalism, Hinduism, and Tonghak, this connection and realization of the higher being or Ultimate Reality could be disrupted only by the egoism in people's hearts and, more important, "outside forces" or negative elements. To Ch'oe, being human meant possessing a heart that is capable of both good and evil.[29] Ch'oe and subsequent Tonghak leaders believed that many socially constructed traditions, rules, and customs polluted the human mind and soul and consequently prevented individuals from realizing their divine potential.[30] In a manner similar to transcendental beliefs in peeling away outside conventions to reveal the inner higher being in humans, Ch'oe believed that individuals needed to reform their internal consciousness by stripping away negative, learned teachings and practices while enriching the mind with Tonghak beliefs and teachings. Truthful words (ideas) and false words, according to Ch'oe, existed in society.[31] Ch'oe wrote that in order to experience and connect with Ultimate Reality, people must reject the false, such as elements of Confucianism and Catholicism, accept the true, and reshape the mind.[32] The key to detoxing the mind and encountering a religious experience, therefore, resided in one's abilities to train the mind with "truthful" beliefs and practices.

How to internally encounter and realize Ultimate Reality undoubtedly becomes an issue of language or mediation between individuals and religious experience. All religions, according to Joachim Wach, establish media that facilitate religious transformations. Constructed by humans, rites and rituals play an especially significant role in connecting people to the "creative sources of life" in that they mentally and physically draw individuals to focus on religious elements.[33] Rituals, for Ch'oe, served as a key component of drawing and joining the individual to Ultimate Reality. Many rituals arose from experimentation and practice after his first religious experience in April 1860. He suggested that the path to Ultimate Reality lay first in cultivating and enriching one's mind through "sitting quietly" and meditating on one's essential nature.[34] Another important step in becoming part of Ultimate Reality involved reciting the incantation created by Ch'oe:

Chigi (Ultimate Energy) that is present and now, I wish for it to enter all.
With Chigi inside of me, I am one with all (heaven and all things).
Never forgetting, I am aware of all.[35]

Finally, Ch'oe believed that by consuming various talismans and performing particular dances, such as the sword dance, a person could overcome spiritual and physical ailments and experience enlightenment and divinity.[36] In all these acts, Ch'oe believed that individuals were fulfilling their meaning in life in that they were cultivating their ability to realize their divine nature.[37]

Ch'oe thought that in this divine state, a connection with Ultimate Reality would allow individuals to be in an enlightened space where everything would be known. In this space, all ordinary knowledge and experience would be shattered, and the subject-object dichotomy would no longer exist. Instead, the enlightened individual would know all and be in a continuous connection with all in the universe.[38] Because of this experience, individuals would be released from finite concerns, such as material wealth, the issue of success, and especially death. Experiencing Ultimate Reality and being released from concerns eventually would allow people to have meaning in this world and stimulate individuals to meaningful activities. Socially speaking, Ch'oe also believed that mass religious transformation would lead to the regeneration of society and thus protect Korea from encroaching Western powers. Ch'oe recognized that Koreans were uncertain about the future of Korea because Western powers were interfering in the affairs of East Asian states. However, he believed that through religious transformation, people would be spiritually protected from any dangerous outside forces.

Tonghak leaders who followed Ch'oe further articulated and expanded this notion of oneness with Ultimate Reality. Ch'oe Si-hyŏng (1827–1898), the second Tonghak leader, agreed with Ch'oe Che-u that Ultimate Reality existed in all humans. Ch'oe Si-hyŏng, however, reworked the concept of Ultimate Reality in two ways. In his early writings, Ch'oe Si-hyŏng first began to allude to the idea that Ultimate Reality and humans were the same. For example, he said, "A human, in other words, is Ultimate Reality. Ultimate Reality, put differently, is human."[39] In another text, he wrote, "Humans are Ultimate Reality [Hanul]."[40] Before Ch'oe Si-hyŏng, Ch'oe Che-u never said that humans were Ultimate Reality; instead, they possessed the power to become part of Ultimate Reality, which resided inside all. Ch'oe Si-hyŏng, however, elaborated on this idea by saying that humans were already Ultimate Reality and therefore already naturally divine regardless of one's efforts. In Ch'oe Si-hyŏng's mind, humanity and Ultimate Reality were on the same level.

Ch'oe Si-hyŏng further developed the idea of Ultimate Reality by expanding the grounds on which Ultimate Reality rested. For him, Ultimate Reality not only resided in humans but also existed in all things and acts in the everyday. Although Ch'oe Che-u, of course, believed that Ultimate Reality as the guiding force in the universe existed in all objects, he never articulated this type of existence as Ch'oe Si-hyŏng did. Using the term "all things and humans embody Ultimate Reality" (*ich'ŏn sikch'ŏn*), Ch'oe Si-hyŏng understood Ultimate Reality as the principal force in the world that dwelled in simple objects and structures, such as food, tools, and homes, as well as in everyday acts, such as greeting one another, helping one another, and working.[41] In his description of his new philosophy, he wrote: *"Ich'ŏn sikch'ŏn* is the fundamental law of heaven and earth. Under this philosophy, we are all interconnected (objects and humans). Since all thing and people embody and express Ultimate Reality, respecting all means respecting Ultimate Reality. . . . Eating anything means you are eating and embodying Ultimate Reality."[42] Under this new religious tenet, nothing was outside the force of Ultimate Reality. The everyday world thus became the contact point between the self and religious experience.

For Ch'oe Che-u, Ultimate Reality was a force that existed everywhere and was immanent in all things, but he never wrote about or articulated Ultimate Reality in the same way as Ch'oe Si-hyŏng. Although Cho'e Che-u believed that Ultimate Reality was a force that existed everywhere and was immanent in all things, he focused on its existence in humans. Only with Ch'oe Si-hyŏng's writings did it become clear to Tonghak followers that Ultimate Reality took on a pantheistic nature in that it was immanent in all, including the smallest objects and practices. This belief now meant that not only humans but also all things from nature to simple objects were sacred. Objects such as finished goods and buildings and acts such as eating a meal, drinking water, or interacting with nature now no longer carried simple meanings but instead became sacred objects and acts. The profane world was now broken, and the everyday world took on a new significance because it became the realm in which individuals could meet and experience Ultimate Reality.

If we place these religious conceptions of the relationship between humanity and Ultimate Reality in their historical context, Ch'oe Che-u's and Ch'oe Si-hyŏng's ideas laid the seeds for starting to alter the established discursive framework of the late nineteenth century. The two Tonghak leaders also expanded the meaning of religion for many Koreans because they emphasized the idea that individuals could have the agency to transform themselves spiritually. Under Confucianism and other traditional religions in Korea, individuals were bound to a cosmic order in which stability depended on the balance between good and evil. People became good and overall stability was maintained when individuals acted in accordance with their place in a hierarchical society and followed established rules. Under this religious structure, people needed only to follow rules and regulations since only the larger cosmic order held the power to transform and maintain individuals and society. The Tonghak religion, however, established a new form of religion in that it gave individuals the power to consciously transform themselves and gain immediate access to universality or Ultimate Reality. Instead of individually and socially being captive to a larger power, followers of the Tonghak religion were given the agency to become divine. Tonghak emphasized and affirmed humanity's power to undergo religious experience, be reconciled with Ultimate Reality, and change the world. Tonghak thus became a "participatory religion," as described by Stanley Tambiah, in which people held the consciousness and power to partake in, maintain, and expand a religion.[43]

Ch'oe Che-u's and Ch'oe Si-hyŏng's religious ideas also expanded the meaning of the everyday world. Since the world in every aspect embodied Ultimate Reality, the world and all things were sacred in Tonghak philosophy. According to Mircea Eliade, when space and objects become sacred, they no longer are homogeneous and neutral. Instead, they embody religious meaning and become the grounds in which individuals encounter religious experience. Maneuvering in sacred space and interacting with sacred objects lift individuals into another realm maintained and moved by Ultimate Reality in which they take on a new form of being that appears more authentic. Under these conditions, the sacred world overcomes the profane world, and individuals are able to discover authentic meaning while overcoming their fears of nothingness.[44] For Tonghak followers, the everyday world became a sacred site where the real was unveiled and individuals could experience Ultimate Reality not only by reading and meditating on Tonghak scripture but also through simple acts, such as spending time outdoors or eating. This idea about the sacred value of the everyday world was consistent with the shamanistic belief that spirits resided in the world. However, it differed from shamanism in that Tonghak ideas on the everyday world emphasized the manifestation of sacred forces through human activities, while shamanism stressed aspects of natural world as the habitat of spirits.

Tonghak in Action

Although Ch'oe Che-u offered new ideas on the form and practice of religion that tested the existing discursive field of knowledge, he never called for the total dismantling of the Confucian political order. In fact, despite the fact that his belief that all could be connected to Ultimate Reality or were Ultimate Reality would lend itself well to calls for political, social, and economic equality, Ch'oe made no calls to replace social hierarchy with a new system that would promote equality in every way.[45] Far from rejecting the standard mode of thought, Ch'oe appropriated Confucian concepts and language to refine his religious beliefs. Ch'oe's motivation for introducing Tonghak was less about challenging the Chosŏn government and its logic of governance and more about helping people transition to new conditions in a society anchored in a weakened Confucian political order.

Between 1860 and 1863, Ch'oe attracted a large following in the P'yŏngyang region and southern parts of Korea. Ch'oe's proselytization campaigns greatly concerned government officials. Worsening social, economic, and political conditions had already begun to expose the contradictions in the Confucian world order and had therefore undermined the state's power and authority to order reality. In place of Confucianism, many Koreans then turned to new religions, like Tonghak and Catholicism. To the state, these religious groups represented serious threats because they were spreading alternative "truths" that challenged Confucian orthodoxy. The state therefore carried out massive campaigns to wipe out these groups and their heterodox beliefs. While the government persecuted Catholics through multiple campaigns that culminated in its eradication by 1866, it carefully kept Ch'oe and the Tonghak under close surveillance. At first, investigators sent by the government appeared to be confused about the nature of Tonghak as they talked with Ch'oe and saw his followers performing various acts, such as presenting offerings at mountain altars and cleaning their mouths and bodies continuously. Unclear about Tonghak's exact nature, they reported that it resembled shamanism and Daoism.[46] Their puzzlement over Tonghak most certainly resulted from their inability to categorize Tonghak within the state's definition of established religions because of Tonghak's nature as a moral bricolage. The growing popularity of Tonghak and the state's inability to decipher it caused the state to become uneasy about Ch'oe, and he was arrested in 1864 for spreading a heterodox religion. The government executed him soon after his arrest and punished several Tonghak leaders.

Before his execution, Ch'oe appointed Ch'oe Si-hyŏng first as his deputy and later as his successor and leader of Tonghak in the fall of 1863. Some scholars have cast doubts on Ch'oe Si-hyŏng's assumption of the head position in Tonghak because other followers competed to become the leader of the religious organization after the founder's death.[47] Despite the debates, experts agree that Ch'oe Si-hyŏng was a high-ranking leader who assumed important responsibilities in rebuilding Tonghak. In his position, Ch'oe needed to deal with the issue of how to make Tonghak into an organized and functioning religion. Tonghak members in the early years relied on Ch'oe Che-u's teaching and guidance, which were sufficient given the relatively small size of the Tonghak group at this time. But as the group grew larger and with the execution of its founder, it became imperative to transform Tonghak into an organized religion with established doctrines, rites, and rituals in order to ensure its survival and create a movement that would effectively bind individuals together and spread its message.

Joachim Wach wrote that all religions express and organize themselves through three means: theoretically, practically, and sociologically.[48] Through these means, it becomes possible to encounter the experiences promised by the religion. Ch'oe Si-hyŏng began to organize the Tonghak religion around these three means because he knew that it was important to establish several avenues through which individuals could experience Ultimate Reality. Theoretically or intellectually, Ch'oe continued to develop Ch'oe Che-u's original ideas concerning the relationship between humans and Ultimate Reality. Like Ch'oe Che-u, he often wrote about and discussed the idea that Ultimate Reality existed in all and was the vital force in the universe.[49] However, he began to explore and introduce the concept that humans in fact were Ultimate Reality. Under this concept, humans no longer needed to strive to become Ultimate Reality because they already were divine. Yet, along the lines of Ch'oe Che-u's thoughts, Ch'oe Si-hyŏng believed that individuals still needed to cultivate the Ultimate Reality force inside their souls because negative ideas and conventions in the social world prevented or inhibited individuals from fully becoming Ultimate Reality.

While expanding the idea of Ultimate Reality, Ch'oe Si-hyŏng also articulated to the Tonghak followers Ch'oe Che-u's thoughts and beliefs concerning the origins of the universe and other existential questions. Ch'oe Si-hyŏng accomplished this task mostly through the publication of Ch'oe Che-u's various writings. With the help of Tonghak leaders such as Kang Si-wŏn, Yu Si-hŏn, and Sin Si-il, he collected Ch'oe Che-u's writings. In 1880, the first collection of essays was published as *Tonggyŏng taejŏn,* and the founder's poems were published as *Yongdam yusa.* It was reported that Ch'oe Si-hyŏng helped publish three hundred copies of both texts between 1880 and 1883.[50] By publishing these materials, Ch'oe not only introduced Ch'oe Che-u's ideas to the public but also provided texts that reaffirmed the importance of cultivating Ultimate Reality and reaching a divine state.

In the area of practice, Ch'oe Si-hyŏng became the first to establish and institutionalize Tonghak religious beliefs and creeds. In so doing, Ch'oe took the teachings of Ch'oe Che-u, further articulated them, and consecrated them as the official ideas and practices that all Tonghak members needed to follow. By establishing the new doctrines, Ch'oe set up the sacred nature of the religion. Sacred ideas and acts are those that are separated from the profane world and are given religious significance.[51] When sacred ideas and practices take on these characteristics, they serve to point to and allow us to experience the real (the infinite, God, and Ultimate Reality). Put differently, interacting with the sacred allows individuals to access a part of a larger objective structure that is considered real, authentic, and a force behind all in reality. Through the sacred, individuals believe that they are a part of an infinite world instead of a finite one.[52]

Sacred rituals in Tonghak became a key medium for facilitating an individual's path toward religious experience because they served as an opening to the sacred world described in Tonghak.[53] Indeed, rituals are a distinct form of acting that brings one to the ultimate source of power.[54] Along the lines of Ch'oe Che-u, Ch'oe Si-hyŏng advised Tonghak followers to perform a daily ritual of silent meditation. After 1875, Ch'oe expanded the ritual of meditation by mandating specific acts. He first ordered followers to begin meditation at 9:00 p.m. Followers were instructed to place before them a bowl of water, which was "the symbol of the original elements of Heaven and Earth," and meditate by repeating the Tonghak prayer written by Ch'oe Che-u. After their meditation, followers were then told to drink the water in the bowl.[55]

In 1878, Ch'oe instituted the most important ritual in the Tonghak religion: the weekly public worship service. During the service, followers listened to a short sermon, sang songs, and meditated silently. Throughout the whole service, worshippers chanted, "Think heaven, think of matter." At the end, people drank from the sacred water placed in front of them to connect with the original source of creation. Through this service, Ch'oe helped create an atmosphere in which people could overcome their personal concerns and collectively encounter and undergo similar religious experiences—experiences that would not occur alone.

Although sacred rituals would play a significant role in people's lives, Ch'oe Si-hyŏng established a set of sacred ideas or rules that were to govern the most important day of their lives: the world of the everyday or of work and leisure. These rules took on an ethical dimension that was intended to structure followers' lives and help them encounter the religious experiences promised by Tonghak ideas. Having the "right" ethics was important because, in the end, they would combine to establish the right conditions that Tonghak leaders believed would enable followers to realize their religious potential. In 1875, Ch'oe began his quest to build the ideal conditions by instituting simple sacred rules for Tonghak members to follow: (1) avoid committing idolatry; (2) abstain from eating meat and fish and drinking and smoking; and (3) use a bowl of water in all worship.[56]

Ch'oe eventually began to believe that all Tonghak ethics needed to be grounded in a sacred idea that had a profound impact on the highly stratified Chosŏn society: the principle of treating and respecting each individual as divine (*sain yŏch'ŏn*). According to Ch'oe, "Humans are Ultimate Reality. All are equal. Differences do not exist between humans, so the distinctions between high and low runs counter to the will of Ultimate Reality."[57] Since each individual possessed Ultimate Reality and was divine, Ch'oe believed that people were equal and needed to treat each other with the utmost respect and without discrimination. Under this tenet, Chosŏn ideas about class and society no longer applied to Tonghak followers; instead, they needed to uphold a society that disregarded political, economic, and social discrimination. Essentially, the principles of *sain yŏch'ŏn* challenged the feudal principles of

Chosŏn society.[58] This sacred rule articulated a new social belief that ruptured and challenged the Confucian symbolic order, which was based on the idea of social hierarchy.

Relying on the concept of *sain yŏch'ŏn* for guidance, in December 1888, Ch'oe Si-hyŏng instituted a set of sacred rules that mandated that Tonghak followers adopt certain practices in their everyday lives, including the following: "Treat all members of your family as if they were Ultimate Reality," "Give thanks to God in the morning and at every meal," "Recognize [treat] everyone as Ultimate Reality," and "Do not disrespect anyone, for you would then be disrespecting Ultimate Reality."[59] Following these rules would transform individuals and bring them closer to encountering an authentic state of religious experience. Equally important, because Korea was in a state of flux with the Confucian symbolic order crumbling, these Tonghak sacred rituals and rules combined to form a structure that took on the role of guiding individuals and governing social relationships.

Socially speaking, these sacred rituals and ideas were never simply given. Instead, Tonghak leaders and followers made and sustained the sacred. As Emile Durkheim noted, sacred ideas and practices are made by groups of people who set them apart and "keep them bounded by actions." They remain sacred as long as the group continues to place meaning on them and continues to act on them.[60] In this process of acting out the practices and following the ideas, not only is the sacred nature surrounding ideas and practices sustained, but also the practices and beliefs combine to help form a "conscious collective" among the believers in which individuals have a similar, particular view of the world.[61] In the end, sharing a similar conception of the world that is created by sacred beliefs and practices brings individuals together and fosters a community. In short, a collective of believers is formed. Moreover, this sharing gives an identity to a group and demarcates groups from one another, allowing followers to find identity and place.

Ch'oe Si-hyŏng and other Tonghak leaders understood, however, that a community of believers cannot be maintained by sacred rules and practices alone. Sustaining a community that upheld Tonghak principles required the creation of an effective leadership system. In 1862 and 1863, Ch'oe Si-hyŏng built a top-down leadership organization in which central Tonghak leaders selected and appointed other leaders to oversee local chapters. Through this system, the top leadership maintained surveillance and control over the local areas. The central leadership of the Tonghak group further solidified its control over local areas and established a more efficient organizational structure through the implementation of the *p'o* system in 1884. Under this system, the supreme leader of the Tonghak was at the top. Under him and his assistants was a regionally based organization (*p'o*). At the bottom, in villages and local communities, was a local congregation (*jup*).[62] A leadership council presided over regional and local congregations. The council was made up of a chief (*kyojang*), a teacher (*kyosu*), a chief administrator (*tojip*), a judge (*chipgang*), a counselor (*taejong*), and a censor (*chongjŏng*).[63] This council served as the leadership structure in regional offices and local villages wherever Tonghak members lived and thus maintained a disciplined environment in which Tonghak doctrine was practiced.

As the main form of leadership, the *p'o* structure also aimed to help realize the goal of creating and sustaining the ideal community in which individuals would treat each other without any forms of discrimination while working and living together as a collective unit. In a sense, the collective life (*tonggwi ilch'e*) would be an organic unit in which individuals lived and worked together closely like a family. Like the physical body and its many parts, each person would have a special skill and would use that skill to maintain the organic unit of the whole body of believers. Although everyone would be interconnected and considered one, the supreme Tonghak leader and the other leaders were the main figures who would guide the people. Bonded by the ideas of love, respect, and equality, Tonghak followers would be one unit in which they worked together to maintain an environment in which Ultimate Reality could be realized in all.

A Religious Revolution?

By the 1890s, there were 339 regionally based organizations and local congregations and close to 300,000 members associated with the Tonghak group.[64] The surge in Tonghak's popularity and the threat of Western and Japanese imperialism after 1876 led many Chosŏn leaders to fear total destabilization on the Korean peninsula. Fearing the loss of order and stability, government leaders quickly started harassment and persecution campaigns against Tonghak followers and leaders. The state's official repression campaign began when the governor of Ch'ungch'ŏng Province outlawed the Tonghak religion in 1892.

Ch'oe Si-hyŏng and the northern leaders (individuals mostly from the P'yŏngyang region or the northwest region) demanded that the governor of Ch'ungch'ŏng reestablish the legal status of Tonghak and asked the governors of Chŏlla Provinces to exonerate the name of Ch'oe Che-u. Rejected by both governors, Ch'oe petitioned King Kojong in April 1893 to legalize Tonghak and grant protection to Tonghak members from local officials. Unable to attain any concessions, Tonghak leaders returned to their homes and refused to take any armed actions against the government. The continuing oppression of Tonghak members, however, forced Ch'oe Si-hyŏng to call a general meeting of all Tonghak leaders to discuss how to respond to the government's campaign against Tonghak in April 1893.[65] Alarmed by the gathering, the state promised to punish oppressive local officials and asked the Tonghak members to return home. Ch'oe agreed to the state's demands and disbanded the meeting.

Although Ch'oe abided by nonviolence, a group of Tonghak followers embraced violence in order to create a new society for Tonghak followers. This group of Tonghak members mostly came from the southern provinces in Korea and was led by Chŏn Pong-jun.[66] A descendant of a landed gentry (yangban) family, Chŏn turned to the Tonghak religion at the age of thirty. He studied under Ch'oe Si-hyŏng and later headed a regionally based organization in Chŏlla Province. In his position, Chŏn encountered the corruption of government officials who demanded forced labor from peasants, unfairly taxed many peasants, and demanded grain from villagers. Unable to express his concerns to the governor of Chŏlla, Chŏn and other Tonghak followers attacked government offices in the province in February 1894, thus beginning the Tonghak Revolution and further turning the nineteenth century in Korea into a period of mass peasant uprisings.

Chŏn was able to mobilize enough followers and resources to capture most of the areas in the Chŏlla Provinces by May 1894. Along the way, many slaves, daily workers, and peasants joined this movement. An examination of the demands made by the Tonghak leadership shows that their main grievances were against the state. They demanded abolition of unfair taxes, punishment of corrupt local officials, and the prohibition of grain exports.[67] Understanding the gravity of the situation, the government brokered a cease-fire with Tonghak members in June 1894 and promised to cancel all debts and end all forms of discrimination. The truce between the government and Tonghak, however, ended in the fall of 1894 when the government failed to carry out the brokered agreement. Feeling betrayed, those who had revolted earlier took up arms against the state. This time, however, their fight coincided with the Sino-Japanese War, which erupted in August 1894. Seeing foreign troops on the peninsula and threatening the sovereignty of Korea, Tonghak and non-Tonghak followers decided to wage war against both the Korean state and Japan, which had forcibly seized the Korean king's palace.

In this new struggle, Chŏn gained the support and help of Ch'oe Si-hyŏng and his followers. In the first revolution, Ch'oe and his northern supporters had refused to use violence to achieve the goals of the Tonghak group and had left Chŏn and his southern followers to fight alone. Persuaded by his advisers, Ch'oe agreed to support Chŏn's second revolution and joined forces with Chŏn. The Tonghak army quickly captured the city of Kongju, which was only one hundred miles away from Seoul. After this victory, however, the Tonghak army met government and Japanese troops and was quickly defeated in battle. Soon after, the government captured and executed Chŏn. In the summer of

1898, the government captured and executed Ch'oe. Before Ch'oe died, however, he appointed Son Pyŏng-hŭi as the next Tonghak leader.

The Tonghak Revolution was a significant event that mobilized many Koreans to address the problems arising from the breakdown of the Confucian political order. Yet despite originally being started by Tonghak members and later supported by the main leaders of Tonghak, the Tonghak Revolution was less about achieving a new spiritual kingdom based on Tonghak beliefs and more about establishing religious freedom and overcoming foreign imperialism.[68] In fact, the main participants in the revolution were non-Tonghak individuals who did not see the movement through religious lenses. Even the Tonghak core leadership, such as Ch'oe Si-hyŏng, never thought of starting a mass social movement to create a new world where the ideal spiritual state could unfold; only after Japan threatened Korea's sovereignty did Ch'oe support the emerging revolution. The Tonghak religion shifted the epistemological terrain by offering a new reality with ideas and practices, but it never promoted a form of activism to transform social, economic, and cultural realms in order to achieve religious goals. The organization's call to build a new religion-based society, or a new heaven on earth, came only in the 1920s as capitalism ruptured Korean society.

The Arrival of Protestant Christianity

When the Tonghak Revolution ended in the 1890s, Protestant Christianity entered and further ruptured the established religious environment of Chosŏn Korea. A Catholic missionary, Father Chou Wên-mu, and Korean converts first spread Christianity among the population in the last quarter of the eighteenth century, but Catholicism was severely repressed in 1866 through state-led persecution campaigns. After 1884, the state allowed Protestant missionaries in the expectation that they would help Korea become civilized and enlightened like Western countries. From 1884 to 1937, Protestant Christian groups built an infrastructure of churches and economic, social, and cultural institutions that made Protestant Christianity into a large and influential force in colonial society and later turned South Korea into a country with one of the largest population of Christians. More than in China and Japan, Protestant Christianity had a deep impact on the formation of economic, social, and cultural ideas, practices, and structures in Korea at a time when people sought meanings for changes produced by Japanese colonialism,

The first Protestant missionaries arrived in Korea in the 1880s at a time when the fervor for missionary activities was at its height in the Western world. Throughout the nineteenth century, colonial projects were taking shape in many parts of the non-Western world. As colonial powers focused on restructuring the political and economic infrastructures of colonized countries and also on exporting raw resources to the homelands of colonial powers, many Protestant Christian groups decided to be the force that would develop the inner qualities of individuals or civilize the colonized by converting them to Christianity, which they believed undergirded the ideas and practices that made Western countries so strong.[69] Hoping to civilize the natives, American and European Protestant Christian groups built missionary stations throughout parts of Africa, China, India, and the Middle East and began teaching them the tenets of Christianity. Wanting to form a stronger presence in Asia by establishing a permanent mission in Korea, the Presbyterian Church in the United States of America (PCUSA or Presbyterian North Church) sent Dr. Horace Allen to Seoul in 1884. Allen served not only as a representative of the Presbyterian Church but also as a physician to members of the foreign legations. Soon after Allen's arrival, Horace Underwood (PCUSA) and Henry Appenzeller of the Methodist Episcopalian North Church (Methodist North Church) arrived in Korea in 1885. The Presbyterian North and the Methodist North eventually became the two largest missionary organizations on the peninsula.[70]

Familiarizing themselves with Korean people and culture, missionaries soon mapped out ways to evangelize and convert Koreans. Through councils and organizations, the missionary groups developed various approaches to evangelizing Koreans and converting them into true believers.[71] To create an effective plan, both Presbyterian and Methodist missionaries relied on the Nevius Plan.[72] Dr. John L. Nevius was a Presbyterian missionary in China who created a new "way in mission methods."[73] Unlike traditional missionary methods, in which foreign missionaries established, financed, and maintained churches and institutions, Nevius proposed that churches and other Christian institutions be self-supporting and governed by natives themselves. Moreover, natives, instead of missionaries, would be at the forefront of spreading the Christian message in local areas. Centering all activities and responsibilities on the native believers would not only build Christian confidence and responsibility in the native believers but also supply a space in which native believers could freely express themselves and spread Christianity without any hindrances from missionaries. To him, having missionaries create and operate everything only created an environment in which natives were dependent on the missionary.[74] Under his new plan, with natives leading and working at the forefront, Nevius envisioned the rapid and solid growth of an indigenous Christian movement.

Wanting to produce a strong movement, Presbyterian and Methodist missionaries adopted the Nevius Plan in 1892. Missionaries first introduced the Christian message and then allowed natives to create and self-support their own churches and other Christian institutions. Moreover, the missionaries stressed that "Koreans must be led to Christ by their own fellow country-men."[75] Although they relied on the Nevius Plan for guidance, the missionar-ies tailored this plan to their ambitions by specifically emphasizing that peas-ants and women would be their target audience.[76] The first two rules of the missionary plan were "It is better to aim at the conversion of the working classes [those in the rural areas] than that of the higher classes, and second, the conversion of women and the training of Christian girls should be an es-pecial aim."[77] Specifically aiming to convert peasants and women displayed the astute and practical nature of missionaries. Since peasants made up the majority of the population and women were vital because of their influence over children, missionaries knew that converting members of these groups would not only quickly turn Korea into a Christian nation but would also secure future generations of Christians.[78] This tactic of missionaries in Korea was quite different from other missionary campaigns, such as those in Japan, which specifically concentrated their efforts in urban areas. By targeting peas-ants and women in the countryside while also establishing a presence in the few cities on the Korean peninsula, the foreign missionary groups made a firm statement that they aimed to have a strong presence in the rural areas.

Using this plan as a source of guidance, the missionaries built mission stations in various cities and used them as bases from which to travel out and preach to those in the surrounding rural areas. Focusing on the northwestern and southeastern sections of the peninsula, PCUSA missionaries built mis-sion stations in cities such as P'yŏngyang in 1893 and Taegu in 1895. Method-ist North missionaries, who resided in the central parts of Korea and parts of the northwest, established bases in cities such as Wŏnju and Seoul. The other denominations constructed bases in the remaining areas of the peninsula: the PCUS in Chŏlla Provinces, the Australian Presbyterian Church in South Kyŏngsang, the Methodist South in Kangwŏn Province and parts of Kyŏnggi Province, and the United Church of Canada in Hamgyŏng Provinces. From these bases in cities, missionaries traveled to the countryside, evangelized to local Koreans, selected individuals to lead the local church, and gave them the responsibility to build a church and finance their mission.[79] Missionaries periodically visited local churches and received monthly progress reports from local Christian leaders.[80] Between 1892 and 1905, missionaries helped build close to 321 churches and 470 stations.[81]

To bolster their church activities, missionaries from all denominations constructed an elaborate social service structure. Building schools and Bible institutes became a priority since teaching youths and adults how to read and write would enable individuals to read, study, and understand Christian writ-ings. More important, educational institutions would be the main means to disseminate religious ideas and beliefs and introduce knowledge and subjects taught in Western schools. As the two largest missionary groups, PCUSA and Methodist North missionaries led the introduction of a new and elaborate educational system in Korea. In P'yŏngyang, PCUSA missionaries built a number of primary schools. They also established secondary schools for girls, such Sungui Girls Academy (1912), and secondary schools for boys, such as Sungsil Academy (1897), Sungdok Academy (1907), and Sungin Academy (1907). Sungsil Academy eventually turned into a college or university (Union Christian College or Sungsil University) and became a leading educational institution that would play a vital role in the Presbyterian rural campaign.[82] To train future Christian leaders, Presbyterian North missionaries also established the Presbyterian Theological Seminary in 1902 and the P'yŏngyang Seminary for Women in 1908. In Seoul, Methodist North missionaries constructed a vast array of schools, including Paejae Boy's School in 1885 and Ewha Girl's School in 1886, which later became Ewha University. Horace Underwood and his wife established the Presbyterian Missionary Orphanage in 1886 and the Presbyterian Girls School in 1890. Later, Presbyterian North and Methodist North missionaries worked together to build Chosen Christian College (Yonsei University today) in 1915. Besides the schools in P'yŏngyang and Seoul, missionaries from all organizations erected schools for youth wherever they evangelized and local Bible institutes where older adults studied the Bible.[83]

Alongside the educational system, missionaries expanded health services in Korea by introducing Western medicine and establishing medical facilities, which provided services to anyone regardless of class. In P'yŏngyang, Presbyterian North missionaries built the Caroline Ladd Memorial Hospital in 1905, while other Presbyterian North missionaries worked to construct Severance Medical College and Nursing School in 1905. In many mission stations, ranging from PCUS (Presbyterian Church in the United States) missions to Canadian Presbyterian missions, small medical facilities existed that offered basic medical services to local people.[84] Providing medical services and education to many people, missionary stations functioned as more than just religious institutions. Through churches, schools, medical facilities, and other institutions, foreign missionaries established a comprehensive framework that allowed them to spread Christian teachings and influence society.

The Revival Movement

As missionary groups were establishing an institutional structure on the peninsula to spread the Christian message throughout Korea, many Koreans were finding language and symbols in the Christian message that could give meaning to the various changes that they were experiencing. According to observers of events from 1890 to 1910, Koreans encountered changes when fighting between Chinese and Japanese forces erupted on the peninsula in the summer of 1894. The Sino-Japanese War ravaged the Korean peninsula until the spring of 1895, severely damaging many areas. According to one missionary, in the city and surrounding areas of P'yŏngyang, "Korean property was destroyed, fields were ravaged, and many of the unhappy people, caught between the upper and nether millstones, suffered from wounds as well as fear."[85] People were reported to be in a state of shock, disbelief, and disarray as they tried to deal with these changes. Many were in a traumatized state because the unanticipated events did not fit a "real or imagined context," leading many to mass confusion.[86] Robert Speer, a leading American missionary official, toured Korea in the late 1890s and noticed that "dissatisfaction with the old life, its failures, miseries, disaffection, were wide spread."[87] Arthur Brown, touring the country in 1901, believed that Korean people were faced with distress.[88]

Japan's declaration of Korea as a protectorate in 1905 only increased political uncertainty on the peninsula and unsteadiness in many Koreans. In a matter of thirty years, Korea lost its political independence and the symbolic order that gave significance and justification to established ideas and practices. According to one magazine article in 1905, "A crisis has been reached. The political situation brings the entire people to a state of unrest."[89] What may have exacerbated this chaotic state was the official dismantling of the Confucian order through the 1894 Kabo Reforms.[90] The government's official distancing of itself from a Confucian past that had ordered reality and had made it meaningful for hundreds of years most certainly caused some Koreans to question the value of Confucianism in helping them make sense of the changing material reality. Consequently, many Koreans turned to different religions, including shamanism, Chŭngsan-gyo, and Taejong-gyo, to find "an image of such a genuine order of the world which will account for, and even celebrate, the perceived ambiguities, puzzles, and the paradoxes in human experience."[91]

The changing environment convinced missionaries that they should take advantage of the situation by starting large-scale revival movements because they witnessed people seeking and wanting new experiences that overcame their distress.[92] Missionaries also wanted to start revival meetings as a way to depoliticize Korean Christians who were beginning to view the church as a political agent that could combat the Japanese. Because the politicization of the church would lead many Koreans to focus less on spiritual development and jeopardize the church's standing under colonial rule, missionaries in 1905–1906 held hundreds of revival meetings where they preached and led all-night prayer meetings with the hope of having "their [Koreans'] thoughts taken away from the national situation to their own personal relation with the Master [Christ]."[93]

Although the 1903 Wŏnsan Revival was an important event for missionaries, the P'yŏngyang Revival in 1907 became the watershed moment that fundamentally transformed the future of Protestant Christian activities in Korea. In January 1907, PCUSA missionaries organized several large tent meetings and prayer meetings in P'yŏngyang, which was considered the center of Christianity in Korea. At first, the revivals evoked very tepid responses from people who attended the various meetings, leaving both missionaries and Korean Christian leaders deeply disappointed and with "heavy hearts."[94] The mood of the revival, however, quickly transformed into a state of euphoria when five to six hundred individuals participated in an all-night prayer meeting and "man after man would rise, confess his sins, break down and weep, and then throw himself to the floor and beat the floor with his fists in a perfect agony of conviction."[95] The emotions from this meeting spread to other parts of the city and soon throughout the whole country.[96] During this period of revivals, boys and girls at schools began to cry out, "Is there any hope, is there any forgiveness for us?"[97] At some churches, men and women cried uncontrollably as they asked for the forgiveness of their sins.

Throughout the P'yŏngyang Revival and other subsequent revivals, missionaries consistently called on Koreans to confess their sins and ask God for forgiveness because they believed that sin was the root of all social problems. Koreans responded to this call and revealed the transgressions they had committed against God. Some Christians asked for forgiveness for petty crimes, such as stealing.[98] Many men confessed to hating others, adultery, misuse of funds in churches, pride, envy, murder, and lusting after women.[99] The majority of people, however, confessed to sinning against the colonial occupiers by having "hatred of the Japanese, and even . . . murderous thoughts and plans towards them."[100] According to observers, the environment at the revival meetings was like a huge storm in which Koreans spent days and nights publicly confessing their sins and seeking God's forgiveness and approval.[101] One observer described the heightened state of emotion in the revival meetings: "He [a Korean man] beat the hard wooden flooring till his hands bled, he shrieked and begged for mercy. 'Is this what sin is?' said the awe-stricken multitudes. 'We never knew it was so awful. We had thought it a trifle, but, behold, here is what God thinks.'"[102] To Koreans, it was sin that was causing their pain and suffering; hating the Japanese, stealing from others, and committing other moral transgressions were the root of all of their problems and separated them from God.

Urging Koreans to declare their sins and ask for forgiveness publicly, missionaries made sin into a symbol that explained why Korean society was in a poor state and Koreans were suffering so much. At the time of the P'yŏngyang Revival, Koreans lived in a state of trauma in which all the political, social, and economic events and changes, especially the 1905 Protectorate Treaty, could not be explained by existing signs and symbols. The existing languages failed to explain the origins of the turmoil in Korean society. Unable to supply reasons for their current predicament, people suffered and were in a state of confusion and disarray. By telling Koreans to concentrate on revealing their sins and transgressions, religious leaders enabled Koreans to make a connection between their individual sins and the overall state of their country; humans were alienated from God and therefore were separated from his love because of sin.

With this meaning of sin, Koreans were able to name their suffering and pinpoint its origins.[103] Knowing the root cause of their problems gave Koreans the opportunity to endure their current predicament. As Clifford Geertz points out, religious symbolism enables humans to cope with suffering by "placing it in a meaningful context, providing a mode of action through which it can be expressed, being expressed understood, and being understood, endured."[104] The revival meetings became a time when individuals learned a new language with which to speak of their suffering and were able to identify the source of their problems. Through this process, people could overcome the unknown and were now equipped with the knowledge not only to overcome their confused, traumatic state but also to endure and engage "present concerns and future possibilities."[105] Christianity offered a path for people to tackle and overcome suffering.

The P'yŏngyang Revival and the overall revival movement became a defining moment for Protestant Christians because they showed Koreans the value of Christianity in helping them negotiate the new challenges in their lives, which helped legitimize the new religion in society. As missionaries preached about sin and the need for repentance, a large number of people turned to Christianity.[106] To capitalize on the success of the P'yŏngyang Revival, missionaries made calls to inaugurate a new evangelical campaign to create the first Asian Christian nation in Korea, which many missionaries believed would be the staging point for the spread of Christianity throughout Asia.[107] Presbyterian missionaries responded to this call by first solidifying the Presbyterian Church's presence in Korea by establishing an independent Presbytery of Korea, which would include the Presbyterian North, the Presbyterian South, the Canadian Church, and the Australian Church, on September 17, 1907.[108] Soon after the establishment of the Presbyterian Church, Presbyterians joined the Southern Methodists' Million Man Movement (1909–1910) with hopes of carrying out ambitious conversion campaigns.

Remaking Koreans

The P'yŏngyang Revival became a defining moment for the Protestant Christian movement in Korea in that it gave missionaries and Korean Christians hope about the future. Drawing from the excitement during the revival, church leaders envisioned harnessing the energy of the people in order to establish a new ideal Christian nation. To do so meant transforming the religious terrain for Koreans by moving them away from the profane world and into the sacred world of Christianity and a new history with a positive and liberating future with God. The missionaries' ideas about what constituted a Christian and what constituted sacred ideas and practices stemmed from their own backgrounds and the religious environment in the nineteenth-century United States. During the 1700s and 1800s, religion in the United States was dominated by the onset of the Great Awakening (1730–1770s) and the Second and Third Great Awakenings (1800–1830 and 1880–1910, respectively). From these three awakenings, a new form of Christian theology emerged: Evangelicalism or Revivalism. Aiming to simplify the Christian message in a time of economic, political, and social changes in the United States, Christian leaders formed evangelical theology, which postulated that people were in a natural condition of sin, and therefore salvation could be procured only through their acceptance of Jesus Christ as their savior. Evangelicalism promoted this simple message as the crux of Christianity instead of emphasizing "church membership, participation in the sacraments, or theological investigation as central to Christian faith."[109] Evangelicals did not subject the Bible to any forms of deeper theological investigation and instead believed that it was inerrant and directly from the mouth of God.[110]

Evangelicalism focused on and placed the power, burden, and responsibility of conversion and gaining salvation on the individual. Evangelicalism, however, demanded more than just conversion. According to Jerald Brauer, evangelicals (or, as Brauer calls them, Revivalists) also expected people to respond to the experience of conversion by displaying it in their actions, which meant living moral lives. Displaying a moral life, under Evangelicalism, became a priority in Christianity, while less regard was given to studying and interpreting doctrine and theology. Evangelical leaders stressed the need to live a moral life because it validated a person's conversion experience as authentic rather than stemming from emotional experiences in church and revivals.[111] In their view, an authentic spiritual conversion would lead a Christian to live naturally a moral life that displayed God's grace and will. Living a moral life first required spreading the Christian message and converting nonbelievers. Moreover, people should not drink, smoke, or dance.[112] Since laziness was a sign of sin, evangelicals stressed the need for people to possess a strong work ethic.[113]

Evangelicals considered the world a place of evil and a breeding ground for sin. Therefore, in order to maintain and preserve their moral life, evangelicals called for followers to refrain from getting involved with political and socioeconomic issues and to focus instead on cultivating one's moral and religious life and spreading the Christian message. Evangelical leaders especially emphasized a "culture of the self" by exhorting believers to focus inward rather than outward. This culture of the self was part of a larger trend in the 1880s United States that emphasized the regeneration of a new spiritual self as a way to overcome the banality and impotence of modern culture. This trend arose in response to the rapid growth of organized corporate capitalism and how it rationalized and standardized work and daily life in a way that narrowed the "the range and intensity of human experience."[114] Far from affording greater autonomy and the expansion of the self, the rationalization of economic life and culture "promoted a spreading sense of moral impotence and spiritual sterility—a feeling that life had become not only overcivilized but also curiously unreal."[115] Seeking alternatives to "modern unreality," Americans, especially the bourgeois, turned to various means to achieve authentic spiritual experiences, such as Eastern religions, medieval religious beliefs, a pastoral life, and preindustrial craftsmanship.[116] What they hoped to achieve through these means for spirituality was the birth of an authentic self who enjoyed deep and intense experiences.

The majority of missionaries in Korea emerged from this environment in the United States, especially Presbyterian North and Methodist North missionaries. Coming into Korea, these missionaries carried and firmly believed in the evangelical message of conversion and salvation and the need to create a culture that would maintain an authentic Christian personhood. Even more than evangelical ministers in the United States, missionaries in Korea placed great emphasis on the mind and body conforming to strong moral standards.[117] They quickly dismissed any ideas and practices that challenged the evangelical message and therefore disrupted the reality envisioned by Evangelicalism as "heretic" or "sinful." Arthur Judson Brown, a leader in the Northern Presbyterian Church Foreign Missionary Board, succinctly characterized the typical missionary in Korea:

He looked upon dancing, smoking, and card playing as sins in which no true followers of Christ should indulge. In theology and biblical criticism, he was strongly conservative, and he held as a vital truth the premillenarian view of the second coming of Christ. The higher criticism and liberal theology were deemed dangerous heresies. In most of the evangelical churches of America and Great Britain, conservatives and liberals have learned to live and work together in peace; but in Korea the few men who hold the "modern view" have a rough road to travel.[118]

Brown highlights the fact that missionaries in Korea tended to be more extreme in their religious views than evangelicals in the United States.

Among missionaries in Korea, Samuel A. Moffett best represented the type of missionary described by Brown. After graduating from McCormick Presbyterian Theological Seminary, Moffett arrived in Korea in 1890. He established the Presbyterian North mission in P'yŏngyang and became one of the leading missionaries in Korea. In his position, he advocated a message of finding salvation and authentic religious conversion only through the acceptance of Jesus Christ as one's savior.[119] More than anything, according to Moffett, "Salvation from sin . . . is the essence of the Gospel message."[120] Moffett's description of Christianity took the tone of evangelical leaders in the United States in that he believed that evangelical projects should spread a simple message of conversion, have people read the Bible and believe in its inerrancy, and push people to evangelize to others. Moffett also believed that converted individuals should show a transformation of character that showed "true repentance and hatred of sin, g[ave] strength to resist temptation and overcome sin, and up[held] a consistent Christian life."[121] Christians needed to differentiate themselves from nonbelievers and validate their conversion by living a strong moral life that involved abiding by certain rules, such as ceasing to drink, swear, smoke, and commit adultery and rejecting Confucian ancestral rituals and other religious practices. Being a moral, upright Christian also required converting others since it validated one's sincerity to Christianity. Finding this an important aspect of Christianity, Moffett supported a policy of requiring Christians to proselytize others in order to gain membership in a church. Drawing from these beliefs, Moffett outlined how to attain salvation and how to live a life blessed by God.

Sharing Moffett's vision of the ideal Christian, most missionaries and Korean Christian leaders set up a cultural nexus that would establish norms that demarcated the sacred from the profane and thus realize the moral and blessed life in all believers. Living and maintaining a moral life called for the creation of ethical standards. Through Bible studies, church sermons, and missionary schools, Koreans learned Christian tenets, such as "Love your neighbor" and "Love your enemy."[122] These tenets demanded that Korean Christians overcome their initial emotions and embrace their enemies, including the Japanese. Koreans also learned about the dangers of tobacco, drinking, and uncleanness.[123] In Presbyterian churches, most pastors and missionaries withheld membership or baptism if one smoked, drank, failed to keep the Sabbath, committed adultery, or engaged in ancestral rites.[124] The world was full of vices, and therefore, keeping Christian discipline through these rules was imperative for the birth of a new Christian society.

Church officials exhorted followers, instead of engaging in sinful acts, to partake in sacred acts such as praying, attending church functions, and fellowshipping with other Christians.[125] Moreover, religious leaders told Christians to read the Bible daily. To show that one's conversion was authentic and genuine, Korean church leaders and missionaries demanded that followers spread the message to others. In fact, many made this act a precondition of baptism and church membership. George Heber Jones, a Methodist North missionary, criticized prospective church members who failed to share the Christian message with others. Describing the standard practice of the Korean church, he wrote, "It has become the universal rule in Korea that the ticket of admission to membership in the Christian Church is another soul won to Jesus Christ."[126] For the Presbyterian Church, Charles Allen Clark wrote, "It has certainly been a custom of the evangelistic missionaries that they would not baptize any person unless he had at least shown that he had tried to win someone else."[127]

Living and representing the blessed and moral Christian life also demanded a disciplined daily life that would keep followers on track to reach and sustain true redemption. In particular, missionaries and Korean Christian leaders called on followers to maintain an industrious, idleness-free daily life. Coming from the nineteenth-century United States, where work was considered a moral virtue, missionaries in Korea held steadfast to the thought that possessing a strong work ethic allowed individuals to develop positive characteristics, such as fortitude, foresight, and self-control.[128] Developing these characteristics through hard work, individuals would be focused and disciplined and therefore able to avert sin. Missionaries laid further importance on displaying a strong work ethic because it showed that one was under God's grace. Indeed, missionaries and Korean church leaders believed that working hard validated the sincerity of a person's faith and an individual's salvation. Influenced by this environment in the nineteenth-century United States, missionaries in Korea hoped to make Koreans into productive workers.[129]

Many missionaries thought that making Koreans into hard workers would not be easy. Although they respected the spiritual vigor of Koreans, missionaries commonly characterized them as "lazy," "ignorant," and without any judgment, foresight, or energy.[130] Finding the current lifestyles of Koreans unacceptable for a healthy Christian life, the missionaries constructed several programs to build a strong work ethic in Koreans. Methodists, the Presbyterian Church, and the Young Men's Christian Association (YMCA) led the drive to make men and women into hard workers through industrial education departments (IEDs). Missionaries decided that industrial work was the most suitable means to teach the work ethic because it was considered the appropriate mode of production in a modern society. In fact, both missionaries and Koreans thought of industrialization as a requirement to become "civilized and enlightened."[131] Transforming Koreans into productive industrial workers was a process open to both young males and females, but it was anything but equal. IEDs taught vocations to males that involved machinery, while women were expected to learn occupational skills that would require only the use of their hands.

Practicing what students learned took place in factory-like settings in buildings that housed IEDs. The largest factory spaces were located at the IEDs in the Anna Davis School, the John Wells School, the Songdo Textile Department, and the YMCA. Because the Anna Davis School, the John Wells School, and the Songdo Textile Department taught students how to manufacture textiles, these IEDs set up rows of hand, foot, and power looms on the main floor of the IED buildings. Alongside technical skills, the IEDs also taught students rudimentary business skills. At the John Wells School, students learned how to use the abacus and perform simple arithmetic and elementary bookkeeping.[132] Teachers at the school also taught students "modern business methods."[133] The YMCA IED offered lectures on such themes as "the dignity of labor," "the value of money," and "methods in the modern business world."[134] These classes and lectures provided a definition of success and showed how business transformed a person into an upstanding Christian.

For most women, missionaries believed that exhibiting a strong work ethic meant staying home, attending to matters associated with the domestic domain, and taking care of the family as wise mothers and good wives. Given this gendered view in which women were expected to occupy only the private space of the home, missionaries believed that it was necessary to teach Korean women modern ideas and practices to maintain a proper household because Korean women lacked any education, especially on hygiene, and practiced feudal and backward customs. Alongside teaching women how to read and write, missionaries also taught them about the Bible and basic Christian beliefs, which they were expected to pass on to family members. Secondary schools in Seoul and P'yŏngyang also offered women courses on domestic science, such as how to cook, clean, and keep proper hygiene. In P'yŏngyang and Kwangju, PCUSA missionaries set up programs where women learned how to raise children properly through instruction on hygiene, how to feed their babies, and how to discipline their children. At times, to motivate women to work harder, PCUSA missionaries held "better-baby contests" where missionaries decided which women were best at raising their children.[135] Missionaries expected these teachings to mold Korean women into productive mothers and wives who would supervise the religious training of their family and make sure that members of their households were productive Christians.[136]

Combining all the rules and moral teachings proposed by the church, this cultural nexus became a system that was to inform Korean Christians about what was right and what was wrong. Through this cultural system, Christian followers were expected to learn what ideas and practices were sacred and permitted and what were profane and prohibited. In effect, then, Koreans not only underwent proselytization but also a course of development in which their identities, personalities, and worldviews were targeted for reshaping. Missionaries sought to change the everyday lives of Koreans by unfixing and reforming the very identities and characteristics that had led to their heathen, uncivilized state and loss of independence to Japan. Like other colonized people in the world whose bodies and minds were influenced by colonizers and missionaries, Koreans thus found themselves experiencing a process that inscribed "a new conception of space, new forms of personhood, and a new means of manufacturing the experience of the real."[137] It was ultimately a process with IEDs and different types of Western-style reforms that was informed by the norms of modernization. For the missionaries in Korea, the standards of a proper Christian personhood derived from what they had seen and experienced in Western societies—specifically the elements of modernity that they believed had allowed for prosperous countries in the West. In the minds of missionaries, a process of shedding harmful customs and incorporating certain norms of modernity that were popular in the West would ensure the single-mindedness, perseverance, and discipline needed to sustain and further expand the ideal Christian life. Japanese authorities had usurped political power by 1905, but missionaries played a significant role in trying to detach converted Koreans from their past lives and instill new habits through their own modernization programs.

From the reconstruction of the Korean self through the Christian cultural nexus, many missionaries and Korean Christian leaders expected followers of Christianity to be devoted solely to developing their personal relationship with God and spreading the gospel to others. Many Protestant Christian leaders and institutions thus considered questioning the process of modernization and engaging in various forms of activism (political, economic, and social) distractions that diverted Christians from their primary mission of becoming true followers of Jesus Christ. Moreover, several missionaries and Korean Christian leaders constantly preached that the material world was unimportant and full of evil, thereby emphasizing the idea that material concerns (political and economic) were second to spiritual concerns.[138] The everyday world for Christians was devoid of religious expression and significance and filled with little more than sin. If economic and political problems arose, the church taught Koreans to pray, ask God for the forgiveness of sins, and wait for the next kingdom when Jesus returned to earth; Koreans were taught not to question and to attempt to solve major problems in society caused by modernization. Arthur Judson Brown described the nonsocial aspect of Christianity in Korea:

Another characteristic of Korean Christianity is comparative in-difference to the social application of the gospel. The thought of the Korean churches is fixed on the next world. The present world is regarded as so utterly lost that it cannot be saved in this dispensation; nor is it believed that the Divine plan contemplates such an end. The duty of the church now is to preach the gospel "for a witness," to gather out the elect, and to leave the world till Christ shall return. . . . Efforts to clean up the community and to bring about better social conditions are regarded as a use of time and strength that could be more usefully employed in other ways. "What are you doing in the way of social reform?" a Korean missionary was once asked. "Nothing," was the reply, "we are too busy preaching the gospel."[139]

The Presbyterian North missionaries best represented Brown's description of church leaders in Korea. Some Methodists and members of the Canadian Presbyterian Church tended to believe in liberal forms of theology that embraced some forms of social activism.[140] The majority of missionaries and Korean Christian leaders, however, disapproved of followers becoming too involved with political and economic affairs.

As Timothy Lee points out, missionaries "conceived as the ultimate goal of their missions the saving of souls, not the amelioration of Korea's social or political ills."[141] Because nationalist activities and sentiments by followers could jeopardize the church's relationship with the Japanese colonizers, "whose toleration was crucial to their evangelistic work in Korea," and divert the church from its main priority of converting Koreans,[142] Protestant missionaries not only kept out of nationalist politics but also exhorted followers to avoid worldly affairs like anticolonial struggles. Moreover, they spoke out little, if at all, against the problems caused by modernization, especially poverty and the dislocation of people's lives. Homer B. Hulbert, Dr. Frank W. Scofield, and a few other missionaries criticized Japanese colonialism, but the majority of missionaries and Korean Christian leaders called for followers to promote Evangelicalism and cultivate their personal relationship with God.[143] For the Christian community, the transformation of Korea should take place first in the individual and not in society.

Before 1919, certain Christians questioned the missionaries' solution to Japanese imperialism of quietly accepting Japanese rule and focusing solely on spiritual matters. Inspired by the life of Jesus Christ, several well-known nationalist leaders not only fully gave themselves to the church but also used their resources and power to organize nationalist campaigns to strengthen Korea politically, economically, and socially.[144] Nationalist figures who were devoted Christians, like An Ch'ang-ho and Sŏ Jae-pil, believed that Christian principles should inform a new civic morality or public virtue for Koreans and organized movements that embodied Christian values. Attributing America's greatness to Christianity, Yun Ch'i-ho (1864–1945), a well-known Methodist, spoke out about the need of Christian-based educational and social reforms to produce a stronger national community. An, Sŏ, Yun, and others like them believed that by embracing Christianity and adopting Western-based reforms, such as industrial capitalism, Korea would become a modern, powerful country like those in West and would be able to resist Japanese imperialism. Perhaps no one at that time was more willing to carry out this model of religious and social development than Yi Sŭng-hun (1864–1930). Yi is known for his nationalist activities in the Sinminhoe (New People's Association), and for promoting Christianity through various institutions, such as Osan Academy (1907), which he founded as a Christian school.[145] As a leading merchant, Yi played an active role in organizing a number of business ventures with fellow Presbyterians. In 1908, for example, Yi helped start Sangmudongsa, one of the first general merchandise stores in Korea. In 1909, Yi also led the movement to start joint-stock companies through the P'yŏngyang Chagi Chusik Hoesa (Pyŏngyang Porcelain Company), which raised 60,000 won and employed sixty-one Koreans by the time it closed in 1919.[146] Behind all these business ventures was Yi's hope that Korean companies would be able to compete with Japanese businesses coming into Korea and resist Japan's takeover of the economy and the country.

These efforts of Korean Christians like Yun and Yi to address nationalist issues showed that certain followers resisted calls by church leaders to be less concerned with worldly issues. But these Korean Christians never challenged missionaries and church leaders on the issue of religious social activism and pursued their nationalist endeavors outside the purview of the Protestant churches. Moreover, Christian theologies originating from Protestant institutions at that time played little role in inspiring Korean Christians to organize political, economic, and social movements because they never encouraged any type of social activism, especially activities that confronted and overcame social and economic problems caused by modernization. In fact, Korean Christians who were active in nationalist affairs promoted social and economic reforms in the hope that Korea would follow the model of development in Western countries and thus would experience the modern stage of history. Korean Christians like Yun Ch'i-ho carried out Western-style reform projects, especially the fostering of industrial capitalism, in order for Korea to become civilized and enlightened or modern.[147] In fact, rather than point out the negative consequences of capitalism, they stressed only its positive value because they regarded it as "unselfish in spirit."[148] Far from questioning the norms of modernity, these figures called for the speeding up of modernization in Korea. Few Korean Christian nationalists articulated and carried out a type of social activism that featured an alternative vision of modernity.

Protestant institutions and officials held firm to their rejection of Christian-based social activism in society and simply asked followers to wait for redemption in the future when they met God in Heaven or experienced Jesus' return to earth. This rejection of social activism and hope in a future heavenly kingdom, however, played a special role after Japan annexed Korea in 1910 and officially claimed it as a colony. Under this new system, Japan controlled Korea, and a Japanese resident general served as the administrative leader of Korea. The established political order that many Koreans had known for years had come to an end. Many Korean Christians refused to violently overthrow the Japanese and tackle socioeconomic problems facing the majority of people and therefore continued to pray to God to forgive their own sins and deliver them from their plight. But Koreans were in despair and found that they needed help to understand and overcome their situation. During this time, a number of Koreans emerged from the missionary-established seminaries and promoted new theologies that would spiritually tackle the political and economic problems experienced by Koreans.

Kil Sŏn-ju was a leading Presbyterian minister who graduated from the Presbyterian North's P'yŏngyang Presbyterian Theological Seminary in 1907. Even today, Christians regard Kil as one of the most prolific revival preachers in the history of Christianity in Korea. Until his death in 1935, he preached about the fundamentals of Christianity and the future arrival of a new kingdom by using language that was filled with symbols Koreans recognized. Using the Bible as his main source, Kil created the idea that God and Jesus Christ would someday establish a kingdom, or a "paradise of peace" on earth. Kil taught others that when Jesus returned, there would be peace on earth and true love among all people; he thereby indirectly said that colonialism would end. The arrival of Jesus and the establishment of this new world, however, could not be revealed to or known by humans. According to Kil, people needed to prepare for the arrival of Christ by reading the Bible, praying, and sharing the gospel.[149] Until the arrival of Jesus, people should spiritually cleanse themselves and strive to become disciplined Christians focused on God. Kil expected followers to separate from the profane world and privilege instead the idea of cultivating a spiritual life in order to reach religious goals. He urged Christians to wait for Jesus to return despite the fact that he was one of the signers of the Declaration of Independence under the 1919 March First Movement.

Kil's beliefs were an example of classic escapist theology, for he exhorted individuals to focus solely on themselves, strengthen their relationship with God, and patiently wait for deliverance from their political, economic, and social problems. He supported the idea that there was nothing people could do to change the political, economic, and social conditions in which they lived. Kil taught Korean Christians to stop concerning themselves with the problems around them and, instead, to wait for God to bring about fundamental changes. With this theology, Kil offered followers a way of living in which they could escape the profane world and pay little attention to the forces and structures that destabilized their lives. Putting Kil's views in historical context, Chung-shin Park argues that those views were not escapist theology because Kil told his followers to wait for the creation of paradise on earth rather than wait until death to be resurrected and live with God in heaven.[150] Park believes that Kil, in fact, presented a nonescapist theology that encouraged people to be a part of this world rather than focus on death and the afterlife. Park's interpretation, however, fails to take into account that escapist theology does not simply encourage a longing for death and union with God in heaven. Rather, it emphasizes the cultivation of one's spiritual life because its health and vitality bring positive change to all other areas of one's life; thus it stresses that the source of producing fundamental changes in society comes through reforming one's personal life rather than through engaging in issues in society and seeking to transform political, economic, and social structures. Escapist theology puts more emphasis on spiritual forces than on individuals as the agents of political, social, and economic changes. Kil's beliefs were in fact escapist because he told his followers to retreat to their own spiritual domains, focus on enhancing their spiritual side through refining their moral lives and daily habits, and wait for Jesus Christ to come and offer them deliverance.

From the late nineteenth century to 1919, Christianity and Tonghak enabled many Koreans to gain a new perspective on the world and taught them how to act in their everyday lives. With Evangelicalism's focus on the self and Tonghak's concepts of the sacred nature of humanity, both religions served the needs of people living in changing political times that featured the decline of the Confucian order. In short, both religions furnished languages, practices, and institutions that positioned Koreans to encounter new experiences and to be able to interpret and give meaning and significance to the political transformations surrounding them. In so doing, however, officials in the Protestant Church and Tonghak never called for followers to engage in forms of faith-based social activism. Activities and movements under the auspices of official Christian and Tonghak organizations were organized and carried out with the purpose of spreading religious messages, converting people, and molding them into disciplined followers instead of addressing political problems in society and securing the material lives of Koreans. Certain followers of Christianity and Tonghak partook in various types of nationalist activities, including the Tonghak Revolution, but these activities were organized and conducted outside the official confines of both religious institutions. In spite of the absence of faith-based social discourse and movements within official Protestant and Tonghak institutions, Christian and Tonghak beliefs and practices still helped people negotiate changes at that time.

The economic, social, and political worlds continued to change after 1919 with the advent of nationalist movements and the commercialization of agriculture. In this new environment, Christianity, Tonghak in the form of Ch'ŏndogyo, and all religious beliefs came under attack for being irrelevant and outdated because they devalued the social and ignored extreme poverty and social inequality caused by capitalism. In this new historical period, religious ideas and practices that had been valued in the past were no longer deemed valuable and important in the present by many critics of religion. In particular, because peasants, who represented the majority of the population, were experiencing fragile living conditions in rural Korea that were crumbling as a result of the forces of capitalism, intellectuals, reformers, and nationalists questioned how religious institutions could stand idle and only preach the merits of conversion and spiritual salvation. Economic, social, and cultural changes thus forced religions institutions, especially the Protestant Church, to rethink their position on the social and modernization.

2

~×~

Economic and Social Change
under Japanese Colonialism

This chapter examines the transformation of the Korean rural economy and society from 1910 to 1937 and its impact on the lives of peasants, who accounted for 80 percent of the Korean population. In so doing, it adds to the rich scholarship on Korean rural affairs and the commercialization of agriculture during the Chosŏn and colonial periods by including writings and observations on rural life by intellectuals and religious figures from the colonial period. Numerous studies of rural Korea have provided valuable statistical and quantitative data that show how rural life changed under colonialism, but these studies have left out valuable qualitative resources in the form of voices of Koreans who at that time articulated how capitalism affected rural society and was experienced by peasants, as well as debating the role of peasants and rural society in the Korean nation. Korean Christians and missionaries, who had a wide-ranging and visible presence in rural areas, especially provided firsthand narratives of rural life with nuanced interpretations of economic, social, and cultural changes in the countryside. Including the discourse on the agricultural economy, peasants, and rural life based on these narratives, therefore, is important for gaining a complete understanding of 1920s and 1930s rural Korea and understanding the reasons behind the organization of rural campaigns by religious groups, such as Ch'ŏndogyo and Protestant Christians, especially because these narratives shaped their perceptions of capitalism, peasant life, and overall rural conditions.

Using a historical approach, this chapter outlines the way Koreans from 1910 to 1937 talked about the rise of new economic and social forces in rural Korea and their impact on landlords and peasants during the 1920s and 1930s. In particular, it discusses observations on how modernization and the commercialization of agriculture under colonial rule fundamentally transformed peasant lives through the weakening or erosion of long-standing ideological, social, and cultural structures that had offered them guidance and protection. This chapter stops short at 1937 because the YMCA, Presbyterian, and Ch'ŏndogyo rural movements carried out most of the major campaigns from

1925 to 1937, and the colonial state's handling of agrarian affairs shifted after 1937 because of the decision to mobilize Koreans for the war in China.

Institutional Developments in the Economy

The shifting context of peasant living occurred because of a growing capitalist economy that rapidly developed under Japanese rule but originated before the colonial period.[1] Historical evidence has shown that the agrarian economy featured new developments starting in sixteenth-century Chosŏn society that signified the emergence of capitalism in Korea.[2] By linking capitalism to agricultural developments, historians like Kim Yong-sŏp have aligned themselves with scholars of European history who have long argued that capitalism in Western countries first evolved through changes in the agricultural economy, such as transformed class relationships, new forms of technology, and larger scales of operations.[3] These historians of Korea and Europe have shown that the start of capitalism was not contingent on industrialization.[4] Although these Korean historians have connected the origins of capitalism in Korea to early agricultural developments, they still acknowledge that the maturation of capitalism started only after Korea's connection to the global capitalist system through the 1876 Treaty of Kanghwa.[5]

Capitalism became more widespread and systematic when Japan formally colonized Korea in 1910. The colonial government in Korea, which was officially known as the government-general, fused political goals with economic objectives to create a political economy that would meet the needs and goals of the Japanese empire. As the center of an integrated Northeast Asian political economy, Japan especially used its colonies to supply agricultural goods and labor to the Japanese mainland.[6] In order to meet the domestic needs of the Japanese, the colonial government introduced reforms and programs to reshape the Korean agricultural economy immediately after annexation in 1910. To establish a new tax base and solidify land as a marketable commodity, the government conducted the cadastral land survey (1910–1918). This comprehensive survey played an important role in reshaping the structure of the economy on two levels. First, it officially recognized the private ownership of land.[7] Theoretically and symbolically, the Chosŏn state (1392–1910) or the king, backed by Confucian principles, had owned all the land and therefore had forbidden any form of private landownership.[8] With the cadastral survey, this established idea lost meaning because the colonial government officially sanctioned private ownership of land. In fact, the government protected landowners' rights to buy, sell, or trade land or use it to secure loans. Thus land became a marketable commodity and gained new meaning and significance in a society that had primarily understood it as something used to grow crops. Writing in 1931,

Ch'in Yŏng-ch'ŏl pointed out that the cadastral survey thus clearly marked
the acceptance of the private ownership of land.[9] Second, the cadastral survey
significantly transformed established economic customs by authorizing single, individual ownership of land and rejecting and making illegal all customary tilling rights, especially cultivating rights that allowed peasants to use
land for an indefinite amount of time (*t'ojikwŏn* or *hwari*).[10]

Starting in the 1920s, the colonial government issued a series of laws and
undertook reforms that were intended to strengthen land rights and bolster
commercial activities in the Korean agricultural market. On April 1, 1920, the
colonial government repealed the Corporation Law, which had required government permission to start a company for commercial purposes. In order to
import cheaper rice, the Japanese government in August 1920 removed agricultural tariffs on products entering Japan from Korea. Finally, the colonial government reformed the rural banking system. Financial reforms started in 1918
with the establishment of the Industrial Bank of Chosŏn (Chosŏn siksan
ŭnhaeng), which served as the primary source of rural credit for landowners,
especially because it offered long-term, sizable loans. In 1928, the government
consolidated local credit associations (*kŭmyung chohap*), which had begun in
1907, to create a centralized credit association, the Chosŏn Organization of
Credit Associations (Chosŏn kŭmyung chohap hyŏphoe). The government envisioned credit associations offering peasants small, low-rate loans.[11] These institutions served as the primary sources of government-backed funding for the
commercialization of agriculture.

Alongside legal and financial reforms, the agriculture market grew with
the expansion of the road, rail, and port systems.[12] Japanese authorities supervised the construction of over 28,000 kilometers of road by the end of 1938. The
height of road construction took place from 1907 to 1912, but the colonial government continuously devoted resources to the construction and maintenance
of roads until 1945. The overall rail system was wide reaching, with trains going not only to all the cities in Korea but also to other countries, including
China. By 1939, 5,411 kilometers of rail had been laid down throughout the
peninsula. Besides transporting people, trains became a popular way to move
goods for export. The final destination of most of these goods was port cities,
where they were shipped to areas outside Korea. By 1945, the colonial government had built twelve trading-port cities.[13]

Programs designed by the colonial government to increase the productivity and output of agricultural crops served as the final component of a system
to expand the market for agricultural goods. The state carried out three programs from 1920 to 1940: the Thirty-Year Plan (1920), the Fourteen-Year Plan
(1926), and the Rural Revitalization Campaign (1932). The colonial government expected landlords and peasants to work together to achieve the goals of

the programs through developing irrigation systems, introducing new forms of seeds and technical information on farming, enriching soil on farms, and increasing the application of commercial fertilizer. The Rural Revitalization Campaign, in particular, addressed not only agricultural productivity but also issues related to the home and the family.[14] All these programs were developed and overseen, in part, by graduates of Suwŏn Agriculture and Forestry School, which was the colonial government's school for agricultural education. Founded in 1911, this school educated young Korean and Japanese men on modern farming technology and knowledge, natural science, and the principles of capitalist agricultural economics. The colonial government expected graduates to be rural leaders at the local level and to carry out state agricultural policies.[15]

The reforms and implementation of the programs occurred at a rapid pace and systematically laid the foundation for a commercialized agricultural economy that became a major supplier of agricultural goods to Japan and East Asia, according to observers of rural Korea from 1920 to 1937.[16] Discourse on the 1920s and 1930s colonial economy specifically pointed out that with the authorization of private landownership, the commodification of land, and the rise of a market economy, a capitalist society (chabonjuŭi) was developing in Korea.[17] Instead of just an isolated force in urban areas, capitalism and its powerful elements, according to Yi Sŏng-hwan in 1923, penetrated all areas of the peninsula, including the vast rural areas.[18] Yi Sun-t'ak wrote in 1926 that the forces of capitalism rushed into rural areas and reshaped economic relationships and exchanges through the development of the commercialization of agriculture and a new financial system.[19] Those writing about the changing economy and society, of course, understood that capitalism had yet to mature fully in colonial Korea, but they emphasized the fact that market principles slowly but forcefully began to undergird the agricultural economy, and capitalist forces started to reshape long-standing structures and relationships in society.[20]

Observers of rural life in Korea pointed out two new features under this new economy. First, some Koreans commented on the pace of capitalist development. An article in Tonggwang in 1931, for example, talked about how capitalist development in Korea differed from that in other countries. The author of the article referred to Karl Marx and his idea that the capitalist economy as a system evolved over many stages in history.[21] This process was gradual rather than sudden in various Western countries. The author of the article pointed out, however, that capitalism and its forces entered Korea rapidly and quickly transformed it from a feudal to a market economy.[22] Second, various figures observed that unlike the previous period, the agrarian economy was now greatly influenced by forces outside local environments and Korea itself. For example, Yi Sun-t'ak pointed out that with the Korean domestic market integrated into the global world market, foreign capital poured into the country and dictated how the Korean agricultural market operated.[23] In this case, as Helen Kim noted, financial control of the economic life of the Korean people no longer rested in their own hands but in the hands of foreigners.[24]

According to Yi Hun-gu in 1936, the prices of agricultural goods were no longer determined just by local, regional, or even national factors but also by forces outside the country. Yi wrote, "The price of rice, the most important agricultural product of Korea, is directly affected by market conditions in Osaka and Tokyo." He stressed that the Osaka market particularly determined "the rice quotations in the Far East."[25] Many peasants encountered these influences and price fluctuations from the outside through the five-day market (changsi). Five-day markets still served as vital sites where a large number of peasants who could not travel to port cities or local railroad stations sold their harvested crops to merchants and purchased basic commodities for living from those merchants. These markets first gained popularity during the Chosŏn period, and there were 1,356 of them by 1926. Each five-day market had separate places where people bought and sold grain, specialized goods such as fish and livestock, and goods for daily consumption.[26] At these markets, merchants were well aware of larger agricultural trends and the broader price fluctuations of commodities inside and outside Korea. This information informed the transactions between merchants and peasants. The five-day markets "functioned as networking markets that effectively connected these rural areas to the global market."[27]

Before colonization, Koreans worked within an economic system that was mostly shaped by domestic or internal forces. Often, only local activities constituted economic activity and structures, and people and economic activities were mostly immune from outside forces. In this situation, those who farmed had a fair amount of control over their economic lives, even peasants, who needed to deal only with landowners and small issues such as rent. Starting in the 1920s, however, Koreans faced the process of "disembedding," in which activities and relations were "lifted out" from the local contexts and areas and reshaped by larger, outside forces. Under this process, many local places became "phantasmagoric," which meant, according to Anthony Giddens, that "locales [were] thoroughly penetrated by and shaped in terms of social influences quite distant from them."[28] In this condition, Korean peasants and farmers encountered a situation where they could not see what now structured their economic and social lives since the outside influences and elements were not immediately present in the local areas. Koreans lived within a new economic system whose motions and forces followed an invisible logic and path that was separated and abstracted from the practices and relationships in people's immediate everyday life.

Transformations of Tenant-Landlord
Relations and Peasant Life

Capitalism in rural Korea transformed not only the economy but also social relationships, according to observers of rural life during the 1920s and 1930s. The transformation of social relationships was significant for colonial society because an increasing number of rural inhabitants were becoming peasant tenants who rented some or all of their land for farming from the smaller landlord class. After the cadastral survey, 77.2 percent of the rural population was leasing part or all of their cultivated land.[29] According to statistics in 1926, in comparison with 103,653 landlord households, 1,185,674 farm households (pure tenants) rented all their lands, and 934,208 households leased half of their farmland and owned half of their cultivated lands (semitenants).[30] The number of pure tenants only increased after the start of an economic depression in 1928 as many independent farmers who owned all or part of their land suffered economic problems, sold their land, and became tenant farmers.[31]

By the late 1920 and early 1930s, a significant number of peasant tenants entered into new forms of social relationships with landlords, which had long been undergirded by customs and traditions established since the Chosŏn dynasty. Traditionally, large landlords in Korea came from the *yangban* class, the social elites and landed gentry who were second only to the royal family in the Confucian social hierarchy system. Enjoying many privileges at the state level, the *yangban* also exerted great influence and power at the local level because the state relied on the *yangban* landed elite to uphold rules and regulations that would bolster and maintain the Confucian order at the local level through various ruling bodies in villages, such as mutual-assistance associations (*kyes*) and community compacts (*hyangyaks*).[32] *Yangban* landlords were also expected to exhibit model behavior in their economic relationship with peasant tenants. Confucian principles, such as goodwill and benevolence, were to structure the economic exchange between the *yangban* landlord and the peasant.[33] In a subsistence economic system where trading agricultural goods on the market took less precedence than growing, cultivating, and harvesting crops for one's own consumption, the economic arrangement between landlords and tenants was therefore relatively simple.[34] In exchange for using the lands, peasants gave half of their harvested crops to the landowners.[35] The continual payment of rent usually assured tenants the use of the land for an extended period of time. Tenants also insured themselves from being removed from the land through customary rights such as *t'ojikwŏn* or *hwari*.[36]

Writing in 1920s and 1930s Korea, agricultural experts and intellectuals called the landlord-tenant relationship in Korea a "paternalistic relationship" (*onchŏngjuŭi*) or a "lord-servant relationship" (*chujong*).[37] The underlying principle of this relationship demanded that landlords be an ideal role model and exhibit benevolence and kindness to tenants, especially during periods of economic hardship.[38] In villages, for example, Confucian tenets expected members of the *yangban* class to maintain proper behavior and rightful actions in order to reinforce the Confucian social code.[39] In addition, when natural disasters or other serious problems made it difficult for tenants to pay rent, landlords were expected to provide various forms of rent relief since profit making was not their main concern. In this capacity, according to Yi Hun-gu, "Landlords were the protectors of the weak tenants against certain kinds of social abuses and against special misfortunes."[40] Because tenants were entitled to these rights, a certain level of trust existed between landlords and peasant tenants in which peasants expected protection and care while living and working on rented farmlands. Of course, there were many instances when the relationship between landlords and peasants under Confucianism was far from ideal as corrupt government officials and *yangban* landlords exploited peasants. But the government and customs expected this benevolent code of behavior to structure a trusting relationship between the landlord and the peasant.

After 1910, as the capitalist economy further developed in the countryside, a new mentality on the value of land, farming, and the agricultural market began to emerge among many Korean landlords of *yangban* descent. Reports on rural life observed that many landlords began to see land as an investment and the production and marketing of agricultural goods as a means to amass wealth. Making and sustaining profits began to be the driving force behind agricultural activities for these landlords. In outlining the changing character of landlords in 1920s colonial Korea, many intellectuals commented that landowners became selfish as they accumulated wealth and strove to make money and profits.[41] "Individualism" and "capitalist thought" became the dominant modes of thought that informed the actions and practices of many landowners.[42] Many landowners no longer appeared to be seeking to be morally and ethically upright, nor did they intend to maintain social stability. Instead, they sought wealth in order to acquire new lands and invest in the burgeoning textile industry in the early 1930s. These reports gave the impression that many landlords were transitioning to this new economic environment by shedding their traditional roles and identities.

Officially, the colonial government classified landlords into two categories: type A landlords, who rented all their land, and type B landlords, who rented out most of their land while keeping a portion for self-cultivation. Type B landlords came in many forms, including owners of agricultural estates (*nongjang*), who took a direct role in managing tenants and overseeing crop production, and agricultural entrepreneurs, who hired wage laborers and employed capitalist methods in operating their farms.[43] Greater in number, type

B and Japanese landlords, in particular, believed that agricultural cultivation and production were intended for commodity production and should be further commercialized.[44] Thus they approached peasant tenants in ways that differed from those of previous periods. First, adopting a rational economic approach to agriculture, many of these landlords directly intervened in tenants' daily farming routines in order to regulate their work. They placed tenants under close surveillance as a way to transform peasants into productive workers who maximized the productivity of soil and labor.[45] Close supervision of the work of tenants started with carefully choosing the right person to cultivate their land base. For example, Oh Kŏn-ki, a major landowner in the 1930s, required prospective peasant tenants to fill out an application and based his choice of tenants on their personal and family background and references.[46] After carefully selecting peasant tenants who had the most potential to be productive farmers, many landlords required them to follow their orders regarding which crops to plant, what kind of manure and fertilizers to use, and what kind of techniques to employ for farming.

In order to regulate work and maximize labor productivity, certain landlords structured daily activities of peasant tenants through schedules.[47] They used timing mechanisms to make sure these schedules were carried out properly. James Dale Van Buskirk, a foreign missionary during the colonial period, nicely summarized the use of timing mechanisms in one village that would be used to regulate everyday work and behavior: "A bell rings at six in the morning as a signal for everyone to get up and begin the day. It rings for lunch, and again an hour later as a summons back to work. It rings at night as a signal for work to stop, and finally at ten o'clock it sends any to bed who may be up so late."[48] Backed by the colonial government, many landlords displayed a new form of surveillance and discipline that sought to penetrate and control the everyday lives of these peasants.

Second, many type B and Japanese landlords increased the amount of rent, often beyond the customary amount of half the total crop yield. Commenting on the rising rental rates during the 1920s and 1930s, one Korean observer wrote that landlords demanded high amounts of crops for rent.[49] Two major studies confirmed this practice of landowners. In 1926, John H. Reisner, an agricultural expert at the Nanking University in China, surveyed rural conditions throughout the peninsula and wrote that "in spite of the fact that the legal rate of the division between the landlord and tenant is 50 / 50, all the evidence secured by the investigations . . . indicate that the actual division is about 60 to 70% for the landlord and from 40 to 30% for the tenant."[50] In the early 1930s, Yi Hun-gu, a professor of agricultural economics at Sungsil University in P'yŏngyang, also conducted extensive research on rural Korea that confirmed that landlords charged high rents. On the basis of his findings, Yi believed that Korean tenants paid "the highest rent for leased land in the world," especially in comparison with Japan, where tenants usually paid 35 to 40 percent of their crops.[51]

Ignoring the plight of peasant tenants when they demanded that their financial burdens be alleviated during unexpected times of misfortune was the final sign of the changing relationship between peasants and type B and Japanese landlords. According to government-general reports in 1933 and 1938, these landlords often rejected tenants' demand to lower rent during periods of bad harvests caused by natural disasters. Moreover, it was reported that landlords—unbound by customs and living with new economic demands—did not hesitate to replace underperforming tenants with new tenants.[52] Observing the overall way landlords treated their tenants during the colonial period, Koreans often commented that the paternalistic (onchŏngjuŭi) relationship between landlords and tenants had ended.[53] In 1935, Yi Hun-gu wrote that capitalism was destroying the paternalistic feelings landlords held toward their peasant tenants.[54] Although many intellectuals and commentators during this period exaggerated the decline of paternalistic relations, they perceived that a fundamental shift had occurred in the relationship between landowners and peasants in the new agricultural market economy.

To many observers of rural life during the colonial period, the new ways in which certain landlords treated their tenants showed the establishment of a new type of relationship in a market-oriented society: social relations that were formal and contractual. These landlords primarily viewed their relationship and transactions with tenants as an impersonal economic exchange between two parties instead of a relationship bonded by religious and social beliefs. In fact, according to a study of tenancy practices in the South Chŏlla Province in 1921 and 1922, landlords and tenants recognized that economic and material interests, instead of moral or social beliefs, grounded their relationship.[55]

Cultural Rupture of Peasant Life in 1920s and 1930s Korea

Economic and social developments gave way to new forms of thought and behavior that differentiated 1920s and 1930s rural Korea from previous eras in the countryside. To many intellectuals and nationalists at that time, all these changes were clearly visible in villages throughout the peninsula. For peasants, a village served as the vital place where, according to Lee Yong-ki, they "lived their daily lives, conducted production activities, formed primary human relationships, and were socialized."[56] As the main site for living, working, and socializing, a village was more than just a place of multiple homes; it was a space of multiple relations that constituted identity, meaning, and value. Villages in colonial Korea essentially were places of localities. "Locality" refers to the organizing structure that establishes and shapes the social consciousness of individuals.[57] In this capacity, a locality allows for various means through which people construct themselves and their identities.

A typical village consisted of a cluster of several houses, while larger villages included well over a hundred farmhouses.[58] After the colonial government reorganized administrative districts in 1914, there were 28,000 villages nationwide. Residents of these villages were mostly peasant tenants and their families and lived separately from their farmlands. Peasants commonly walked together to their respective farmlands and worked cooperatively to weed and harvest crops during the busiest points of the farming season. After work, villagers gathered to listen to stories, play games, and talk to one another.[59] In addition to recreational events, villagers also assembled to perform religious and cultural customs, rites, and rituals. Villagers developed close and intimate relationships by living, working, and participating in recreational activities together.

Various systems of knowledge and belief structured daily life in villages, but Confucianism was the dominant force in the lives of villagers. Particularly after 1392, when the new Chosŏn dynasty instituted Confucianism as the state's ideology, Confucian ideas, practices, and institutions became more pronounced and visible at the local level. Villagers did not just follow Confucian ideas and practices because of government pressure; they relied on Confucianism as a system of values that organized daily experiences and give them guidance. Customs and institutions were established in villages to materialize Confucianism as a lived reality, and ancestor worship and funeral rites were two of the most popular customs. Ancestor worship was given value and importance because, according to Martina Deuchler, it was "a medium through which the living could express filial piety by requiting the ancestors' favors and keeping their memories alive."[60] Funeral rites were equally important because they too were mechanisms to embody and show filial piety. Ancestor worship and funeral rites involved elaborate ceremonies that required the participation of the first son. Under both customs, the eldest son represented siblings and "came to be recognized as the ideal link in the continuum of generations."[61] Through these customs, the performance of rituals by the eldest son allowed for links between the past and present and overall continuity in daily life.

The mutual-assistance association (kye), in particular, served as a valued Confucian institution to orient and socialize village life because it promoted a "social contract of localized mutual interdependence."[62] Fostering this type of social relationship under the kye served not only to meet the physical needs and security of villagers but also to produce and maintain harmony and stability, as defined by Confucianism. A 1913 study of kyes and their charters, for example, noted that kyes outside Seoul emphasized the cultivation of "harmony of mind on the part of people" and the promotion of "kindness and harmony" as "the most important thing."[63]

*Kye*s aimed to achieve ideal social relationships through three forms: (1) associations to provide funds and resources for "public works, education and the relief of the poor"; (2) associations to collect and distribute funds for the support of events and customs, such as weddings, funerals, and ancestor worship; and (3) associations for "investment financing, providing for tree planting . . . irrigation, and for the lease of oxen and ploughs."[64] Overseen by an elected leadership, each *kye* required villagers either to contribute money to a collective pool or to provide labor or other resources when needed. Because achieving the goals of the association required proper behavior and effective operations, *kye*s demanded strict order and discipline and exact bookkeeping and accounting. *Kye*s operated with the same precision, efficiency, and discipline found in any commercial enterprise, but they distinguished themselves by emphasizing mutual support instead of profit.

As these rites, customs, and institutions anchored villages, they materially expressed the beliefs and ideas of Confucianism. The continual performance of these practices thus allowed for the reproduction of the village locality. According to Arjun Appadurai, "locality is ephemeral unless hard and regular work is undertaken to produce and maintain its materiality."[65] During the Chosŏn period, Confucian-based localities in villages always faced the threat of weakening and disappearing, especially in the face of elements from different systems of knowledge and belief, such as shamanism and Buddhism. Changes to village localities continued throughout the Chosŏn period, but the continuity of key Confucian beliefs, customs, and institutions came under greater threat during the 1920s and 1930s because of changes caused by the process of modernization overseen by the colonial government. From 1920 to 1937, writers provided vivid accounts of the transition from the old to the new in the countryside, including Yi Ki-yŏng, who wrote *Kohyang* (Hometown, 1936). In *Kohyang,* Yi described the protagonist's shock at how fast his hometown in the countryside had changed: "In five years, my hometown has surprisingly changed! Behind the railroad station, there are large streets connected to the town. . . . The railway system is becoming like a spider web in which houses and hotels stand left and right of the tracks."[66] Yi further noted that the rural town had a new silk factory whose chimney spewed out black smoke. Through the creation of an elaborate infrastructure system, material and ideological influences from the outside arrived in villages and set off a series of changes that reconstituted the environment that conditioned people's daily lives.

Against this backdrop of alterations and changes during the 1920s and 1930s, a number of *kye*s appeared to deteriorate and disappear. In 1931, Helen Kim pointed out that many *kye*s lost a considerable amount of power and influence under colonial rule.[67] Their decline appeared to be the result of many factors. First, according to Hong Pyŏng-sŏn, many *kye*s had been mishandled and abused over the years.[68] Although Hong never identified the factors behind the abuse and mishandling of kyes, the changed economic, political, social, and cultural environment from 1920 to 1937 most certainly created new conditions that affected their makeup and operations. Second, the decline of kyes could be explained through the colonial government's strict regulation of the rural credit infrastructure. From 1920 to 1945, the colonial government actively pursued control of the rural credit system by cracking down on non-regulated financial organizations, like kyes, and authorizing the establishment of rural credit societies (kŭmyung chohap). Finally, many kyes disappeared because the colonial government replaced them with rural revitalization committees under Governor-General Ugaki's Rural Revitalization Campaign (1932–1940). These committees abolished kyes and became the main institution of surveillance to carry out the campaign in villages.[69]

Communal life in villages never totally collapsed as a result of the breakdown of kyes and the loss of the corporate taxation system,[70] but the absence of kyes left many villages without key institutions that had long anchored and played a fundamental role in structuring and maintaining localities. Alongside institutional changes, the migration of villagers to cities on the peninsula and urban centers outside Korea further contributed to the transformation of localities. Writing in 1929, Cho Min-hyŏng pointed out that thousands of peasants left their villages to travel to Japan and Manchuria, starting in the early 1920s and especially after the agricultural depression in Korea starting after 1929.[71] Peasants traveled outside villages in search of work because they were unable to meet the demands of the market economy as farmers. The high cost of agricultural supplies, taxes, and food, combined with the high rents paid to landowners, often created a situation in which a significant number of peasant tenant families had barely enough money to make a living and went into serious debt.[72] One study conducted in the South Cholla Province in 1922 found that 96.9 percent of the tenants who were interviewed ended the year in debt.[73] According to Hoon Koo Lee (Yi Hun-gu), in a study of 1,249 farms in 1931, tenants on average had an income of 57.42 yen with expenditures at 62.99 yen, leaving an average deficit of 5.57 yen.[74] Peasant debt only increased because of their inability to repay loans with high interest rates that they had obtained to sustain daily life. Landlords exacted high rates of interest on their loans to peasants, historically between 20 percent and 30 percent a month.[75] Peasant tenants also received high-interest-rate loans (average rate between 12 and 48 percent) from the nearly 12,153 loan brokers on the peninsula.[76]

Peasants began to seek work outside the countryside to improve their economic situation in the late 1910s under the supervision of the colonial government.[77] The number of peasant migrants, however, increased during the 1920s and 1930s.[78] By 1931, there were so many Korean peasants in Japan and

Manchuria that Sakai Toshio wrote, "Like nomads roving about in search of greener pastures, Korean workers wander the heavens and earth in search of labor, appearing in Manchuria or the wilderness of Siberia. Or, crossing the straits to Japan, they come as a white-robed army, a veritable Asian multitude."[79] Those peasants who were unable to travel outside the country migrated to the growing cities on the peninsula. During the colonial period, urban areas transformed into sites of vibrant commercial and economic activity with the construction of textile factories and an emerging service industry. Serving mainly as the connecting point to the outside world, cities also became the centers of contemporary culture where people encountered ideas, practices, and trends from outside Korea. Offering opportunities and new experiences, cities attracted a growing number of inhabitants from the rural areas. From 1910 to 1940, the percentage of Koreans living in cities jumped from 3 to 14 percent. The population of Seoul, P'yŏngyang, and Wŏnsan tripled, while the population of Taegu and Pusan doubled.[80] Cities in Korea became places of great attraction for experiencing a modern life through new and contemporary forms of employment, architecture, consumption, and entertainment.[81]

More than just magnets for peasants looking for work, cities inside and outside Korea were particularly attractive to the rural youth, who imagined them to be centers for new possibilities of living. Village youth in Korea were restless and longed to escape what they perceived to be the mundane and hopeless life of farming. Aware of the new jobs and enjoyments available in the cities, many country youth saw farming as useless and rejected traditions and customs that had served as the foundation of villages for hundreds of years.[82] Korean youth inevitably compared the conservative countryside with the outside world and found it lacking. They were captivated by foreign cultural elements and saw cities as places where they could achieve economic success while also partaking in fresh and exciting cultural activities.[83] Given the opportunity to leave the countryside for the possibility of living a life full of excitement and enjoyment in cities, a large number of village youth left the countryside and traveled to urban areas, according to many observers of 1920s and 1930 rural life.[84]

Writings from the colonial period described how the exodus of people from the countryside left many villages in a "ghost-like" state. Yi Hun-gu wrote that those who wrote about village life talked about how many of them had become deserted.[85] Indeed, in a matter of one evening, some villages lost several of their residents who fled in the middle of the night to escape their creditors.[86] Many villages were described as lifeless spaces of psychological disorder and distress for villagers. According to one report, many villages were devoid of life and activity.[87] With men and youths mostly traveling, many of the remaining functioning and operating villages were populated only by women and the elderly.[88] In the absence of villagers, especially men and young adults, customs and practices that had sustained village locality could no longer be performed. Practicing basic Confucian customs such as ancestor worship, for example, was difficult without older males who traditionally led the services. Consequently, according to one survey of villages throughout the peninsula, villages reported "that ancestor worship was ceasing," and that "in many villages . . . all customs and traditions were changing with greater or less rapidity." The survey reported that "economic and other conditions" produced these changes.[89] The exodus of peasants who were expected to carry on traditions to urban centers most certainly caused village localities to become precarious.

In order to prevent the collapse of village life and localities, some village elders discouraged migration and attempted to prevent young men and women from leaving. Although some elders recognized the need of some villagers to leave and find work in cities, they realized that young men and women were necessary for the continuity of village life. Attempts to stop young men and women from leaving the village caused tension between elders and youth. During this period, Korean writers well articulated this tension. Yu Ch'i-jin, a well-known playwright during the colonial period, highlighted this conflict in his 1935 play *The Ox,* which tells the story of a peasant family struggling to keep its farm. In one scene of the play, a father and son fight over the son's insistence to sell a valuable ox, which he later does without the father's permission:

> *Son:* Father, don't get so angry. Please give me some travel money. It's unreasonable for you to try and make a farmer out of me. A guy like me likes going places, riding boats. Idling around here suffocates me.
> *Father:* Even if you were born a boatman, will your bones break from lending a hand to your father when he's busy like this?
> *Son:* Father, look. Our ox, why don't you sell it and give me the money? I'll go to Manchuria and come back a rich man. All I need is one thousand five hundred *yang.*
> *Father:* What? Sell the ox? Listen to this child. He has no sense left in him. . . . You can't look down on our ox because it doesn't do anything. It still tills the soil for us and works for our neighbors when we exchange our work.
> *Son:* Father, I heard there are a lot of well-paid jobs in Manchuria. We've got to get a taste of them.[90]

This tension between father and son and the son's actions highlighted the breakdown of norms in village life, especially the belief that the young needed to follow in the footsteps of their ancestors. Although the play is only a fictional story, this tension played out in many villages and led to youth challenging established ways, therefore further shaking the foundation of localities.

Interpreting and Responding to the Rural Crisis

Throughout the 1920s and 1930s, especially after 1928, the discourse on rural life in colonial Korea focused on the rapidly declining economic, social, and cultural conditions of peasant tenants. An article in *Kaebyŏk* (Creation) declared that the countryside and people were in a "miserable state."[91] According to a Christian leader who observed rural affairs, "Right now, the lifestyle of the peasant is unstable."[92] Peasants and those living in the countryside faced the task of finding a way to survive by adapting to the new social and economic conditions brought forth by the commercialization of agriculture. With the absence of certain established forms of security that had once protected the social and economic rights of peasants and had provided them with assistance in hard times, many peasants refused to sit idly and turned to other ways to restore stable living conditions. In some villages, for example, peasants established cooperative unions to combine labor and resources to increase production of agricultural goods, while peasants in other villages learned about contemporary farming skills and used them to increase their harvests. The most popular means for peasants to overcome their difficulties was through mobilizing the people and holding public protests against those who controlled the lands they rented. Starting in 1920, the number of protests increased annually, except for a decline in the number of protests between 1929 and 1932. In 1935 and 1936 alone, there were 25,834 and 29,975 protests, respectively.[93] Disputes and conflicts in the 1930s went beyond the issue of rent reduction; they also centered on land reform and the inequality caused by capitalism.

All nationalist groups believed that solving rural issues was a necessary step toward overcoming class conflict that pitted Koreans against one another and establishing a united front that would challenge colonial rule and build a powerful nation-state. Helping, organizing, and gaining influence over peasants, in particular, were major objectives of nationalists because they saw peasants expressing a new level of national consciousness after the 1919 March First Movement. As various groups pursued rural campaigns, the colonial government continuously tried to exercise control over the volatility of rural affairs, especially the conflicts between peasants and landlords. In particular, the colonial government inaugurated the Rural Revitalization Campaign in November 1932 to bring order to what appeared to be an uncontrolled environment. Spearheaded by the new governor-general, Ugaki Kazuhige, the rural campaign introduced various programs, such as establishing over 28,000 model villages by 1939, providing low-interest loans through financial cooperatives (*kŭmyung chohap*) and mutual-aid associations for production (*siksan'gye*), and organizing over two thousand schools where peasants learned to read and write Japanese and new vocational skills.[94] The state expected these social and economic programs to help peasants improve their farming skills and abilities to market their harvested goods in order to lift them out of poverty. The state also carried out a plan to "regenerate the spirit of peasants" because it attributed the poor conditions experienced by peasants to their lack of discipline and industrious behavior. Ugaki pointed out that Koreans lived without any respect for "thrift and labour" because they lacked morals and ethics.[95] The colonial government promoted traditional customs, especially those related to Confucianism, as a way to condition peasants morally and to nurture filial piety, frugality, and diligence.[96]

Above all, the primary purpose behind the colonial government's new rural campaign was to exert more disciplinary power and control over peasants. Through the programs under its rural campaign, the state hoped that the regeneration of the Korean spirit would naturally lead to proper behavior and thought as defined by the state. Simply put, it expected the formation of disciplined subjects who had internalized colonial power and had become loyal to the empire. This pursuit to establish a Foucauldian-like power structure was in line with the 1930s trend of campaigns throughout the Japanese empire, including Manchukuo and Japan, to discipline subjects through projects of governmentality.[97] In colonial Korea and elsewhere in the empire, the introduction of contemporary knowledge, practices, and institutions by authorities served only as a means to exert new forms of surveillance and power, contain disturbances and conflicts, and mobilize labor and resources for Japan.

After the March First Movement, leftist groups, ranging from Marxists to socialists, conducted rural campaigns to achieve national liberation and build a modern society based on political, economic, and social equality. Reasons for starting rural campaigns arrived from different areas. Paek Nam-un (1894–1979), a Marxist who taught economics at Yŏnhŭi Junior College, articulated a framework of Korean historical development that served as a basis for leftist rural movements. In *The Socioeconomic History of Chosŏn* (1933) and *The Socioeconomic History of Feudal Chosŏn* (1937), Paek explained that leftists should join peasants with the goal of overthrowing Japanese colonialism through a "Chosŏn Revolution" because colonial policies had preserved feudal customs and structures in rural Korea, which had distorted the evolution of capitalism and had prevented material transformations that would lead to a communist society. To Paek, only a revolution for national liberation could overcome the

economic and social contradictions in agrarian society and restore the historical trajectory that would lead to communism.[98] The 1928 December Theses
also furnished reasons for leftists to seek an alliance with peasants. Adopted
by the Communist International and taken up by Koreans, this document
stressed that "the Korean proletariat will not be able to take over the leadership in the national-revolutionary movement if the Korean communists will
not link up organically the agrarian problem with the national revolution."[99]

Despite constant surveillance by the colonial government, leftists established a large presence in rural Korea through peasant associations, including
Red Peasant Unions that taught peasant how to read and write, introduced
leftist ideology, and collectively organized peasants against their unfair treatment by landlords.[100] But despite this commitment to the peasant cause, it
appeared that many leftists rejected the peasantry as the vanguard of the revolution and the leading class in the nation-state. Many leftists viewed the
industry-based proletariat as a revolutionary force, as was well articulated by
Sa Kong-pyo in 1929: "In the Chosŏn Revolution . . . the main force is only the
proletariat class. . . . Of course, the proletariat is still weak. . . . Yet it is not
possible for peasants to be the main force in the revolution since they are no
more than a relic of the feudal landlord society. They cannot organize themselves as a single firm force for revolution."[101] Because their lives were and continued to be shaped by forces from a past era, peasants, in the view of several
leftists, lacked the appropriate consciousness to usher in the necessary changes
to advance society toward the next stage of historical development. Indeed,
because peasants traditionally lived and worked apart from one another, "their
objective grievances could not become collective ones" that would spark
changes and a revolution.[102] The proletariat, however, could lead Korea toward
a revolutionary future because the mode of production shaping them allowed
the growth of a collective class consciousness necessary for making a social
revolution. Articulating the amount of faith leftists had in the proletariat, Kim
Yŏng-du, a leftist leader, wrote in 1928 that "all of the serious and grave problems in Chosŏn will be finally resolved only through the point of view and
hand of the proletariat."[103] The absence of an industrial capitalist base and a
large proletariat class never deterred certain leftists from investing their hopes
for a new future in the proletariat because they had great confidence in Marx's
theory on historical development. Thus, for them, veering away from the
principles of Marxism would only prevent the construction of a communist
society with the proletariat class at its base.

Bourgeois nationalists rejected the leftist vision of Korea because they envisioned the country evolving into a modern society centered on the bourgeois
and industrial capitalism. Bourgeois nationalists such as Yi Kwang-su, An

Chae-hong, Kim Sŏng-su, and An Ch'ang-ho grounded this vision of the future in their interpretation of the historical development of Western society, especially in Europe. Their views on this issue were well represented in *Tonga ilbo* (Dong-a ilbo), which served as the mouthpiece of bourgeois nationalists. A May 1921 article, for instance, highlighted how industrialization and the bourgeois paved the way for the creation of a democratic society in the West. According to the article, as a new bourgeois class, which consisted of merchants and industrialists (*sanggongŏpcha*), matured and increased its economic and social power under capitalism, its members sought to extend their power into the political realm. The bourgeoisie organized themselves in cities and confronted the traditional political system, which was controlled by nobles through the feudal system.[104] What articles like this in *Tonga ilbo* pointed out to their readers was that economic progress through the development of capitalism and the bourgeois class gave way to democracy and political advancement—a narrative of modern development that was known throughout the world during the 1920s and 1930s. The bourgeois class was valued because it possessed the passion and creativity to test the limits of traditional power structures and build a new society for the greater benefit of all.

Achieving an industrial capitalist society became the most important objective of many bourgeois nationalists. Leaders from the P'yŏng'an and Chŏlla Provinces organized the Chosŏn kyŏngjehoe (Chosŏn Economic Society) in December 1919 and the Chosŏnin sanŏp taehoe (Conference of Chosŏn Industrialists) in July 1921 to forge a collaborative approach to building a new economy.[105] As a way to influence the public directly, bourgeois nationalists also conducted mass economic campaigns, such as the Native Products Promotion Movement, which pursued "economic development based on laissez-faire liberalism"[106] and began with the Chosŏn mulsan changnyŏhoe (Society for the Promotion of Chosŏn Native Products) in P'yŏngyang in August 1920.[107] As a way to encourage "healthy" forms of consumption, bourgeois nationalist leaders also promoted frugality "as a rational and planned act of consumption."[108] Finally, in order to transform Koreans into an urban bourgeois, a "Life Reform Movement" criticized the wearing of traditional types of Korean clothing and emphasized new home designs that rationally planned spaces with clear functions.

For bourgeois nationalists, working with peasants was a necessity since they represented the largest group in society and were becoming heavily influenced by leftists. Some bourgeois nationalists, like An Chae-hong, recognized the importance of coming to the aid of peasants in order to help them transition to the new society and economy envisioned by the bourgeois.[109] To combat peasant poverty, bourgeois nationalists like An suggested various reforms, such as strengthening peasant tenant rights, building cooperatives (*hyŏpdong chohap*), and introducing advanced farming technology. Instead of large-scale comprehensive rural movements, bourgeois nationalists conducted literacy movements through the Chosŏn ilbo Literacy Movement (1929–1934) and the Tonga ilbo V Narod Movement (1931–1934). The Chosŏn ilbo movement relied on young students to travel to villages throughout the peninsula and teach peasants how to read and write. Students used a basic Korean language textbook, *The Script Han'gŭl* (*Han'gŭl wŏnbo*), which promoted several virtues, such as "Knowing is strength. You need to learn to live" and "Let's teach according to one's skills." Over four hundred students helped build close to forty-six schools on the peninsula.[110] The Tonga ilbo movement took its name from the 1874 Khozhdenic v narod (To the People) movement in Russia.[111] Whereas the Russian movement pushed a radical agenda of turning peasants into a revolutionary force who would create a socialist society, the Tonga ilbo movement pursued the goal of modernizing peasants through teaching literacy skills and lecturing on hygiene and sanitation, music, and drama.

Diversity certainly characterized Korean leftist and bourgeois nationalist rural movements, but most groups in both categories still held to a modernist view of history as linear progress that precluded a vision of a Korea anchored in the peasant, the agrarian economy, and pastoral living. As these two groups pursued their respective goals, their visions of historical development were sharply contested by agrarianists who favored the restoration of an ideal past based on the principles of agrarianism (*nongbonjuŭi*). A diverse group of individuals who included Confucian scholars, local village leaders, and intellectuals, agrarianists claimed that the country's agricultural heritage with peasants should be at the center of the nation-state. According to them, peasants would be self-reliant and thus free from any outside influences, such as foreign capital, through an agriculture-based economy that emphasized collective farming and mutual assistance. Besides economic benefits, agrarianists argued that preserving Korea's agricultural heritage ensured the preservation of Korea's national identity because agriculture and peasants were considered the foundation of the nation and a long part of Korea's history. They regarded agriculture and peasants as concrete manifestations of the country's national spirit and thus the authentic signs of the nation.

In the face of what they considered the destructive nature of modernization, agrarianists adopted an anticommercial and anticapitalist position and sought a return to "a golden age" (*hwanggŭm sidae*) when Korea was anchored in agriculture and peasants and untouched by capitalism, industrialization, urbanization, and foreign influences.[112] They wanted to return to this heavily fictionalized agrarian past as their way of arresting change, escaping the linear progression of time, and surviving the crushing effects of the mass changes in society. In order to restore this ideal past, agrarianists emphasized the return of traditional beliefs, customs, and institutions, especially Confucianism, from the golden age. Although there was never a single organized agrarianist campaign, it appeared that the majority of agrarianists pursued the restoration of the past through the construction of ideal villages (*isangch'on*). The principles of self-sufficiency, moral reconstruction, and collectivism were behind these drives to build ideal villages.[113] Agrarianists expected Confucian customs and institutions, such as *kyes*, *tonggyes* (village mutual-aid societies), *tonghoes* (village associations), and *hyangyaks* (community compacts), to channel these principles. Restoration of *kyes*, in particular, became popular. A village in Kyŏngsang Province, for example, organized a traditional *kye* with the hope of raising capital to fund various activities. In order to improve its fishing business, a village in Hwanghaenamdo also revived a *kye* to organize villagers into a collective body that worked together. According to a special issue of *Sinmin* (New People) on utopian agrarian villages in 1929, agrarianists had restored a number of traditional institutions and practices through ideal-village projects.[114]

In their beliefs, agrarianists were antimodernists who rejected the view of the present as a temporality of potential in which changes would lead to a new and brighter future. Modernization, in their view, was foreign and full of destructive changes that eroded traditions and national identity. Hence refuge from these consequences required isolation from society and a descent into the past by restoring mythical historical conditions when Korea had flourished through agriculture and peasants. This idealization of agriculture and peasants as the way to negotiate and overcome modernization occurred also through artists whose paintings featured the peasantry and rural life. Beginning in the late 1920s, artists called for a form of Korean art that emphasized and portrayed the authentic identity of Korea. These artists rejected Western-style painting and portrayal of foreign subjects in favor of a style centered on local colors (*hyangt'o*), which emphasized "Koreanness." They promoted *hyangt'o* through organizations such as Nokhyanghoe (Association of Green Country) and Hyangt'ohoe (Local Color Association). Art critics, such as Kim Yong-jun and Yun Hi-sun, "generally agreed that it [*hyangt'o*] could be summarized as the portrayal of Korea's climate, seasons, nature and life on the farm."[115] In effect, *hyangt'o* was an agrarianist drive by artists to preserve values and heritages unique to the Korean nation as a way to shield themselves from the changes caused by modernization.

Rural Korea in the 1920s and 1930s became the primary site of a transforming capitalist system that reshaped long-standing social and cultural structures and people's overall daily lives. Most peasants, in particular, were forced to transition quickly to the new requirements and demands of the market economy. Although there were a number of examples of peasants who took advantage of the new economic opportunities and became wealthy, there were far more examples of peasants struggling to negotiate the vast challenges that resulted from the commercialization of agriculture. The decline and weakening of village localities that had provided them material and ideological support further compounded the severity of their situation. Peasants experienced the contradictions of capitalism in which the market economy promised greater autonomy and opportunities but created an unsettling environment and uneven power relations.

During the transition from a subsistence economy to a profit-oriented one, Korean peasants experienced for the first time what Karl Polanyi called "a cultural disaster." Studying how capitalism first affected societies, Polanyi wrote that the introduction of a market economy in a society was particularly culturally destructive because a capitalist economic system was foisted on a differently organized society. As market economies formed in different societies, they introduced foreign forces, elements, and principles that reorganized society and altered the culture that had fundamentally grounded and directed their everyday life. Witnessing these effects, Polanyi believed that the transformation of one's culture in a violent manner was more devastating than simply losing it.[116] In colonial Korean society, many peasants experienced the ruptures described by Polanyi. As long-standing traditions, relationships, and institutions weakened, changed, or simply disappeared, peasants found that the culture of their past could no longer guarantee guidance and security in the present. With this cultural transformation, peasants thus experienced "the transforming power of capitalism—its tendency to undermine radically the past and the present."[117] As the growing political economy greatly disrupted the Confucian order, it showed the power of capitalism to "dis[solve] all stable links and traditions" and affect the "stability of the symbolic order that provides a definitive identification for subjects."[118]

Observers of rural life noticed that the way of life and thinking, or culture, of peasants was in a state of flux. According to writers on Korean rural life, many peasants faced a challenging situation because of the new political economy. Byron P. Barnhart, a YMCA official, described this new situation facing all Koreans in the countryside: "Life is changing rapidly for the Korean villager. New things are coming in and he finds new demands are knocking at his door. Life is dictating new terms to which he must adjust."[119] The important question for established religious institutions was how they were going to respond to all these changes, especially in light of their lack of interest in political, economic, and social issues. The changes stemming from the forces of modernization presented religious groups with the challenge of whether they would adapt religious languages and practices to the changed living environment and build a new form of modernity that would organize and make meaningful people's experiences in the changing present.

3

A Heavenly Kingdom on Earth

The Rise of Religious Social Ideology

Until and immediately after the March First Movement, many Koreans held religion in high regard because a small number of religious followers had played significant roles in promoting nationalist causes and speaking out against Japanese imperialism. Above all, numerous Protestant Christians and Ch'ŏndogyo believers became forceful advocates of building a new nation and protecting the country from foreign aggressors through the modernization of Korea based on the principles of civilization and enlightenment. Despite the crackdown on nationalist movements after Japan formally colonized Korea in 1910, many Protestant Christian and Ch'ŏndogyo believers secretly continued their nationalist endeavors. Their efforts to free Korea from colonial rule culminated in the 1919 March First Movement. Both Yi Sŭng-hun and Pak Hŭi-do, well-known Christians, played major roles in organizing and leading this movement. Yi reached out to key religious figures, especially Ch'ŏndogyo followers, and urged them to collaborate in staging a mass demonstration against colonial rule in conjunction with King Kojong's funeral. Pak, as a youth organizer, helped draw over six thousand students to the demonstration by organizing young men and women to spread news about the planned protest. Alongside Yi and Pak, some well-regarded Protestant Christians and Ch'ŏndogyo followers participated in this transformative event by signing the Declaration of Independence that formally renounced Japanese colonial rule. All the signers of the declaration were leading followers of a religion,[1] and a significant number of demonstrators belonged to a religious group, so religious figures figured prominently in the March First Movement. Although certain nationalist activities and campaigns were organized and carried out by individual followers outside the supervision of religious institutions, followers of Protestant Christianity, Ch'ŏndogyo, and Buddhism became widely respected by fighting to safeguard the nation.

After the March First Movement, Koreans questioned how religions would approach issues of nationalism and independence in light of the colonial government's new Cultural Policy (Bunka Seiji) that allowed for limited freedoms of speech and organization but ultimately created a new regime of surveillance and discipline that aimed to control tightly the daily lives of Koreans. In line with the principles and goals of the Culture Movement (Munhwa Undong), religious followers transitioned from a direct political struggle with the colonial state to the pursuit of building a new national community. Still seeking independence from Japan, religious leaders and followers nevertheless maintained that it was imperative first to concentrate on organizing movements that addressed the severe material and ideological disorder in daily life and the fracturing of the social body that the forces of modernization caused. Whereas a few individual religious followers, in particular Korean Christians, initiated social reforms to modernize Korea before 1919, a large number of young and old religious believers after 1920 participated in social movements designed and carried out by leading religious institutions that responded directly to the ruptures and dislocations caused by modernity.[2] For the first time, Koreans saw the rise of religion-based reconstruction campaigns after 1925 that seriously questioned the norms of modernity, addressed the extreme changes and problems caused by modernization, and set out to reform and stabilize the economic, social, and cultural lives of people, especially peasants, whose lives were seen as full of instability and dislocation because of capitalism. These campaigns, especially those led by the YMCA, the Presbyterian Church, and Ch'ŏndogyo, were grounded in socially oriented religious systems of belief that valued the present and society because religious experiences were based in the everyday life of the now. In order to continuously ensure sacred experiences, these systems of belief further called on religious followers to build a healthy and stable society that would allow the unfolding of a heavenly kingdom on the peninsula (chisang ch'ŏn'guk) and therefore the creation of a spiritually based nation-state. Far from retreating from nationalist politics, many religious followers channeled their energy and focus into achieving a new modern personhood and national community through movements organized by religious institutions that embodied new social beliefs and envisioned an alternative vision of modernity.

This chapter starts the process of explaining the origins of large-scale reconstruction movements by established religious institutions through a detailed investigation of the ideas that undergirded and guided these drives. In particular, this chapter studies the ideas of Yi Ton-hwa, Hong Pyŏng-sŏn, and Pae Min-su (Pai Min-soo), which served as the religious justifications and rationales for the Ch'ŏndogyo, YMCA, and Presbyterian rural movements, respectively. Faced with a transforming colonial system and antireligion movements that questioned how religions would respond to the mass political, economic, social, and cultural changes, Yi, Hong, and Pae conceptualized religion as an appropriate system for creating and sustaining a dynamic and durable modernity.

Of particular interest is analyzing how each figure similarly defined time (present), space (everyday life, society), and "heavenly kingdom on earth" (chisang ch'ŏn'guk) in a way that linked all three categories; all three figures framed chisang ch'ŏn'guk as the crucial medium that linked time and space. Through their efforts, they configured religion as a powerful source for social activism and for negotiating people's experiences of modernization. They thus helped adapt religion to the contemporary period.

An understanding of Yi's, Hong's, and Pae's ideas is crucial because they were among the few leaders from leading religious institutions not only to articulate a socially oriented religious system of belief that became widely disseminated but also to apply their ideas through mass movements. Unlike most religious leaders in colonial Korea, Yi, Hong, and Pae purposefully reinterpreted religion in a way intended to help people overcome the crises caused by modernization. Their ideas appeared in over a hundred books, journals, and newspapers read by a wide range of people, from intellectuals and nationalist leaders to peasants. Beyond the printed word, Yi's, Hong's, and Pae's religious beliefs also heavily influenced people through rural campaigns that they had a leading role in designing and implementing, which gave them an advantage over a number of nationalist leaders who lacked the means to realize their beliefs. Yi's, Hong's, and Pae's beliefs therefore illustrate well how religions grappled with modernization.

Cultural Change and Antireligion Movements in the 1920s and 1930s

After the March First Movement, the colonial government swiftly introduced a series of reforms under its new Cultural Policy (Bunka Seiji). Scaling back its military-style rule, the colonial state appeared to launch these reforms in order to relax its overall control over the daily lives of Koreans. Although it gave more autonomy to Koreans, the colonial state actually pursued these reforms as part of a larger drive to increase its power and influence. The March First Movement proved that oppression alone was inadequate to prevent opposition to colonial rule. Colonial officials, including Saito Makoto, the new governor-general; Mizuno Rentaro, the administrative superintendent; and Moriya Yoshio, the secretary of the governor-general, argued for an alternative form of governance that deemphasized "repressive means of control that would wait for someone to violate the law."[3] In place of coercive measures, the colonial government hoped to discipline the habits and behaviors of Koreans and transform them into docile, obedient subjects who possessed correct thought and expressed proper behavior. The state set out to discipline Koreans through various reforms that included medical and hygienic programs and educational and moral campaigns that exposed Koreans to new forms of knowledge. It also introduced new surveillance programs that included laws giving the police wide latitude to censor any publication it perceived as questioning or threatening colonial rule. With a budget that doubled from 77,560,690 yen to 157,342,289 yen between 1919 and 1921, the colonial state established new institutions that implemented these programs and campaigns, such as schools, hospitals, sanatoriums, and museums. With the state intervening in people's daily lives and exerting power at the micro level, the Cultural Policy represented a form of government that aimed to prevent any future uprisings.[4]

As part of its mission of governing, the colonial state reorganized the policies on religion that had been in place since 1910. From the start of colonial rule, Article 2, Section 11 of the 1889 Japanese constitution structured the relationship between state and religion: "Japanese subjects enjoy freedom of religion, with the provision that no one is allowed to disturb public peace or public order or to evade the duties incumbent on all subjects of the Emperor."[5] Although the constitution permitted Koreans to practice religion openly, it also authorized the colonial government to adopt measures that would ensure that religion would never become a threatening force. The colonial government classified a religion as either legitimate / official or miscellaneous as a way to oversee and manage the practice of religion. Christianity, Buddhism, and Shintoism were assigned to the former category, while new religions, such as Ch'ŏndogyo and Taejong-gyo, fell into the latter category. The state never classified shamanism as a religion and instead sought to eliminate it because it was seen as a corrosive tradition.

From 1910 to 1919, the Department of Home Affairs tightly controlled the affairs of official religions. Under the June 1911 Temple Law, for example, the colonial state reorganized Buddhism into a centralized system, took control of temples, and managed personnel and daily affairs by supervising the elections of Buddhist leaders and requiring permits for all activities. The state also applied this intrusive method of rule to its management of Protestant Christianity. Although established Protestant Christian churches and institutions and foreign missionaries never promoted nationalist causes, the colonial state perceived religion as a threat because of its strong institutional presence in the country, the influence of foreign missionaries over Koreans, and nationalist activities conducted by followers.[6] The state's fears of Christianity became apparent when it arrested several missionaries and Korean Christians over an alleged plot to assassinate Governor-General Terauchi, known as the Conspiracy Case of 1911–1915. The case fell apart, but it revealed that the state was serious about controlling the church and taking any measure to prevent it from causing disturbances.[7] The state also used educational laws in 1915 to curb church power by prohibiting private schools, which included missionary

educational institutions, from teaching religious subjects and performing religious rituals on school grounds. Finally, the state tried to limit the influence
of churches by supporting the growth of the Congregational Church of Japan
in Korea.[8] In 1913, Yang Ju-sam, a Methodist pastor, unsurprisingly declared
that the state aimed to "repress, if not to suppress," the church.[9]

Under the state's new Cultural Policy, colonial officials still wanted to
deter the "tendency of religion to become easily involved in political issues,"[10]
but they sought to pacify religion through a less combative relationship with
religious organizations. This new relationship started with shifting oversight
of religion from the Home Affairs Ministry to other government branches.
The Educational Bureau oversaw Buddhism, Christianity, and Shinto, while
the Police Bureau supervised miscellaneous religions.[11] Next, the colonial
government repealed some earlier policies that had restricted the practice of
religion, such as the educational laws that had required permits to operate a
private school and had prohibited religious teaching and activities at these
schools. The state also tried to create a more hospitable environment for religions by no longer pressuring churches to join the Congregational Church of
Japan and by organizing meetings between religious leaders and colonial
officials as a way to open healthy lines of communication.

In this new relationship with religious groups, the state still wielded
strong influence and control over religious life. For example, it tried to prevent religions from straying beyond spiritual matters by continuously track-
ing their activities and growth through comprehensive surveys.[12] Alongside
surveys, the colonial state used new censorship rules to ensure that the language
in books and journals published by religious organizations never expressed
political rhetoric or opposition to colonial rule. Finally, the state increased its
drive to promote Shinto and indoctrinate Koreans with its nationalist religious
messages by constructing the Chosŏn Shrine in Seoul in 1925 and supporting
the establishment of ten Shinto sects throughout the peninsula.

Until 1937, the Cultural Policy allowed for a space where followers could
practice religion under limited forms of autonomy. The creation of this space
indicated the state's desire to move away from full-on suppression of religion
in favor of regulating how it would be practiced. Regulating religious practices would still enable the state to keep religion in check because of the new
reforms and measures initiated under its mission of governmentality. The
state hoped that this new space for the practice of religion would encourage
an ever-increasing number of religious activities in ways that would shift
people's attention and energies away from politics. Indeed, the state hoped
that Koreans would be distracted from their "suffering under colonial rule" by
religious activities[13] and become depoliticized, passive subjects who were numb
to immediate political, economic, and social concerns. The state, however,

recognized that distraction alone would never fully pacify subjects, so it cracked down on any religious groups if they appeared to be threatening colonial rule, such as one hundred new religions, including Kongja-gyo and Paebaek-gyo, because they allegedly conducted nationalist activities.

Operating in a challenging political environment, religions also had to be sensitive to happenings in the national community because they were part of a greatly changed nationalist culture. The easing of restrictions on speech and organization led to nationalist groups organizing new mass movements centered on the idea of "reconstruction" (*kaejo*). Reconstruction, according to Michael Shin, "embodied the hopes of new social forces for fundamental change."[14] Leftists regarded reconstruction as a series of radical reforms "ranging from social democracy to social revolution" that directly challenged colonial rule.[15] For bourgeois nationalists, reconstruction represented a process to forge a new culture that served as a medium for the formation of a national community that would be equipped with the knowledge, skills, and practices to negotiate and manage the challenges of modernization.

Far from being just a local nationalist trend, ideas of the Korean Culture Movement were found in many parts of the world during the 1920s. Neo-Kantians in the West and Asia interpreted culture as a mechanism for overcoming the rupturing ideological and material changes stemming from capitalism.[16] As a mechanism, culture directly connected people to the nation, which was considered an infinite spirit that was the source of authentic meaning and value and thus the stable ground of signification. It was hoped that through experiencing the nation, people would communally enjoy historical continuity and a meaningful form of existence that grounded their identity. In this capacity, culture was expected to establish a national community, serve as a "refuge from the disruptions caused by the dominance of the market in social life," and furnish stability for a modern life.[17] For many people outside and inside colonial Korea, resolving the tensions and strains of modernization required cultural reforms.

Koreans were well aware of these drives to build a new culture worldwide, as is evident in an April 1, 1920, *Tonga ilbo* (*Dong-a ilbo*) article, "World Reconstruction and the Nationalist Movement in Chosŏn," which argued that "the most pressing task was to bring the nationalist movement [in Korea] in line with the trends of world reconstruction."[18] To the bourgeois nationalist camp, heeding *Tonga ilbo*'s call for cultural reconstruction in Korea was imperative because the forces of modernization destabilized society and especially left rural Korea full of uncertainty and unease. Some Koreans, such as women in the new women's movement, celebrated modernization because it produced liberating changes, but others considered it the source of the breakdown of long-standing institutions and customs that had long grounded the

Korean identity and had provided economic and social stability. Articles on colonial life, in particular an editorial in the April 1923 edition of *Kaebyŏk*, argued that new developments in colonial society destroyed traditional forms of community and caused the loss of structures that had upheld society and provided forms of social mediation between individuals.[19] Conflicts appeared in the absence of mechanisms that smoothly governed social relations and caused social divisions that threatened the unity and survival of the nation.

Seeing the serious economic, social, and cultural consequences of modernization, participants in the Culture Movement saw reforms as means to revitalize the economic, social, and cultural lives of people and repair broken social relationships. These reforms were to produce deep and fundamental, rather than cosmetic, changes that would allow Koreans to experience the nation and the creation of a new national identity and community. The Culture Movement wanted to fix society and people's lives in a way that had the long-term effect of maintaining a healthy national body and ensuring the survival of the nation under modernization. The turn to culture signified a move away from the discourse and goals of "civilization and enlightenment" (*munmyŏng kaehwa*), which had emphasized a capitalist modernization program through the adoption of Western knowledge and institutions. Supporters of civilization and enlightenment had advocated this type of program without recognizing the vast problems that resulted from the forces of modernization, especially capitalism. The Culture Movement sought to address this oversight of civilization and enlightenment discourse by transforming Koreans into totally new national subjects who could continuously manage the challenges produced by modernization and experience the spirit of the nation that gave them meaning, identity, and thus stability. Culture Movement leaders knew that transforming people and society required an immense amount of time and effort. Thus they called for a move from a direct political confrontation with the colonial state to carrying out economic, social, and cultural reforms. They argued that cultural reforms still served a nationalist purpose because they were building a durable national body that would thrive in the world and ensure Korea's sovereignty after independence.

From the Culture Movement to campaigns organized by leftists, reconstruction projects swiftly moved ahead in the 1920s. Bourgeois nationalists and leftists pursued different agendas for constructing a new nation, but both agreed that reconstruction should take place in the present and in society and criticized anything that derailed these temporal and spatially bound reconstruction projects. In the early 1920s, the Left and the Right accused religion of being a destructive force that threatened any nationalist movement, and they waged large-scale antireligion campaigns. These campaigns in Korea coincided with the appearance of antireligious sentiments throughout the world. The Soviet Union became the site of state-led antireligion campaigns in which Stalin ordered the arrest of religious figures and the confiscation of religious property. During the 1919 May Fourth Movement in China, leftist intellectuals and students relentlessly criticized religion for being out of date and inhibiting the progress of humanity. They started antireligion organizations such as the Anti-Christian Student Federation (1922) and the Great Federation of Anti-religions (1922). In 1925, people in the United States showed their discontent with religion during the period of "religious depression," which saw unfavorable views of Christianity growing, a steep drop in financial support of missionary work, and a decline in the number of new church members.[20] In 1927, the most influential attack on religion came from Bertrand Russell's lecture "Why I Am Not a Christian," which had a profound impact on Western society. Journals informed Koreans about these criticisms and the organized protests against religion.[21] *Kaebyŏk* even featured several articles on how Russell's philosophies could be applied to reconstructing Korea.[22]

Interpreting religion as a "mystifying" force, Korean leftists shared these antireligion sentiments felt throughout the world. In 1921, at the Koryŏ Communist Party's convention in Siberia, Korean communists publicly condemned religion as antirevolutionary and called for an ideological struggle against all religions. In Korea, through *Kaebyŏk* and *Pip'an* (Criticism), a left-wing journal, communists denounced religion. Their articles attacked religion, especially Christianity, for supporting capitalism and imperialism.[23] Some articles attacked religion for promoting an escapist life. In the November 1925 issue of *Kaebyŏk*, Pae Sŏng-nyong stressed that "religion is a fantasy that makes people thirst for the eternal heaven and yearn for the otherworld while making them disattached from the everyday social world."[24] Religious followers believed that true happiness and peace arrived through spiritual experiences and ultimately through physical death, which would allow a reunion with God. With a mind-set that focused only on spiritual matters and anticipated the next world, religious believers dismissed reality on earth and ignored problems in society. In fact, because religions portrayed society as the space of evil, followers found even more reasons to reject the present and separate themselves from society by escaping to the world of spirituality. Pae argued that because of this influence, religion was an obstacle to carrying out nationalist movements.

Leftists' complaints against religion stemmed from their conception of people's place in history. According to a leftist who criticized religion in 1931, the Left advocated a materialist form of history that emphasized people as the power and source behind changes in society, while religions supported an idealist or spiritual conception of history in which a "spiritual force" undergirded and transformed the world.[25] Leftists heavily criticized the religious conception of history because it deemphasized humans as the primary agents and

makers of history and instead promoted a powerless form of human subjectivity. Until 1937, leftists thus attacked religion out of fears that it would turn
Koreans into passive subjects and prevent the mobilization of the masses to
achieve social revolution and independence from colonial rule.

Alongside communists and socialists, bourgeois nationalists attacked religion and religious groups, especially through the mass dailies whose articles
reached and influenced people all over the peninsula. *Tonga ilbo* published edi-
torials that condemned Christians for refusing to provide social and economic
welfare for the poor and needy.[26] *Chosŏn ilbo* (*Chosun ilbo*) criticized religious
groups for their unwillingness to value society and assume an active role in
reconstructing society. Since the Protestant Church also rejected contemporary science and social-evolutionary theories, *Chosŏn ilbo* concluded that the
church was a conservative institution that refused to adapt to changes in
society.[27]

Chosŏn ilbo's and *Tonga ilbo*'s criticisms of religion were already well articulated by Yi Kwang-su, a leading nationalist leader and the prominent modern novelist. For Yi, the Christian church particularly exemplified what was
wrong with religion because it promoted an "ecclesiastical supremacy," a theology that called for followers to focus solely on their relationship with God by
devoting themselves to spiritual matters and cultivating a spiritual life away
from society. This theology stressed that by pursuing a sacred life inside the
church, followers would enjoy a spiritual experience and be sheltered from the
forces of evil that ruled the everyday world. Guided by this theology, missionaries and Korean Christian leaders taught followers "to read the Bible daily, to
sing hymns, to go to church, to obey the directions of the pastor," and that "this
is regarded as the whole and only responsibility of humans." Korean Christians therefore "look[ed] upon other duties as unimportant" and "treat[ed]
with contempt all duties toward state and society, as the 'work of the world.'"
When Christians faced problems, they were thus told to rely on worship and
prayer rather than practical forms of knowledge. Emphasizing this point, Yi
wrote, "They [Christians] think prayer alone can save a ship from a storm or
an unfit man from defeat in the struggle for existence."[28] Yi criticized this way
of thinking and living because it molded followers into passive, ignorant subjects who believed that they were held captive by spiritual forces. He appeared
to soften his criticism of religion and Christianity somewhat in the mid-1920s,
but his critique nevertheless encapsulated the overall sentiment and anger
many bourgeois nationalists held toward religion.

Criticisms of religion appeared to have some resonance with parts of the
population, especially the youth. Rejecting the old and embracing the new, the
youth population channeled its energy into carrying out nationalist projects
after the March First Movement. Youths responded well to the leftist argument

that religion was a relic of the past that prevented Korea from achieving the modern stage of history and spoke publicly against religion. In March 1923, the National Youth Party Convention argued for the death of religion. Participants in the convention proclaimed "religion as such a prejudice, which harms the development and expression of individuality, contradicts the truth of science, and . . . serv[es] as an opiate for the conquered."[29] In April 1924, participants in the National Chosŏn Youth Party called religion a hindrance to class struggle. At the National Chosŏn People's Movement Convention in April 1925, participants described religion as "mystical" and declared that "religion is opium."[30] These conventions spoke out against all religions, but many participants reserved most of their anger for the Protestant Church. In part, this fury stemmed from what appeared to be a close relationship between the church and the colonial state—a perception that arose after the police quashed antireligion protests outside a Sunday-school conference.

Antireligion discourse and campaigns caused deep disquiet in religious communities. Religious leaders saw how these attacks were leading followers to question the application of traditional doctrines in the present and the role of religion in society. Internal dissent, for example, arose within Buddhist circles as lay leaders questioned the antisocial stance promoted by Buddhism and other religions.[31] Criticisms of Christianity appeared through followers acknowledging the shortcomings of the Protestant Church in society. In 1926, Korean seminary students at Union Methodist Theological Seminary, for example, called attention to the "failures" of the church, such as the "failure to give due regard to the economic needs of the people . . . [failure of] faith without works. The greatest of all superstitions is the belief that God will intervene miraculously, which is mere credulity, and results in inactivity and death."[32] Skepticism about Christianity's place in the modern world also appeared in questions asked by followers in various venues, such as "What is Christian Socialism?" "Did Jesus only speak of spiritual food or did He not also speak about the present economic problems?" and "Why doesn't the church take some interest in evolution?"[33]

At youth conferences, participants asked whether religion could effectively guide them through the vast developments in society. The YMCA held several student conferences where young men and women partook in lively discussions over issues that pertained to the fundamentals of their faith. At the 1926 YMCA Student Conference in Kongju, attended by sixty students from Korea, Peking, and Tokyo, participants debated the questions "Does God exist?" and "What is the Bible?" and issues such as "old and new customs," "marriage, love and divorce," "how to marry," and "liberty and obedience." At the heart of their debates and discussions, these participants were questioning whether and how Christianity could be applied to their lives when they were experiencing many new developments and changes.[34] This line of intense questioning continued into the following year at the 1927 YMCA Student Conference, held in P'yŏngyang with over one hundred participants. There, students expanded their debate topics to include political and economic questions, such as "To what extent is Christianity imperialistic?" and "How far do Christianity and Capitalism go together in exploiting the countries of the East?"[35] Everywhere in the church, youths were questioning church fundamentals. Indeed, a 1925 report by the Australian Presbyterian Mission stated that "the deity of Christ, the necessity of atonement, the authenticity of the Bible, the very existence of God . . . all these are called in question."[36]

In this climate of protest and questioning, some followers rejected religion in favor of ideologies that more readily categorized and gave meaning to their new experiences. This discontent with religion can be seen in the life of Kim San, who attended church and a Christian school before 1919. He rejected all forms of religion because of their unwillingness to aid the people socially and economically and unite them in the drive for independence. Kim specifically criticized the Christian church and Western missionaries because they taught a conservative theology, which explained that the colonial situation originated from the sinful nature of Koreans and that the power to realize independence rested with God, who first demanded penance from people. In this form, Christianity had very little relevance for Koreans like Kim who sought to overcome colonialism and social instability through their own hands. Frustrated, Kim wrote, "I thought there was certainly no God and that the teachings of Christ had little application for the world of struggle into which I had been born."[37]

In this complex environment, religion came under severe attack. After the March First Movement, as the newly energized Korean population entered a period of developments that fundamentally disrupted their lives, many Koreans, young and old, wanted concrete means to deal with Japanese colonialism and create a meaningful modern society and nation simultaneously. They attacked and rejected religions because of their inability to make sense of the present and address their concerns properly and effectively. Closer examination of this situation shows that religious groups faced a problem where a disjuncture existed between what the established religious messages offered and what people experienced and believed they needed to give meaning to these experiences and guide them to reconstruct colonial society. Religious organizations faced the issue of "cultural distance" in which their established religious beliefs and practices, which had once been meaningful, no longer had any relevance or significance for people entering a new historical period.[38] Several religious institutions realized that the antireligion campaigns were symptoms and an indication of the severity of the upheavals caused by modernization. The issue that religious figures now faced was how they were going to respond to the problem of cultural distance and reshape beliefs to meet the new needs of the people.

Yi Ton-hwa and the Transformation of Ch'ŏndogyo

By the time antireligion campaigns began, Ch'ŏndogyo had already undergone a period of reform. The reorganization of the institution started when Son Pyŏng-hŭi (1861–1922), the third Tonghak leader, renamed it Ch'ŏndogyo (Religion of the Heavenly Way) in 1905. This new beginning for Tonghak resulted from Son's attempt to distance the institution from Japanese colonialism. In 1904, Son, Yi Yong-gu, a prominent Tonghak leader, and several followers had become active in the Ilchinhoe, which supported greater Japanese involvement in Korea as a way to promote Asian unity. Son left the Ilchinhoe, but Tonghak's reputation had already come under question as the public criticized followers for their association with a pro-Japanese organization that supported the 1905 Protectorate Treaty. Seeking to quiet these criticisms and wrest control of the organization from Yi, Son persuaded the Tonghak leadership to rename the religion Ch'ŏndogyo under his leadership.[39]

Son viewed the reorganization of Tonghak as an opportunity to position Ch'ŏndogyo as a major player in nationalist politics. To achieve this goal, the organization issued the Charter of Ch'ŏndogyo in 1906—a new organizational plan that centralized decision-making power in the leader and established a new bureaucracy that included an office of religious inspectors who communicated the leader's commands to local followers and required followers to be obedient to the leadership. Alongside these new rules and regulations, the church established Seoul as its headquarters to be physically closer to the king and the national government and partake in "nationalist discussions."[40] Finally, in February 1906, Ch'ŏndogyo founded a printing house known as Pomunsa that was responsible for publishing *Mansebo,* a newspaper, and *Ch'ŏndogyo wŏlbo,* a monthly magazine.[41] Through these developments, Son spread his message on reforming the country, which promoted industrialization, military expansion, and educational, health, and sanitation programs. Embodying the ideas of civilization and enlightenment, Son's plan of reform stressed that religion would serve as a major civilizing force that would achieve social enlightenment for Koreans.[42] Son argued that instead of being a force of opposition, religion could work with the government to resist Japanese imperialism. Although he believed that religion should play a major role in society, Son never ordered the organization to start any major social movements. Instead, the Ch'ŏndogyo leader and followers individually carried out reforms by participating in nationalist activities like the March First Movement.

Son's ideas laid the foundation for the organization's social activism in the 1920s.[43] However, he advanced a narrow form of social activism that mostly focused on political outcomes. From 1905 to 1919, Son reinterpreted Tonghak teachings to apply them to protecting the nation and preserving Korea's independence by advancing the normative model of modernization. His reconceptualization of Tonghak traditions gave less importance to addressing and solving the economic, social, and cultural consequences of modernization, such as mass poverty, rising social inequality and division, and the fragmentation of identity that Koreans began to experience more because of the rapid growth of capitalism starting in the 1920s.

The primary responsibility for adapting Ch'ŏndogyo thought to the changing 1920s and 1930s and providing a concept of religion that would meet the new needs of the people was left to Yi Ton-hwa (1884–?). Yi became a Tonghak believer in 1903 in P'yŏngyang, served as a close confidant of Son Pyŏnghui, and became the main theorist of the Ch'ŏndogyo organization.[44] After the March First Movement, Yi joined the new faction (sin pa) in the organization and served as one of the original founders of the Ch'ŏndogyo Youth Party in September 1923.[45] His ideas were widely published in journals, such as Kaebyŏk, Sinin'gan (New Human), and Chosŏn nongmin (Chosŏn Peasant), and a number of books, including Innaech'ŏn yoŭi (The Essential Teaching of Innaech'ŏn, 1924), Sinin ch'ŏrhak (New Person Philosophy, 1931), and Ch'ŏndogyo ch'anggŏnsa (The History of Ch'ŏndogyo, 1933), which was the seminal book on the history of Tonghak and Ch'ŏndogyo. Through his writings and speeches, Yi became the leading voice of the organization who was concerned about the welfare of Ch'ŏndogyo followers and the entire public.

Yi rearticulated conventional Ch'ŏndogyo language in response to the vast changes erupting on the peninsula in the 1920s, which had created a period of transition between the old and new. During the late nineteenth century or the enlightenment (Kaehwa) period, the new had entered Korea as foreign forces, beliefs, customs, and practices. The new reshaped the social, economic, and cultural terrains of Korean society, but old or established ideas, practices, and structures continued to influence the lives of many Koreans. This situation started a period of transition in Korea in which the new stood alongside the old, thus causing unevenness in society. As a way to explain this development, Yi pointed to the way people kept time. Koreans had used the Chinese lunar calendar to track the days and months of the year, but they also began to use the Western solar calendar after the arrival of foreigners in Korea during the late nineteenth century. Using both the Chinese and the Western calendars, Koreans thus experienced the "year changing twice." Yi interpreted unevenness as a phenomenon that fostered a chaotic environment full of uncertain changes, conflicts between the old and the new, and things being overturned.[46] People suffered economically and socially and became disoriented and mentally confused. Specifically, "doubt and agony" beset people's lives,[47] and individuals "wandered and roamed about in society." In this condition, phenomenon people (hyŏnsangjŏk saram) lived with "uncertainty" about the present.[48] Yi's description of unevenness and the changes resulting from it spoke to the power of modernization to unsettle society by producing material and ideological dislocations that caused Koreans to become cautious about and even scared of the present.

According to Yi, these attitudes and approaches to the present arose because people lacked systems of knowledge and practice that interpreted changes. He faulted religious organizations for leaving people without the conceptual language to make sense of the uneven social world and how to live in it. Religions were unwilling to reflect on established religious doctrines, question them, and readjust them in ways that made them valuable resources for dealing with current issues.[49] Yi explained to the religious community that reexamining doctrines and beliefs was a natural process in the history of religions. Religious doctrines had always undergone reinterpretation in order to meet the purposes and needs of that specific period.[50] Yi wrote that religious truth never changed, but "what change[d] [was] the adaptation of the religious teaching to the developments in society."[51]

Yi argued that standard categories of Ch'ŏndogyo should be adapted to the new environment and thus allow the religion to become a religion of modernity (hyŏndae chonggyo).[52] As a religious principle first articulated by Son Pyŏng-hŭi in 1907 and one of the foundational ideas of Ch'ŏndogyo, "humanity is Ultimate Reality" (innaech'ŏn) became the mechanism through which Yi reinterpreted the religion. Yi regarded innaech'ŏn as a religious concept based on pantheism in that it emphasized how a single force created, embodied, and sustained all.[53] Instead of Sangje, Ch'ŏnju, and Chigi, which earlier Tonghak leaders had used, Yi named this force Hanŭllim or Uju. Han represented "great," while ŭl stood for everything in the universe.[54] With these two parts as its foundation, Hanŭllim signified the primary force that created, united, and sustained all things and served as an objective power that was "ubiquitous and pervasive." As the original and primary force in the universe, Hanŭllim embodied "truth, goodness, and beauty."[55] According to Yi, Hanŭllim represented a perfect being that established and powered everything and endowed the material world with meaning and value, especially goodness.[56] Hanŭllim, in short, represented the source of signification.

Instead of viewing Hanŭllim as a transcendental being like God (Hananim) in Christianity, Yi interpreted it as an immanent force.[57] Influenced by the ideas of Ch'oe Che-u, he configured Hanŭllim as a force that existed within and found expression in all things from the material (mulchil) to the spiritual (*chŏngsin*) or from the "heaven and stars to the particles on the earth."[58] Its immanent nature meant that there was no division between the spiritual and material realm.[59] Because Hanŭllim was an eternal force that was the origin and end of all reality, Yi added that it had no beginning or no end.[60] As a never-ending force in the everyday, Hanŭllim was thus immune to the messy changes and transformations erupting in the material world.

Under this interpretation of Hanŭllim, not only did unity exist among all forces, things, and people in the universe,[61] but also everything equaled the original and creative force of Hanŭllim. This interpretation thus emphasized that humans were also theoretically Hanŭllim and therefore divine.[62] Indeed, according to Yi, since Hanŭllim directly "conceived" people rather than human parents, an individual was a manifestation of and a form of Hanŭllim from the very beginning of life.[63] Accordingly, people were part of a larger totality that extended beyond the material world and were endowed with a divine state of being and a "sacred consciousness" or a direct perception (*chikgakgye*) through which they could be aware of and experience the objective, unchanging values of Hanŭllim.[64] As a result, individuals could experience truth, goodness, and beauty as well as know and experience the forces that created and moved the universe. In this sacred state, Yi emphasized, the self became whole and complete.[65]

Yi specifically conceptualized and introduced the concept of Hanŭllim to help Koreans in the 1920s and 1930s confidently live in the changing world. Yi wanted Koreans to know that because they possessed a sacred identity, value, and consciousness that were constant, people should no longer fear the material and ideological ruptures in society. With a sacred consciousness that illuminated ultimate truth, people could confront the changes, "break up the chaos and darkness" in society, and be in a position to navigate through any transformations.[66] Yi hoped that because of this consciousness, Koreans would no longer interpret and experience the present (*hyŏnjae*) as an undetermined period when events and developments quickly vanished and receded into the past, but as a meaningful period when people encountered spiritual experiences and enlightenment.[67] With the present as a temporality in which people gained meaning and value through their connection with Hanŭllim, Yi believed that the present should be regarded as a moment of the "eternal" (*musimuchong*) rather than a finite period in time.[68]

Defining humanity and the present as sacred permitted Yi to reconfigure the modern period as a dynamic temporality in which people continually experienced spiritual enlightenment, certainty, and continuity in their lives. For Yi, however, the realization of this type of life rested on individuals first uncovering their divine nature. He clarified that *innaech'ŏn* never said that humans were already Hanŭllim; instead, individuals possessed the potential to become Hanŭllim: "The principle of *innaech'ŏn* does not imply that a human's present mind and behavior are that of Hanŭllim. It means that humans have the abilities to realize the spirit of Hanulnim. Put differently, under *innaech'ŏn* doctrine, humans become Hanŭllim."[69] Stressing that Koreans were presently alienated from their sacred nature, Yi wrote, "By observing people's present actions and spirit, one can tell that they are not Hanŭllim."[70]

Yi pointed to conditions in society as the reason that Koreans had become estranged from their divine nature. Specifically, destructive political, social, and economic developments left them in a state of spiritual abstraction. In present-day Korean society, discrimination, poverty, and violence were some of the developments that warped people's physical and spiritual conditions.[71] Many of these problems originated from what Yi called "false conventions, customs, and traditions of the world."[72] In particular, these false ideas and practices stemmed from capitalism. Yi explained that because the purpose of capitalism was to "continue the concentration of power of capital" rather than to work "for the benefit of humanity," this economic system privileged capital as the subject and humanity as the object. Capitalism consequently arranged society in a way that pitted humanity against capital, and humanity suffered as the forces of capital dislodged it as the center of society.[73] Destructive systems like capitalism and their ideas and practices distorted people's sacred personalities (*inkyŏk*) by fashioning characteristics and habits that prevented people from experiencing and exhibiting the qualities of Hanŭllim, such as goodness and beauty.[74] With Hanŭllim suppressed, people were separated from their divine nature.

Seeing the root of spiritual alienation in the way society was shaped instead of in evil spiritual forces such as shamanistic spirits, Yi exhorted Ch'ŏndogyo and all religious followers to carry out campaigns for the spatial reconstruction (*kaejo*) of Korean society to restore people's divine nature. Koreans should specifically construct a heaven on earth (*chisang ch'ŏn'guk*) that served as a spiritual space on the peninsula.[75] Yi argued that in this new space, all harmful systems that caused destruction and spiritual alienation should be replaced by systems that promoted healthy and stable material conditions and daily lives. Through this process, an ideal environment would emerge that would allow the divine to be realized within humanity and in all of society, which he explained as follows:

> Innaech'ŏn was created in order to make this world a heaven. But this does not mean that *innaech'ŏn* was created because the world had already become a paradise. That is, humans have the potential to become Hanŭllim, and the present world has the potential to be a heaven. . . . According to the materialist theory of Marx, a

person's mind does not originate from within oneself. Rather, it is created and shaped by the historical traditions and customs of the outside world. Consequently, a human's mind, according to Marx, is formed by the social system, customs, and habits, which have been transmitted to us for a thousand years Therefore, a new mind [Hanŭllim] could be created only by breaking down or eliminating conventions and traditions.[76]

Yi shared Marx's belief that humanity could overcome alienation only by transforming the material world. He thus designated political, economic, social, and cultural structures as objects for transformation.

In this new heavenly space, the material world would be informed by and anchored in a new culture (*sae munhwa*) of ideas and practices appropriate for the current times or living in the modern period, according to Yi. Just as religion should adapt to present times, the relevance of ideas, practices, and institutions at that moment should be constantly reevaluated. Yi pointed out that what might have value in one period might no longer have value in a different period with new environments and challenges.[77] In challenging Koreans to adopt an attitude toward innovation that was rooted in and conscious of the present, Yi in particular expected all ideas, practices, structures, and systems to reconstruct society in ways that promoted and ensured the development and security of people's personalities.[78] Constructing the ideal personality required addressing every aspect of life (*saenghwal*), which included "eating and clothing," "law, politics, science, and economics," and "religion, ethics, and art."[79] It also necessitated attention to people's mental / spiritual state (*chŏngsin*), which included morals, ethics, and religion. In pursuing this goal, Koreans, according to Yi, would be part of a worldwide trend because many countries had embarked on a mission of culturalism, which criticized people's excessive attachment to the material and sought to improve people's mental and spiritual state throughout the world. In part, Yi learned about and embraced this trend through reading the works of Bertrand Russell.[80] Like Russell, he stressed that improving people's mental and spiritual side would occur through a new culture[81] that not only unleashed people's creative potential because a human was a naturally "creative person" (*ch'angcho saram*),[82] but also gave people free rein to nurture their personalities.

Yi stressed that certain ethical principles should determine and structure the form of culture. In particular, he emphasized the concept of treating and respecting each individual as divine and stressing that everyone is equal (*sainyŏch'ŏn*) as an essential principle for governing all social relations.[83] He also stressed the importance of structuring the new culture around the principle of social oneness (*tong kwi il che*). *Sainyŏch'ŏn* and *tong kwi il che* guaranteed the construction of a community based on love, trust, and equality that collaborated on improving all aspects of people's lives. For Yi, creating this type of community was essential because it was through social relations that "a person's self materializes" and one could expand his or her abilities and capabilities.[84] Although this idea of the individual evolving only in relation to others was a popular notion in philosophical circles, it set Yi apart from several Korean nationalists who argued that the modernist project of self-enlightenment should start and end with the individual. In 1925, for example, Chang Paek-san declared, "Before any kinds of revolution, revolutionize yourself first," while Yi Chun-sik wrote that "true reform lies in individuals innovating, criticizing and encouraging themselves."[85] By insisting that community and healthy social relations were necessary for improving individual personalities, Yi sought to prevent the social chaos that would result from people pursuing their own wants and desires and to undercut the dark side of modernization in which "privileging individual self-realization and promoting adversary culture unleashes hedonistic impulses irreconcilable with the requirements of a well-ordered society."[86]

With a new culture anchored in a healthy and vibrant community, Yi expected the creation of a "heaven on earth" where "distinctions between high and low classes would be absent, differences between the rich and poor would no longer exist, hostility and war would disappear, jealousy, malice, and hatred would be gone . . . goodness will underline all activities, no restraints will be placed on obtaining food and clothing, there will be no restraints on human agency, there will be no struggle between good and evil . . . and sickness will disappear." Moreover, it would be a place without unevenness because "a condition of prosperity and decline and rising and falling would be absent."[87] Yi imagined this spiritual place to be full of peace, social harmony, and stability that would enable Koreans to develop their personalities, experience Hanŭllim, and acquire a "sacred consciousness" that would allow for a vibrant life under modernization.

Promoting spatial reconstruction in response to the consequences of modernization distinguished Yi from earlier Tonghak and Ch'ŏndogyo leaders. The first leaders of Tonghak, such as Ch'oe Che-u and Ch'oe Si-hyŏng, favored cultivating the self through prayer and worship and following moral and religious principles as the primary means to achieve spiritual enlightenment. Through these activities, a divine being would be uncovered, and a new utopian world would emerge.[88] Early leaders never advocated first building a new material world. Son Pyŏng-hŭi had called on followers to embrace contemporary Western-based reforms and modernize Korea. In so doing, however, he never thought of the type of impact modernization would have on society and the problematic changes resulting from it. Yi, however, unlike earlier Tonghak leaders, stressed the importance of first constructing a new world to overcome the problems of modernization and articulated an alternative vision of modernity through his religious writings. Although he considered meditating and praying important religious practices, Yi thought of spatial production as a way to control modernization and its mass changes and foster an environment where people uncovered their divine identities.[89] He rearticulated traditional religious language to emphasize religion-based social activism as a practice through which to question modernization and build a new world to achieve religious goals. His reinterpretation of the means and pathway to achieve the spiritual goals of Ch'ŏndogyo simply represented a process of transforming the form of religion while keeping its content the same. Far from straying or breaking from long-standing Tonghak and Ch'ŏndogyo thought, Yi adapted foundational language and practices to people's needs in the 1920s and 1930s.

Yi's emphasis on spatial production provided for a new vision of the nation-state. Indeed, he believed that in an environment where everyone became a sacred being, a new heaven on earth would realize a new nation (*minjok*) where common ideas and practices and especially a common spiritual identity united people.[90] Similar to the ideas emerging from the Culture Movement, Yi's concepts of culture, ethics and morals, and community and society became tools through which Koreans could organize their experiences in the changing present, build a new Korean identity, and establish a national community that would handle the modern period's challenges in a productive and safe way. What distinguished Yi from organizers of the Culture Movement was the belief that building a new culture should lead to establishing a form of modernity rooted in religion.

Hong Pyŏng-sŏn's Transformation of Protestant Christianity

Alongside Yi Ton-hwa and Ch'ŏndogyo, several Protestant Christian groups and Korean Christian leaders rearticulated theologies and crafted alternative practices that gave meaning to the ever-changing present and valued society as a fundamental means to experience God and shape spirituality. The rearticulation of theologies and practices was part of an overall movement by some Christians to align themselves with the mission of the Culture Movement—to refrain from direct political struggles and to carry out comprehensive reforms in response to modernization. The following statement to the Christian Youth Federation in 1925 by Sin Hŭng-u, the leader of the YMCA, well encapsulates the rationale of Christians in supporting the Culture Movement:

For about a decade, we Koreans lived our lives in silence, but stimulated by the culture brought in from abroad over recent years we launched an uprising. Yet, nothing was gained as a result, and in the end the Korean people incurred only harm and loss. In the future, we must put a stop to this blind activity and exert ourselves fully on behalf of our nation and society. . . . So it is my hope that you will put short-term considerations behind you and grasp hold of the long-term.[91]

Seeing direct political protests like the March First Movement as ineffective for producing long-term effects, Sin and Christian reformers alike believed that the next stage of the nationalist movement should include comprehensive reforms that would help people manage their changing economic, social, and cultural environment for the long term.

After 1919, Korean Christian socialists were among the earliest reformers of the church who demanded that Christians become socially conscious. Yi Tong-hwi and Pak Hŭi-do, for example, challenged Christians to combat newly emergent social and economic ills in society and published the magazine *Sinsaenghwal* (New Life) to encourage them to construct a just world based on political, economic, and social equality.[92] Yi Tae-wi, a YMCA leader who regarded Christ as a social reformer, exhorted Christians to stop fighting with socialists and instead collaborate to build a new kingdom on earth. Korean youth, in particular, were drawn to Christian socialism through the writings of the Japanese Christian socialist Kagawa Toyohiko, whose materials were introduced to the Korean public in 1925. Toyohiko's socialism of love, which combined Marxism with the teachings and examples of Christ, motivated certain Korean Christians to fight economic inequality and social injustice in order to form a new society through which people could experience God's love.[93] The various messages of Christian socialism were timely since followers appeared to grow more discontented over the state of the church. A Korean pastor in P'yŏngyang who returned to his church after two years of imprisonment in 1922 well articulated this brewing discontent when he confessed "that he needed reconstruction before he could enter again upon his work." He claimed, "Old time sermons, long and filled with doctrinal discussions, would not now satisfy his people. They demand teaching that fits into their present day needs."[94]

Christian socialism had a limited impact on the church because of its lack of institutional powers and influence. Interestingly enough, it took an international event, the Jerusalem Meeting of the International Missionary Council (IMC) in 1928, to awaken the Korean church socially. As one of the largest ecumenical Christian organizations, the IMC held large-scale conferences where Christian leaders from around the world debated issues confronting the global Christian movement and set standards for Christian thought and living. The political and economic upheavals of the 1920s and the subsequent rise of leftist movements around the world motivated participants in the Jerusalem Meeting to discuss Christianity's response to Western imperialism, the rise of nationalism, the problems of industrialization, and economic and racial divisions.[95] Christianity in Korea became one of the main topics for discussion because Edmund de Schweinitz Brunner presented his report on rural conditions and the Korean church at the conference. It pointed out that missionaries and church institutions overlooked the limits of existing religious language to represent people's new lived experiences. Brunner wrote that historically, missionaries had adapted well to changes, but "to-day the point of greatest interest and of greatest stress is economic and social, and this time the church is unready." He declared that "the church has failed . . . to take into account the changes in the ideals and thinking of the people." The church even discouraged new knowledge or "worldly knowledge," including "scientific learning," by denouncing "the new intellectual tendencies as 'foam.' "[96] Brunner's report emphasized that the church ignored changes, upheld orthodoxy, and refused to adapt Christianity to the present.

Besides Korea, conference participants debated issues facing churches in Africa, India, and China and concluded that the political and economic problems of the 1920s caused great physical suffering. Arguing that spiritual life was rooted in social conditions, conference leaders stressed that current economic and social injustices were separating people from God and his love and beauty in the present.[97] In order to bring people closer to God, conference delegates issued multiple declarations that called on Christians to improve social, political, and economic conditions. By linking a person's spirituality to the conditions of society, the Jerusalem conference instituted a new standard for Christian living. No longer should Christians reject and retreat from the world, focus only on spiritual matters, and wait for deliverance in the future. Instead, they must engage the world and build a peaceful society.

The social declarations coming from the Jerusalem conference set new standards for Christians in Korea. Korean Christian leaders who attended the conference disseminated conference ideas throughout the peninsula.[98] Large-scale publications, such as *Kidok sinbo,* and specialized journals, such as *Ch'ŏngnyŏn,* also exposed Koreans to the IMC's message of fighting social and economic injustice and forming a new society that would protect both people's material and spiritual lives.[99] By the late 1920s, this social message deeply influenced certain Christian communities and unsettled otherworldly conceptions of Christianity.[100] Influenced by the IMC's messages, the antireligion movement, and Christian socialist discourse, some Korean Christians constructed a social gospel (*sahoe pogŭmjuŭi*). Similar to the social gospel theology in the United States, the social gospel in Korea called on Christians to reform social, economic, and political structures in a way for love, equality, and justice to prevail.[101] Inspired by this new theology and the principle of Christism (Kidokjuŭi), which called for Christians to follow Christ's example of addressing people's spiritual and physical needs, prominent Korean Christian leaders organized the Kidok sinuhoe (Christian United Fellowship) in 1929. Members of this group argued for establishing a heaven on earth where people would experience liberty, peace, truth, and love in the present.[102] This spiritual kingdom not only would meet people's material and spiritual needs but also would create a new nation where God would serve as the source of unity and stability.[103]

Developments in the Christian community, such as Christian socialism and the social gospel, helped frame society as an important object of religious discourse and introduce the concept of Christian-based social activism. Christians who supported these developments used the symbol of Christ to create new theologies that explained their ideas and actions. Creating new theologies based on Christian doctrines and symbols, which according to Paul Tillich is "a statement of truth of the Christian message and interpretation of the truth for each generation," was important because these new theologies religiously justified the application of socially oriented ideas and practices in the modern period.[104] As these new ideas circulated around Korea, people still yearned for theologies that could more concretely articulate the role of religion under modernization and inform a religion-based modernity.

Hong Pyŏng-sŏn (1888–1967) became a leading Christian who constructed a framework to explain the relationship between religion and modernization. Hong was well aware that Koreans had experienced a new and changing environment called "the modern" because he himself was a product of all these changes. Born in Seoul, Hong attended Kyŏngsŏng haktang, a Japanese Protestant church-run school, where he specialized in Chinese classics. Upon graduation in 1908, Hong traveled to Japan to study theology at Doshisha University in Kyoto and returned to Korea in 1911. Unlike other Korean students returning from Japan, however, Hong used his theological training and his Korean background to assist Watase Tsuneyoshi, the director of the Kumiai Kyōkai's (Japanese Congregational Church) mission in colonial Korea. As Tsuneyoshi's personal assistant and translator, Hong participated in evangelical campaigns to spread Tsuneyoshi's theology and to persuade Koreans to join the Kumiai Kyōkai. For reasons unexplained, Hong left the church in 1914 to join the Southern Methodists. Before joining the YMCA in 1920, Hong taught at Pierson Memorial Bible School and Paehwa Girl's School. Considered one of the most active secretaries at the YMCA, he became the director and architect of the YMCA rural movement in 1925 and held the position until he left the organization in 1939.

From his first days at the YMCA, Hong wrote extensively on modernization's impact on society and religion. He believed that Korea had entered a new historical period called the modern (*hyŏndae*) characterized and distinguished by change.[105] Hong pointed out two specific principles that were promoted in the modern period. Valuing humanity, or people's personalities (*inkyŏk*), represented the first key feature. More specifically, Hong wrote that under the modern, "the value of each person was equal and people should be free from discrimination by money, law, systems, and customs." Grounded in this value, the modern thus stood for a period of "great diversity of form and figure of people's personalities." The second key feature of the modern was harmony between the material (*mulchil*) and the mental / spiritual (*chŏngsin*). Hong declared that under the modern, people "cannot live by mental / spiritual alone and cannot live by material alone" but instead must incorporate both into their lives.[106] What begs attention here is that despite popular criticism of religion as being antimodern, Hong stressed that religion did and should play an important role in a life under the modern period.

Hong's description of how the modern evolved helps explain why he argued that religion was a fundamental component of modernity. From his historical study of modern development in the world, Hong concluded that "people have been lost" and that people and personalities had been displaced and ignored.[107] Despite individuals being promoted as the most important figure under the modern, forces of "civilization" (*munmyŏng*) caused the deterioration of lives. As a collection of new ideas, practices, and systems that powered the modern, civilization promised positive developments and changes that would lead to the birth of an enlightened society and people in the modern period. Capitalism, for example, was to provide a brighter future for humanity, but it ended up introducing a new value system that caused people to become concerned about material development above anything else, including ethical and spiritual cultivation. Under this new economic system, people became materialistic (*mulchiljuŭi*)—focused solely on obtaining and increasing material wealth.[108] Materialism, according to Hong, stemmed from an "ideology of happiness and pleasure." Equating happiness and pleasure with the acquisition of money and goods, this ideology severely warped people's nature and subjectivity in that people became cheaters, stealers, mischief makers, and murderers[109] and no longer controlled their own lives because they were controlled by material desires; they were, in fact, "slaves to money."[110] To Hong, civilization controlled and determined people's thoughts, emotions, and bodies because it represented the subject while people served as the object. Writing in 1920, Hong declared, "In today's civilization, the person has become the slave of civilization. People have not become the owners and controllers of how civilization is used." Consequently, "People are living an empty and vain life [hŏyŏng]" that is totally separated from a life that promotes and emphasizes the individual.[111]

Hong maintained that civilization had diminished people's power and value and prevented the moral and ethical development of individuals under the modern in the West, but he also argued that Korea had already started to experience the ill effects of civilization. Hong placed the start of the modern period in the late nineteenth century,[112] which is unsurprising since Japan forcibly opened Korea at that time and connected it to the world market. This period marked the beginning of the rapid entrance of ideas and practices into Korea from the West and Japan that were drastically influencing "households and structures in society."[113] A number of Koreans, according to Hong, at first widely accepted and welcomed civilization because it offered the "tools" to build a new future.[114] Indeed, many Korean state leaders, intellectuals, and nationalist leaders, like King Kojong, Yun Ch'i-ho, and Yu Kil-chun, adopted the civilization model to help construct a new modern society and citizenry. Through this model, they hoped for a new nation-state that would ward off Western and Japanese imperialism and uphold Korea's sovereignty. Presumably from watching groups dashing to carry out reforms based on the civilization model, Hong decided that Koreans were fully part of a process of becoming "civilized" or, more specifically, "modern."[115]

Hong pointed out that Koreans too were experiencing the destructive consequences of carrying out reforms based on the civilization model. He appeared very concerned that capitalism had engendered the same materialistic lifestyle in Korea as it had in other countries experiencing civilization. In 1925, he wrote, "We have become money lovers. We believe that we cannot live without money." Hong further pointed out that ethics and religion took a back seat to money and material concerns.[116] Privileging material wants and desires over all, Koreans cared little about their personality and character.[117] To Hong, materialistic desires gave way to social conflicts.[118] Here he most certainly was referring to the growing clashes between landlords and peasants. Hong interpreted this turbulent relationship between landlords and peasants as a manifestation of uneven capitalist development in which the landlord class disregarded the plight of Koreans because of their desire for money, wealth, and power. In light of these developments, Hong feared that Korea's present course under modernity would be held captive to the forces of civilization and leave Korea in a ruined, fractured state.

The type of changes resulting from the forces of civilization troubled Hong, but it was the pace and scope of these changes that caused his greatest worries about how the modern was evolving in Korea. Change, according to him, was happening rapidly and transforming everything, and he was thus led to configure it as a leading characteristic of the modern: "The Modern [*Hyŏndae*] means time never rests and all things change; things of various nature change. There is not one thing that does not transform under modernity. Materials that do not transform are lifeless. The Modern as a word means change. It, of course, does not mean the past. That the past changes and something new arises is the Modern."[119] In a modern society, nothing was immune to change under the steady emergence and development of political, economic, and cultural forces, especially capitalism. It no longer could be taken for granted that traditional beliefs, institutions, and customs that had long structured people's lives would remain unchanged, intact, or relevant in the present or in the future. Hong wrote that Koreans found the rules and forms that shaped their lifestyles shifting dramatically.[120] Under the modern, the present became a temporality in which the new immediately slipped into the past; what was seen as immutable became subject to forces that diminished its place, meaning, and significance in the present. Because of these vast changes happening in a specific moment, Hong emphasized the present as the featured temporality of the modern. Indeed, instead of the term *kŭndae,* Hong used *hyŏndae,* which also meant the present or contemporary, to define modern.

To Hong, in this transformative environment, Koreans suffered physically and mentally. He characterized people's lives as unstable, chaotic, and full of confusion.[121] Describing how new influences affected Koreans in 1931, he wrote, "About forty years ago, the new ideas and elements from Japan and the West greatly influenced Korean households and society. These forces from the outside, however, created chaotic conditions." In fact, conditions were so chaotic that people could not figure out which direction society was heading.[122] In a condition where Koreans lacked the means to interpret and give meaning to their new lived experiences, people did not know what was right or wrong, true or untrue.[123] Modern life, according to Hong, was consequently "becoming more chaotic and busy. . . . [Koreans'] lives are filled with agony, despair, and strife. It is like a revolution."[124] Although he interpreted the modern as a period full of destructive, unsettling, and overwhelming experiences, Hong refused a wholesale rejection of civilization and the modern in favor of a return to the past because he believed that humanity must continually progress toward improving and elevating life. He declared, "We have to raise our life. We have to advance it. We must work hard to raise and expand the boundaries of our culture."[125] Achieving this form of progress required people to make room for the new in their lives so it could expand and strengthen their minds and bodies.

Because he recognized that embracing the new was challenging because of its destructive possibilities, Hong publicly introduced a conceptualization of the ideal modern life that curbed destructive forces and ensured the enrichment of humanity and the highest development of society. For Hong, this type of modern life required religion in that he envisioned that religious experiences through material practices in the everyday would serve as the basis of this new modern life. Theologically, Hong supported the established Christian principle that all people should live a truthful life or a life with God.[126] However, where Hong diverged from mainline Christian thought was the area of where and how people experienced God. He located the grounds of religious experience in the present everyday world instead of exclusively in conversion, prayer, and worship[127] because God, or truth (ch'am), existed at the center of people's lives and between individuals in the present.[128] Specifically, people experienced God in life (saenghwal), which Hong defined as everyday activities in society.[129] Working, playing, eating communally, and helping others were some of the means through which God manifested himself. According to Hong, "Life is the ground in which the spirit is revealed or announced. Through everyday life [ŭisikchu] or eating, dressing, and sleeping . . . every action is where the spirit [God] is revealed."[130] By constituting the everyday as the grounds for meeting God, Hong connected religious experience to the social.

Everyday life in the present took on new meaning through Hong's interpretation of religious experience. No longer should everyday life be considered the space of evil from which people should withdraw. Instead, it should be regarded as the site of goodness and sacredness because it was the means to encounter God. Hong's theology stripped the everyday of its ordinary value as the realm of regularity and boredom and gave each daily activity and practice divine status and meaning. Describing the religious nature of everyday life, he wrote that the spirit existed "when we eat . . . when we buy things, when we are looking, when we are doing office work, when we are farming . . . when we meet beggars . . . anytime."[131] These activities and others served as the portal through which the profane disappeared and the sacred appeared.

Hong's beliefs also reconfigured God as a being immanent on earth instead of a distant being separated from humanity. In many ways, he derived this idea about God from Karl Barth (1886–1968), one of the leading Christian theologians in the twentieth century, whom Hong greatly admired.[132] Barth wrote that God indirectly unveiled himself to humanity through signs and symbols and veiling forms, such as Jesus Christ. God's willingness to reveal himself showed that he desired a strong partnership with humanity in order for people to take part especially in the creative process to unveil and spread the divine on earth.[133] Alongside Barth, Watase Tsuneyoshi of the Kumiai Kyōkai most certainly helped shape Hong's conception of God because Hong had spent many years with Tsuneyoshi while working as his translator in Korea.

Like Hong, Tsuneyoshi stressed that God was not a distant being but instead "represented and reflected something at once more amorphous and diffused, something that consisted of spirit but without definitive structure or form."[134] In this form, God was less the personified deity as conceived and popularized by traditional Christianity and more a force that embodied all things, including human consciousness.[135]

From his conception of God and everyday life, Hong particularly stressed that the act of creation represented the best means through which not only to develop one's personality but also to encounter and experience God. He regarded all humans as "creative creatures" (changjojŏk tongmul).[136] He wrote that "the universe is God's creation," but everything in society resulted from people's labor; people created culture, society, and all things, such as "music, art, literature, buildings, the Bible, philosophy, politics, laws, and morals."[137] At the same time at which Hong stressed human consciousness developed through acts of creation, he also pointed out, "It is in your human creations that one's freedom and liberty is realized." To Hong, then, performing mental and physical labor to create things was a process not only for the concrete expression of the self but also for self-realization and cultivation; it was a process that led to a complete life, which Hong outlined in the following diagram: creation—ability / power—satisfaction—happiness—life. In the end, he thought that the act of creating was most effective in shaping consciousness and expanding personalities because it connected people to God and revealed God's beauty in the world. Hong thus wrote that "the world that is created by you is where you experience heaven . . . [creation] is where the heavenly kingdom resides and is exhibited."[138]

Framing religious experience as an active external process, Hong declared, "Religion is all about life or living. Religion dies if it is not about living out its principles. Religion is not about sentences and words."[139] Because people enjoyed a sacred state of being through material practices in the everyday, Hong was confident that Koreans would experience and be endowed with the qualities God embodied: beauty, love, and truth.[140] In fact, he believed that all things in the universe possessed spiritual meaning and significance because God as the ultimate creator of the universe gave everything meaning and value.[141] Because of this, people were part of the eternal and immutable force of the universe and had an authentic life full of value (kach'i).[142] In particular, he stressed that through their connection to God, people possessed truth (ch'am or chinri).[143] To Hong, truth was important because it was the basis of all knowledge (chisik), which determined what was right and wrong, enabled people to overcome the falsehoods and chaos in society, and allowed people to become free.[144] With a life anchored in value and truth that were constant, Hong believed that Koreans would be able to live a modern life full of authenticity and stability; religious experiences in the everyday would provide meaning and continuity through which people would overcome their fear of changes under modernization.

Through his theology, Hong presented a way for Koreans to live a productive and healthy life under modernization. Although God's presence in the world was unchanging and permanent, Hong posited that meeting and experiencing God in the present everyday were contingent on the material conditions in society because he believed that a relationship existed between the mind (spirit) and the body (material).[145] Because the material world shaped an individual's mental and spiritual state and determined the way in which people underwent religious experiences, destructive political, economic, and social developments and structures prevented people from experiencing the divine. Hong pointed out, for example, that when people faced poverty and hunger, the drive to overcome these problems often outweighed an interest in religion or becoming spiritual.[146] Attacking and excising gross materialism were especially imperative since it was the root of vast social problems and led to a vain and empty life (hŏyŏng saenghwal).[147] To Hong, anything that drove a wedge between God and humanity, such as materialism, was considered "sin" (choeak).[148] Like Paul Tillich's conceptualization of sin, Hong reframed it to include not only personal infractions but also obstacles in society that caused people's lives to become unsafe and unstable, estranged people from God, and distorted people's spiritual conditions.[149] Understanding the power of sin to distance people from experiencing God in the everyday, Hong asserted that experiencing the sacred and maintaining a thriving modern life required ideal material conditions.

Because his theology emphasized that the ideal environment for spiritual authenticity and growth could not be simply willed but instead must be created by people, Hong called for social activism and the reconstruction of colonial society. For him, reconstruction should lead to a modern life that was "simple" (kandan) and centered on humanity (in chungsim).[150] Moreover, this new life "must be made according to the requests and demands of a modern life." It could not be based solely on the past or the past life.[151] To ensure this development, Hong stressed that the spirit of social structures or "politics, education, and production should be centered on religion."[152] In particular, people's lives and society should be structured around the morals and ethics of religion or, more concretely, guided by righteousness (ŭi) and love (ae).[153] From this path of moral and ethical development that emphasized "forgiveness, mutual love, no discrimination, and mutual interdependence," Hong envisioned the creation of a heaven or a new world.[154] Indeed, through development that led to the beautification of society, a heaven on earth (chisang ch'ŏn'guk) would emerge in people's everyday lives and lead to a heavenly paradise (nagwŏn).[155] This heavenly kingdom represented the ideal space through which Koreans would live and experience a modern life.

Like Korean intellectuals who theorized the meaning of the modern, Hong viewed the changes caused by modernization as the root causes of the disjuncture between material reality and ideology and called for social movements to build a new religion-based modern life and society in order to overcome this division. For Hong, this type of modern life would enable Koreans to experience God in everyday life and to partner with sacred forces to create a just world that embodied the values and qualities of God.[156] Moreover, they would experience the present as a meaningful moment within the larger history that God had created and sustained instead of as a fleeting and undetermined temporality. These concepts became part of a map through which Koreans could conceptualize, understand, and negotiate the modern. Hong hoped that by using this map, Koreans would be motivated to carry out reconstruction projects in ways that readjusted limits and refitted the material world to allow for the framing of meaningful and productive economic, social, and cultural ideas and practices. From this position, he expected Koreans to be open to changes and to live confidently in the present.

Love, the Everyday, and the Theology of Pae Min-su

Although Pae Min-su (1896–1968) spent less time theorizing the origins and meaning of modernity than Yi Ton-hwa and Hong Pyŏng-sŏn did, he still constructed a theology that argued for a religion-based modern life. Pae committed himself to finding a way for Koreans to live safely and fruitfully in the modern world because he himself experienced the benefits and drawbacks of all the changes produced by modernization. Pae was an ordained minister in the Presbyterian Church who carried a deep interest in nationalist affairs from a young age. He protested against Japanese rule and participated in nationalist movements, including the March First Movement. By the early 1920s, however, Pae focused on his education when he enrolled in Sungsil University in P'yŏngyang, a school created and operated by the Presbyterian Church. At school, while learning about the meaning of Christianity and its relationship to society, Pae met Cho Man-sik, and they worked together to improve peasant lives through the Presbyterian-based Christian Rural Research Institute (Kidokkyo nongch'on yŏn'guhoe) from 1928 to 1931.[157] Pae later attended McCormick Theological Seminary in Chicago from 1931 to 1933. In the summer of 1933, he returned to Korea and immediately went to the countryside to help rebuild rural society as the head of the official rural reconstruction movement of the Presbyterian Church.

In rearticulating traditional Protestant symbols and language while developing his new theology, Pae called into question mainstream Presbyterian thought at a time when conservative Presbyterian leaders were hardening their beliefs in the face of changes. Many conservative Presbyterian leaders continued to hold to the belief that Christ would return to earth and deliver Koreans from social and economic oppression and Japanese rule. Led by powerful pastors such as Kil Sŏn-ju and Samuel Moffett, Christians diligently searched for clues in the Bible about Christ's return and prayed to God for deliverance from colonial rule. They demanded that followers pray, read the Bible, and individually focus on spiritual matters in anticipation of Christ's return to earth. To these leaders, retreating from the everyday world into a world of spirituality was the most productive way to live in the changing society. For Pae and a group of young Presbyterian leaders who called for the church to address both the spiritual and material needs of Koreans, the challenge lay in how they would seek reforms without totally alienating conservative Presbyterians and causing deep divisions in the church.

Pae approached this delicate process by reaffirming several traditional evangelical principles but also reconceptualizing what parts of the evangelical message should be stressed and how it should be experienced and delivered. Pae's theology, which he called evangelicalism (*pogŭmjuŭi*), rested on the three fundamental beliefs in traditional evangelical Christianity: (1) God loved the world and sent Jesus Christ, his only son, to save people from their natural condition of sin; (2) salvation came only through the acceptance of Jesus Christ as one's savior; and (3) people had to live a spiritual life based on God's laws and rules in the Bible after conversion.[158] But Pae differentiated himself from mainline Evangelicalism in the Presbyterian Church in that he downplayed the importance of formal conversion and instead stressed that all people could and should know and meet God in order to experience authentic love, which was ultimate truth.[159] In Pae's theology, experiencing God's love was a transformative experience that turned people into new, spiritual beings who would be forever connected to God. This transformative state aligned individuals with God's attributes and purposes and gave them joy and happiness. What people acquired through God's love was a new value that gave them a sacred identity and state of being. Pae framed spiritual love as the means to bridge the gap between humanity and God or to overcome the alienation between the sacred and the profane. In a sense, Pae's conception of love mirrored Paul Tillich's idea of love as "the drive toward the reunion of the separated."[160] For both Tillich and Pae, love reunited humanity with God and reestablished the lost intimacy between the two. A reconnection with God enabled a new state of being without any ambiguities in people's lives because they gained a new spiritual identity and value.

For Pae, discovering and experiencing God's love permitted people to live spiritually enriched, authentic lives, which was a principle found in evangelical

theologies of the Presbyterian Church. But his theology further differentiated itself from mainline Evangelicalism by stressing that God's love manifested itself through human interactions instead of through formal conversion and the personal cultivation of the spiritual self. Most Presbyterian
leaders and pastors, both Western missionaries and Koreans, privileged the
personal conversion experience as the primary means to experience God and
his love, while Pae emphasized that people experienced God and his spiritual
love through humanity. He wrote that to be one with God, humans must love
one another.[161] In fact, loving the other served as the primary mode to achieve
spiritual transformations. Pae drew this idea on love from Henry T. Hodgkin,
a missionary in China during the 1920s who wrote about the relationship between Christianity and human society, especially about the importance of
realizing love in human relationships because be believed these relationships
produce experiences through which a person encounters God.[162] In his book
The Way of Jesus, which Pae cited several times in his writings, Hodgkin stressed
the necessity of love between humans in order to experience God: "God is love.
It is by means of loving acts and words that men know God and experience His
life. As we love, the life of God comes into us."[163]

Declaring that experiencing God arrived through human relationships
based on love, Pae offered Presbyterians and the overall Christian community
an alternative way to think about and value their daily lives and the present.
Like Hong's ideas, Pae's religious beliefs interpreted everyday life as a dimension
where meaningful human relationships served as sacred paths to God. Moreover, instead of representing a period that simply quickly gave way to the future,
the present stood for a valued moment in time; people could find true happiness
and become spiritually whole in the now instead of in the future when they died
or when Christ returned to earth. Defining the present in this way was especially important because, according to Pae, "too often the Kingdom of God, as
taught by Jesus, has often been conceived in terms of the future life only [other-
worldliness]."[164] To Pae, God's kingdom resided in the here and now.

By emphasizing sacred love though human interactions in the present,
Pae consequently valued society and healthy social relationships. Unsurprisingly, he grew gravely concerned over how the changing environment of the
1920s and 1930s appeared to be twisting, distorting, and ruining the bodies,
minds, and souls of Koreans. Pae interpreted the ideological and material
transformations and ruptures in society as results of the forces of capitalism.[165]
He pointed out that this new economic system wreaked havoc on people's lives
in ways that left them suffering a great deal of mental and physical anguish.
Throughout the peninsula, for example, destitution, famine, and bankruptcies
plagued "vast hordes of people."[166] In part, the economic lives of Koreans, especially peasants, worsened because of their inability to adjust to the changing

economic conditions in society.[167] Moreover, natural disasters such as floods exacerbated conditions that were already severe.[168] In a society conditioned by new economic structures and forces, Pae argued that Koreans lacked any forms of security, as was evident in the increasing number of beggars and unemployed.[169]

Pae stressed that to overcome this material insecurity, seeking money and accumulating material wealth became people's only concerns. Indeed, under this new economic system, Koreans valued only money and desired profits.[170] In order to stress this point, Pae declared, "In looking at modern society's economic system, money dominates and controls the life and death of humans. . . . Money is the blood that gives life to people."[171] Because money controlled everything, Pae grew convinced that Koreans did anything to acquire more material wealth. In fact, people were even commodifying their own friends and family for the sake of accumulating more money and goods.[172] Pae colorfully expressed this observation by declaring, "By worshipping gold and accumulating wealth, men make merchandise of the flesh and blood of their fellow-men."[173] It would be a mistake, according to Pae, to characterize those who were materially insecure as the only group of people controlled by materialistic desires. Even those who were materially secure or wealthy pursued the goal of acquiring more money and wealth. To this end, people from the high to the low believed that the fortune of life "is counted by the amount of money gained." Therefore, when people "have enough material things they are happy and optimistic."[174]

These happenings in the colonial period led Pae to believe that capitalism established a new value system that controlled Koreans' lives—a system that caused excessive materialism and the deterioration of morality, ethics, and social relationships. Indeed, according to Pae, people "lov[ed] gold" and became "enslaved" by it.[175] This development unsettled him because people not only faced tough economic challenges but also lost all control over their lives as they became lost in their material wants and desires. Consciousness and behavior no longer were conditioned and controlled by people themselves but instead by a system. What was being lost from all of this was people's humanity.[176]

To overcome the subjugation and distortion of Koreans' lives, Pae argued for the production of a new space or "heaven on earth" (*chisang ch'ŏn'guk*) through economic, social, and cultural reconstruction.[177] This new spiritual space would embody the ideas of Pae's theology through the construction of healthy social relationships that would allow people to experience and live out spiritual love and become whole and complete individuals once again. This type of social relationship should be constructed from a stable and harmonious material environment that addressed people's daily economic struggles and released them from their bondage to materialism. Pae therefore challenged

Christians to "conquer the inequalities of the present economic order and the materialistic living it produces."[178] He wanted them to build a heaven on earth where people's lives were reconstructed in ways that allowed the spiritualization of economic life.

In this new spiritual space, Pae stressed that economic and social living should be strictly organized.[179] Specifically, he wanted "material livelihoods" (*mulchil saenghwal*) of individuals to be organized on the basis of economic standards.[180] Pae felt that if people's livelihoods were not organized, especially in changing and chaotic surroundings, people would lose focus and fail to achieve certain goals.[181] In many ways, his thoughts on an organized life echoed the ideas held by many Christian leaders in the West who promoted the total organization of people's lives to prevent capitalism and economic forces from drawing people away from the spiritual ideal. Sherwood Eddy, a YMCA official in America and a leading Christian social activist, for example, rejected liberalism and wrote that individual lives should be organized around certain principles in order to realize specific economic and spiritual goals.[182] For Pae, in a world conditioned by capitalism and other forces of modernization, organization was necessary for religious experience; organization provided order, and, in turn, order furnished a stable environment for spiritual enlightenment.

The principle of mutual cooperation (*sangho pujo*), according to Pae, should be at the base of all economic and social standards.[183] Because mutual cooperation challenged people to love and help one another, individuals would be able not only to collectively establish economic security but also to experience God and enrich their state of spirituality. In fact, Pae pointed out that through mutual cooperation, Christ's love would be concretely realized.[184] Stressing this principle, he pushed for an ethical way of life that considered and valued the other. Under his vision of a new economic and social system undergirded by mutual cooperation, people no longer could consider others simply as strangers and ignore them. Instead, they were required to recognize others and be concerned with their problems in order to be spiritually whole.

For Pae, a heavenly space on the peninsula would form through mutual cooperation. Instead of discord and division, solidarity and unity would be lived out and would be continually reinforced in people's minds and bodies as they helped and cared for one another. Pae added that this disciplined environment of mutual cooperation would prevent the destructive side of money from upsetting social relations and ruining people's moral and ethical foundations. Instead of money being "the root of all evil," it would "turn to the root of all goodness when we use it in loving service for each other."[185] In a new social context anchored in the ethic of caring for the other and mutual dependence, Pae was confident that money would be a productive and healthy medium.

Pae's theology offered an alternative framework to represent and negotiate modernization for people inside and outside Protestant Christianity. He believed that this theology was appropriate for the new conditions in society, but he also recognized that he faced criticism from Presbyterian officials who adhered to conservative theologies and were suspicious of any change in the church. To limit attacks on his theology, Pae stressed that he agreed with conservatives that the Bible promoted eternal principles or "truths." However, he added that these principles "may be applied differently at different times according to varying social conditions."[186] Pae justified the call to build a new world since it would still realize the truth of God's love, but through a different context and means. He also defended himself from attacks by grounding his beliefs in the life of Christ, who, according to Pae, had used his ministry not only to teach spiritual truths but also to provide for people's concrete needs. Christ, for example, healed the sick, fed the hungry, and fought against all forms of injustice.[187] Christ's actions showed that he believed that the spiritual was connected to the material.[188] Because Christ promoted a social agenda, Pae thus declared that Christians should "go to the hungry, ill-clad, and weak country people and minister both to their material needs and to their deeper spiritual needs."[189]

As Koreans from the rural to the urban experienced changes and ruptures as a result of modernization, Yi, Hong, and Pae reconceptualized existing religious language in ways that pointed to how people should experience and consider their lives under modernization. Far from fearing and rejecting changes, all three religious leaders stressed the importance of valuing this new moment in time as a temporality for potentiality; under this temporality, Koreans should nurture and experience new forms of consciousness, agency, social relationships, and community through an everyday life rooted in the present. Although many critics of religion inside and outside colonial Korea lambasted religion as an archaic force that prevented the unfolding of an ideal modern life, Yi, Hong, and Pae argued that religion was appropriate for a life in the modern period. In fact, through their systems of belief, all three figures stressed that religion was necessary for a life under modernization because it (1) gave absolute and constant value and meaning to people experiencing fast-paced and transformative changes in the present; (2) helped people become whole and complete since it discouraged materialism and encouraged the cultivation of individual personalities through ethical, moral, and spiritual training; (3) provided a moral and ethical system that could structure the new forms of social interaction and thus establish social unity; and (4) called for the continual development of society and created a form of agency that inspired political, economic, social, cultural, and religious innovations. In their conceptions of religion, these three religious leaders saw qualities that were no different from the features found in many modernist ideologies and philosophies at that time, especially the emphasis on being focused and rooted in the present and continuously developing humanity and society. These new systems of spiritual belief showed religious followers, in particular, that they could experience and celebrate a religion-based modern life. These new belief systems demonstrated that being modern was less about adopting certain popular styles, trends, and material practices and more about possessing an attitude of experiencing and engaging the present as a temporality for new possibilities for living and working.

Although Yi, Hong, and Pae came from different religious backgrounds, they arrived at similar interpretations of and conclusions about religion because they were all responding to the mass and rupturing changes caused by the forces of modernization, in particular the ideological and material changes caused by capitalism. To all three leaders, developments as a result of capitalism were so overwhelming both mentally and physically that religious ideas and practices needed to be reconceptualized in ways that provided Koreans with appropriate guidance to liberate themselves from fear, anxiety, and pain. In particular, these three leaders articulated the idea of a heavenly kingdom on earth as a way for Koreans to negotiate and overcome the transformation in society. The concept encouraged Koreans to build a new society as a way to domesticate and manage changes so that they could enjoy religious experiences in the everyday life of the present that connected them to eternal sacred forces. In many ways, all three figures made this connection between time and space through the concept of a heavenly kingdom on earth as a result of and a response to capitalism in colonial society and thus linked religion to economics, a view that had not been articulated before 1920.

By calling for the transformation of society in order to establish a sacred space for living, Yi's, Hong's, and Pae's systems of belief, in particular, empowered religious followers to create and participate in social movements and thus expanded the ways in which they could pursue the construction of modern Korea. Indeed, alongside religion-based social movements, followers of Christianity and Ch'ŏndogyo could now confidently participate in various nonreligious nationalist drives on the basis of the belief that these social, economic, and cultural drives could aid in the construction of a heavenly kingdom on the peninsula. There were individual followers of both religions who were already involved in nationalist projects, but they participated in these movements without any institutionally established religious ideas grounding their actions. With Yi's, Hong's, and Pae's ideas coming out of Ch'ŏndogyo, the YMCA, and the Presbyterian Church, respectively, the actions of these believers were reframed as sacred with a spiritual purpose. Beyond those already involved in nationalist movements, these new religious ideas provided restless religious followers who were seeking ways to make their changing experiences in the present more meaningful and to deal with modernization and colonialism simultaneously with the reasons and motivations to live a full life in society and to tackle issues such as poverty and social inequality. At their core, Yi's, Hong's, and Pae's systems of belief furnished religious language suitable for representing and communicating living experiences in the now and overcoming the limitations of established religious language and the overall "tension between the received interpretation and practical experience."[190] In so doing, then, their systems of belief were frameworks through which people could work out a new capacity for "desiring, for forming intentions, and for acting creatively" and become agents of material change who could exert some "degree of control over the social relations in which one is enmeshed."[191]

As these new religious ideas offered new possibilities of organizing experiences and conceptualizing new forms of agency, community, and the nation for Koreans, they also added a new dimension to religion's relationship to the colonial state. Colonial officials had long tried to limit the power and influence of religion and deter followers from becoming involved in political, economic, and social issues. The ideas of Yi, Hong, and Pae, however, now challenged the colonial state's control of religion because they encouraged followers to be involved in tackling issues and problems in society for spiritual purposes. The colonial state faced the possibility of a new slew of Ch'ŏndogyo and Christian followers organizing Koreans to achieve social and economic equality. What became threatening about this situation was the fact that anticolonial sentiments could increase if religious followers connected the problems in society to colonialism. Indeed, Yi's, Hong's, and Pae's systems of belief objectified society in that they made it into an understandable and transparent object through ideas that uncovered what made up society, how it operated and ordered people's lives, and the direction it was heading. With society thus objectified, it no longer seemed foreign and distant but instead demystified and known; society became, as Paul Ricoeur put it, a "realm of the manageable."[192] Yi, Hong, and Pae never called for the overthrow of the colonial government, but their religious ideas held the potential to inspire new forms of activism, depending on the context in which Koreans learned and applied these ideas.

Part II

❧

BUILDING A HEAVEN ON EARTH, 1925–1937

4

⌒☟⌒

The Path to the Sacred

Korea as an Agrarian Paradise

After the 1919 March First Movement, peasants, agriculture, and the countryside figured prominently in nationalist discourse. In 1929, Sa Kong-pyo
declared in *Leninjuŭi* (Leninism), a leading leftist journal, "If we do not boldly
take up peasant problems in the revolution and fail to fight for the political
and economic demands of peasants, there is no possibility for the revolution
to advance."[1] Sharing the leftist view on the urgency of solving the vast troubles
besetting the agrarian economy and peasant life, bourgeois nationalists called
for wide-ranging reforms to attack the destitution of peasants.[2] For leaders like
An Chae-hong, overcoming the agrarian crisis represented the crucial step
toward transitioning society from total ruin to a new and prosperous time
centered on the bourgeoisie, industrialization, and urbanization. Differences
aside, pushing followers to combat the rapidly declining conditions of peasants
in order to achieve a future that lay outside the peasantry, agriculture, and the
countryside connected most leftists and bourgeois nationalists.

Although many leftist and bourgeois nationalists held to a model of development that would leave behind Korea's agrarian heritage, agrarianists
hoped for a restoration of the past, which featured an idyllic agrarian society
anchored by peasants. Returning to this idealized moment in history became
the agrarianists' approach to protecting Koreans from the changes caused by
modernization and also their approach to preserving the nation. They regarded
agriculture, farming, and a pastoral way of life as the source not only of fostering and preserving peasant autonomy but also of the national spirit, which
grounded Korean ethnic identity. To reestablish the past in the present, agrarianists rejected anything new and foreign in favor of restoring and strengthening traditions, especially those that were Confucian based, that had eroded
because of capitalist developments.

Because the colonial state government carefully watched all nationalist
rural movements, peasants found themselves caught between movements with
a temporal emphasis on the future (leftists and bourgeois nationalists) or the
past (agrarianists). Peasants, however, found alternatives to these two sides in

the YMCA (1925), Presbyterian (1928), and Ch'ŏndogyo (1925) rural movements, which were rooted in the present. From historical studies, each of these movements constructed a model of modernity that sought to protect, enhance, and expand Korea's agrarian heritage simultaneously through the adoption of contemporary ideas, practices, and institutions. For all three movements, these models afforded an organic form of modernity that valued and defended place through the careful incorporation of changes into peasant lives. These changes were expected to enable peasants to manage the vast material and ideological transformations in society with confidence and security, as well as to achieve new possibilities of thought, practice, and social organization. But far from demanding that peasants shed their identity as agricultural cultivators and their way of life in pursuit of new experiences and opportunities, these movements believed that changes and developments would occur through a process that would still preserve the agrarian economy and a pastoral existence. From the reconstruction and revitalization of the rural economy and society, the three movements expected that peasants would live a dynamic modern life rooted in the present and the birth of a spiritually based modern nation-state.

Although their model of modern development and emphasis on the present set them apart from all other movements in the countryside, the Presbyterian, YMCA, and Ch'ŏndogyo rural movements were still linked to all the other rural movements because each one from the left to the right was searching for solutions to the economic, social, and moral crises caused by the forces of capitalism. In fact, all rural campaigns in Korea were connected to numerous drives throughout the world that sought ways to address and overcome the severe consequences of capitalist development, such as alienation, economic inequality, social division, and ecological degradation, and materialize their visions of society. Inside and outside Korea, "the city" and "the machine" in particular became popular symbols through which people interpreted and negotiated the challenges, ruptures, and dislocations caused by capitalist development.[3] Intellectuals, writers, and reformers configured the city and the machine as symbols that expressed a promising future complete with revolutionary forms of consciousness and "higher kinds of social organization and cooperation" through industrialization, urbanization, and technological innovation.[4] European leftists, for example, saw in industrialization and urban spaces the means to forge a working class whose collective consciousness would power struggles for human and social liberation. In 1920s and 1930s China and Japan, the city and the machine became symbols of hope as intellectuals framed cities as sources of economic, social, and cultural innovation. With its diverse opportunities for employment, dynamic consumer culture, and new forms of entertainment, the city was represented as a place of vitality that encouraged diversity, spurred imagination, and heightened senses and perceptions.[5] For believers in these symbols, achieving progress and reaching the highest state of humanity required accepting capitalism, industrialization, and urbanization.

As reactionary symbols against "the city" and "the machine," "the country" and "the garden" expressed a hopeful return to a glorious past of pastoral living in the face of rapid capitalist development. Through these symbols, the countryside became known as the authentic space for living because it was a natural area of beauty and tranquility that was full of stability.[6] In the countryside, people experienced the most meaningful and rewarding forms of work through farming because they not only interacted with nature but also cultivated their personalities and talents through a life of self-subsistence, like Jeffersonian yeoman farmers.[7] Barrington Moore points out that this idyllic image of the countryside and rural life led people to think of them as "organic and whole" instead of artificial.[8] Because the country and the garden represented rural life as authentic, communal, and beneficial, these symbols inspired a slew of movements that sought to restore the agrarian paradise that had been lost to industrial capitalism and urbanization. The Nōhonshugi movement in Japan, Chinese rural movements influenced by the concept of *yinong liguo* (country founded on agriculture), and the agrarian conservative movement led by the Christian Social Party in Austria, for example, pursued restoration of the pastoral ideal in order to find protection from the mass material and ideological changes originating from the changing economy.[9] Unlike the city and the machine, the country and the garden became symbols that rejected capitalism, industrialization, and urbanization in favor of a return to an agrarian past.

These two sets of symbols furnished representations of the future and the past that became refuges and sources of meaning for people struggling with the alienating and disrupting effects of everyday life under capitalist development. But as people yearned for an urban future that had yet to be realized or desired a rural past that was clearly romanticized and had never existed, these representations developed a dichotomous form of consciousness in individuals that stressed new versus old, progress versus tradition, and breaking versus restoring. As this global trend became expressed through leftists, bourgeois nationalists, and agrarianists and their rural movements in colonial Korea, the Presbyterian, YMCA, and Ch'ŏndogyo rural movements staked out a middle ground between these two sets of symbols in order to reconcile their differences and forge an alternative approach to capitalism. Although all three movements never rejected capitalism, industrialization, and urbanization outright, they criticized them as unfit systems that greatly diminished any hope of realizing their visions of society. For them, an agriculture-based economy, farming, and a pastoral way of life were the best means to manage the challenges of capitalism in ways that afforded peasants some material stability and a dynamic process of spiritual development. Rural life represented the form that would allow for the birth of a spiritually based modern life and society. But instead of simply advocating a return to an agrarian past and the restoration of rural traditions, all three movements stressed the need to develop rural Korea through the introduction of innovations in the areas of ideas, practices, and social organization. The last two chapters of this book will examine in detail how the three religion-based rural movements attempted to redevelop the peasantry and the agrarian economy. This chapter will thus limit its scope of analysis to the beginnings of the three rural movements and the reasons behind their support of an agriculture-based life.

The Farming Life as the Ideal and the Rise of the YMCA Rural Movement

From 1920 to 1937, the countryside became the site of large-scale campaigns by various groups to reconstruct rural Korea and gain control over peasants. Under the new Japanese colonial policy that permitted limited nationalist movements, these rural campaigns, including movements by the Red Peasant Union, *Tonga ilbo*, and former Confucian scholars, carried out economic, political, social, and cultural programs in the hope of materializing their visions of the nation-state. They wanted to transition from "ideology as 'systems of ideals' to ideology as lived, habitual social practice" in order to unite material reality and ideology.[10]

In this crowded field of competing rural movements, the YMCA positioned itself as a leading institution to reform and modernize rural life through comprehensive programs that gave form to the ideas outlined by Hong Pyŏng-sŏn. Laying the groundwork and infrastructure for the movement was Sin Hŭng-u (1883–1959), who became Hong's shrewd partner in reconstructing rural Korea after being appointed national general secretary of the YMCA in September 1920.[11] Like Hong, Sin rejected conservative otherworldly theology in favor of a theology that valued the social. Believing "in God who is revealed in nature, history, Jesus and experience,"[12] he stressed that God manifested himself in multiple ways, including ones in the social realm. Experiencing God, however, was contingent on the relationship between the individual and society because Sin believed that harmful forces and developments in the world, which were material manifestations of sin, separated people from the spiritual divine. Refusing to abstract a person's state of spirituality from that person's material existence, he especially blamed destructive economic forces for separating humanity from God. Consequently, Sin's theology called for economic and social justice that featured the creation of a society structured

around "democratic economics" and the "total equality of human livelihood."[13] This ideal society would "guarantee to all an ascending equity and
security in the economic, cultural and spiritual life" in order for people to be
permanently united with God.[14] Sin's interpretation of Christianity privileged
society as the primary space for religious experience and called for a society
with just economic, political, social, and cultural structures that would provide for thriving modern lives.

   Sin's theology served as a lens through which he interpreted the impact of
modernization on the Korean countryside. In 1923, in his first major act as
national general secretary, Sin joined Hong and other YMCA leaders in conducting ethnographic studies of peasant life to find out how peasants were re-
acting and adapting to the vast changes caused by capitalist forces. From these
excursions to the countryside, "careful observations were made and were fully
discussed on the return."[15] Discussions centered on how peasants lacked the
appropriate skills, knowledge, and overall resources to deal with the transforming rural economy and thus lived in extreme poverty with high debt
and dwindling food supplies.[16] "Barren," "in utter despair," and "little happiness" were some of the descriptions YMCA members used to characterize the
physical and mental toll of capitalist development on peasant lives.[17] Leaders
concluded that in these conditions, peasants could not experience God and
enjoy a vibrant spiritual life. Referring to truth (ch'am) as God, Hong wrote,
"In the countryside . . . people are living; however, there is extreme poverty,
very little to eat, no one is learning anything, and no one is living a truthful
(ch'am) life."[18] John H. Reisner, a professor of agricultural economics at Nanking University in China whom the YMCA invited to Korea in the spring of
1926 to write a report on rural life, helped the YMCA arrive at its assessment.
In his report, Reisner noted that a number of factors contributed to the plight
of peasants, including Japanese colonialism, the lack of landownership, high
debt, limited access to fertilizers and the latest farming technology, and a lack
of supplementary income.[19]

   The instability of rural society and its effect on the national body moved
YMCA leaders to emphasize the need for the spatial reconstruction of rural
Korea. Leaders recognized that peasants required a modern culture that positioned them to stabilize their material lives and experience spiritual happiness.
Influenced by his concept of a heavenly kingdom on earth (chisang ch'ŏn'guk),
Hong urged the YMCA to shift the organization's attention and resources from
urban vocational and recreational programs to introducing economic, social,
religious, and cultural reforms in the countryside. Sin agreed with Hong's
stance on reorienting the YMCA's mission because he believed, in part, that
this transition would help advance religious reconstruction in Korea. For Sin,
helping people manage and make sense of economic uncertainty and social

strife required new developments in religion: "To say that we live in a changing and much changed world is to say the most obvious. In order to meet new
attitudes and new situations we must find new methods."[20]

Sin began laying the groundwork for a rural movement in 1924 by traveling to America and consulting with John Mott and Fletcher Brockman about
the rural program.[21] At the time of his trip, YMCAs throughout the world
were transforming into institutions for economic and social justice. In the
1920s, certain YMCAs in the United States promoted social gospel theology
and called for social justice. Sherwood Eddy, who became a well-known national secretary of the YMCA in 1911, traveled extensively throughout the
world to spread a social gospel that stressed political, social, and economic
equality.[22] Several YMCAs in Asia started social movements in the countryside.
In 1915, the central YMCA office in India, under the leadership of K. T. Paul,
inaugurated a wide-scale rural movement that conducted literacy campaigns,
taught peasants how to improve agricultural production, and introduced
health reforms. In China, James Yen established the Department of Popular
Education in the Chinese YMCA and oversaw an extensive rural literacy
campaign from 1920 to 1923. Yen later incorporated many of the movement's
techniques and materials, including his textbook *People's 1000 Character
Primer*, into his Mass Education Movement, which he organized in 1923.
Against this backdrop, Mott and Brockman supported the Korean YMCA's
decision to start a rural movement. They agreed to send YMCA secretaries to
Korea who "would be men of agricultural training, of Associational experience, of social vision, and of spiritual vitality."[23] From 1925 to 1932, the International Committee of the YMCA sent five association secretaries to Korea.[24]

In a January 1, 1925, *Tonga ilbo* article, Sin announced the start of the
YMCA rural movement by proclaiming that the organization would be "cast-
ing aside the city and standardizing the development of the countryside where
80 percent of the population lives."[25] The YMCA formalized this rural movement by establishing the Department of Rural Affairs (Nongch'on bu) in
February 1925, and Hong was appointed as its director. From the central headquarters in Seoul, Hong both directed the rural movement and coordinated and
supervised the work of YMCA branches and associations.[26] By 1925, the
YMCA had established urban branches in Seoul (the national headquarters
of the Korean YMCA), Kwangju, Taegu, Chŏnju, Sŏnch'ŏn, P'yŏngyang,
Shinŭiju, Wŏnsan, and Hamhŭng. Collectively, the branches employed nearly
forty Koreans and had a total of 2,914 members.[27] Besides urban branches, the
YMCA also oversaw nineteen YMCA student associations with over 4,000
members at various secondary schools and institutions of higher learning.
These students became essential figures in the rural movement because the
YMCA relied on them to travel to the countryside and carry out programs.

Financing for the rural movement came from various sources. The YMCA national headquarters in Seoul and its local branches and associations had a long history of financial support from local sources, such as membership dues and contributions from individuals and corporations in Korea.[28] The YMCA even received financial assistance from the colonial government during the Korean YMCA's first years of operation. Financial contributions by various sources in the United States, however, represented the bulk of its support.[29] Since 1903, the YMCA had received money from wealthy industrialists and individual Christians in America. Sin's salary, for example, was mostly paid by a yearly gift from a Mrs. Denman.[30] This financial structure was overseen by Sin and B. P. Barnhart, who was a foreign secretary in Seoul, while Hong was left to run the rural campaign. In this position, Hong held the power, especially over labor and resources, to realize his religious, social, economic, and cultural ideas and a new "heaven on earth." Hong reported to Sin, but he had great autonomy to direct the movement in any way he saw fit because Sin was preoccupied with his duties as director of the YMCA, his responsibilities in organizations such as the Hŭngŏp kurakbu and the Sin'ganhoe, and his travels abroad.[31] In the end, Hong was able to carry out his ideas without much interference because Sin agreed with Hong on the purpose and goals of the rural movement.

The official platform of the YMCA rural movement, which outlined its objectives, was made public in April 1926:

> We conceive the main objectives of the rural work to be spiritual, cultural and economic. We shall seek first to help men live in right relations with God and each other and to realize the spiritual values in their daily tasks. We shall endeavor to eliminate illiteracy in the villages and to stimulate such other educational processes as may prove suited to the needs of the agricultural population. We shall promote better economic conditions, through improved farming methods, the development of household and village industries and legitimate and brotherly expressions of the cooperative spirit.[32]

By stressing the importance of restoring spirituality in the daily lives of peasants, the YMCA committed its rural movement, above everything else, to being a religion-oriented mission to unite people with divine forces. But unlike traditional evangelical campaigns, the YMCA rural movement would focus less on conversion and more on reconstructing material conditions in the countryside to help people encounter religious experiences. Specifically, then, "to help men live in right relations with God and each other and to realize the spiritual values in their daily tasks" meant the total reconstruction of the economic, social, and cultural structures of peasant life. Rural reconstruction would lay the path to the sacred and consequently produce a new spiritual culture for peasants to live confidently and securely in the now.

The YMCA used the following questions raised in the 1926 platform to guide its search for an appropriate model of modern development for rural reconstruction: "Will the teaching [model] that is offered be based on the assumption that the type of industrialism which has developed in western countries is inevitable, or on a belief in the soundness of the principles of brotherhood of which Jesus Christ stood? Will this teaching come promptly before the formative period has passed, or will it be postponed until the task will have become many times more difficult of accomplishment?"[33] The second question, in particular, showed that YMCA leaders knew that rural society was far from being tied to a specific route to modernity. Under the colonial government's supervision, capitalist development was rapidly reshaping social relationships and forms of production, consumption, and exchange in rural Korea. But YMCA leaders believed that reforms and changes introduced by the state had yet to create a permanent form of the economy and society and thus left both entities undetermined. In this moment of flux, then, YMCA leaders confidently expressed their view that the rural movement could take hold of the rural economy and society and reshape them in ways that allowed for the healthy development of the peasant's body, mind, and soul.

To the organization, nothing was already predetermined in rural Korea despite Korea's colonized status. So, in answering the first question presented in the platform, the YMCA decided against industrial capitalist development even though a great many people inside and outside Korea believed that it was the system that had enabled countries to become modern, civilized nation-states. Hong and Sin best articulated the YMCA's reasons for rejecting this popular route toward modernity. On the basis of their studies of industrial capitalist development in the West, these two leaders expressed deep reservations about industrial capitalism because of its destructive impact on people's consciousness and behavior and on the social body. To them, capitalism's value system, which solely promoted the pursuit of money, was the source of these consequences. To help explain this system, Hong turned to the ideas of Adam Smith, whom he considered the most significant figure to define and promote capitalism:

> Adam Smith's position was that "one's occupation should be chosen freely. Whatever you do, it should be done according to your wishes. Acquiring profits should be the standard." Here Smith says that in the world, what should be satisfied or fulfilled is the ambitions of each person to acquire profit in any business. . . .

Originally people were egotistical and selfish, so Smith's ideas only encouraged more selfishness and egoism. In each Western country, an ideology, which has been soaked deep in the bodies of individuals, has emerged that stresses that the most important thing is to make a lot of money through one's authority and freedom.[34]

From his interpretation of Smith's ideas, Hong saw capitalism as encouraging not only the accumulation of money and profit but also self-interest. What therefore deeply troubled him about capitalism's value system was that achieving material goals, especially the accumulation of wealth, became the standard for good living over the pursuit of enriching and expanding one's moral, ethical, and spiritual self.[35]

   Sin and Hong were not so naïve that they thought that people should refrain from trying to earn money to support their daily life, but they recognized that lives centered solely on the goal of pursuing wealth lowered the overall ethical and moral standards of society. Indeed, more than anything else, people became consumed by materialism (*mulchiljuŭi*) under capitalism; that is, they became self-centered and worshippers of money and goods.[36] In this state, people desired only the accumulation of wealth and material goods instead of seeking to expand their moral, ethical, and spiritual self. Rejecting the value of being virtuous, people consequently measured and determined a person's character and worth on the basis of that person's material possessions. According to Sin, people, for example, called individuals "king" if they possessed an abundant amount of money and goods[37] and respected only wealthy individuals. In pointing out this transformed behavior of people under capitalism, Hong and Sin believed that this economic system controlled people's lives. Emphasizing this point, Hong wrote, "People have become the slaves of money. People are not the owners and the controllers of money."[38] Here he tried to show that the values and structures of capitalism controlled people to the point that individuals were enslaved by this system. Beyond the warping and stunting of moral, spiritual, and ethical growth, Hong and Sin criticized capitalism for diminishing people's agency as they become subservient to their desire for money.

   Although capitalism itself harmed people's bodies and minds, Sin and Hong argued that capitalism's connection to industrialization caused the most fundamental changes that ruined modern life in the West. For both leaders, industrialization was a process that changed the character of modern social life because of "the energizing impulse of a complex division of labour, harnessing production to human needs through the industrial exploitation of nature."[39] This process, according to Hong, started with the Industrial Revolution (Sanŏp hyŏngmyŏng), which spurred technological innovations such as the cotton spinning wheel, the steam engine, and trains.[40] The Industrial Revolution expanded commerce and the overall economy, but it started a period of chronic social strife. Social fragmentation, in particular, originated in a new division of labor that resulted from the site of production moving from farms in the countryside that ran cottage industries to large factories in cities that used advanced machinery to manufacture goods on a mass level.[41] "From this time on," according to Hong, "cottage industries in which goods were manufactured at home with small tools disappeared, and all those people [farmers who ran cottage industries] went to work in the factories and became wage laborers."[42] In factories, wage laborers worked for capitalists who owned the capital required to start and operate factories.[43] Under industrialization, then, a division of labor materialized with a proletariat class who sold their labor power and a capitalist class who owned and controlled the means of production.[44] For Hong, what distinguished the upper class (capitalist) from the working class (proletariat) was that the former was driven by profit, owned factories, and acquired great wealth while the latter held little economic power and few resources and lived in poverty.[45] The stark difference between the upper and working classes formed an uneven relationship between the two where the former controlled the latter. Because of this uneven relationship, conflicts erupted between the two classes and led to social division.[46] Because industrial capitalism fractured society instead of unifying it, Hong wondered how industrial capitalism could be relied on to foster social cohesion and national unity, which were essential for national liberation from colonial rule.

Alongside its sowing social conflict and division, Hong and Sin criticized industrial capitalism for diminishing workers' autonomy, subjectivity, and value. Sin, in particular, asserted that the capitalists controlled the working class to the point that they stunted the workers' personal growth. In factories, workers were always on guard since owners constantly kept them under close surveillance. Because factory owners determined a laborer's future in the company, workers feared that inappropriate words and actions could threaten their job security. Workers consequently constrained themselves in thought and practice out of fear of upsetting owners. In fact, workers refused to express themselves freely and became "cowardly and selfish" as they attempted to please capitalist owners.[47] In this condition, workers were trapped in a system where "[they] are just like in a jail without any freedom. . . . [They] feel pressure on [their] back all year around." This environment, Sin added, was so destructive that a worker suffered the "death of his personality."[48]

Whereas Sin stressed that owners limited the growth of workers, Hong argued that machines (*kigye*) in factories made workers less significant because they replaced people as the primary source of labor and value. Hong made it clear to readers that industrialization reduced human labor to an appendage of machines. Just as Karl Marx had argued that "in handicrafts and manufactures, the worker makes use of a tool; in the factory, the machine makes use of him," Hong wrote that human labor existed only to serve machines.[49] As a consequence, people, according to Hong, "became the slaves of machines, and individuals overall had nothing to do and their lives became low."[50] With people no longer serving any use but to operate machines, he wrote that "the value of people gradually diminished and fell."[51]

On the basis of their observations of what workers experienced in factories under industrialization, Sin and Hong pointed out that workers lost all control over their lives; surveillance, rules, and discipline by owners combined with factory machines to create a mechanism of power that was independent of workers and conditioned their bodies and consciousness in destructive ways. According to Sin and Hong, workers still believed that they could find relief from the factory's suffocating environment in the enjoyments of the city, which was the primary place where industrial capitalism had evolved. Cities became objects of fascination for every person because they were seen as places that offered a "brilliant, splendorous, magnificent, and wonderful life that was pleasing to the eye."[52] Through consuming the newest commodities and experiencing the latest trends in cities, people thought that they could experience the modern life. But, as Hong and Sin pointed out, this image of the city was a pure fantasy because actual developments showed the city's malignant nature. First, a city encouraged a futile life based on materialism. Indeed, in their "luxurious life," capitalists wasted time and money as they went out to eat and bought "fashionable goods" that had no real value. Members of the working class longed to be like these capitalists even though they were always short of money and struggled to find enough to eat.[53] Because everyone in the city pursued a life of conspicuous consumption, Hong thought that the culture of the city led to artificial lives. Second, Sin and Hong described cities as inhospitable places to live; according to Hong, they were "dirty . . . very busy and unsafe."[54] Because cities were a poor environment beset with poverty and class conflicts, Hong and Sin considered them "uncomfortable" places that harmed minds and bodies.[55]

In studying the historical development of industrial capitalism, Sin and Hong discovered an economic system that introduced a vast number of rupturing changes that made the healthy development of society impossible. Connected to capitalism, industrialization further damaged society because it increased social inequality and division and created places of living and work that were dilapidated and polluted. Hong expressed that many Europeans, overwhelmed by the consequences of industrial capitalism, left cities for the countryside to escape "civilization" and live a "simple and frugal life."[56] Sin offered a more detailed explanation of why Europeans sought a return to rural life:

After the start of the Industrial Revolution, as machines and
steam power were more widely used, products became cheaper
and big capitalism arose. . . . The entire population went to the
cities, leaving the villages empty. In the industrial system, people
became machines and lost sight of their humanity. Moreover,
comparing city slum life with the villages, we can say that city life
was pure hell on people's bodies and morals. . . . After World War
I, people screamed out for more decentralization. People called
out to "go back to nature." In England, many people went from
factories in cities to villages with small industries.[57]

What Hong and Sin saw in industrial capitalism was a process where destructive consequences unfolded in society and ravaged people's minds, spirits,
and bodies. From seeing people in countries first embracing and then rejecting industrial capitalism, they agreed that Korea should avoid this outcome
by adopting an alternative model of rural development.

In their pursuit of an appropriate model of development, Sin, Hong, and
the entire YMCA staff supported the model of economic development that
was already native to Korea: an agriculture-based economy with farming,
small cottage industries, and a pastoral way of living.[58] As the leader of the rural
movement, Hong in particular strongly supported an agrarian route to modernity because a pastoral existence provided for a "simple" life that was stable and spiritual.[59] What allowed this life to develop in the countryside was
the concept of self-sufficiency or self-sustenance (*chajak chagŭp / chagŭp chajok*). From 1920 to 1937, several nationalist campaigns heavily promoted *chajak chagŭp,* which they defined as a process where Koreans should buy and
consume only Korean-made goods in order to construct an industrialized national economy independent of foreign influences.[60] Although many Korean
nationalists connected *chajak chagŭp* to the creation of a powerful industrial
capitalist base, Hong considered *chajak chagŭp* a long-standing practice associated with a pastoral life that encouraged creativity and a strong sense of
morality. From his study of rural life in Europe and Korea, he saw that rural
cultivators experienced a totally different life from factory workers because
they organized their daily lives around the principle of *chajak chagŭp.* Indeed,
unlike factory workers who sold their labor and manufactured goods that were
sold in the market, rural cultivators were autonomous in that they controlled
their own labor power and made goods for self-consumption. Describing this
independent life of the farmer, Hong wrote, "Under the principle of *chajak
chagŭp,* people farmed at their homes, made things and whatever they made,
they did so in an intimate and personal [*ch'inhi*] way. . . . Whether it was in the
village or at home, they lived by making and creating everything."[61]

To Hong, a pastoral life based on *chajak chagŭp* achieved positive results for rural cultivators. Whereas a society based on industrial capitalism caused members of the capitalist and working classes to become enslaved by materialist desires and to pursue superficial goals, a pastoral life through *chajak chagŭp* enabled rural cultivators to enjoy a "simple [*dansun*] and clear" life.[62] Simply put, rural cultivators took pleasure in being frugal and plain (*kŏmso*).[63] Far from being uneventful and colorless, a frugal life afforded a fruitful way of living without shallow luxuries, extravagant goods, and distractions that would lead to crass materialism. Instead of encouraging waste of both time and resources, frugal living promoted the judicious management and conservation of resources (*chŏlyak*).[64] Hong consequently believed that with these attributes, *chajak chagŭp* gave farmers the means to be authentic, responsible, and productive; it provided healthier means for people to cultivate their personalities than anything found in cities conditioned by industrial capitalism.

Hong's lofty description of a pastoral life based on *chajak chagŭp* showed that he privileged this type of existence above all. This was hardly surprising because it provided the means to materialize Hong's vision of an ideal modern life that was moral, creative, and spiritual. First, because people on their own raised and harvested crops and manufactured goods primarily for self-consumption instead of for the market, Hong believed that rural cultivators were more concerned with "eating and living" than with earning large sums of money. Unlike those who owned or worked in factories, rural cultivators worked for more enriching purposes than to raise their material status by seeking money and profits, which Hong believed corrupted people's moral and ethical life.[65] Second, since rural cultivators made everything in an intimate and personal way with their hands, a pastoral life enabled individuals to become creative builders. Hong arguably imagined rural cultivators as being able to use their imagination to create items freely for themselves and their families. He thus greatly valued the capacity of a pastoral life to unleash people's creative nature because he believed that the act of creation was a vital medium through which people experienced God in the everyday.

Beyond its self-sufficient nature, the high level of autonomy people achieved with a pastoral life also served as a motivating factor for Sin and Hong to embrace an agrarian future for Korea. Both men heavily criticized the wage-labor system because workers held no control over their economic lives and found themselves confined in every way. They greatly valued farming, however, because it gave people control over their labor power and overall mode of production and consequently enabled them to be economically independent, unlike wage laborers. This independence gave individuals the autonomy to manage their own economic affairs. Hong, in particular, maintained that this autonomy afforded rural cultivators the means to prevent outside forces from determining their financial situation. For example, by practicing *chajak chagŭp,* rural cultivators could avoid purchasing and becoming reliant on expensive commodities manufactured in the city. In this capacity, they would be free from outside control, powers, and influences.[66]

Equally important, autonomy through a pastoral life gave people the space to think and act freely and enabled them to cultivate their personalities. Sin valued economic independence because people could work and live without worrying about owners and thus could focus on developing their moral character or personality. Writing to high-school graduates in colonial Korea about the merits of economic independence, Sin declared, "Therefore, for your livelihood, it should be independent. When it becomes independent, you will be more moral; in that, you will respect man more and be more tolerant. You will also have the chance to display and express your individual personality."[67] What Sin respected in farming and its independent livelihood was the fact that individuals could become morally upright, like Jeffersonian yeoman farmers, without any restrictions.[68]

Sin and Hong's characterization of an agrarian life anchored in the principle of *chajak chagŭp* connected them to a long line of American and European intellectuals who romanticized farmers as well-rounded citizens who could perform any task and possessed a wide range of knowledge. Their grand appraisal of an agrarian life certainly downplayed the adversity of farming, such as the need for demanding labor and experiencing natural disasters that ruined crops, as well as the extreme challenges of living a purely self-sufficient life. But despite these drawbacks, Hong, Sin, and the YMCA mostly saw the advantages of an agrarian life outweighing all aspects of a life conditioned by industrial capitalism. History had shown Sin and Hong that industrial capitalism failed to deliver the promise of an improved modern personhood and society, while an agrarian life offered benefits that would lead to a healthy society unified around the goal of continuously improving people's personalities and subjectivity and achieving a perfect nation-state. Their historical findings moved Hong and Sin to commit the YMCA to reconstructing Korea into an idyllic agrarian society with independent farmers who were spiritual, moral, and ethical at its base.

The Quest for a Sacred Agrarian Life and the Presbyterian-Based Rural Movements

As the YMCA reoriented its mission toward reconstructing rural society, Pae Min-su collaborated with prominent Korean Presbyterian leaders, such as Cho Man-sik, Yi Hun-gu, and Yu Chae-gi, to organize their own movement to rebuild rural society. Through the Christian Rural Research Association

(Kidokkyo nongch'on yŏn'guhoe, CRRA) and the official Presbyterian Church Rural Movement (PCRM), these leaders carried out a design to modernize the rural economy and society and establish a rural-based heavenly paradise where peasants' material and spiritual needs were addressed. From its beginning to its end, the PCRM was never without controversy because conservative Presbyterian leaders opposed it on the grounds that it represented an unorthodox way to minister to the spiritual needs of peasants. Instead of economic and social programs, these conservative leaders argued that overcoming the dislocations, ruptures, and physical hardships caused by the forces of capitalism only required peasants to hear the gospel and undergo personal conversion to become born-again Christians. Samuel Moffett, the best-known Presbyterian missionary, in 1928 captured the overall sentiment of conservatives on dealing with changes in society in the following words: "We have a profound conviction that education, reformation, social improvement, industrial and scientific advancement with progress in civilization, however greatly to be desired and however to be fostered, can never change the heart of man nor be the means for the evangelization of the world."[69] For Moffett and conservative Presbyterian leaders, traditions should stand firm in the face of change and take precedence over reconceptualized ideas, practices, and institutions that had been adapted to meet new challenges in society.

The conflict between supporters of the rural movements and conservative leaders was over theological control or how to express and practice Christianity. PCRM leaders wanted to push the church to embrace and practice a socially oriented theology, while conservative leaders sought to maintain the status quo of saving people through repentance and conversion. This theological split proved very difficult to overcome because each side believed that it was the rightful interpreter of the language and symbols of Christianity. Bridging the gap was made even more difficult because this struggle was not just about dictating theology but also about controlling and determining how the manpower and vast resources of the church should be used. In 1928 and 1929, the Presbyterian Church had close to 127,142 adherents, 1,734 paid staff members, 2,551 churches, and 278 self-supported schools. To support its programs, services, and staff, the church collected close to $365,369 in offerings from Korean followers and received financial contributions from an array of sources, including international donors.[70] Any side in this debate that controlled this vast array of services, institutions, and money would have the power to deploy the church's resources to achieve its views on Christianity.

The power struggle between the two sides took a slight turn in favor of PCRM leaders after the 1928 Jerusalem meeting of the International Missionary Council (IMC). At the meeting, the workshop titled "The Christian Mission in Relation to Rural Problems" specifically tackled the issue of rural unrest due to growing social and economic developments and the weakening of the rural church. Participants in this workshop concluded that reforming all sides of a person, not just the spiritual side, was necessary to stabilize the lives of Christians and rural churches. Their decision to connect the spiritual to the material was quite clear when the workshop issued objectives for Christian organizations to consider in designing an effective rural program, including "healthy living in a healthful environment" and "the effective cultivation of the physical resources necessary to the food supply and the sound economic development of people in villages and in the open country."[71] The IMC's workshop on rural affairs never rejected evangelization but instead called for spreading and realizing the principles of Christianity through a holistic program that addressed the material needs of those living in the countryside. Reframing evangelization in this manner gave Christian leaders all over the world a theological justification to design and implement plans to fight poverty and bring stability to people's social and economic lives.

One of the Korean delegates to the IMC conference, Chŏng In-kwa (1888–1972), one of the best-known and most powerful Presbyterian pastors, carried back the conference's decisions on rural evangelization to the Presbyterian Church. Because the IMC was a highly respected organization, Chŏng persuaded enough high-ranking Presbyterian leaders to carry out the IMC's rural guidelines by establishing an official rural board in the Presbyterian Church in 1928.[72] Charged with the responsibility of coordinating a rural movement to help peasants, this rural board announced in 1928 that the PCRM would feature the construction of model villages and the establishment of various social institutions, including educational facilities. It also decided to publish a monthly magazine, *Nongmin saenghwal* (Farmer's Life), which became the voice of the movement. The first issue of *Nongmin saenghwal* in June 1929 serves as a window for understanding the reasons for starting the PCRM. The introduction declared that the Korean agricultural economy and farming were in extremely poor shape, and peasants lacked any "means to live."[73] An article by Yun Chŏng-ho provided a long list of reasons for the decline of the rural economy and the weakening of peasant life, such as (1) the loss of a *chagŭp chajok* life and the rise of an exchange economy (*kyohwan kyŏngje*) through which peasants accumulated debts as they bought goods from city merchants and manufacturers, and (2) the diminishing financial power of peasants because they lacked the resources and organizations to market their crops at high prices and also the loss of cottage industries.[74]

Led by an executive committee of seven church leaders in P'yŏngyang with branch offices in various provinces, including North P'yŏng'an Province, Hwanghae Province, North Kyŏngsang Province, and South Chŏlla Province, the PCRM expected churches to organize local campaigns and to use *Nongmin saenghwal* to teach peasants the latest skills, knowledge, and practices in agriculture. Although the first years of the PCRM (1928–1933) were relatively low key, the number of PCRM activities exploded after Pae Min-su became the leader of the movement in 1933. Under Pae's leadership, the PCRM transitioned from a decentralized to a centralized movement that directly organized several large-scale rural campaigns throughout the peninsula. To design and carry out comprehensive reforms, Pae collaborated with like-minded Presbyterian leaders, such as Yi Hun-gu, Cho Man-sik, and Yu Chae-gi, to build a "heavenly kingdom on earth." A leading Presbyterian nationalist figure who organized numerous nationalist movements, including the Native Products Promotion Movement and the Sin'ganhoe, Cho Man-sik (1883–1950) first exposed Pae to the vast issues facing peasants.[75] Unlike mainstream Presbyterian leaders, Cho espoused Christism (Kidokjuŭi), which emphasized spreading God's love by addressing the economic and social problems of the poor and the construction of a spiritually based Korean nation. Yu Chae-gi (1905–1949), a Presbyterian minister who became a close adviser to Pae during the PCRM, was heavily influenced by the ideas of Kagawa Toyohiko, a well-known Japanese Christian Socialist whose writings first appeared in Korea in 1925.[76] Just as Christ had done in his own ministry, Yu stated that Christians needed to reach out to the poor and oppressed and minister to their needs.[77] For Yu, the quest for social salvation outweighed the goals of any evangelical campaign that focused only on conversion.

The close relationship among Pae, Cho, and Yu first developed outside the PCRM when they joined forces to establish the Christian Rural Research Association.[78] Founded in 1929, this organization grew out of their desire to develop solutions to combat the deteriorating living conditions in the countryside that they all had personally witnessed. Indeed, far from being a heavenly kingdom, according to Yu, "in reality, the Korean rural area, in the present age, can be called hell. Spiritually, it is hell. Materially, it is hell."[79] Under Pae's leadership, the CRRA designed its mission around the goal of being on the front line in designing practical solutions to combat the vast problems in rural Korea.[80] The organization stressed that all solutions must attack the source of the rural crisis, that is, peasant lives structured for a feudal economy despite the rapid emergence of a capitalism-based agrarian economy. All solutions, in other words, should strive to construct spiritually based modern lives that were appropriate for this period of new economic and social conditions. In designing effective solutions, the CRRA followed the following principles: (1) research the problems facing the Korean countryside; (2) realize Christ's love through all rural projects; and (3) raise leaders for this movement.[81]

Although these principles informed several new designs for rural society, the campaign to produce spiritual spaces through Jesus villages (Yesuch'on), in particular, became the cornerstone of the CRRA's plan to reconstruct and revitalize peasant lives. The design to construct Jesus villages called for multiple approaches to reforming villages where not only economic, social, and cultural programs but also religious programs that stressed the Christian message of love were offered to peasants. Through a collaborative effort, these programs, according to Yu, were expected to establish an entirely new environment that turned villages into places of refuge where people discovered material stability and spiritual joy in the everyday: "People would live without sin and according to Jesus' love. Materially, there would be no hunger; people would love one another and assist each other. People would freely work under the spirit and people would find enjoyment everyday. . . . In the peaceful village, on Sundays, people would follow the church bell and worship the saints gathered in the church."[82] Yu's emphasis on mutual love among people strongly suggests that the CRRA called for social relationships in Jesus villages to be based on Pae's principle of mutual assistance (*sangho pujo*). Adopting this principle was hardly surprising, since CRRA leaders believed that mutual assistance fostered love among individuals, which would then enable people to experience God's love.[83] With the ethic of mutual assistance at the center of a Jesus village, the CRRA hoped to convert villages into sacred places of community.

For Pae, the construction of Jesus villages represented a vital component of achieving his vision of a heaven on earth (*chisang ch'ŏn'guk*) on the peninsula.[84] He imagined that daily life in Jesus villages not only would be materially secure but also would become a portal to a new realm of spiritual being instead of a workday of regularity, boredom, and alienation. People in these villages would acquire constant value and identity as they experienced God in their daily lives. With these effects, then, Pae expected that Jesus villages would be places where peasants could withstand and negotiate the unpredictable dislocations caused by modernization. As Jesus villages sprouted throughout the peninsula, he envisioned a future where the entire countryside would no longer be hell but instead a divine, protected place.

The CRRA's emphasis on spatial reconstruction mirrored the discourse on 1920s and 1930s projects in Europe that dealt with modernization through the "spatialization of time (Being) over the annihilation of space by time (Becoming)."[85] Like European intellectuals, Pae, Yu, Cho, and the CRRA valued spatial reconstruction as a means to control changes in ways that safeguarded the welfare of peasants and connected them to a transcendental force (God) that provided a stable state of being. But despite the urgency of carrying out projects of spatial reconstruction, the CRRA never started a major rural campaign before it was dismantled in 1932.[86] Instead, the CRRA mostly conducted research on rural life and designed programs like the Jesus villages. These designs and the organization's research, however, were important because they were integrated into the PCRM after Pae's appointment as its leader. The Jesus villages plan, for example, was adopted as an official PCRM program to redesign rural life.[87]

Alongside its research and design, the legacy of the CRRA also continued through Yu Chae-gi and several former CRRA members who joined Pae at the PCRM. In the Presbyterian rural movement, Yu and former CRRA members worked with figures such as Yi Hun-gu (1896–1961), Ch'ae Pil-gǔn (1885–1973), Pak Hak-chŏn (1905–1972), and Kim Sŏng-wŏn (?–?).[88] Yi Hun-gu, in particular, stood out for his abilities to analyze and articulate the root causes of peasant poverty and design appropriate programs to ease peasant poverty. Having studied agriculture and agricultural economics at Suwŏn Agricultural and Forestry School, Tokyo Imperial University, and the University of Wisconsin, Yi believed in a socially oriented theology and the creation of a society anchored in a strong agricultural economy. In 1933, after receiving a doctorate in economics from the University of Wisconsin, he taught agricultural economics at Sungsil University in P'yŏngyang. Through Sungsil, Yi became affiliated with the PCRM and played a major role in the movement by becoming responsible for publishing *Nongmin saenghwal*, teaching farming techniques to peasants and young students, and writing treatises on agricultural development in colonial Korea.[89] While Pae supplied the theology behind the movement, Yi furnished the economic and social theories that guided the PCRM's drive to revive the countryside. According to Pang Kie-chung, who wrote an extensive study on Yi, he was "an active theorist providing the rationale of the Christian rural society movement and national-capitalist solutions for the Korean agricultural problem."[90] Pae, Yu, and PCRM leaders came from different backgrounds and specialties, but a commitment to provide social relief to peasants through reconstruction projects united these leaders.

What further drew PCRM leaders together was their vision of reviving the agricultural economy and turning peasants into independent farmers as the way to create a modern Korean society. The leaders' pursuit of this path of development was based on a number of factors, including reasons derived from historical investigations. While YMCA leaders relied on their study of Western development to help shape their movement, PCRM leaders turned to the history of Christianity as presented in the Bible, where they found spiritual teachings that guided and justified their drive to build a sacred society anchored in agriculture. PCRM leaders, in particular, drew inspiration and guidance from the Bible's narrative on agriculturalism (*chungnongjuǔi*), or the love of agriculture and farming. First, from this narrative, they learned that God had endorsed farming as the first form of labor for humanity. Indeed, Ch'ae Pil-gǔn pointed out that farming (*nongsa*) was the original type of work recorded in the Bible, and man devoted himself to farming.[91] Yi Hun-gu added that because the Hebrew nation supported an agriculture-first policy, farming and farmers were well respected.[92] For Ch'ae and Yi, the early history of Christianity showed that farming was considered a valuable, worthy form of labor that was anything but trivial. "If you think along these lines," according to Ch'ae, "then farming is very noble and a biblical occupation."[93] Approved by God and cherished by early Christians, farming, in the minds of Ch'ae and Yi, should therefore be valued as a sacred form of labor by present-day Koreans and become the centerpiece of a modern society.

Second, the PCRM came to respect farming above all other forms of labor because it served as a medium for experiencing God. Land, according to Yi, originated from and was sustained by God. He cited various verses in the Bible, including Genesis 26:3, to support his argument: "Stay in this land for a while, and I will be with you and will bless you. For to you and your descendants I will give all these lands and will confirm the oath I swore to your father Abraham."[94] Believing that land came directly from God, Yi consequently characterized it as "God's palace" and, more specifically, "the door to God."[95] Because God created, controlled, and ordered the universe, land and the natural environment represented portals through which farmers could encounter and experience God.[96] By planting seeds, cultivating soil, and tending to crops, farmers would gain direct access to God and thereby transform farming into a divine form of labor. Yi added that simply by being in nature, farmers also had the opportunity to undergo religious experiences since they dealt with "rain, snow, wind, and frost."[97] Pak Hyŏng-yong agreed with Yi since he stressed that one could acknowledge or recognize God's existence in nature.[98]

For the PCRM, Christian doctrine framed farming as the connective tissue between humanity and God that enabled individuals to encounter sacred forces continuously and experience a joyful life. PCRM leaders, however, recognized that people had not simply received "blessings from God" through this relationship but also had "conscientiously sung praises to God."[99] By singing "praises to God," people acknowledged God's grace and lived a life of holiness as a form of thanksgiving. PCRM leaders most certainly believed that giving thanks through a holy life required the respect and care of nature because it was God's creation. In fact, Yi pointed out that *chungnongjuŭi* in the Bible stressed that individuals should respect all of nature, including trees, fruits, and all agricultural products.[100] In the end, the organization's emphasis on the proper treatment of nature was hardly surprising because the destruction of nature would leave people without a vital medium through which to experience God.

Finally, the PCRM also supported an agrarian model of development because of the social impact of farming and agriculture as outlined by the Bible. From interpretations of the Old Testament, PCRM leaders learned that farming promoted the sharing of goods and caring for others. Exodus 23:10–11, according to Yi, showed how this communal philosophy was practiced among the Hebrew nation. In those verses, people were told to farm their lands for six years but to let them remain unplowed and unused in the seventh year so that the poor could collect food from them. These verses stressed that this practice should be applied to all lands that underwent agricultural cultivation, including vineyards and olive groves. From this practice, communities ultimately developed. Indeed, Yi wrote that landowners and agricultural workers, who gathered food from the unused lands, came together to celebrate events and religious ceremonies.[101] This philosophy of sharing with and caring for others was certainly appealing to PCRM members because many of them, especially Pae and Yu, argued that a person could experience God and his love through community.

From biblical history, PCRM leaders learned to view and value farming not only as a process that mediated the relationship between humanity and God but also as a system that had enabled the formation of communities. Because farming moved people from a profane to a sacred communal life that was full of joy, PCRM leaders were further confident that people who worked in agriculture would enjoy a sound physical and mental life because they would be surrounded by natural beauty in the countryside. Using lofty language to describe rural Korea, a PCRM-authored article described the countryside as "natural," "clear," and "quiet."[102] Yi himself described the countryside as clean and beautiful and "full of natural music."[103] To the PCRM, with these attributes, the landscape of the countryside was peaceful and a source of physical, mental, and spiritual therapy. What the countryside represented to the PCRM was a site and symbol of authenticity. Unsurprisingly, then, PCRM writings pointed out that people experienced pure and moral lives that were full of truth within this genuine environment.[104] Yi, for example, pointed out that a farmer had qualities or a disposition that could be characterized as "pure minded" (sunhu).[105]

PCRM leaders agreed that an agriculture-based modern society afforded a rich and stable moral, ethical, and spiritual life. There were, however, certain concerns about how well farming and a pastoral life would enable economic and material stability overall for Koreans, considering the current state of rural society. Yi Hun-gu quickly quashed those concerns by arguing that a life centered on agriculture and farming would enable peasants to deal best with the demands of capitalism and forge material security, especially if they became independent agricultural cultivators who also operated small cottage industries. By becoming independent farmers, Korean peasants would enjoy economic independence, which would enable them to deal with the changes surrounding them.[106] Without any interference from controlling powers, peasants would also be able to produce and keep their own wealth and experience stability in their lives. Ultimately, promoting the development of independent agricultural cultivators would not only economically benefit Korean peasants but also boost the overall agricultural economy; Yi had argued that agricultural cultivators, who were directly tied to farmlands, were in the best position to achieve the highest level of agricultural productivity and use farming lands in the best ways.[107] For Yi, an agricultural economy with independent farmers would produce a level of evenness where everyone would experience economic equality and freedom and would have the same abilities and resources to tackle issues of capitalism successfully.

Of course, as the PCRM pursued modernity through the route of agriculture and religion, it encountered a number of challenges and setbacks. Yet in the face of these obstacles, PCRM leaders never wavered from this model of development because they were confident that their decision was based on careful, reflective thinking. Far from being unsure, PCRM leaders were certain that they had chosen the right direction for reconstructing Korea on the basis of the knowledge they had acquired through the study of history. They specifically turned to the history of Christianity and the West to help shape their actions, but they also relied on Korean history. From studying their national history, PCRM leaders became further convinced that reconstructing Korea into an agrarian, spiritual paradise was an appropriate course of action because it would preserve and continue the identity and history of Koreans, which had long been shaped by agriculture. Declaring that "Chosŏn is an agricultural country," Yi Hun-gu pointed out that agriculture had always been part of the life of Koreans since the first days of Tan'gun, the mythical founder of Korea, and that all governments had valued agriculture and endorsed agriculture-first policies in the Three Kingdoms period, the Koryŏ dynasty, and the Chosŏn dynasty.[108] Pae also declared that agriculture was deeply intertwined into the lives of most Koreans: "We are farmers. We have for more than a thousand years lived an agricultural lifestyle."[109] Stressing the way in which farming and agriculture had long been part of the life of Koreans and the nation strongly suggests that Pae and Yi considered agriculture an essential component of Korean identity. Agriculture constituted what it meant to be Korean. In this case, the PCRM arguably foresaw the turning of Korea into an industrial capitalist country, which was seen as a foreign system and as a process that would radically dislocate and change the identity of Korea. During a period when modernization caused mass disruptions and stripped peasants of vital traditions and customs, the leaders of the PCRM most certainly feared that the loss of the agricultural identity would cause further disorientation in the lives of peasants, destroy the nation, and derail any hope of building a modern spiritual kingdom on earth. Pae therefore confidently declared that "since 80% of all the people are farmers, it is not an exaggeration to say that the whole of

Korea is made up of farm villages. If these farmers can live, then all Korea can live; if these farmers become Christian, the whole country will be Christian."[110]

The Ch'öndogyo Rural Movement: Agriculture, Wealth, and National Independence

The Ch'öndogyo organization's decision to focus on reconstructing rural society was unsurprising, considering its roots in the countryside. Since 1905, Ch'öndogyo had developed into an elaborate organization whose influence spanned the countryside. While provincial and district headquarters were located in large villages or cities, local congregations (*p'os*) were found deep in the countryside, where they attracted the majority of Ch'öndogyo followers. Even after the defeat of Tonghak forces in 1894, the number of Ch'öndogyo members dramatically increased during the 1910s. From 1910 to 1916, the number of Ch'öndogyo believers jumped from 27,760 to 1,073,408, with a large number of followers in the northern provinces of P'yŏngyang, Hamgyŏng, and Hwanghae.[111] By 1919, Ch'öndogyo claimed that it had between 1.5 million and 2 million members.[112] The organization's membership numbers were somewhat remarkable since overall membership declined in the Protestant Church between 1910 and 1919.[113]

Through its administrative framework, Ch'öndogyo sought to shape all these new members into religious subjects who would embody the organization's teachings, including the principle of "humanity is Ultimate Reality" (*innaech'ŏn*). Hence followers received religious training and a basic education from Ch'öndogyo leaders in local areas.[114] After the March First Movement, the organization wanted to become one of the leading organizations in the new Culture Movement by not only addressing the spiritual needs of Koreans but also influencing and shaping national trends and the overall society.[115] As a way to coordinate the Ch'öndogyo drive to reconstruct Korean society and the national body, Yi Ton-hwa collaborated with Ch'öndogyo leaders on establishing the Ch'öndogyo Youth Department for the Study of Doctrine (Ch'öndogyo ch'ŏngnyŏn kyori kangyŏnbu) in September 1919.[116] Reorganized several times, this institution became known as the Ch'öndogyo Youth Party (Ch'öndogyo ch'ŏngnyŏndang) in September 1923. Ch'öndogyo leaders expected the organization to develop into a modern party with a coherent ideology and a wide-ranging organizational system to spread the party's message and achieve its goals.[117] The party worked tirelessly to establish a major presence throughout the peninsula. By the late 1920s, it was able to organize over two hundred branches throughout the country and attract close to 8,000 members.[118]

The establishment of the party shifted Ch'öndogyo's mission from waging a political struggle for independence against the colonial government to constructing a new culture that would allow for a spiritually based modern life. An article in the September 2, 1923, issue of *Tonga ilbo* articulated this shift by announcing that the principle of a heaven on earth (*chisang ch'ŏn'guk*) would guide and drive party activities. It added that the party would "bring to fruition a new system that would be in harmony with the natural constitution of the individual" and "establish a new code of morals and ethics that would be in accord with the spirit of treating one another as divine [*sain yŏch'ŏn*]."[119] Put differently, the party planned to establish a new society that would embody the principles of *innaech'ŏn* and *sain yŏch'ŏn*. What became clear from the *Tonga ilbo* article was that the party expected to carry out Yi Ton-hwa's message of constructing a new world in order to achieve the religious ideal under modernization.

While *chisang ch'ŏn'guk, innaech'ŏn,* and *sain yŏch'ŏn* served as the guiding principles behind the party's effort to reconstruct the nation-state,[120] the party relied on various means to spread its religious message and carry out economic, social, and cultural reforms. For example, in August 1926, the party organized several departments responsible for crafting policies to reform a specific sector of society. Party members expected that all aspects of society would be studied through the departments, as is evident in the numerous subjects that departments covered, such as infants, children, youth, students, women, peasants, and laborers. In order to assist certain departments in carrying out specific reform projects, several agencies were also established, such as the Children's Group, the Youth Group, and the Students' Group.

The party recognized that designing and carrying out reforms through departmental initiatives alone would never achieve the organization's goals, so educational reforms became an additional feature of its reconstruction efforts. Teachings on Ch'ŏndogyo ideas and different forms of analysis of the new developments in society were spread through books, journals, and newspapers that were part of the party's extensive publication system. Some of the party's well-known publications included *Kaebyŏk* (Creation), *Sinyŏsŏng* (New Women), *Hyesŏng* (Comet), and *Sinin'gan* (New Human). With the possible exception of Protestant Christian organizations, no other group in Korea published more materials than the Ch'ŏndogyo Youth Party did, and it had a fundamental impact on shaping the burgeoning print culture of the 1920s. Consumers in this new print culture feverishly bought and read the various publications of the party, especially *Kaebyŏk,* which became one of the most popular journals and sold 7,000 to 8,000 copies a month. What journals like *Kaebyŏk* offered to Koreans was the means not only to learn about Ch'ŏndogyo beliefs but also to read about the latest social, economic, and cultural issues facing Koreans, such as gender inequality, poverty, the rise of the modern woman, the Westernization of Korea, and antireligion movements. From these publications, the public acquired the language and symbols to visualize modernity in colonial Korea and to map out ways to negotiate the country's ever-changing economic, social, and cultural terrains.

In the party itself, a unified position on modernity was difficult to achieve at times because members debated the most appropriate path to modernity in Korea. As a large organization, the Ch'ŏndogyo Youth Party had a diverse group of members. Some argued that Korea's present and future course should be centered on urban and industrial development; others stressed the value of a modern nation-state organized around agriculture, the countryside, and peasants. Arguing for one side or the other continued until 1937, but a powerful group of party leaders, including Yi Ton-hwa, persuasively argued to the entire party that Korea's path to modernity should be tied to its agrarian heritage. These leaders appreciated the various results of urbanization and never rejected it and industrialization outright, but they perceived an agriculture-based economy, society, and way of life as the healthier, more effective means through which Koreans could negotiate modernization and establish an ideal modern life. Rejecting the idea that anything associated with the rural was antiquated and inhibited change, the leaders strongly believed that the means to build and sustain a spiritually based modern Korea existed in an agrarian economy and a pastoral life.

These leaders gained the opportunity to carry out their experiment of turning rural Korea into a modern agrarian paradise through the party's establishment of the Korean Peasant Society (Chosŏn nongminsa) on October 29, 1925. As the main organization to design, organize, and carry out the plans of a new rural movement, Chosŏn nongminsa had the task of modernizing rural Korea because the agrarian economy and peasant lives appeared to be anything but ideal. Articles written by leaders had pointed out that most rural households experienced extreme poverty and overall instability in their lives.[121] Because peasants lacked protective measures, such as customary tilling rights,[122] and the overall means to help them navigate through the changing economy, Chosŏn nongminsa established a wide-ranging organizational structure to enhance every aspect of rural life.[123] The organization's governing structure consisted of four levels: the central headquarters (*chungang*), the county (*kun*), the township (*myŏn*), and the village (*ri*). Leaders oversaw and controlled all activities from the organization's headquarters in Seoul, but they created a decentralized system for an organic (*yugijŏk*) movement at the local level. In fact, wanting the movement to evolve as naturally as possible and its reforms to remain over time, the central headquarters encouraged branches at the village level to exercise self-rule and some autonomy, especially in making decisions.[124] In 1928, the organization decided to limit membership only to the "independent farmer, independent farmer / tenant farmer, tenant farmer, a farm laborer, a person who engaged in farming and industry, and any worker who engaged in physical labor in the countryside."[125] Members had the "right to speak, the right to bring up a resolution, the right to vote and the right to be eligible for elections."[126]

Overall, Chosŏn nongminsa committed itself to educating and training peasants. To do so, the organization refused to uproot the lives of peasants entirely and turn them into something other than farmers because of the organization's commitment to building an agriculture-based nation-state. The December 1925 inaugural issue of *Chosŏn nongmin* (Chosŏn Peasant), the official magazine of the organization, articulated the organization's vision of Korean society and its plan for its rural movement.[127] Yi Sŏng-hwan, who worked with Yi Ton-hwa to start the organization and later became its first leader, announced the founding principles of the movement:

1. Our Chosŏn is a peasant (*nongmin*) country (*nara*).
2. From this moment and on, we shall use all of our power and strength to help the peasant.
3. The coming age is the world of the peasant.[128]

The first principle declared that the peasant and agriculture represented the essential features of the Korean nation in the past and present by connecting *nongmin* to Chosŏn and *nara*, while the third principle stressed that these two features should and would continue to constitute the nation in the future. According to the second principle, however, only through Chosŏn nongminsa leadership would the first principle remain true and the third principle become true. The organization essentially promised to serve as the mediating power that intervened in history to improve and sustain rural life in ways that ensured that Korea's past, present, and future were rooted in agriculture and the peasant.

While the YMCA studied Western history and the PCRM analyzed the history of Christianity, Chosŏn nongminsa justified its pro-agrarian position through a historical study of Korea. From this history, the organization concluded that agriculture and the peasant were "the very body of the nation" because they constituted and defined the Korean ethnic identity from the past to the present.[129] The direct connection of agriculture and the peasant to the nation derived from the historical recognition that Korea had been an agricultural country with peasants at its base since its inception. Yi Sŏng-hwan, for example, pointed out that agriculture and the peasant had been at the center of society for over four thousand years.[130] In light of its pivotal role in Korean society over time, agriculture was seen as embodying the national spirit of Korea (*kukka chŏngsin*).[131] Because peasants were the only people who actually engaged in agriculture, they too were considered essential features of the nation; indeed, Yi described peasants as "the repository of Korean ethnicity."[132] Leaders in Chosŏn nongminsa thus naturally emphasized the peasant as the most important figure in Korean society and history. In fact, Yi Ton-hwa considered peasants the "head of the family" in society—that is, the head of the nation.[133]

Despite their essential place in Korean history, peasants had long been mistreated and abused, according to Yi Sŏng-hwan and Yi Ton-hwa. Yi Sŏng-hwan wrote, "In Korea, even though the peasant is the master, he has not been treated as if he is the master." Instead, society characterized peasants badly and treated them as if they were "country bumpkins."[134] The poor treatment of peasants happened despite traditional philosophical teachings that placed farmers high in the social hierarchy system—even higher than artisans and merchants. People, especially government officials, ignored these teachings that called for the farmer to be honored and showed little reverence to peasants.[135] Yi Ton-hwa wrote that the peasant's stature had diminished even further in civilization discourse because it depicted the peasant as one of the least important figures in a modern society—below the scholar, the merchant, and the artisan. Under modernization, then, the peasant's status dropped dramatically, and farming was considered worthless.[136] For Chosŏn nongminsa, the devaluation of peasants and the steady erosion of their material lives were certainly causes for great concern. The organization's leaders questioned how Korea's national spirit could survive in the present and future with the decline of agriculture and the peasant—the two essential features of the nation. To the organization, what was necessary for the continuity of the nation under modernization was to bring stability to rural Korea and the lives of Korean peasants through the development and enhancement of the agrarian economy.

Beyond nationalistic concerns, Chosŏn nongminsa greatly valued agriculture, in particular, because farming (*nongsa*) was essential for the healthy development of society on two levels. First, agricultural (*nongŏp*) goods met people's most basic needs, such as food and natural resources.[137] Farming, in other words, gave people the means to survive. Kim Pyŏng-hyang pointed out that "everyone's life requires drink, food, and air every minute," and agriculture satisfied those demands.[138] Because of this value, Yi Ton-hwa unsurprisingly characterized farming and agriculture as the vehicles that supported human life.[139] Second, farming and agriculture played vital roles in building and sustaining the economy. Agriculture especially supplied the natural resources for building homes and manufacturing finished goods.[140] Kim Pyŏng-hyang summed up nicely the value of agriculture to the economy:

Raw resources [*wŏllyop'um*], which are obtained through agricultural production, have a direct relationship to people's lives. Farming cultivates foodstuffs and stuff to drink. Moreover, farming through the raising of livestock gives us leather, fur, meat, and milk. Through cultivation, farming supplies raw resources for silk thread and fabrics. . . . It also provides materials for cotton spinning. . . . Timber, which is provided through the lumber industry, has broad uses as a natural resource for industry.[141]

He specifically pointed out that the source of production, especially manufacturing, was agriculture. Arguing against Koreans who were confident that technological innovations would no longer require agricultural goods for industrial production, Kim emphasized that industries would still depend on agriculture for raw resources because industries could not produce any "organic materials."[142] Here Kim was specifically criticizing those Koreans who thought of farming and agriculture as relics of the past that would only inhibit the development of a modern economy. Instead of being obstacles that inhibited progress, farming and agriculture, to Kim, served as the essential means to a flourishing economy and society. In believing that agriculture and farming served as valuable resources for a healthy society and economy, Kim shared Yi Sŏng-hwan and Yi Ton-hwa's belief that agriculture was the foundation of life.

In many ways, the Chosŏn nongminsa's position on agriculture and farming embodied the principles of physiocracy. Founded in France by François Quesnay and Anne-Robert-Jacques Turgot during the second half of the eighteenth century, physiocracy was one of the first theoretical models to furnish a total view of the economy that explains the creation and circulation of wealth and value. What distinguishes this model of the economy from other models is its emphasis on agriculture as the source of wealth. According to physiocracy, farmers, after subtracting what is necessary for consumption, are left with an agricultural surplus or excess known as the "net product" that is transferred to landlords as rent. Landlords consume part of this rent and use the remaining amount to purchase goods from artisans. Artisans then receive a portion of the net product not only from landlords but also through direct exchanges with farmers. In the end, artisans use parts of the net product to manufacture finished goods that they sell to or exchange with landlords and farmers.[143] Stephen Gudeman points out that "the Physiocrats portrayed the economy as a total, circulating system of wealth" and configured agriculture as the very source of wealth.[144] Although prominent figures like Adam Smith and Karl Marx criticized the theory as too simple and full of illusions, many admired this economic model because physiocracy showed that "agricultural production had this unique and marvelous power of yielding a 'net product' that economy was possible and civilization a fact."[145] For those who supported an agriculture-based economy and society as the route to modernity, physiocracy proved that agriculture and farming were the most appropriate means to build a successful socioeconomic system.

Chosŏn nongminsa used the language of physiocracy to legitimize its position on agriculture and farming. In colonial Korea, especially in Chosŏn nongminsa circles, the principles of physiocracy were well known because they were introduced in general newspapers and journals, such as *Tonga ilbo* and *Samch'ŏlli* (Three Thousand Ri), and in journals published by the Ch'ŏndogyo Youth Party, such as *Kaebyŏk* and *Nongmin*. An article in the July 1933 issue of *Nongmin* specifically defined physiocracy (*chungnongjuŭi*) as an ideology that described agriculture as the "foundation of society" because "it is the main force to produce and promote authentic wealth." The article further added that physiocracy spoke of agriculture generating wealth not only through farming but also through commerce by "supplying raw materials to industries." At the end, the article particularly emphasized that physiocracy assured followers that agriculture, rather than industrial and commercial development, would establish "a paradise with a rich nation and happy people."[146] This explanation of physiocracy clearly and succinctly articulated the ideas that Chosŏn nongminsa leaders held about agriculture. Because physiocracy was a modern theory of economic development, Chosŏn nongminsa therefore publicized this definition of physiocracy to show Koreans that agriculture-based development was suitable for modernity and was far from being a traditional system that was appropriate only for premodern societies.

In addition to agriculture, Chosŏn nongminsa leaders further agreed with physiocrats that rural cultivators, whether farmers or peasants, should be greatly appreciated and valued because they performed the labor that generated wealth for society. Yi Ton-hwa, for example, argued that the peasant should be called "the master" because he harvested rice, raised cows, and grew beans—the basic goods necessary for a thriving economy.[147] In order to show how much peasants contributed to Korean society, Yi Sŏng-hwan pointed out that peasants harvested nearly "15,000,000 *sŏk* of rice, 8,000,000 *sŏk* of barley, [and] 4,500,000 *sŏk* of beans" and raised "27,390,000 won worth of livestock" in 1925.[148] Because Chosŏn nongminsa viewed the peasant as an essential figure who helped transform agriculture into a productive form of capital and wealth, Yi Ton-hwa publicly announced that "if the peasant dies, Korea will die. If the peasant lives, Korea will live."[149]

For Chosŏn nongminsa, wealth generated through agriculture and the labor performed by rural cultivators gave farmers and peasants practical benefits. Wealth, for example, would bolster a self-sufficient life (*chagŭp chajok saenghwal*) for rural cultivators, thus giving them further autonomy and control over their lives in the unruly capitalist economy.[150] Their abilities to maintain this type of life would then enable them to continue experiencing "sound and healthy" (*kŏnjŏn*) lives because they were interacting with nature in the countryside[151]—which, as a place of peace, beauty, and stability, was considered a natural source of physical and spiritual therapy.[152] Besides influencing individual lives, agriculture-based wealth, more important, would make Korea autonomous and thus sustain national independence. To Chosŏn nongminsa leaders, agriculture would supply the essential wealth that would help Korea avoid being dependent on the forces of capital controlled by foreign banks and capitalists and regain its sovereignty. A 1923 *Kaebyŏk* editorial spoke of this need for and importance of autonomy and self-sufficiency via agriculture in Korea:

> Agriculture is the place that preserves eternal sacred value since it maintains human life. . . . If the world were self-sufficient in the way that agricultural society is, there would be no need to rely on banks, it wouldn't be affected by fluctuations of capital, and wouldn't be subject to the abuses of modern civilization, such as class discrimination and economic pain. That is why the sacred value of agriculture becomes all the more crucial in modern society. . . . Even were Korea to develop commerce and industry, they would be subject to foreign forces of capitalism and therefore would not benefit Korean civilization. The only way to engage in economic war is therefore to preserve agriculture and establish our unique agricultural civilization in ways that prepare for a self-sufficient utopian agrarian nation which would be the basis of our new society.[153]

The editorial embellishes aspects of a pastoral life, but it speaks well of Chosŏn nongminsa's desire for a pastoral life to achieve wealth and self-sufficiency as a way to national independence.

Because (1) agriculture and the peasant were the material manifestations and symbols of the Korean nation, (2) agriculture, farming, and the peasant made vital contributions to society, and (3) agriculture sustained national independence, Chosŏn nongminsa committed itself to constructing a spiritual kingdom on the peninsula through an agriculture-centered path of modern development. This agrarian vision of Korea guided the Chosŏn nongminsa rural movement from beginning to end, even in the midst of internal developments. In 1929 and 1930, the leadership of the Ch'ŏndogyo Youth Party had sought more control over Chosŏn nongminsa in order to use it as the primary vehicle to achieve its vision of society. Instead of letting it operate autonomously as a branch of the party, officials directly took over Chosŏn nongminsa.

Despite the change in leadership, the organization continued its mission of building an agrarian, spiritual paradise. Chosŏn nongminsa, in fact, became even more committed to this mission by expanding its rural campaign to include new economic programs, such as the construction of cooperatives.[154]

Agriculture, Agency, and Temporality in Colonial Korea

In the 1920s and 1930s, rural Korea became a battleground where leftists, bourgeois nationalists, agrarianists, and the colonial government competed with one another to gain hegemonic control over peasants and achieve their ideal visions of the nation-state. In this crowded field of rival campaigns, the YMCA, Presbyterian, and Ch'ŏndogyo movements distinguished themselves from all other rural movements through their commitment to an agrarian model of development to establish a modern nation-state. Each of them studied different types of history to arrive at their model, but they all shared the belief that the principal features of an agriculture-based economy and a pastoral life not only served as the source of ethnic identification but also provided the control, organization, and overall environment to ensure a life of material prosperity, moral and ethical growth, and spiritual enlightenment. They invested all their power and resources in rural reconstruction because a stable, agriculture-based economy and pastoral life delivered a form of agency that was appropriate for building a spiritual modern nation-state as first imagined by Hong, Pae, and Yi.

In laying out this narrative of development, all three movements argued against sacrificing the peasant, agriculture, and the countryside for the sake of becoming modern. To them, a promising future with a dynamic state of spiritual being, individual autonomy and prosperity, social equality and harmony, and national unity should be achieved without fundamentally separating Korea from its agrarian heritage, which still played a fundamental role in shaping Korean lives in the 1920s and 1930s. Cultivating and emphasizing the importance of an agriculture-based life and society were in accordance with Yi, Hong, and Pae's belief that being modern required a life rooted in the present. In refusing to break radically with the present in order to establish an entirely new future centered on industrialization and urbanization, the three movements called for a process of modern development that was organic in that it valued a smooth continuity between the past and the present in order to develop new possibilities for the future. The movements' temporal framework for modern development thus became an alternative to those articulated by most leftists and bourgeois nationalists.

The three movements' temporal framework for modernity also represented an alternative to the colonial government's vision of Korean modernity.

Before and after annexation in 1910, Japanese government officials and intellectuals argued that Korea lagged in modern development because it lacked an industrial capitalist base, urban development and culture, and disciplined, hygienic, industrious subjects who displayed entrepreneurial skills. Because Japan was imagined or even fantasized as having become a successful modern nation-state through a process of transitioning from a rural-based society to an industrial-capitalist and urban-based society, these same intellectuals and officials emphasized that Japan represented the perfect role model that could help modernize Korea—a line that became the justification for colonizing Korea. Thus the turn to an agriculture-based plan for modern development by the YMCA, Presbyterian, and Ch'ŏndogyo movements arguably signified a rejection of Japan's model of modernity for Korea. For YMCA, Presbyterian, and Ch'ŏndogyo leaders, rural reconstruction offered a way to write Japan out of Korean modernity and challenge its claim over Korea by actually materializing a healthy and functioning rural-based modern society. In so doing, this narrative of modern development gave Koreans new language with which to resist and escape the logic behind colonial rule—a logic that had been indirectly legitimized by Korean nationalists who believed that modernity arrived only through industrial capitalism and urbanization. Indeed, by supporting and carrying out this vision of modernity, these Koreans, according to Se-mi Oh, "duplicated the structure which already produced the inferior status of the colonized."[155] By challenging the colonial government's narrative of modernity, the language coming out of the three rural movements became an alternative form of resistance to direct political struggles at a time when the colonial government tightly controlled the speech and movements of Koreans.

The application of agrarian language to the struggle against colonialism was part of an overall trend in colonized areas during the 1920s and 1930s. Partha Chatterjee points out that it was common for many anticolonial struggles to create a cultural, spiritual domain from which to resist foreign occupiers by adopting and promoting anticapitalist, anti-industrial, agrarian rhetoric.[156] Many conservative agrarianists in colonial Korea created this domain by attracting peasants to their beliefs that emphasized agriculture and the peasant as the sources of wealth and national identity. In some ways, their beliefs mirrored the ideas held by the YMCA, Presbyterian, and Ch'ŏndogyo rural movements. But although both sides shared a belief in the value of rural Korea and in saving it, the YMCA, Presbyterian, and Ch'ŏndogyo rural movements rejected the agrarianists' plan for solving the crisis in rural Korea by returning to the past through the restoration of traditions and refused to fix present-day rural Korea in a static past. Instead, they sought to introduce a series of reforms that not only respected and safeguarded Korea's agrarian heritage but also reconfigured peasant life in ways that allowed new possibilities of existence that were appropriate to the contemporary period. The three movements planned to lay down a new system for work and living that cultivated the peasants' "middle state"—a state of life in which they continued to exhibit "ease, equality, and innocence" and the "spontaneity and freedom" of a pastoral life while being able to apply creatively the latest ideas, practices, and forms of technology to achieve a life full of continuous progress.[157] By developing this middle state, the movements hoped to avoid peasants exclusively experiencing what Leo Marx characterizes as a "primitive life," which fostered simplicity, autonomy, and tranquility but was also harsh and laborious, or a "progressive life," which promised rationality, enlightenment, and advancement but also led to massive problems, such as "undignified restlessness, ambition, or distrust."[158] The middle state, to leaders of the three movements, would arrive through combining the most ideal features from both types of life. In order to create a suitable environment for the development of this middle state, the three movements searched for a system that would afford material prosperity alongside moral and ethical growth under capitalism. Faced with this pressing issue, the three movements turned to the Danish cooperative system as a way to manage capitalism and ensure a healthy and holistic pastoral life.

5

Spiritualizing the National Body

Sacred Labor, Community, and the Danish Cooperative System

When the YMCA, the Presbyterian Church, and Ch'ŏndogyo started their respective rural movements, Korean peasants found themselves in a challenging situation in which many lacked the resources and power to meet the new demands and requirements of a powerful capitalist economy. Without the tools to negotiate the new conditions, a growing number of peasants had no choice but to sell their labor and become wageworkers, especially when the economy suffered many setbacks in the 1930s because of the Great Depression.[1] Compared with the 1920s, when certain peasants were able to strengthen their holdings in relation to landowners and take advantage of the expanding agricultural market, many peasants became part of the agricultural working class from 1932 to 1938.[2] The commodification of peasant labor played out well for the colonial state, which supervised the transfer of surplus labor from Korea to cities in Manchuria and Japan.[3] Korean immigration to Japan steadily increased from 1920 to 1944 (1920: 40,755; 1930: 419,000; 1944: 1,000,000) as more and more people hoped to exchange their labor for wages. In Japan, a lucky few immigrants found permanent work at factories, but most were forced to become day laborers who experienced an unstable livelihood plagued with poverty, discrimination, and oppression. According to an observer of rural life, an increasing number of peasants encountered "a rapid process of dispossession" in which they first turned into "owner-tenants, then into tenants, and finally into proletarians, squatters, beggars and vagabonds."[4] Koreans working in Japanese cities faced the very harmful consequences that leaders in the YMCA, Presbyterian, and Ch'ŏndogyo rural movements predicted and feared would happen in a society shaped and dominated by the structures and principles of industrial capitalism.

What was emerging in colonial Korea between 1920 and 1937 was a capitalist system that forced many peasants to flee from their agriculture-based livelihoods and commodify their labor in order to find relief from material insecurities. This transforming economic landscape threatened the YMCA, Presbyterian, and Ch'ŏndogyo drives to build a modern spiritual, agriculture-based society. Their difficulty in building their ideal society was that the colonial economy was becoming a complex, multifaceted system that moved people, goods, and capital in ways that appeared to be controlled by the colonial government but were often uncontrollable. The challenge for all three groups was to develop mechanisms that directly intervened in and arrested this unruly process of capitalist development and reoriented the economy toward the achievement of the agrarian and religious ideal. In particular, these movements required a proven organizing system that could stabilize and strengthen rural life under capitalism and ensure that farming would continue to be a pleasing and enriching form of labor.

To meet this challenge, all three movements advocated the creation of a comprehensive cooperative (*hyŏpdong chohap*) system. Each group prominently featured cooperatives in its movement because of the capabilities of the cooperative to pool the labor and resources of individual peasants and create enough economic power to manage and negotiate the challenges and demands of the market economy. Through a collective effort, cooperatives seemed to offer the best means to stem the collapse of agrarian society and the further commodification of peasant labor. Cooperatives further appealed to YMCA, Presbyterian, and Ch'ŏndogyo leaders because they created a collective body of individuals that aimed to protect and elevate life. The leaders believed that cooperative members working side by side would create harmonious social relations through which the members would become committed to caring for and helping one another. The underlying goal of the cooperative went beyond simply reaching economic and material success toward communally achieving a life of well-being grounded in morals and ethics. The pursuit of profit and money was the means to cultivate the good life under the cooperative. In this capacity, YMCA, Presbyterian, and Ch'ŏndogyo leaders interpreted a cooperative as a mechanism that framed and conditioned labor as a practice for developing and expanding personalities. A cooperative would prevent labor from undergoing the process of commodification and becoming a means solely for existence in which a person "works in order to live. He does not even reckon labour as part of his life, it is rather a sacrifice of his life."[5]

This chapter outlines and analyzes the YMCA, Presbyterian, and Ch'ŏndogyo rural movements' endeavors to construct cooperatives based on the Danish cooperative model throughout the peninsula. During the 1920s and 1930s, the Danish cooperative system was praised throughout the world for modernizing an agriculture-based economy and fostering a new society of well-rounded Danish farmers who enjoyed rich daily lives. This system was well respected because it not only gave farmers the means to compete in a capitalist economy but also forged a communal structure through which labor functioned as a creative, self-realizing practice that continuously elevated the human condition. Incorporating principles from the Danish cooperative system into their own designs of cooperatives, the three movements established new frameworks in which peasants could adapt their local environments to changes and processes originating from capitalism and create new conditions that would allow for the healthy advancement of agrarian life and society. They expected the cooperative system to achieve this effect through the architecture of place—designing and establishing new localities in villages that allowed for a secure interface between the macro and the micro context. Through a new locality, peasants would be equipped with the means to deal with larger-scale forces in secure and powerful ways that would strengthen local identities, practices, and relationships while giving peasants access to new experiences that would allow for the growth of the middle state.

Space of Hope and the Danish Cooperative Model

During the 1920s and 1930s, cooperative economic systems grew in popularity as an alternative to the mainstream economic models of industrial capitalism, socialism, and fascism. Especially after the onset of the Great Depression, when economic turmoil and conflict abounded at the everyday level and ruptured the social fabric of societies, people searched for means to forge a stable economic life in what Karl Polanyi called "market societ[ies] that refused to function," and they took cooperatives seriously as a viable alternative economic system to bring economic and social order to disordered environments.[6] More than just a sudden alternative in the 1920s and 1930s, cooperatives had had long histories in countries throughout the world. In many parts of the globe, cooperatives grew in popularity as people looked for a system that avoided turning labor into a coercive process that made humanity one sided, fragmented identities, and created forms of alienation that were occurring under industrial capitalism. Starting in the middle and late nineteenth century, various discourses and movements, such as Edward Carpenter's pastoral visions in his "Simple Life movement," the "decentralized communitarianism of the anarchist Prince Kropotkin," the British Arts and Crafts movement under John Ruskin and William Morris, and the American Arts and Crafts movement that emphasized the "guild spirit," called for experimenting with various systems that would counter the mechanization of labor under industrialization and guarantee work, such as farming and manufacturing, as a sustainable, productive, and rewarding process.[7]

Imagining ways for people to shield themselves from the dangers of industrial capitalism, European social advocates and intellectuals believed that a cooperative system would enable artisans and laborers to protect the value of their labor and their autonomy. Consumers and producers could pool their resources to bypass profiteers and usurers and create an economy based on morality.[8] In nineteenth-century England, for example, social advocates and members of the working class set up consumer cooperatives to acquire everyday goods at low prices. Guided by the question "What can we do to save ourselves from misery?" flannel weavers in Rochdale, in particular, recognized that combining their labor and capital could create a new power through which they could improve their lives and "do something."[9] Under the direction of Friedrich Wilhelm Raiffeisen and Franz Hermann Schulze-Delitzsch during the late 1840s, credit cooperatives in Germany started as a way for small producers to raise capital and resources collectively at a time when big industries were beginning to power the German economy.[10]

A number of non-Western societies have had a long history of operating successful cooperatives. Many cooperatives in East Asia originated from Buddhist movements in which cooperative-like organizations were established to build and maintain Buddhist temples and monuments. Mutual financing associations in China, for example, became major supporters of Buddhist activities. These religion-oriented cooperatives served as the foundation of a new crop of cooperatives that appeared in early twentieth-century China in order to grapple with the new challenges coming out of the fractured political and economic environment. By 1935, there were more than 25,000 cooperatives in China, mostly credit cooperatives, with a total membership of a little more than a million individuals.[11] Elsewhere, some of the most vibrant cooperatives thrived in local areas of Japan during the eighteenth century. Cooperatives in Japanese villages collectively organized the resources and labor of individuals under the logic and purpose of saving others rather than of solely increasing profits. Japanese cooperatives served as tools to realize principles of moral contracts, which promoted strengthening and protecting the quality of human life. In this capacity, these cooperatives fused economics with morality as they worked to improve human life. During the age of industrial capitalism in the late nineteenth century, many local villagers refused to follow Meiji state guidelines that credit and loan cooperatives operate on the basis of the modern economic logic of profitability. Interwoven into the lives of ordinary citizens, cooperatives played a fundamental role in enabling people to survive in a society shaken by the forces of capitalism throughout the early 1900s. In Japan, there were no fewer than 333,634 cooperatives at the local levels by 1910.[12]

Although cooperatives in Europe and Asia proved to be effective institutions for ordinary individuals, Danes had created what many observers considered a utopian agrarian society through a comprehensive cooperative system. The birth of an ideal agrarian society in Denmark was especially remarkable in light of the political and economic crises that had weighed Danes down heavily during the eighteenth and nineteenth centuries. In 1807, for example, the decision to side with Napoleon in the Napoleonic Wars led to the Second Battle of Copenhagen, in which British troops destroyed most of the capital city, and to the loss of Norway to Sweden in 1814. The loss of Slesvig and Holsten (Schleswig and Holstein), a valuable area of land in southern Denmark, to Bismarck's Prussia only further shrank what once had been a wide-encompassing Danish state in 1864. The Napoleonic Wars were so costly that they led the Danish state to declare bankruptcy by 1813. The entrance of new agricultural players, such as the United States and Canada, both of which offered products at cheaper prices, into the global agricultural commodities market during the mid-nineteenth century and the declining prices for grain during the 1870s led to diminishing incomes in many Danish homes. By the late nineteenth century, the volatile economic and political conditions caused Denmark, according to Frederic Howe, to be at its lowest ebb in history.[13]

The movement to stabilize the Danish state and society and the everyday livelihoods of Danish farmers, who represented a large percentage of society, started from three different drives that spanned the decades since the eighteenth century. First, the Danish state initiated a series of land-reform laws starting in 1784 that dismantled the feudal system by 1919.[14] Second, Nikolai Frederik Severin Grundtvig (1783–1872), who was a major Danish religious figure and educator, articulated and spread the idea of establishing folk schools that would play a major role in fostering a new class of farmers who were well rounded in work, education, and culture. Grundtvig thought of folk schools as places where students would obtain an education through which they could become critical thinkers, acquire practical knowledge and skills for successfully forging a livelihood, and learn more about their Danish heritage. The final component that paved the way for the revival of the Danish economy and society came in the form of a comprehensive cooperative economic system. As land reforms released Danish farmers from the bonds of feudalism and folk schools equipped them with valuable education, cooperatives gave Danish farmers concrete organizing mechanisms to pool labor and resources. Linked with the land reforms and the folk schools, the Danish Cooperative Movement (Andelsbevægelsen) served as the linchpin that allowed local rural communities to compete in the global agricultural market and therefore turned Denmark into the ideal modern agrarian society in the world.[15]

During the 1920s and 1930s, global discourse on cooperatives by economists, intellectuals, politicians, and ordinary citizens tended to center on the dramatic revival of Danish society through cooperatives. People from England, Japan, Korea, Canada, and the United States, among other countries, traveled to Denmark in order to study its cooperatives. An American official observed in 1923 that those traveling to Denmark were farmers and farm organization officials, college professors and teachers of every grade and rank, graduate students digging doctorate dissertations out of life and not out of dust bins, legislative committees and commissions, congressmen and field investigators from the agricultural department at Washington, members of the English parliament and details from the Home Office, settlement workers, social secretaries, public welfare officers, research students representing the social-work foundations of America, authors assembling material for books on Denmark, Scandinavian-American scholarship students, and so on.[16]

In Denmark, foreigners were mostly likely amazed at the impressive figures for agricultural exports. Through cooperatives, the value of exports of agricultural products increased from $25,500,000 to $150,000,000 between 1881 and 1912.[17] Even after the onset of the Great Depression, the value of agricultural exports increased to $220,600,000 in 1933, which was a significant portion of the total export trade of Denmark that year. Denmark served as a classroom for foreigners to study the operations of the Danish cooperative system in order to rejuvenate their own countries' economies and overcome the inherent problems of capitalism, especially at a time when communist collectivization in the Soviet Union, which was quite violent, was widely touted.

Koreans participated in this global discourse on Denmark by prominently featuring the country in their own discourse on Korea's reconstruction. Before 1919, Koreans conducted some discussions about Denmark, most likely sparked by Japanese commentaries on Danish living. Starting in 1920, the discourse on Denmark exploded. Almost daily, *Tonga ilbo* featured articles about Denmark ranging from the country's physical education programs to its agrarian reforms. Articles in monthly journals, such as *Kaebyŏk, Sinmin,* and *Tonggwang,* and numerous books analyzed Danish reforms.[18] Readers of these materials encountered similar narratives about Denmark's path to economic, social, and cultural revival that started with the political and economic disasters that the country had encountered and ended with the rebirth of a "heavenly Denmark" through the folk-school system and the cooperative movement. Hoping to raise a new Danish-like spirit of revival within Koreans, nationalist leaders carried out various types of Danish-style reforms. For example, Pak In-duk (Induk Park), a leading Korean feminist, wrote after visiting Denmark, "I kept thinking as to how my people could get the living spirit similar to that by which Denmark was revived. The step to be taken obviously was to try out some of their working principles in among our people." To reach this goal, Pak wrote the book *Danish Folk High Schools* and founded a Danish folk high school for women in 1933.[19]

YMCA, Presbyterian, and Ch'ŏndogyo writings prominently featured this narrative as a guide for reconstruction. Among the groups, Hong Pyŏng-sŏn became the strongest admirer of Denmark who wanted this trajectory to be replicated in Korea. As one of the few Koreans to visit Denmark and study the folk-school system and cooperative system up close, Hong came to be known as the foremost expert on Denmark and cooperative economics.[20] His reputation as an expert on Danish affairs grew through his public lectures on Denmark and numerous publications on cooperative economics and Denmark's cooperative system, physical education programs, and family dynamics, including *Chŏngmal kwa Chŏngmal nongmin* (Denmark and Her Farmers), the authoritative book on Danish history that detailed Denmark's revival.[21]

Hong's work and messages on Denmark influenced a wide number of Korean social activists during the colonial period.[22] His influence even extended into the Presbyterian and Ch'ŏndogyo rural movements. *Nongmin saenghwal*, the official journal of the Presbyterian rural movement, featured an article by Hong that urged readers to start Danish-style cooperatives as a solution to the problem of reforming peasants' minds and bodies. To learn more details about Denmark and its cooperative system, he urged people to read *Chŏngmal kwa Chŏngmal nongmin*, which was prominently advertised in the back of the same issue as Hong's article.[23] In *Nongmin*, the official Ch'ŏndogyo rural journal, Hong also published several articles that touched on Denmark and cooperative economics. These articles gave a detailed history of Denmark, Grundtvig, and folk schools; supplied reasons for building cooperatives; and encouraged collective responses to solve Korea's problems.[24] Asking Hong to write articles strongly implies that Presbyterian and Ch'ŏndogyo rural leaders specifically sought out his expertise on Denmark and cooperatives and based many of their Danish-style programs on his ideas.

Because Hong was the leading expert on Denmark during his time and strongly influenced Presbyterian and Ch'ŏndogyo rural leaders' impressions of Denmark and its cooperative system, it is appropriate here to analyze his thoughts on the Danish cooperative system. To Hong, Denmark was unique because it built itself into a modern agriculture-based country while other countries pursued industry and trade.[25] He was amazed by how Danish farmers were able to use cooperatives at the local level to react effectively to global competition and challenges. The influence of cooperatives extended beyond the economic realm because they also enabled farmers to enjoy rich moral, ethical, spiritual, and cultural lives—to "liv[e] in heaven with an ideal life." With cooperatives revitalizing the agrarian economy and Danish society, Hong declared that "Denmark was a state that could provide valuable knowledge to peasants throughout the world."[26]

Hong explained that as a communal economic organization, a cooperative promoted self-rule and was egalitarian and democratic. In a typical Danish cooperative, members pooled and shared resources, mandated equal responsibility in work, and, in the case of marketing cooperatives, redistributed profits in proportion to the amount of goods given to the cooperative. Members of a cooperative had equal say and power, which was exercised through equal voting rights for each person regardless of the size of that person's original investment.[27] Unlike a modern corporation, adopting a policy of "one person, one vote" ensured the cooperative's nature of economic equality. In his investigation of Danish cooperatives, Hong discovered that the success of a cooperative lay in its ability to organize labor and capital among a small group of people so that the combined resources could wield greater power in the global market. This type of collective formation to ensure high economic productivity and financial security materialized through three types of cooperatives: consumer cooperatives, marketing cooperatives that produced and sold goods, and credit unions.

Consumer cooperatives pooled members' money to purchase supplies and goods directly from wholesalers or manufacturers.[28] Hong pointed out that the Danes had learned about consumer cooperatives from the English cooperative model, which had been started in 1844. But what distinguished the cooperative movement in Denmark from movements in other countries was that the Danish consumer cooperative inspired the systematic formation of other cooperatives to meet all the other economic needs of Danish farmers. Soon after consumer cooperatives developed, marketing cooperatives emerged in order to bolster the production and quality of goods, which would help ensure consistent revenue for farmers. Danish farmers in the dairy, beef, pork, and egg industries relied on cooperatives to organize the manufacturing, packaging, and selling of their goods. Farmers delivered goods to their cooperative, where specialists inspected and packaged them. These goods were then sold and shipped directly to customers. Cooperatives functioned through discipline, regulation, and the levy of fines against members who produced inferior goods.[29]

Although consumer and marketing cooperatives met the consumption and production needs of Danish farmers, credit unions were the most important cooperative institutions because they supplied the necessary capital for consumption and production, according to Hong. Credit unions collected money from their members and let members borrow money at a low interest rate. Loans were then disbursed to members, who were expected to repay them in a timely manner.[30] Hong thought that this institution was pivotal in reviving the life of Danish farmers because it gave them access to capital without obligating them to pay high interest rates. Farmers therefore had the autonomy and confidence to engage in different kinds of economic activities.

Through cooperatives, Hong believed, Danish farmers as a group had found a way to act autonomously while also achieving economic stability. Able to buy and sell as a group, cooperative members no longer needed middlemen or intermediary merchants who took away valuable profit. Farmers in cooperatives could negotiate prices directly with wholesalers and thus act in their own interests as a group. Cooperatives also helped insulate farmers from the oppressive forces of capitalism by preserving their ability to act autonomously. Through the three kinds of Danish cooperatives, farmers controlled their own labor and generated as well as circulated money and other forms of capital at the local level. Farmers in cooperatives overcame alienation from their means of production and became financially independent from banks and other external sources of capital or money.[31] With local forms of capital in circulation, farmers made economic decisions in a way that did not disrupt local affairs, thereby overcoming the volatile nature of capitalism and achieving stability. Hong believed that Danish cooperatives had contained the most revolutionary aspect of capitalism—the destabilization and upheavals caused by capital circulating from area to area in order to seek new ways of gaining profits.

In addition to the economic benefits that they could bestow, Hong respected Danish cooperatives because they were ideal social mechanisms that fostered a community based on the moral principle of improving the quality of human life. Cooperatives were fundamentally different from modern corporations that operated purely for the pursuit of profit: "In a bank . . . the most important objective and purpose is to gain profit and divide the earnings. In a cooperative, the purpose and objective is helping individuals and uplifting their lives. The most important thing for a bank is money, while the person is the most important element in a cooperative."[32] By bringing people together to work closely with one another and share responsibilities, cooperatives were institutions that materialized the ethic of mutual aid and sought to elevate the human condition.[33]

Trust (*sinyong*) bound Danish cooperative members to one another and upheld the collective identity of the cooperative, according to Hong. Trusting relationships were cultivated and upheld because of the risks involved in conducting a business in which everything was jointly owned. The ramifications of one person's actions were great in that if one member failed to perform her or his duties, all members would be adversely affected economically. Hong pointed this out when he wrote that when a Danish cooperative, for example, borrowed money from a bank or credit cooperative, it was the responsibility of all members to repay the loan. If production failed, members would suffer the consequences of losing their "land, house, cows, and pigs and anything else they could sell to pay back the loan." In order to be successful and prevent catastrophes, cooperative members "had to work together through trust and had to believe through trust."[34]

Hong recognized that Danish cooperatives wove social relationships built on trust among members. He also saw that trust was predicated on belief. "Believing" meant being certain that each member of one's cooperative would work hard to improve the livelihood of all members. Hong's interpretation of trust in Danish cooperatives resembles Anthony Giddens's definition of trust: "confidence in the reliability of a person or system, regarding a given set of outcomes or events, where that confidence expresses a faith in the probity or love of one another, or in the correctness of abstract principles."[35] Hong was confident that by believing in one another and in a system that affirmed trust, cooperative members would feel that risks would be minimized and dangers would be averted. Hong further believed that if members of a cooperative felt secure, they would willingly work with one another and take part in activities that would help them succeed as a cooperative. Bearing this in mind, Hong wrote, "Without trust or belief between people, nothing would be possible."[36]

Much of Hong's keen interest in the social benefits of Danish-style cooperatives can be attributed to the growing social alienation he saw around him. He argued that capitalism caused the deterioration of human cooperation and social solidarity among Koreans who became less concerned about and dependent on one another and instead focused on money to structure their lives. Hong noted, "Today, in terms of the structure of the economy and society, money is at the center."[37] In such an environment, acquiring money was the most important objective in life. Koreans thought that money would give them access not only to resources but also to social power because money now influenced everything. This was evident to Hong, who saw "people bow in front of people who have money."[38] Presbyterian and Ch'ŏndogyo rural leaders shared Hong's growing anxiety about money's power and influence under capitalism, which helps explain why they all were attracted to the Danish-style cooperative system. On the Presbyterian side, Yu Chae-gi pointed out that capitalism promoted "the acquisition of profit for the accumulation of capital." He added that there was no "love" in profit, and it caused only conflict.[39] Yi Hun-gu expressed concern about the enormous power a single person who controlled a corporation by owning the majority of its stock could wield to rule over and oppress many individuals.[40] Yi Ton-hwa, the Ch'ŏndogyo leader, echoed Yi Hun-gu's fears about the dominating power of capital by pointing out that "capital is the subject while humanity becomes the object" under the standards of capitalism.[41]

To the leaders of the three movements, the consequences of a maturing capitalist system that privileged money and profit were oppression, the erosion of human subjectivity, and the fracturing of society and the nation. These leaders believed that the construction of cooperatives in Korea could stave off these developments, just as it appeared that cooperatives had done in Denmark. Yi Hun-gu wrote that Danish cooperatives had moved people to shed forms of individualism and realize a life based on cooperation, observing that "cooperation fever among Danish citizens is imposing," while Sin Hŭng-u admired the way members of a Danish cooperative took responsibility for one another, especially when a member's economic endeavors were in jeopardy.[42] Hong added that Danish cooperatives helped people realize that even activities outside work should be done in a cooperative manner. He believed that there was no ideological or class division in Danish society because of cooperatives.[43]

Leaders of the movements emphasized that the structure of Danish cooperatives fostered a cooperative ethic and a unified social body over time. First, Hong and Paek Min of the Ch'ŏndogyo rural movement observed that rules regarding membership ensured communal ties. Both noted that membership in a Danish cooperative was restricted to people who lived in the same neighborhood or district. Paek wrote that because members of a cooperative lived close to one another, they already likely shared common interests.[44] Second, Hong argued that Danish cooperatives fostered the growth of communities because members discussed and decided together the purpose of the cooperative and their individual responsibilities.[45] Third, Hong and Paek viewed the contract that individuals who joined a cooperative were required to sign as a fruitful mechanism that helped maintain communal ties by obligating members to work together in order to achieve the goals of the cooperative.[46] Finally, Yi Hun-gu stressed that the cooperative's democratic governing system would prevent any one person from dominating others and thus overthrowing the cooperative's mission of improving the lives of all its members.[47] Institutional features of the cooperative made rural leaders feel confident that money and the pursuit of profit would not take precedence over people, while the day-to-day work required to maintain the cooperative would bring its members into close relationship with one another.

It appears that all three groups hoped to institutionalize a moral economy through a Danish-style cooperative system. Their vision of a moral economy, unlike that defined by James Scott, emphasized the importance of being financially competitive and profitable in the emerging capitalist agricultural market.[48] Making profits, however, only for the sake of obtaining money was far from what they had in mind when they encouraged cooperative enterprises to earn profits. Rather, they maintained that profits should be redistributed to cooperative members and reinvested in the cooperative's businesses in order to ensure the cooperative's viability. In this case, this conception of a moral economy encouraged moral integrity and economic interest, although the former outweighed the latter. The three movements hoped to form a moral economy that equipped peasants to be economically successful in a capitalist economy while promoting love, close social relationships, and religious experiences. They imagined that the creation of a cooperative-based economy would establish a gemeinschaft form of capitalism that limited the excesses and faults of a market economy.

All three organizations argued that Denmark's cooperatives proved that cooperatives as modern institutions could successfully establish a vibrant rural society in which farmers had the power to negotiate and control capitalist development and could foster a moral and ethical community. Paek Min declared in 1932: "There is no other country than Denmark that has developed more cooperatives. Therefore, Denmark is a collaborative based society." He wrote that cooperatives, along with folk schools and a physical education program, had helped Danes become wealthy, had contributed to the growth of their minds and bodies, and had turned Denmark into the most famous agricultural country in the world.[49] Han Tong-wu, a Ch'ŏndogyo leader, added that Danes "had constructed the world's model farms."[50] Explaining that the countryside served as the site of the majority of cooperatives in Denmark, Yi Chae-gi stressed that farmers enjoyed economic success and that Denmark was a "heaven" (nagwŏn) through cooperatives. Yi Hun-gu added that Danish cooperatives, which were based on "modern rationality," organized farmers so well that butter, bacon, and egg cooperatives "were victorious over fierce German farmers and were active players in the European market." Farmers benefited so much from cooperatives that Denmark became known as "today's Jerusalem for farmers."[51] To Hong, the success of the Danish cooperative system extended beyond the economic realm because successful cooperative endeavors translated into improvements in other areas of everyday life, including family life, leisure, and spirituality.[52] Consequently, according to Hong, "The life of the Danish farmer is satisfying" and full of "gratification and joy."[53]

Although successful cooperative programs were found throughout the world, such as Germany's Raiffeisen / Schulze-Delitzsch credit cooperative movement, the Hotoku movement in Japan, and the YMCA-led agricultural cooperative movement in India, the three movements turned to Denmark because it was the only country to install a comprehensive cooperative system that enabled it to become the most respected modern agrarian nation-state in the world.[54] By promoting a Danish cooperative system, the three movements stood apart from traditional Korean agrarianists at that time who advocated Confucian communal organizations, such as village associations (tonghoe), village compacts (hyangyak), and village mutual-aid societies (tonggye). Unlike traditional agrarianists who hoped to restore the past through these organizations, leaders of the three movements expected cooperatives to help peasants negotiate capitalism and domesticate changes in ways that would allow for the continual development of agrarian society. To the movements, Danish-style cooperatives served the contemporary needs of peasants, while Confucian communal organizations were inadequate mechanisms to deal with current economic and social problems because they had been built originally to deal with issues and problems in the past Confucian-based society.

The Danish cooperative system furnished all three rural movements a blueprint for successfully transforming Korea from a poor agricultural country into a prosperous agrarian nation-state integrated into the world. This blueprint for development became the cornerstone of their rural reconstruction plan because it promised to give Korean peasants the knowledge, skills, and organization to negotiate communally the various economic and social challenges and changes under capitalism. The cover of Hong Pyŏng-sŏn's book *Nongch'on hyŏpdong chohap kwa chojikpŏp* (Cooperatives: Organization and Methods) sums up well what rural leaders expected from a cooperative-based economy in Korea. It depicts a tree whose roots are made up of various cooperatives, while the tree's trunk is marked as "farmer" (*nongbu*). The fruits of the tree are tagged as "one's own work" (*chajak*), "saving" (*chŏch'uk*), "stable, secure livelihood" (*saenghwal anjŏn*), and "life of enjoyment and satisfaction" (*chaemi innŭn saenghwal*). The cover figured cooperatives as the foundational mechanism to transform peasants into farmers who would then enjoy the fruits of an agrarian life, such as *chajak*.[55]

The YMCA and Cooperatives: Trust, Social Relations, and Model Villages

Material instability fueled peasant discontent and protests, which led to a dramatic increase in the number of tenant disputes from three hundred in 1932 to nearly thirty thousand in 1936. Believing that these disputes revealed peasants' desires for fundamental changes in the current political economy, leftists, in particular, moved swiftly to organize peasants for their respective causes. Although leftist movements seriously challenged the religion-based rural movements, the colonial state represented an even bigger threat to the YMCA, Presbyterian, and Ch'ŏndogyo movements. From the beginning, the colonial state permitted the three movements because it thought that religion-based rural movements could draw peasants away from leftist groups and diminish leftist influence. In 1931, John H. Reisner, an agricultural economist, summed up the feelings of the colonial state toward Christian-based rural movements: "In an evening conference with several of the Japanese officials it was very clearly indicated that the government is studying closely what the missionary community is undertaking along the lines of rural advancement, and that it is not only willing but anxious to cooperate wherever possible."[56] Despite this expression of support, the state still represented a threat because its agenda of increasing agricultural outputs and crushing rural unrest rested on advancing the interests of the Japanese empire, not the interests of the three rural movements and the Korean nation. The state was more of a threat than any Korean nationalist group because it could attract peasants to its own rural programs by offering vast resources, including money and the latest farming technology and knowledge. The state's ability to provide capital to peasants gave it a huge advantage over any group. The 1932 rural campaign's cooperative program through the Rural Credit Society (Kŭmyung chohap or Kinyu kumiai), for example, granted any Koreans who organized a credit cooperative a subsidy of 10,000 yen, which could be used for loans as well as for financing the distribution and sale of members' goods.[57]

Having to contend with the colonial state and rural movements by agrarianists, leftists, and bourgeois nationalists, all three organizations recognized that they needed to design and carry out with precision a comprehensive movement with sustainable cooperatives that would reach as many peasants as possible and thrive in the volatile capitalist economy. Until 1937, each organization oversaw the construction of various types of cooperatives, but they also concentrated on building specific types of cooperatives to meet the most urgent needs of peasants that they had identified. To this end, the YMCA focused on credit and marketing cooperatives, the Presbyterian Church Rural Movement (PCRM) supported the construction of credit and consumer cooperatives, and Ch'ŏndogyo started cooperative farms that applied the principles found in Danish cooperatives.

All three organizations dreamed of achieving an ideal agrarian society like that of Denmark, but the YMCA's faithful devotion to the adoption of Danish reforms distinguished it from all other rural movements. The organization's fervor for Denmark came as no surprise because Hong served as the architect of the YMCA rural movement and Sin Hŭng-u matched Hong's enthusiasm over Denmark.[58] Sin declared that through the Danish model of agricultural development, especially cooperatives, Korea would turn into the main supplier of agricultural goods in East Asia, and its survival in the global market would therefore be ensured.[59] Arthur C. Bunce, F. O. Clark, and Gordon Avison, who were foreign missionaries who specialized in rural affairs at the YMCA, also favored the construction of Danish institutions as a way to revive the countryside. Before arriving in Korea, Clark directed the J. C. Penney Farms in Florida from 1925 to 1929, where he carried out a rural movement based on the Danish model. At the YMCA, Clark continued this quest to build a new agricultural society through Danish examples.[60] Bunce, in particular, became a strong supporter of Denmark-style reforms after visiting the country in

1929.[61] Bunce was strongly attracted to the Danish model of agricultural development because he saw that "it develops and encourages individuality and democracy." He was specifically impressed with Danish cooperatives because "the cooperative store and business methods seem to me to have the essential elements of efficiency and a great deal more of character and individuality building ability." Cooperatives empowered farmers so well that Danish farmers were "in power for many years." What Bunce found so appealing in Danish cooperatives was how they limited the controlling power of money and capital and forged a farmer-centered society without social divisions.[62]

What made the Danish agricultural model of development even more attractive to YMCA officials was that it could become a viable alternative for agrarian reform in place of comprehensive land reforms. YMCA leaders, such as Hong and Sin, vocally supported land reform because there was a direct correlation between the lack of landownership and the inability of peasants to overcome their indebtedness and rise out of poverty. In 1928, Sin explained that this arduous task was "political and require[ed] much legislation and expenditure of public funds" that could be carried out only by the state.[63] He acknowledged, however, that because the political realm was controlled by the Japanese colonial state, which showed no inclination to reorganize landownership, it would be nearly impossible to enact land reform. The state's unwillingness to push for land reform would make it very difficult to achieve a Danish-like revival since rural programs in Denmark succeeded in boosting the wealth and power of farmers only because major land reforms broke down feudal conditions and made farmers independent. For the time being, however, the YMCA decided to table any discussion of land reform.

The Danish cooperative system allowed the YMCA to be confident that it could still fundamentally help peasants adjust to their new social and economic environment. Beginning in 1929, the YMCA mostly carried out Danish-style reforms, including cooperatives and folk schools. From the organization's office in Seoul, Hong spearheaded and coordinated the rural campaign.[64] The central office crafted policies and worked with local YMCA branches to implement them. Branch leaders visited villages to carry out program directives, while Sin and Hong traveled throughout the country to oversee the program and help villagers start cooperatives. Although branch leaders worked under a top-down structure, they could revise certain polices and modify programs to meet the specific demands and conditions of the places where they operated. Flexibility characterized the YMCA's approach to building a Danish-style cooperative system.

At the local level, the YMCA built three kinds of cooperatives, replicating the cooperatives in Denmark: credit unions, consumer cooperatives, and marketing cooperatives. Although they served different purposes, each kind adhered to similar principles that Hong articulated through official YMCA journals and public newspapers. He wrote that for cooperatives to be effective, the following rules had to be obeyed: a village should have one of each type of cooperative; capital and resources should come only from villagers participating in the cooperative;[65] and regardless of one's background, particularly one's religion, anyone could join a cooperative. Most important, Hong emphasized that individuals should love and mutually support one another in order for a cooperative to succeed.[66] The YMCA also told cooperative members to discipline one another while working and managing all things together as one (*ilch'i*). Hong exhorted cooperative members to regulate and help one another live morally by working together to extinguish negative and harmful customs, manners, and morals. Gambling, drinking, and vanity were a few habits that Hong considered harmful to one's mind and body.[67] He wanted cooperative members in villages to observe one another constantly and correct these harmful habits and other destructive behaviors because he thought that disciplining the mind and body ensured an organized life. Hong believed that peasants were already familiar with the concept of cooperation because many villages had used *kye*s in the past.[68] The fact that Hong blamed external factors rather than some insufficiency in the Korean character for weakening and destroying some *kye*s strongly suggests that he believed that Koreans had the ability and potential to work together; they needed only an institution to bring them together and foster trusting relationships.

YMCA leaders began to carry out these directives on cooperatives in 1929 and built a network of cooperatives throughout the peninsula, although a large majority of cooperatives were located in Chŏlla and Hamhŭng Provinces. By 1930, YMCA leaders had visited 256 villages with the aim of reconstructing rural life. In those 256 villages, the YMCA helped build and operate 165 cooperatives with more than 3,548 members.[69] Interviewed by Reisner, Hong stated that there were 52 credit cooperatives, each with a capital reserve of 50 to 600 yen; 67 consumer cooperatives; and 46 marketing cooperatives. YMCA members also planned to design and operate district cooperatives in order to centralize the operation of all local cooperatives and coordinate their activities. By 1931, the YMCA had started only one district cooperative in Seoul, which was made up of 40 smaller cooperatives.[70]

In areas where cooperatives operated successfully, there were small developments that appeared to give peasants the opportunity to improve their dire economic situations. To form efficient credit cooperatives, peasants often set aside a small amount of money each month that they contributed to the collective cooperative fund. A 1931 report on cooperative activities noted that twenty-five men in one village near Seoul, for example, gave twenty sen per month to a credit cooperative fund.[71] By building a strong reserve fund, members could borrow money at a low interest rate. Using the credit cooperative rather than traditional moneylenders, who often charged interest rates of up to 50 percent, peasants could now easily access money that they could use to develop their agricultural businesses. Peasants who participated in these credit cooperatives became more productive without going into debt. Consequently, they were able to contribute even more to the cooperative fund.[72] Alongside credit cooperatives, some villages operated successful consumer cooperatives in which they bought vital goods, usually seeds and fertilizer, at low prices because they purchased them in bulk.[73]

Beyond material results, YMCA officials also wrote how some of these cooperatives encouraged and enabled peasants to cultivate their personalities and improve their overall well-being. Hong pointed out that cooperatives pushed peasants to develop continuously their minds and bodies: "They [cooperatives] broaden life little by little and not suddenly. They bring the farmer to a realization of a need of betterment and possibility of attaining such betterment. This challenges action, and from this action comes better economic, social and spiritual life."[74] Hong added that peasants were learning that transformation through cooperatives was a gradual process in which they would develop the knowledge, skills, and practices that would maintain the constant growth of personalities. What made YMCA leaders seem so pleased about individuals growing and developing in all ways was that this process occurred through a cooperative-created collaborative environment. YMCA officials reported how cooperatives greatly improved social relations among Korean peasants. In villages where cooperatives created by the YMCA anchored the local economy, cooperatives became social mechanisms that cultivated tight-knit communities in which people cared for and mutually supported one another. Hong also wrote that "we have found that those cooperatives develop loyalty and brotherhood."[75] A YMCA report stated that a credit cooperative in a village led people to overcome religious differences and construct a new community: "Social solidarity is seen in a quickened hope. Men work together with enthusiasm. . . . In the old days Buddhists and Christians were hostile. In the cooperative they have worked together and they like it."[76]

YMCA observations on the impact of a cooperative on peasants should be carefully scrutinized because YMCA leaders had incentives to portray the cooperative movement in a positive light, especially in order to acquire more financial support from outside donors. When cooperatives experienced problems, however, YMCA leaders frankly wrote about them and any failures. Writing in 1933, Sin noted that peasants were unable to operate cooperatives successfully after YMCA leaders stopped supervising activities. Some peasants, according to Sin, gave up on their cooperatives immediately after YMCA leaders left their villages.[77] Some cooperatives also failed because they lacked accessible forms of working capital. Although Hong argued that members of local cooperatives should use their own capital in order to maintain economic control, he eventually realized that cooperatives needed capital from external sources during periods when demand for capital outweighed supply.[78] Without enough capital, some cooperatives suspended their operations. Easy access to flexible capital was important for adapting to and sustaining activities in a changing economy, so the inability of some cooperatives to acquire sufficient capital caused some of them to fail in the end.

Wanting to overcome these problems and improve the cooperative program, Hong and YMCA leaders overhauled it in 1931. Rather than operating as a stand-alone program, the mission of building cooperatives was incorporated into a new village plan that targeted peasant life holistically through economic, social, religious, cultural, and physical education programs. Underlying this new plan was the belief that every side of a person's life was interconnected. For example, if a person's physical or spiritual condition was weak, she or he would be unable to maintain economic stability. The following quote in a YMCA document that described the new rural program demonstrated how important it was to attend to a person holistically: "It is believed that spiritual resuscitation, which will arouse the will to make endeavor and act, is fundamental to economic betterment, and that with increased social solidarity a life of fuller happiness, well-being and achievement may be realized."[79] YMCA officials presumed that carefully nurturing each side of a person would allow that person to acquire the skills and knowledge necessary for a strong character that would help her or him achieve the "good life" or "a fuller satisfaction of life."[80] They believed that with a strong character, peasants would be able to sustain a thriving cooperative program.

To reflect this new mission, the YMCA changed the name of its rural reconstruction movement from "agriculture work" (nongch'on saŏp) to "village work" (hyangch'on saŏp). Renaming its movement served to inform the public that the YMCA rural campaign no longer solely served to improve a peasant's agricultural skills—a mistake commonly made during the early stages of the movement—but instead expected a complete overhaul of peasant life.[81] The YMCA designed the new village plan to be a multifaceted program. Through the program for economic development, peasants would learn about cooperatives, home industries, crop production, horticulture, farm management, animal husbandry, and marketing agricultural goods, while the spiritual program entailed holding public worship and teaching peasants about the social gospel. To enhance the overall physical welfare of peasants, the YMCA decided to teach them old and new games, such as Korean wrestling, volleyball, and baseball, and to instruct them on "personal, family and village sanitation and hygiene, mother and child welfare, mental health and sex instruction, production and use of health-giving foods, instruction in first aid and home remedies." The YMCA expected to meet the educational needs of peasants through the construction of a library and a night school that offered literacy classes and lectures on general affairs and history. It envisioned educational programs as a means to abolish "harmful and useless customs" and to make a "special effort to bring women to a higher standard," thus developing new forms of conduct and gender relations. For social development, leaders planned for "games and entertainments, community events, field days," and "singing and use of musical instruments."[82]

With the aim of widely affecting rural life through the new village programs, YMCA leaders most certainly hoped to reach their original goal of reconstructing twenty-six thousand villages because they held a grand vision of transforming all of Korea. In order to accomplish this goal effectively, the YMCA devised a precise plan of action through a model-village program. This plan was far from unique; before 1931 the colonial government and Korean landlords had already started several model villages where new ways of organizing peasant labor and the latest agricultural knowledge and practices were applied and tested. These model villages were part of an overall worldwide trend during the 1920s and 1930s in which social reformers experimented with alternative ways of organizing economic, social, and cultural life through a process called the "miniaturization of perfection and control." Under this process, resources and efforts were concentrated at a single point, like a model village, and this "constriction of focus ma[de] possible a far higher degree of social control and discipline." In a controlled and well-ordered environment that could be closely surveyed, "the number of rogue variables and unknowns [was] minimized," which permitted a model village to become a laboratory for experiments in which methods could be shaped and then applied to other places with minimum risks.[83] These features of a model village, as described by James Scott, served as the exact reasons for the YMCA to start model villages.

In the early stages of the model-village program, the Hamhŭng area in northeastern Korea became the most successful place for the construction of YMCA model villages. Led by Bunce, the model-village program was expected not only to advance the YMCA's goal of building a Denmark-like society in Korea but also to decrease leftist influences. Hamhŭng was the capital of South Hamgyŏng and was located next to the Manchurian border, where Korean leftist guerillas often organized peasants and battled Japanese forces. Bunce pointed out that leftists gained peasant support because of "the fact that there is no other liberal organization with a constructive program for bettering social conditions."[84] In 1931, Bunce set up three model villages in the Hamhŭng region with the hope that they would become viable alternatives to leftist programs. Rather than enter villages and totally disrupt daily living, Bunce worked with what existed in each village. When he talked about achieving the ideal model village, Bunce wrote that "all this has been done with local materials, money and labour."[85] Through the combination of outside and local knowledge, Bunce designed and implemented a wide-ranging village plan that attended to the educational, physical health, and social needs of peasants through such programs as a "night school for illiterates," constructing a village library, lectures on "superstition; drink; child marriage and debt," teaching "elementary hygiene," and installing a "clean toilet for each household."[86] The economic program featured the improvement of crop and livestock production. Bunce introduced varieties of seeds, such as sweet clover, alfalfa, and cabbage, and exposed peasants to technological innovations in the areas of plows, seeders, cultivators, and pesticides. He also introduced purebred Berkshire pigs and leghorn chickens and helped build poultry-production plants.[87]

Cooperatives stood at the center of the economic program. Bunce wrote, "We are starting co-operative societies in each village to save money for community enterprises, such as buying and selling, and also to loan its members money at low rates of interest when wanted. The common rate of interest is 36% per annum." Bunce pointed out that these high rates of interest were on loans issued by a peasant's landlord and were "one of the brakes on Korean progress."[88] To circumvent landlord power and control and give peasants flexible access to capital, he organized credit cooperatives. Bunce also experimented with various types of marketing cooperatives, trying to figure out what would best sell on the market and the most efficient networks through which to grow, harvest, market, and distribute agricultural items. He invested most of his time in starting a cooperative in a model village that exported apples to Japan. This cooperative consisted of a group of Korean apple farmers who normally sold their harvested apples to middlemen, often at a loss. In 1931, these apple farmers suffered even steeper losses when the price of apples fell to just about half of what it had been in 1930 with the closing of the Chinese market. He was confident that the Hamhŭng apple industry could be turned around and "multiplied many times" through a cooperative that gave peasants access to the labor, capital, and organization necessary to compete in a capitalist market.[89]

Setting up and running the cooperative involved a two-step process. First, Bunce and the apple growers laid the groundwork for an infrastructure to transport, market, and sell harvested apples. Along with a Korean YMCA official, they assisted with this task by traveling to Japanese cities nearest Korea, acquiring information on freight charges and commission rates from each place, and helping broker deals with wholesalers in Japan to buy apples directly from the cooperatives.[90] Second, the cooperative became an organizing mechanism that unified the apple growers toward achieving the goal of accurately and efficiently running a self-sustaining business, as was reflected in the following passage:

> The cooperative was formed and members were holding their apples. We obtained a full-time salaried secretary, an office, and packing yard. We ordered a thousand boxes and I spent a busy week teaching the grading and packing of apples. We designed a cooperative box label where the variety, grade, weight, grower's name, and a guarantee were all stamped. The apples were brought into the cooperative plant, graded, wrapped, and packed uniformly. The first thousand boxes are gone and the second started.[91]

The cooperative served as a material structure that made sure that members continuously worked together and shared equal responsibility in growing and selling apples in a well-ordered way.

In Bunce's writings, the apple cooperative appeared to have positively affected the economic, social, and mental lives of cooperative members. Bunce wrote that economically, "they [cooperative members] have obtained about double the local price for their apples." In December 1931, he reported that the apple cooperative earned healthy profits per one hundred boxes shipped to Japan.[92] As for social benefits, Bunce wrote that "the Korean farmers have learned to cooperate together. . . . They have realized the reality of international Christian cooperation and friendship."[93] Finally, he witnessed improvement of the psychological well-being of the peasant apple growers. They were apparently confident about the present and future because they no longer believed that they were permanently bound to blind social and economic forces but instead held the means for a stable, thriving life in a modern capitalist economy. Observing the behavior of peasants within the cooperative, Bunce wrote that "they have found out that they [are] not in the grip of insoluble hostile forces."[94]

The experimental apple cooperative appeared to have achieved long-lasting results. Writing in December 1933, Bunce noted that the apple cooperative was thriving without his direct supervision. In a short time, the apple cooperative was already obtaining higher prices for its apples and exporting more than five thousand boxes of apples. It even expanded its cooperative activities to include a consumer cooperative through which members collectively bought spray materials and manure.[95] Because of its success, the YMCA incorporated aspects of the organizational methods of the experimental apple cooperative into its overall plan to reconstruct village life.

Until 1937, the YMCA experienced a number of challenges to building successful cooperatives like those found in Denmark. Uncontrollable variables and changing conditions forced YMCA rural leaders to reframe and rework their cooperative programs and their physical, spiritual, educational, and social programs continuously under the village plan. What became the controlling factor throughout this changing process was the dream of achieving a powerful Denmark-style cooperative system that would be well integrated into the YMCA's village plans of merging complex and various details into a viable, flexible, holistic system. Trying to bring the details into context rather than getting lost in them, YMCA leaders hoped that this new system would erect a new built environment or locality through which peasants in a village continuously elevated their personalities and experiences every day and became modern subjects. Naturally, the YMCA hoped that a peasant would not become just any modern individual but instead would become like a Danish farmer, who experienced labor as an enriching activity and everyday life as a portal to new adventures that widened his or her character.

The Architecture of Capital: Overcoming City and Country Unevenness through Presbyterian-Constructed Cooperatives

Denmark's achievements also gave PCRM leaders confidence that Korea would experience a grand renewal if Koreans closely followed the example of the Danes. In particular, the abilities of consumer and credit cooperatives to raise and secure money and capital collectively drew the leaders' attention because they would prevent capital from being transferred to cities and overcome the unevenness between the country and the city that left peasants with few financial resources and subjected them to the control and influence of powerful figures and institutions in cities. Recognizing this threat to the PCRM's drive to reclaim rural Korea, Yi Hun-gu became the leading expert on theorizing and publicly articulating this crisis of unevenness. Yi's training as an agricultural economist gave him an advantage over all other PCRM leaders because of his ability to connect what appeared to be unrelated developments under capitalism and articulate the processes that were reconfiguring the financial landscape.

Yi helped his readers visualize what was happening between the country and the city by renaming this relationship "unjust / uneven" (*pulgongp'yŏng pulgyunhyŏng*).[96] Yi pointed out that old and new factors contributed to this unjust / uneven environment in Korea. First, peasants sent a large amount of their wealth (*bu*) to cities through land rent.[97] The flight of peasant wealth, which Yi defined as *kokmul*, or the corn, cereals, grains, or crops planted and harvested by peasants, increased over time as more landowners moved to cities.[98] Yi wrote in 1935, "The Korean countryside is made up mostly of tenants while some landowners live in the city. . . . As rent in the countryside goes up, at least half of the wealth that is produced from the land flows into the city."[99]

The loss of peasant tenants' wealth to landowners during the 1920s and 1930s was unsurprising because the majority of peasant tenants had historically paid rent to local landowners for the use of land. What was new in the transaction between peasants and landlords was that peasants now encountered a growing number of absentee landowners. These urban absentee landlords, according to Yi, had many opportunities to buy land, especially during the 1930s, because many well-to-do peasants were unable to keep up loan payments and sold large tracts of land to settle their debts.[100] High prices prohibited most individuals living in the countryside, including other landowners, from purchasing any available land. This situation opened up the land market to outside people, including "successful industrialists who held a large amount of capital and lived in the city." Yi wrote that industrialists in Seoul, Inch'ŏn, and P'yŏngyang became large landowners.[101] Landownership in Korea even became a foreign enterprise as "large capitalists [taejapon'ga]" in industrialized cities in East Asia purchased land on the peninsula and became "large landowners [taejiju]."[102]

These absentee landowners represented a new breed of landlords because they viewed land solely as a source of investment and a tradable commodity that could easily be bought or sold. Because landowners recognized only the economic value of land, they cared little about the farming conditions of their land. Hence they made few, if any, attempts to develop their land properly for the benefit of tenants.[103] Yi pointed out that because landowners in the city cared only about receiving rent, they "gave absolutely nothing back to our countryside."[104] This trend alarmed Yi because urban interests inside and outside Korea were emptying the countryside of valuable wealth and solidifying the financial inequality between the city and the country.[105]

Second, Yi stressed that unevenness also resulted from peasant consumption habits. The wealth of peasants, for example, flowed from the country to the city as they paid urban industrialists and merchants (sanggongŏpga) high prices for items essential for farming. Peasants specifically paid a considerable amount for artificial fertilizer, which was manufactured by industrialists, sold by merchants, and bought by peasants for four times the original wholesale price.[106] Peasants even had to spend a large sum of money for natural fertilizer from merchants and landlords living in the city. Landlords handsomely profited from selling fertilizer by buying it in the city at low prices, supplying it to their tenants on credit, and demanding repayment of double the amount of the fertilizer's original price at the time of harvest.[107] Yi understood that peasants paid high prices for certain goods in order to maintain farming operations, but he criticized peasants for wasting a great amount of their wealth on the conspicuous consumption of goods that were popular in cities. Allured by urban consumer culture and the hope of becoming modern, peasants moved away from a life based on simplicity by purchasing the newest goods, such as furniture and clothing. Yi recognized that some goods could improve peasant lives, but he believed that mass-produced goods, such as phonographs, hair oil, and dressers with mirrors, were unnecessary because they had no other function than to give peasants the appearance of living a modern life. The conspicuous consumption of these goods led only to the loss of money that was going mostly to businesses in cities.[108] Yi was upset that the consumption habits of peasants drained money from the countryside and thus kept rural society under the control of urban centers.

The financial and credit system served as the final factor that explained the uneven relationship between the country and the city. Under this system, according to Yi, peasants could borrow money from six lending sources: the Industrial Bank of Chosen (1918), the Oriental Development Company (1908), the Rural Credit Society (1907), the Rural Mutual Aid Society (1928), *kyes*, and individual lenders.[109] Despite many options, it was still a challenge for peasants to borrow money since the overall lending system heavily favored certain groups over the Korean peasantry. Japanese settlers in Korea and large Korean landowners, for example, received favorable treatment from financial institutions. The Oriental Development Company, which served as a major landholding company that supervised the immigration of Japanese farmers to Korea, issued loans specifically to Japanese citizens. Designated by the colonial state as the primary institution to extend credit to medium- and small-size farmers, the Rural Credit Society also gave preferential treatment to Japanese citizens because, according to Yi, "the credit organization is not of, by, and for the Korean farmers, but largely Japanese in managerial, personnel and operating funds."[110] When financial institutions loaned money to Koreans, Yi noted that they preferred better-established classes, such as large landowners.[111] These lending institutions targeted these groups because they were considered the most rational users of capital, who could successfully expand their businesses without defaulting on their loans. Moreover, as Yi pointed out, landowners could easily obtain loans because they could use their land as collateral.[112]

When peasants were able to get loans, Yi pointed out those lending institutions charged higher rates of interest than for other groups and classes, such as Korean landowners and elites, who enjoyed the lowest rates.[113] Peasants often received loans that carried interest rates as high as 40 percent for mortgage credits and 70 percent for personal credit—rates that were higher than those extended to borrowers from urban institutions, such as the City Credit Society, which was the urban version of the Rural Credit Society. Peasants were charged even higher rates of interest by individual lenders, such as landowners and private lenders, who served as the last lending resort for peasants. Yi asserted that landlords "extract from the peasant farmers as much as they

can by charging high rates of interest," while Japanese usurers charged "exor-
bitant rates of interest."[114] Unsurprisingly, these interest rates pushed peasants
further into debt because they were unable to pay back their original loans. Yi
pointed out that peasant debt had grown so severe that it collectively stood at
600 million yen in 1932.[115]

Besides how it left peasants in a perpetual state of poverty, Yi grew
alarmed over how this system allowed urban-based individuals and institutions around Korea and East Asia to acquire large sums of money at the ex-
pense of rising peasant debt. In 1935, for example, Yi pointed out that the Rural Credit Society charged high interest rates to peasants in order to earn
profits and collect "large sums of money" that would be returned to investors
in cities.[116] Investors in the Industrial Bank of Chosen received this money
because the bank was the parent of the Rural Credit Society.[117] The Industrial
Bank of Chosen entrusted the Rural Credit Society with representing its interests in the countryside because the bank had only city branches. As "the
center for rural credit, especially for loans of long term and large amounts," Yi
wrote that the Rural Credit Society quickly "became nothing other than small
banks for the mass of farmers."[118] To Yi, the ultimate purpose of this lending
process was for "capital from the city [to] indirectly enter the countryside and
work to generate large sums of money."[119] Yi interpreted loans backed by the
Industrial Bank of Chosen as forms of speculative capital that sought profit-
making ventures in order to give financiers in cities a steady flow of money
from principal and interest payments.

Yi noted that speculative capital also appeared in the countryside through
loans by urban-based private banks. Backed by capital from individual moneylenders in cities, these private banks issued loans to peasants at high or usuri-
ous (*kori*) rates. Through these loans, urban capital fully penetrated rural
areas and became "very active" to the point that banks "pulled out the wealth
of peasants" and turned it over to their investors in the cities.[120] Speculative
capital, as described by Yi, demonstrated the most destabilizing feature of
capitalism—the power of capital to make great changes as it quickly moved in
and out of areas in search of profitable investments. Insensitive to local needs
and culture, capital on behalf of urban interests caused the impoverishment
of peasant lives and the growing unevenness between the rural and the urban.

Yi characterized the unjust / uneven relationship structured by absentee
landownership, peasant consumption habits, and the rural financial and
credit system as exploitative[121]—that is, urban interests and institutions pulled
money from the countryside without any consideration of peasant concerns
and needs. Exploitation meant more than just the loss of valuable wealth; it
also meant that peasants were becoming controlled, and conditioned by urban influences. These forms of exploitation only highlighted what Yi believed

was the most dangerous aspect of capitalism—the ability of a single entity to dominate others through the concentration of money and capital.[122] Yi wrote that those who possessed a large amount of capital could exert pressure on holders of small capital and control and determine their fate through the use of their vast financial resources. This situation ultimately led to the demise of holders of small capital because they were unable to withstand the forces of large capital.[123] Applying this situation to Korea, Yi grew concerned that the growing power of cities would limit the economic and social opportunities of rural inhabitants and command the present and future course of rural society. Because capitalism was spatially reorganizing the center of finance and power on the peninsula and creating an uneven environment full of exploitation, PCRM members grew gravely concerned that the organization's vision of a modern agrarian nation-state would never materialize. To prevent this moment in the present from becoming permanent, Yi called on the PCRM to design a new rural economy that kept peasant wealth (*bu*) in the countryside.[124] He argued that with this wealth, peasants would become "prosperous [*buyu*]"[125] through a productive process in which wealth became the capital for various enterprises that would generate further wealth and financial opportunities. Turning *bu* into *buyu*, this process would arrest current trends, reverse the spatial reorganization of finance and power on the peninsula, and create a prosperous agrarian society.

Following Yi's advice, the PCRM decided to build a comprehensive cooperative system that would be modeled after the Danish cooperative system but would focus on the establishment of credit and consumer cooperatives. Both types of cooperatives would prevent the outflow of rural wealth by reconditioning and strengthening the financial and consumption practices of peasants. In terms of finance, credit cooperatives were considered valuable because the money and capital for these institutions originated from members rather than from outside sources and continuously circulated in the local area where the cooperative operated. Yi added that with local capital funding the credit cooperative, members could draw funds from the cooperative using a low-interest loan and use it to pay off any high-interest loans they had accumulated throughout the years.[126] Through cooperative-based credit, not only would peasants be extricated from outside loans that caused continual impoverishment, but also peasant wealth would remain in the countryside because loan repayments would return to the cooperative rather than to urban financial interests.[127] Leaders advocated for the construction of consumer cooperatives because peasants could purchase necessary equipment and supplies collectively from wholesalers at affordable prices.[128] Yi and Yu Chae-gi even envisioned that by purchasing goods at wholesale prices, a consumer cooperative could open up as a business that sold goods to the general public at lower prices than merchants.

Yi predicted that consumer cooperatives would be so successful that they would dominate the market and cause the "self-destruction" of merchants.[129] PCRM leaders pushed for consumer cooperatives because they offered an alternative procurement process that would lead to much-needed savings and power that would otherwise be lost to manufacturers, merchants, and landlords in cities.

During 1932 and 1933, the movement designed and carried out a plan to build an elaborate cooperative system centered on these two types of cooperatives. Before 1932, the PCRM relied on local Presbyterian churches to start cooperatives. In 1929 and 1930, various churches established only five cooperatives.[130] In 1932, the movement organized a central office for credit cooperatives (*chungang sinyong chohap*) that laid down the ground rules for a credit cooperative, such as membership qualifications and capital requirements, and stressed that "all cooperative members shared equal rights and responsibilities."[131] Although the leadership of the PCRM changed with the arrival of Yi Hun-gu, Yu Chae-gi, and Pae Min-su in 1932 and 1933, it maintained some practices and institutions set up by earlier administrators. The new PCRM leadership, for example, still encouraged local churches to start cooperatives, and this encouragement led to the construction of twelve additional cooperatives by 1937.[132] Just like any company or bank, church-created cooperatives appeared to be economically competitive.[133] In Tudalli, a village on the Taedong River directly southwest of P'yŏngyang, villagers formed a consumer cooperative that purchased tools and products, such as oil and fertilizer, at low prices. By purchasing these goods collectively, they lowered their overall costs and saved money that could be used for other important expenses. In addition to consumer cooperatives, peasants also formed credit cooperatives. Credit cooperatives were developed by members who contributed a portion of their fall crops to a credit fund. Members borrowed money from this fund at low interest rates and used it to improve their productivity. Interest rates were set at a fairly low percentage because the cooperative was formed for the purpose of helping people rather than making a profit. Cooperatives in the village of Tudanri apparently emphasized the need for unity and cooperation. One of the cooperative's organizers stated that it was important to have organizations that fostered unity among a group of people.[134]

To make sure information on cooperatives reached peasants at the local level from the central PCRM office, the PCRM under Pae started an educational campaign in which rural leaders directly taught peasants about cooperatives and expected peasants to apply what they learned to building cooperatives without any direct supervision by PCRM leaders. The PCRM's educational campaign took three forms: (1) official PCRM publications, such as *Nongmin saenghwal* and *Nongch'on t'ongsin* (The Rural News); (2) the High

School Farming Program; and (3) training programs. Published monthly in Korean beginning in 1929, *Nongmin saenghwal* was distributed to churches and peasants for free and delivered to organizations and individual paid subscribers. The journal printed all of the PRCM's arguments for adopting a Danish-style agrarian revival, especially Yi's and Yu's, discussions of the different types of cooperatives, and reasons for developing a cooperative-based rural economy. Published only from March to August 1935, *Nongch'on t'ongsin* was another PCRM publication that outlined ideas on Christianity and cooperatives and summarized PCRM activities, including its lecture campaigns. A total of fourteen thousand copies were printed and distributed for free. Directed by Yi and taught by various rural leaders, the High School Farming School taught young men from the countryside about cooperatives. Based on the Danish folk-school system, the school ran every July and August from 1933 to 1936 at Sungsil University in P'yŏngyang. Students were taught various subjects on farming and agriculture and also learned about the social gospel from Pae Min-su and about cooperatives and rural economics from Yi. Finally, between 1933 and 1937, PCRM leaders conducted short-term training programs on subjects concerning farming, agriculture, and Christianity in villages throughout most of the provinces and in parts of Manchuria. These programs were open to all and attracted large crowds. In all, the PCRM held sixteen programs, each one of which lasted from one to two months. In 1936, for example, a total of 8,500 peasants attended one of the lecture series. Pae Min-su and Yu Chae-gi led these programs, and both spoke on the economic and spiritual value of cooperatives.

The written and spoken words from each of the three apparatuses materialized the PCRM's views and beliefs on cooperatives, which were now available to be absorbed and circulated by peasants. Basic knowledge about the purpose, organization, and value of cooperatives was taught to the younger and older generations of peasants.[135] These apparatuses specifically offered the opportunity to teach new rules that cooperatives needed to follow. First, a cooperative should be well capitalized because only well-capitalized businesses thrived and remained independent under capitalism.[136] Recognizing that raising a large sum of capital at one time would be challenging to peasants, Yi Hun-gu suggested a four-installment capitalization plan. First, peasants should use any initial capital to start the cooperative. Second, all cooperatives should abide by all the commercial laws in Korea. The PCRM presumably stressed this rule out of the belief that following colonial laws would allow cooperatives to avoid any unwanted supervision or forced closures by the state. Third, cooperative businesses should set up branches throughout the peninsula, including Seoul.[137] In all likelihood, Yi mandated this rule because he knew that a cooperative at the local level could flourish and survive only by gaining more business opportunities at the national level. Finally, cooperatives should be required to adopt and implement "the most positive points of modern capitalism."[138] Cooperatives should employ knowledge, techniques, and tools that had proved to achieve economic success for individuals and groups in a capitalist economy. In the view of PRCM leaders, what peasants needed to do in order to operate a successful cooperative was to adopt an entrepreneurial way of thinking in which they stayed attuned to and used the most current trends, practices, and ideas to advance cooperatives and the rural economy.

As peasants read and heard this message about developing an entrepreneurial identity, the various media for the cooperative educational campaign also served as appropriate forums to teach and remind peasants that the true purpose of the cooperative was to enhance and secure the welfare and interests of humans above all else—especially above capital. Leaders promoted a cooperative as an institution that was organized around the principle of developing a collective body to provide mutual support rather than structuring economic activities around the sole purpose of achieving profit and earning money. In Yi's words, it was through a single unified body that helped members care for one another together (hyŏpdong ilch'i / kongjo kongbu) that life (saeng) would be supported and sustained.[139] For Yi and PCRM leaders, supporting life meant more than just protecting the biological and physiological existence of individuals; it also meant continuously developing an ideal subject who was multitalented and exhibited a strong character.

"Supporting life" also referred to enabling a person to experience a deep and vibrant religious life. PCRM leaders publicly explained that cooperatives helped achieve this type of life by establishing a sacred culture through which people experienced God in the everyday. Pae Min-su and Yu Chae-gi stressed that the cooperative movement was not only an economic movement but also a drive to bolster and maintain the spiritual lives of peasants.[140] To them, cooperatives offered an institutional and concrete way to foster a close-knit community in which people formed close bonds.[141] Cooperatives positioned people to overcome their fear of strangers and encouraged them to embrace and love "the other," just as Jesus had done in his ministry. Aiding, having fellowship with, and loving others through daily economic activities were spiritually important because these activities were the means through which humanity encountered God. In his discussions of cooperatives, Yu reminded his audience that love of the other was more important than praying and attending Sunday services because by loving one another, people experienced God's love.[142] Because cooperatives fostered a community bonded through love, he pronounced that cooperatives were the ideal way to realize Jesus' and God's love.[143] Yu's theology consequently provided spiritual justification for making cooperatives the cornerstone of Jesus villages.

Pae Min-su's spiritual justification for the construction of cooperatives stemmed from his belief that they materially manifested the concept of mutual cooperation (*sangho pujo*). Pae expressed to people that God manifested himself in the everyday through human interaction. In particular, God revealed himself to humanity in the active love that existed between people when they worked together and helped one another. Pae saw cooperatives as the ideal spiritual body in which people were connected to one another and to God in the same way in which parts of the human body came together. He declared that as parts of a single unified body, cooperative members were so closely connected that if one person in the group experienced pain or difficulties, other members experienced the same things.[144] What Pai conveyed to peasants was that the construction of a spiritual, organic body would come as a result of developing cooperatives.

The PCRM offered a vision of cooperatives anchoring a rural economy in order to achieve economic stability and a vibrant peasant life full of enriching and transformative experiences in everyday life. PCRM leaders told peasants that these experiences would give way to a sacred, yeoman-style life (*saenghwal*) like that of the Danish farmers. What would enable the concrete realization of these various experiences and the organization's vision of an ideal personhood and identity for peasants was the specific type of labor emphasized, cultivated, and maintained by a cooperative. Within the cooperative, working together as a collective whole in order to achieve various material results served as the concrete means to realize an ideal spiritual, moral, and ethical state of being. PCRM leaders expressed admiration for a cooperative system because cooperatives refused to define work as labor that produced money and capital as the sole goal and instead framed and institutionalized work as labor that unleashed the creative and spontaneous nature of humanity and therefore bridged the gap between the real and the ideal. Yi and other PCRM leaders spread the belief that a Danish-style cooperative system sought to reverse the logic of capitalism by generating and using money and capital to ensure the healthy development of the individual, the social body, and the nation rather than the other way around.

The Ch'ŏndogyo Cooperative Economy

The Ch'ŏndogyo organization, under the leadership of Chosŏn nongminsa, also aggressively organized peasants in its pursuit of a Danish-style agrarian revival through the construction of a cooperative-based economy. The Chosŏn nongminsa cooperative movement, however, distinguished itself from the YMCA and Presbyterian cooperative movements by featuring cooperative farming (*kongdong kyŏngjak*). The organization's overall rural revitalization plan involved all types of cooperatives (*kongsaeng chohap*), such as credit, marketing, and consumer cooperatives, playing central roles in organizing a collective response to meet the challenges of the new capitalist economy. The organization, however, particularly valued cooperative farming because it called for peasants to own land collectively, which would overcome the increasingly severe problem of land tenancy and ownership. By most accounts, severe economic conditions for peasants due to the effects of the Great Depression led to a sharp rise in tenancy rates during the early 1930s, primarily because of the loss of land by owner-cultivator peasants, or those who possessed their own land, due to rising debt. From 1929 to 1932, the percentage of land cultivated by tenants increased to more than half of all farming households. By 1932, the number of nonowning peasant tenants increased from 37.7 percent to 53.8 percent. The problem of tenancy became so severe that "two-thirds of all paddy land and half of all upland was farmed by a tenant rather than an owner."[145] Numerous reports on rural affairs revealed that tenants of all kinds constituted 81.9 percent of rural cultivators in Korea.[146] If they failed as tenant farmers, they would be forced to sell their labor and become part of the working class in Korea, Japan, and other parts of the Japanese empire.

Chosŏn nongminsa leaders proposed a cooperative farming program to reverse this dangerous trend that was leading to the further proletarianization of peasants. Chosŏn nongminsa discourse on cooperative farming first appeared during the late 1920s.[147] Originally, plans for cooperative farming called for three to seven families to purchase land and become a single unit of labor, production, and consumption.[148] Cooperative members were expected to perform all duties on the farm collectively, including harvesting agricultural goods and selling them on the market. Although children under eighteen and those older than sixty were exempted from these duties, they still needed to be productive by attending school (children) or performing side jobs at home (elderly).[149] Cooperative farming plans also required members to follow several rules, including manufacturing their own fertilizer and making sure that all agricultural production on the farm was closely controlled and supervised. Chosŏn nongminsa leaders expected concrete, positive results for peasants if they followed these rules.[150] They specifically promised the birth of a prosperous farm through which peasants would become well-rounded farmers who enjoyed material success. Rules aside, leaders strongly believed that labor power would become more powerful and effective through the collective organization of peasant labor and resources—a key factor for achieving a model agriculture-based life.

Between 1931 and 1933, local Chosŏn nongminsa branches took it on themselves to design and build cooperative farming programs in various rural communities.[151] In December 1932, cooperative cultivation began to be trans-

lated into official Chosŏn nongminsa policy when Ch'ŏndogyo officials decided
to make cooperative farming the centerpiece of their drive to build new
Ch'ŏndogyo autonomous villages. In April 1933, Chosŏn nongminsa decided
to implement a cooperative farming program in Ch'ŏndogyo-controlled villages throughout the peninsula.[152] Officially, Chosŏn nongminsa called for
the program to build cooperative cultivation associations (*kongjakkye*, CCAs).
The CCAs embodied the overall ideology of cooperative farming and carried
out several of its principles.[153]

The CCA, according to the rural leader Yu Ho, would become a system
under which a person would transition from a current livelihood full of "deficiencies" to a "new, current, and improved" life.[154] To achieve this result, the
principle of group work based on mutual cooperation anchored and powered
the CCA. In order to maintain an environment of mutual cooperation, there
were several rules that leaders suggested should be applied to the CCA. Yu, for
example, proposed that a CCA be made up of five or more families, which
roughly corresponded to the number proposed originally by leaders who designed cooperative farming programs.[155] Others suggested that the CCA be
organized in a way to limit "failing attitudes" and maximize labor time.[156] In
April 1933, the organization issued the "Rules on Cooperative Cultivation Association" ("Kongjakkye kyuyak"), which outlined the official rules and
directions for building a CCA.[157] According to the document, the primary
objective of the CCA was for "Ch'ŏndogyo followers to be devoted to collaborative production and work in order to realize the spirit of mutual cooperation and raise the economic condition" of association members. As a single
unit, members should purchase land, cultivate the land cooperatively, and
engage in joint production and labor. Moreover, all labor, resources, and
goods should come from the CCA. Chosŏn nongminsa envisioned that
through a system based on mutual cooperation, the CCA would turn into a
community with organic connections like a family as its members labored,
consumed, and partook in leisure activities together. Over time, it hoped that
connections among members would become naturalized, which would therefore preserve the communal power structure that would give peasants a powerful form of agency to deal with capitalism.

To help them develop and carry out a successful CCA program, Chosŏn
nongminsa leaders had at their disposal the ideas and practices that had already
been tried out and tested in the Chosŏn nongminsa cooperative program (*kongsaeng chohap*). Designed along the lines of the Danish cooperative system, the
organization's cooperative program featured three types of cooperatives: marketing, consumer, and credit. Between 1931 and 1933, Chosŏn nongminsa leaders
built an elaborate cooperative system in the northern part of Korea by traveling
to villages and teaching peasants various aspects of cooperatives, such as the

history of cooperatives, the meaning and purpose of cooperatives, modern farming techniques, how to build an efficient credit system, and how to market and sell their harvested goods or manufactured goods made in their homes.[158] Chosŏn nongminsa started several regional organizations to coordinate local cooperative activities, such as the Union of the Peasant Cooperative System for the Kwansŏ Region (Nongmin kongsaeng chohap kwansŏ yŏnhap, 1931), which coordinated cooperative movements in P'yŏng'an Province and Hwanghae Province and the Organization of the P'yŏng'an Province Peasant Cooperative System (P'yŏng'an nongmin kongsaeng chohap undong chahyŏp ŭi hoe, 1932), which managed cooperative activities in areas around the city of P'yŏngyang by providing a forum to discuss theories and policies concerning cooperatives.[159] These efforts by the organization resulted in the construction of close to 180 cooperatives with 50,000 members and a total capitalization of 300,000 won.

Chosŏn nongminsa expected the cooperative and CCA programs to be at the forefront of building a Denmark-like agrarian nation-state in Korea. Chosŏn nongminsa leaders, however, clearly pointed out that there were differences between the two programs despite their shared spirit and purpose. Sŭng Kwan-ha wrote that the membership requirements distinguished the cooperative program from a CCA.[160] For example, Chosŏn nongminsa officials set up cooperatives in several non-Ch'ŏndogyo villages, while Ch'ŏndogyo followers were the only participants in the CCA program. Landownership further demarcated the difference between the programs in that CCA members were called on to own land collectively, while peasants were never required to own land as a condition of starting or joining a cooperative. To a certain extent, the cooperative program faced more potential problems than the CCA program because of its different membership requirements. Under the cooperative system, for instance, a peasant's non-Ch'ŏndogyo background and ties to a landowner limited the organization's influence and power over cooperative members. Unsurprisingly, Chosŏn nongminsa and Ch'ŏndogyo leaders pushed for the conversion of cooperatives into CCAs.[161] The CCA represented the ideal and most comprehensive cooperative that incorporated valuable instruments and parts from each type of cooperative. Securing every need of the peasant, especially landownership, it was projected to overcome all peasant deficiencies. Chosŏn nongminsa valued both programs because they would at least lay the foundations for cooperative economics, but the organization still highlighted the differences in order to persuade peasants to start a CCA.[162]

Differences aside, both programs shared the most important similarity of every type of Danish-style cooperative: a communal governing structure.[163] "Kongjakkye kyuyak" promoted this type of governance by requiring members of a CCA to make decisions collectively during a general assembly. Through a common voting system, for example, members elected an executive board consisting of a leader and a secretary. Because these officers held the responsibility of overseeing the CCA and performing intermediary duties between members and Chosŏn nongminsa, such as writing CCA activity reports and sending them to district and central offices, members carefully voted for a new leader every three years, and a new secretary was chosen every year. In addition to voting on the leadership, members voted on how much labor and materials were required in the association.[164] The assembly period also served as an occasion when members openly expressed grievances, discussed issues concerning the CCA, and debated the present and future direction of the association. In this capacity, the general assembly represented a public forum for rational discourse that would allow for informed decisions. Hence, by giving equal standing to all, the CCA endorsed a transparent process of debate and voting that upheld individual rights and strengthened communal bonds.

Directing CCAs to make important decisions and determine their own paths of development strongly suggests that the central office of Chosŏn nongminsa designed a local CCA to be self-sufficient and autonomous. A local CCA was overseen by a district CCA office, which in turn was under the control of the central Chosŏn nongminsa office. Local CCA branches, according to "Kongjakkye kyuyak," were ordered to report their activities and decisions to a district office. Moreover, a local CCA required approval from the district office to change any details or rules in "Kongjakkye kyuyak." Despite these regulations, the local CCA still held the power to plan and decide the details of how to purchase land, cultivate its land, and carry out cooperative production. These details, "Kongjakkye kyuyak" stated, should be decided in the general assembly and made "according to the conditions and circumstances of the area."[165] A May 1934 article about the CCA added that there would be different types of CCAs because each would develop according to the conditions of the area in which it was based. Depending on the area, a CCA, for example, could engage in sericulture or raise garlic and different types of fruits and beans.[166] In general, rural leaders argued that decisions about the constitution and direction of the CCA should be based on what was considered suitable for lives of the CCA members and the conditions of the area where they lived.

Chosŏn nongminsa believed that members of CCAs possessed the local knowledge about the needs of the community to craft an appropriate program. Moreover, it recognized that a CCA could be maintained over time only if members made their own decisions and invested in the program. Chosŏn nongminsa understood the importance of taking place into consideration in making decisions and plans and decided to give local CCAs enough space to construct their own programs. Hence the request that a local branch report its decisions and activities to higher authorities seemed to be less about the center micromanaging and needing to control the local CCA and more about the need to coordinate activities among branches. As long as branches were adhering to the purpose and spirit of the CCA, it appeared the district and central offices gave the local branches great autonomy.

The overall governing structure of the relationship between a local CCA branch and higher offices showed that Chosŏn nongminsa wanted to avert and avoid the disastrous results of collectivization farming in the Soviet Union. From 1929 to 1933, Soviet Union authorities under the leadership of Joseph Stalin initiated a collectivization farming program (*kolkhoz*) that was quite similar to the Chosŏn nongminsa CCA program in that it called for a group of peasants to cultivate collectively a large piece of land and jointly make decisions to improve collectivized farming. However, unlike the Chosŏn nongminsa CCA, Soviet authorities promoted collectivization not only as a way to maintain food security, especially after the Grain Crisis of 1928, but also as a means for the central state to control the countryside tightly and connect peasants to the proletariat mission of achieving communism. Connecting the local to the center would modernize the backward farming life of peasants and subject them to a new level of surveillance and discipline that would rid the countryside of any capitalist influences.[167] By most accounts, a top-down collectivization program led to devastating results for peasants with increasing poverty, famine, and political terror.[168]

In contrast to collectivization in the Soviet Union, which represented an ideological and political process in which the center attempted to control the local, the Chosŏn nongminsa CCA movement endorsed local autonomy. Because Chosŏn nongminsa started its collective farming movement in 1933, after the disastrous results of collectivization in the Soviet Union became well known throughout the world, its leaders had the opportunity to learn from the Soviet Union's collective-farming debacle and craft an alternative plan for collective farming that valued local knowledge, self-sufficiency, and independence.[169] The Chosŏn nongminsa CCA movement appeared to be moving away from the prevailing trend in the world of high modernism and its sweeping vision of implementing a program of development and progress that was based on modern knowledge and dismissed local knowledge. Seeking modernity while respecting the local, Chosŏn nongminsa leaders arranged for a healthy partnership between the center and CCAs in order to build vibrant CCAs that would join with other cooperatives in order to establish a cooperative system that would anchor the revival of the countryside.

Viewing itself as an institution that would help rather than lead, the central Chosŏn nongminsa office provided various resources that were difficult for a local CCA to obtain alone. Chosŏn nongminsa leaders, for example, supported the attempts of local CCAs to acquire land by helping transfer land to peasants from the organization or from wealthy officials in the organization.[170] As a way to transfer more land to CCAs, Chosŏn nongminsa formed the Organization of Rural Work (Nongch'on saŏp tanch'e) in April 1936. This institution served as a landholding company that both loaned peasants money to purchase land and directly bought land that would be turned over to peasants.[171] The Chosŏn nongminsa organization appeared to contradict its original stance on land reform through the Nongch'on saŏp tanch'e. From its beginning, Chosŏn nongminsa and the overall Ch'ŏndogyo organization called for the nationalization of land, which would be owned and regulated by the state.[172] Under this plan, land would then be distributed to families. By buying land from the real-estate market or loaning money to peasants so they could buy land and become landowners, the organization acknowledged and legitimized the existing land system of private property. Although this went against its original land-reform plan, the organization justified its position by pointing to the present circumstances of the 1930s. Leaders of Chosŏn nongminsa decided that it was important to help peasants now rather than wait for fundamental land reforms by the colonial state.

Alongside providing assistance in the acquisition of land, the central office also supported CCAs in various ways, such as sending agricultural experts and Chosŏn nongminsa leaders who taught peasants the latest knowledge on farming and introduced them to the newest technological innovations. With this assistance from the center and work by local members, peasants started and maintained nearly thirty cooperative farms between 1931 and 1945.[173] The average size of communal farms ranged from 400 *pyŏng* (0.3 acres) to 14,000 *pyŏng* (11 acres).[174] A large majority of CCAs followed the directives outlined in "Kongjakkye kyuyak." In the regions of Dukch'ŏn-gun of South P'yŏng'an Province and Kusŏng-gun of North P'yŏng'an Province, for example, CCAs adopted several of the principles featured in "Kongjakkye kyuyak." First, the article of association for the Dukch'ŏn-gun and Kusŏng-gun CCAs contained the rule of democratically electing officers to lead the CCA, which suggests that they also believed in holding open meetings to talk about issues and concerns.[175] Second, both articles of association required members of the CCA to set up a general capital fund for the CCA that presumably was intended to serve as a credit union.[176] Specifically, the Dukch'ŏn-gun CCA article of association mandated that profits should be redistributed to CCA members.

What local CCAs primarily adopted from "Kongjakkye kyuyak" was the overall principle that the CCA should be a self-sufficient, successful economic institution that promoted cooperation. Almost every rule in the articles of association of local CCAs embodied the belief that everything, including work and consumption, must be performed cooperatively. The rules structured communal farming and oriented individuals in ways that demanded that people work together in order to ensure the survival of the CCA. A member who disregarded or failed to fulfill his or her duties would be punished.[177] The rules intended to make members of a CCA responsible for one another's lives and realize the importance of community. To promote financial success, local articles of association required members to know that the CCA was organized to make a profit and to become precise and exact in their economic activities and financial dealings. The Dukch'ŏn-gun articles of association declared that "it planned to make an economic profit." Moreover, it demanded that members keep account of everything and become fiscally responsible.[178] With these rules, local CCAs distanced themselves from traditional communal organizations, like *kye*s and *ture*,[179] and became associations that aimed to deal with present conditions and challenges through the development of a healthy social and financial body that would continually innovate, grow economically, and improve living standards under capitalism.

Given the right to design and carry out the particularities of a program, several CCAs charted their own courses of development that took the local environment into account. Local CCAs, for example, determined which types of crops and plants to raise and harvest on the basis of environmental conditions of the area. The Kowŏn area of South Hamgyŏng Province, which was an agriculturally rich area in northern Korea, featured several CCAs that raised a variety of crops, such as water chestnuts, beans, red beans, and millet, which were indigenous to the area.[180] Alongside local CCAs, the central office of Chosŏn nongminsa deployed local knowledge in coordinating where to locate and establish CCAs. The majority of the CCAs were located in North P'yŏng'an Province, South P'yŏng'an Province, and South Hamgyŏng Province, which were not only the strongholds of the Ch'ŏndogyo party but also, more important, areas where there were few conflicts between landlords and peasant tenants.[181] The rate of tenancy was lower in northern Korea than in the south. With fewer problems and conflicts over land than in the south, areas in the north became fertile grounds to embark on ambitious projects in order to revolutionize ways of working and living.

Transforming peasant lives through the CCA was vital for economic reasons, but Chosŏn nongminsa also expected the CCA to foster a new spiritually based personhood. Leaders were confident that CCAs, as well as all cooperatives, would elevate the ethical, moral, and, most important, spiritual lives of peasants and transform them into complete and whole persons. CCA branches frequently wrote that both programs were never created with the sole intention of allowing peasants to make a greater profit from their cooperative work.[182] Instead, CCAs and cooperatives also served as ideal institutions to cultivate people's religious lives. Ch'ŏndogyo had long held the belief, articulated by Yi Ton-hwa, that people helping one another and forming a community helped create an environment in which people were able to realize their divine nature in the everyday. To Chosŏn nongminsa leaders, it was natural to start building cooperative farms and cooperatives because they promoted mutual cooperation and fostered social solidarity. A cooperative farm, according to Chosŏn nongminsa documents, represented an economic system that created and cultivated the "spirit of mutual cooperation."[183] Alongside cooperative farms, cooperatives were also seen as institutions that created strong communities.[184] Chosŏn nongminsa officials believed that both cooperative farms and cooperatives moved peasants to depend on and care for one another.

Structuring people's daily lives in a way in which work and leisure centered on interacting and helping the "other," cooperatives fundamentally served as institutions that worked to realize the spiritual goal of collective life (*tonggwi ilch'e*). They provided the grounds through which an organic unity formed among cooperative members. Connected to one another like a family, cooperative members moved and operated together as one entity rather than acting as self-interested individuals. Chosŏn nongminsa leaders maintained that through cooperatives, peasants could experience a total transformation in every aspect of their lives. Yu Ho strongly expressed the belief in the transformative power of cooperatives when he wrote that through cooperatives

> [individuals] would lose their fragmented life and become a whole human. They would lose their individualistic life and gain a cooperative, collective life. They would lose their finite life and gain an eternal life. They would go from a limited to a universal life. They would move from a dependent to an independent life. They would go from a copied to an original life. They would go from an uncreative to a creative life.[185]

What cooperative farms and cooperatives did for peasants was to create an economic and social culture that would help turn peasants into new, authentic human beings who manifested the characteristics of the divine force of Hanŭllim, or Ultimate Reality. Through various types of cooperative projects, peasants would become part of a new temporality in which they were linked to eternal spiritual forces. Market forces had distanced them from the spiritually divine, but cooperative projects now provided them with the opportunity to be one with the ideal time and space described by Ch'ŏndogyo doctrine.

Chosŏn nongminsa believed that it could realize its utopian vision of a new nation, society, and personhood by uniting peasants institutionally and materially through cooperative labor. Peasants were already familiar with communal forms of labor because of a long history of communal farming in Korea. During the Chosŏn period, for example, intellectuals and government officials had touted the merits and benefits of the well-field system that had originated in China, under which peasants worked together on a neighbor's farm during times of need and harvest time. Cooperative cultivation's spirit of mutual assistance certainly connected it to this history of communal farming. The Chosŏn nongminsa's cooperative cultivation program, however, diverged by calling for members to be constituted as a single unit that owned and worked on a single piece of land rather than working on separate plots of land and coming together only in order to farm a communal plot. Cooperative cultivation further distinguished itself from past examples of communal farming by its purpose of negotiating the challenges and demands of a capitalist economy. The system of cooperative cultivation geared peasants toward achieving stability and prosperity under capitalism. This system would equip peasants with the knowledge, practices, tools, and resources to raise and market agricultural goods efficiently. According to Kim Hwal-san, cooperative cultivation should transform farming into a "rational process" (hamnihwa) for peasants in which their life and wealth would be safeguarded and protected.[186] It would be a process that would transform peasants into intelligent, well-organized, and productive farmers who were expected to adjust to the changing environment by thinking and acting in ways appropriate to the new economy.

Each organization embarked on different paths to achieve a Danish-style cooperative system on the peninsula, but the belief that Korea's future rested on the Danish agricultural model tied the YMCA, Presbyterian, and Ch'ŏndogyo rural movements together. Among the programs that led to an agrarian revival in Denmark, its cooperative experience supplied the three organizations with a concrete plan for socioeconomic development that would allow Korea to meet the challenges of capitalism, avoid becoming an industrial capitalism-based society, and become a modern, agriculture-based nation-state. Their plans for the reconstruction of peasant lives and the agrarian economy through cooperatives took into consideration and greatly valued the particularities of place. They believed in transforming and enhancing peasant life through a process of change, but they maintained that this process should respect and incorporate local knowledge and practices. Including contemporary knowledge on Danish cooperatives and local knowledge in their designs of a cooperative system, the movements constructed a socioeconomic system that was expected to modify local environments in ways that set up a new framework that was appropriate to place and from which peasants could effectively negotiate economic processes that were shaped by the forces of capitalism from the outside. Rather than reject capitalism outright and forge an entirely different economic system, these cooperative systems abided by the logic of capitalism. This decision exposed the movements to criticisms that they attacked only the symptoms of capitalism and never offered a true alternative system that resolved the core problems of production, exchange, and consumption under capitalism. But at a time when a significant number of Korean intellectuals and nationalists spoke highly of capitalism's value to strengthen the nation without discussing its destructive consequences for society, the movements still provided the needed criticism of this economic system and designed a plan that sought to deal immediately with the economic, social, and spiritual crises caused by capitalism.

What each of the movements achieved with their drives to build a new cooperative system was the laying of a foundation for a new, unified national body. Throughout the 1920s and 1930s, social conflicts that resulted from capitalist developments caused extreme divisions in society. Nationalist movements continuously faced the challenge of how to unify Koreans against Japanese colonialism under an economy that promoted structural inequality through a degrading value system, the uneven distribution of resources and power, and exploitation. In this environment, the ideas, practices, and institutions of the cooperative systems became valuable means to unify people around a common goal and thus repair fractured social relationships. By checking the social ills of capitalism through a community of shared purposes, cooperatives allowed for the possibility of a new economy that fostered a level of evenness from which a cohesive national community could form. The very possibility of realizing this type of political community through these socioeconomic reforms consequently caused the colonial state to maintain close surveillance of the movements.

For the three rural movements, a new cooperative-based economy would ensure the peasant as the foundation of this national community by preventing peasant labor, as a form of practice, from becoming commodified, causing alienation, and serving solely as the means to sustain daily existence. All three religious organizations envisioned cooperatives as mechanisms that would transform labor into a medium that allowed individuals to cultivate their moral and ethical sides and uncover their sacred nature. In a period when an increasing number of peasants were forced to become wage laborers and experience the commodification of labor, YMCA, PCRM, and Chosŏn nongminsa leaders stressed that building a cooperative-based economy was the most attractive option to help peasants overcome economic strife and realize an ideal state of being. A cooperative system would make sure that farming would continue to be a form of labor that not only ensured material security but also elevated and expanded people's identities and subjectivities. These rural leaders put their confidence in cooperatives as the means to reconstitute labor as a form of collective practice that would prevent a dreary and estranged life and would instead communally encourage creativity and authenticity in the countryside and allow peasants to become complete and whole.

6

Constructing National Consciousness

EDUCATING AND DISCIPLINING PEASANTS' MINDS

Beginning in 1910, the Japanese colonial government had already introduced a modern educational system in Korea that operated with the goals of extinguishing the Korean national identity and molding Koreans into loyal citizens of the Japanese empire. Sekiya Teizaburo, the education director in the colonial government, declared that "the fundamental principle of Korean education, stated in a word, is to bring up the Koreans as citizens or subjects of the Japanese empire. . . . The Korean education aims to foster a loyal and patriotic spirit in the minds of the Korean pupils. The laws and instructions concerning education have no other purpose than this." Despite cultural differences between Koreans and Japanese, Sekiya confidently declared that Koreans would ultimately become Japanese through education.[1] Envisioning education as an ideological state apparatus that would reshape the colonial subject's ethnic identity, the government devoted substantial resources to the educational system.

Despite the construction of a modern educational system, geography limited the reach and influence of this new system. Because schools were mostly located in urban areas, people living in rural areas had few opportunities to enjoy a modern education. In his study of colonial Korea, Andrew Grajdanzev pointed out that only 12,331 students from the countryside enrolled in colonial schools, despite the fact that over 15 million people lived in rural areas.[2] The reach of the colonial educational system was further limited by the fact that schools taught only young men and women and therefore were unable to influence the older generation of Koreans. This educational vacuum created an opportunity for leftists and bourgeois nationalists to inaugurate their own educational programs. Movements by various groups ranging from the Red Peasant Union to *Tonga ilbo* not only carried out literacy programs but also introduced peasants to contemporary social and economic theories and technical information on farming that would develop new forms of consciousness and agency.

Protestant Christian groups and Ch'ŏndogyo have had a long history of operating schools in the countryside since the late nineteenth century. Having

191

already constructed an elaborate educational system that rivaled the colonial government's string of schools, Protestant Christian and Ch'ŏndogyo leaders originally considered their schools as institutions through which Koreans would develop their spiritual lives. Although the underlying mission of these religion-based educational systems was to promote a vigorous spiritual life, schools also provided technical, vocational, and scientific education. In line with "civilization and enlightenment" discourse, these three areas of education emphasized industrialization. Religion-based institutions offered curricula that instructed Koreans on how to become successful laborers and entrepreneurs in an industry-based society. What added to the industrial dimension of these curriculums was the fact that these schools were mostly located in cities.

When the YMCA, the Presbyterian Church, and Ch'ŏndogyo (Chosŏn nongminsa) started their rural campaigns, they went against this prevailing trend in education by not only bringing educational programs to the countryside but also centering them on the goal of turning peasants into modern farmers who would enjoy an idyllic pastoral life. For them, education should do more than just provide literacy skills and expose people to religious ideas. It should also open people to a wealth of knowledge about practical matters, politics, economics, and society. Each of the three groups believed that with this type of education, peasants would be able to view the world as a place that could be concretely understood and changed; they predicted that peasants would acquire a new consciousness (ŭisik) through which they would make a connection between their own lived experiences and overall conditions in society. In doing so, peasants would realize that they held the power to improve their own lives. The three rural movements expected this consciousness to empower peasants to enhance their existing conditions in ways that preserved their agrarian heritage but still allowed for innovative diversity that would create new possibilities for living and working. Leaders of the three rural movements envisioned education serving as the mental counterpart to cooperatives, which structured peasant bodies, in achieving the agrarian-spiritual ideal by disciplining the minds of peasants.

The three rural movements designed their educational programs to provide peasants contemporary knowledge and skills that would enable them to thrive, but the programs also served to condition peasants ideologically to believe that developing agriculture and a pastoral life was the right course for the Korean nation-state. From the start of their rural campaigns, each of the movements faced a growing reality where a vast number of peasants were willingly or unwillingly leaving farming for what they believed would be a more secure and prosperous life as laborers in factories or business figures in cities. Using various programs, journals, and newsletters, the movements stressed the importance of peasants in the history of the Korean nation and how they were the front line of creating a new and powerful nation-state anchored in religion and agriculture, with the hope of motivating peasants to stay in the countryside and take part in their rural campaigns.

All three educational campaigns specifically sought to achieve this effect on the growing and restless youth population who had started to reject the customs and ideas of the past and instead sought meaning and significance in the present and future. Korean youths were embracing "modern" knowledge and practices that would help them make sense of and deal with the larger world that was full of changes. James Fisher, an American missionary, accurately described youths during the 1920 as "frank, fearless, and honest" figures who "are making life adjustments which are happier and more satisfying to themselves and others, than the kind of lives that were led by their parents."[3] Young Koreans were so active in trying to discover alternative ways to live and think that many students grew distant and detached from Korean culture.[4] In place of established Korean ideas and practices, young Koreans gladly welcomed ideas and customs from the outside to help them develop new forms of subjectivity.

The behavior of youths greatly alarmed the older generation of nationalist leaders, who envisioned them adopting traditions and becoming the future transmitters of the Korean identity in a unified, independent nation. Without the youth who would physically represent the Korean nation, nationalist figures feared that the nation could not survive in the future. Leaders of the three religious rural movements especially grew alarmed over the recent developments among the youth population because young people in the countryside were beginning to abandon everything associated with the past, including farming and agriculture. Observers of rural developments reported that restless young men and women left villages and traveled to cities in Korea, Manchuria, and Japan in pursuit of new adventures. Seeing no future in agricultural labor, the rural youth grew attracted to the spectacle of the urban space where opportunities existed to reinvent their identities through new forms of work and cultural experiences. To leaders of the YMCA, Presbyterian, and Ch'ŏndogyo rural movements, the absence of young men and women jeopardized their plans to build a powerful agrarian society because without youths, who served to bridge the age gap between adults and the future, farming and Korea's agricultural heritage and identity would be lost.

These problems of the young people were part of a trend that all societies experienced as they underwent a process of capitalist modernization. Franco Moretti points out that in traditional societies, youth as a category was defined as "not yet being an adult." Young men and women were expected to live a "prescribed" life in which they would repeat the same type of life experienced by their parents and ancestors. Because capitalism was breaking down social hierarchy systems, introducing diverse forms of work, and promoting urbanization, the "socialization of 'old' youth" was no longer sustainable as young people set off to explore and experience this new social space. Capitalism gave young women and men new forms of mobility and opportunities for experiences through which they discovered alternatives to their "prescribed youth," which many came to reject. Challenging the established by seeking and embracing the new, young people thus accentuated "modernity's dynamism and instability."[5] Nationalist movements throughout the world in the 1920s and 1930s appreciated the dynamic nature of youths but worried that their behavior could dramatically unsettle society and threaten forms of continuity that were necessary for the survival of the nation-state. Programs and movements were established to control young people and harness their energy to achieve the ideal national community. The YMCA, Presbyterian, and Ch'ŏndogyo rural movements also carried out rural youth programs that physically, mentally, and spiritually disciplined their bodies and minds with the intention of conditioning them to stay in the countryside. These movements constructed special leadership programs to domesticate modernity by molding rural youths into the vanguard who would lead the drive to reconstruct rural Korea.

Literacy and Literature

All three movements deemed it vital that peasants learn how to read and write in order for them to become independent farmers. Only the YMCA and Chosŏn nongminsa, however, devoted resources to creating stand-alone literacy programs in villages, called "night schools" and "peasant schools," respectively; the Presbyterian movement incorporated its literacy program into its other educational programs. The literacy programs of the YMCA and Chosŏn nongminsa ran at roughly the same time—October to March (YMCA) and November to February (Chosŏn nongminsa)—because it was the off season for farming. Starting in 1926, Chosŏn nongminsa concentrated the majority of its peasant schools in P'yŏngyang and Hamgyŏng Provinces, which were close to P'yŏngyang, a Ch'ŏndogyo stronghold. With the help of youths and volunteer teachers, the YMCA had already constructed night-school programs in 108 villages throughout the peninsula with a total enrollment of 5,000 people by 1926.[6] From 1929 to 1935, the number of night schools increased, with over 227 villages serving as sites of YMCA night schools and 10,000 to 15,000 people attending one of them.[7]

The YMCA and Chosŏn nongminsa literacy programs focused on teaching basic reading and writing skills, but they also introduced a variety of information to peasants. Chosŏn nongminsa leaders, for example, used peasant schools to indoctrinate peasants ideologically with "proper ideals and beliefs," specifically the idea of loving rural life.[8] The titles of the textbooks used in their classes show that Chosŏn nongminsa leaders gave lessons on fertilizer, cooperatives, the history of Korea, and Korea's international affairs.[9] In a typical YMCA night-school class, male and female peasants learned math, read the Bible, and studied Korean history.[10] Teaching students how to read and write was itself a process through which students learned about cooperatives and modern farming skills, since they used reading and writing texts that discussed "how to live together, chicken raising, pig raising, horticulture, sanitation [and] disease prevention."[11] To complement peasants' knowledge of farming, outside experts lectured once or twice a week on various topics, such as world events, the "rural problem," hygiene, and infant raising.[12] Early in the night-school program, there were even some instances of students being shown a slide show depicting European and American farming.[13] YMCA leaders later added a new component to their night-school program that formalized the teaching of various subjects. Called the "Triangular Club" (Samgak non'guhoe), its curriculum stressed the value of literacy skills and expanding one's knowledge and labor.[14] At the 120 Triangular Clubs, peasants learned how to read and write and heard lectures on the value of work, hygiene, and agricultural techniques.

The YMCA considered its literacy program one of its most important projects to equip peasants with the resources to deal with their economic situation. According to Hong Pyŏng-sŏn, the head of the YMCA rural movement, if someone traveled to a Korean village, he would find that on average only twenty out of the three hundred households had family members who knew how to read and write.[15] Hong found this situation problematic because illiteracy prevented peasants from directly accessing knowledge and information that would improve their lives. Without knowing how to read and write, Hong believed, peasants could not develop an overall critical consciousness that would enable them to figure out solutions to their problems.[16] In developing a critical consciousness, YMCA leaders specifically set out to cultivate a collective consciousness among peasants by having students not only listen to lectures but also partake in small group discussions where they read various types of materials and shared personal stories and opinions about their lives.[17] As people discussed and debated issues together, Hong hoped that they would learn from one another and expand their ideas and knowledge collectively. He believed that communicating and exchanging personal experiences would lead to the development of a collective consciousness where people shared common feelings and passions (hyŏpdong kangchŏm).[18] In short, Hong wrote that through group interactions and studying ideologies and texts, people would grow more powerful intellectually and more "conscious of things" as a single group.[19] In many ways, Hong's line of thinking echoed the ideas of V. N.

Volosinov, who wrote that "consciousness took shape and being in the material signs created by an organized group in the process of social interaction."[20] Creating this collective consciousness was important for Hong because it would help maintain unity and sustain a community where people worked together to change their surroundings.

The YMCA and Chosŏn nongminsa literacy programs were not only about teaching peasants the practical skills of reading and writing. They were also about giving peasants new means to interpret and negotiate the events and developments in their lives. In particular, reading and writing served as media through which peasants as subjects could acquire signs and symbols that would give appropriate meaning and sense to the object or material reality. Because literacy skills afforded a new process for thinking about and interacting with reality, it was imperative that the organizations use forms of literature that would provide appropriate language to interpret the world. The YMCA and Chosŏn nongminsa therefore designed, distributed, and employed their own textbooks that embodied their ideologies and spiritual beliefs. Their textbooks included not only the traditional books that were used for a specific curriculum but also monthly journals on rural economics, society, and life. Like the YMCA and Chosŏn nongminsa, the Presbyterian rural movement also published journals on rural life that it used in its various educational programs. Although all three groups published journals with the purpose of spreading ideas and news about their movements among their members, leaders, and the public, the journals also educated peasants on how to create a stable and dynamic pastoral life that was viable. Each issue of the journals followed a similar pattern of using a mixed script of Korean and *hanja* (Chinese characters); publishing an array of articles on religion, agriculture, and modernity that spoke of the value of enjoying everyday life in the present, the importance of social activism, and the need to build a modern society based on farming and agriculture; introducing Danish reforms and history and contemporary farming knowledge and technology; presenting historical lessons and fictional stories that emphasized the value of peasants; and providing information on the overall rural movements, especially on events and development in other villages.

Publishing the monthly journal *Ch'ŏngnyŏn* (The Young Korean) beginning in 1921, YMCA leaders, for example, wrote about the state of Korean culture and politics and the Korean economy and introduced Marxist philosophy, social gospel theology, and general theories on literature and culture that were popular in the West and Japan.[21] Intended to be read by intellectuals, young men and women in YMCA programs, and YMCA and YWCA leaders, *Ch'ŏngnyŏn* became a forum through which YMCA members acquired and debated valuable information that would help them become effective teachers to peasants. The journal, in a sense, worked as a mode for learning what was new and a structure through which leaders and members exchanged ideas and communicated with one another.

While *Ch'ŏngnyŏn* functioned as a tool for those working in the YMCA, those working and living in the countryside became the target audience of the journal *Nongch'on ch'ŏngnyŏn* (The Rural Youth). Edited by Hong, this journal mostly served as the primary textbook used to educate peasants, and therefore the majority of articles in the journal were written in Korean rather than in Chinese characters. As an accessible text for peasants, *Nongch'on ch'ŏngnyŏn* published different types of articles with the intention of cultivating the multiple sides of peasants and encouraging them to work together to change their present predicaments. Through the journal, YMCA rural leaders first informed peasants on how to compete in a capitalist economy through articles on cooperatives and modern farming techniques and through vocabulary sections where peasants could learn basic agricultural and cooperative terms, such as "farming" (*nongŏp*), "landlord" (*chiju*), "tenant" (*sojak*), "cooperative farming" (*kongdong kyŏngjak*), and "cooperatives" (*hyŏpdong chohap*).[22] Defining words such as "landlord," "tenant," and "rent" presumably was a way to help peasants grow more conscious of the capitalist logic used by Korean and Japanese landlords to structure their relationship with peasants.[23] We may assume that YMCA leaders saw the acquisition of a new economic language as an important step toward leveling the power relationship between peasants and landlords and merchants. The second type of articles in the journal discussed the tendencies and characteristics of the "modern" and their effect on religion in order to educate peasants on how to live spiritual and ethical lives.[24] Finally, by publishing historical writings on subjects such as the history of the Chosŏn dynasty and rural folktales, the YMCA attempted to develop a historical memory that linked peasants to their past.[25] Arguably, the organization published historical studies and stories on rural life and agriculture in the hope that peasants would realize that they were part of a long agricultural tradition that characterized the Korean nation. YMCA leaders wished that by reading these stories, peasants would become confident about their occupation and see their work not just as labor but also as an essential element in maintaining the nation's ethnic identity. Alongside several books on cooperative economics and Denmark that Hong and Helen Kim wrote, such as *Chŏngmal kwa Chŏngmal nongmin* (Denmark and Her Farmers; Hong), *Nongch'on hyŏpdong chohap kwa chojikpŏp* (Cooperatives: Organization and Methods; Hong), and *Chŏngmalin ŭi kyŏngje puhŭngron* (The Danish Rehabilitation; Kim), YMCA leaders expected peasants to read *Ch'ŏngnyŏn* and *Nongch'on ch'ŏngnyŏn* in order to gain access to a whole new level of conceptualizing and structuring their reality.

To disseminate its interpretations of spirituality and material reality, Chosŏn nongminsa issued several textbooks for its literacy programs. The subjects of these textbooks ranged widely, from arithmetic to history to fertilizer production. Some of the titles are *The Study of Recent Korean History (13)*, *A Reader on Peasants*, *A Reader on Han'gŭl*, *The Peasant Enlightenment Movement*, *Mass Arithmetic*, and *Rules of Cooperative Accounting*.[26] The publication of a vast number of textbooks was in line with the Ch'ŏndogyo Youth Party's strong publication record in the 1920s and 1930s. Overall, Chosŏn nongminsa leaders and officials from the other branches of the party found it important to be active in the growing print culture in colonial Korea because books, newspapers, journals, and pamphlets allowed for the wider dissemination of Ch'ŏndogyo ideas. The production of these textbooks for peasants, however, specifically distinguished the Chosŏn nongminsa's rationale for publications from the other branches of the party, which saw the urban elite as the intended audience of their books and journals.

Published by Ch'ŏndogyo's printing house in Seoul, the articles in Chosŏn nongminsa's monthly journal, first titled *Chosŏn nongmin* (Chosŏn Farmer) and later renamed *Nongmin* (Farmer), introduced topics such as the origins of Korea's agricultural problems, problems of tenancy, how to improve farming techniques, and the state of agriculture in other countries.[27] In a sense, the journal worked as a practical manual to help peasants transition to a new life as modern farmers. Yet in addition to being a practical manual on how to become a better farmer, the journal, like *Nongch'on ch'ŏngnyŏn*, also tried to instill a sense of historical consciousness in peasants through short stories and historical lessons that emphasized the important role of peasants in Korean history. Because Chosŏn nongminsa valued peasants as the material symbols of the Korean nation, this journal naturally promoted stories about peasants that portrayed them as invaluable members in the history of Korea. What Chosŏn nongminsa hoped to accomplish through these stories was to show peasants that they were important, valued figures in society who needed to work hard continually in the fields in order to maintain a healthy countryside and perpetuate Korea's agricultural identity. Yet by juxtaposing articles that emphasized this calling to peasants with articles on contemporary subjects, such as capitalism, Danish farmers, cooperatives, and the latest technological innovations in farming, Chosŏn nongminsa called for peasants to preserve and protect Korea's agricultural identity and heritage by adopting a new attitude that was appropriate to the present and incorporating changes into their lives.

Presbyterian rural leaders published two monthly journals: *Nongmin saenghwal* (Farmer's Life) and *Nongch'on t'ongsin* (The Rural News). First published in 1929 and in Korean, *Nongmin saenghwal* stood out for the English translation of its title, *Farmer's Life*, which appeared in a number of its issues. By translating *nongmin* as "farmer," the organization deliberately stressed that the movement's goal was to transform peasants into farmers—most certainly American-style farmers who were independent, owned land, and produced for the market. With this purpose, the journal became the primary avenue through which the movement introduced important scientific and economic information, concepts on how to improve farming and build cooperatives, and news about rural affairs in Korea and the world. But besides strengthening peasants' economic agency, the journal also heavily featured articles on Christian theology, as well as stories and poems about peasants and agricultural life, in order to raise the spiritual and historical consciousness of peasants. The journal was sent to institutions and individual subscribers for a fee but was given free to many peasants who could not afford it. Alongside *Nongmin saenghwal,* the Presbyterian movement also published *Nongch'on t'ongsin* from March to August 1935. Published under the direction of Pae Min-su, the director of the Presbyterian rural movement, and given out for free, *Nongch'on t'ongsin* specifically informed peasants about the overall state and direction of the Presbyterian rural movement. From this journal, peasants learned about educational programs and which villages and small towns had started cooperatives and implemented programs to revitalize the countryside. Moreover, peasants encountered the theological beliefs of Pae and Yu Chae-gi, especially Yu's ideas on Jesus villages and his philosophy behind realizing God's love through cooperatives. Because the Presbyterian rural movement often distributed both journals widely throughout Korea, they became important in maximizing the movement's influence and reach in the countryside without physical meetings with peasants.

   Although it is difficult to verify the exact number of peasants who read these journals, it appears from each journal's number of published copies that readership levels were high. The Presbyterian rural movement published 20,000 total copies of *Nongmin saenghwal* in 1929 and a total of 38,500 copies in 1932. The movement also printed over 14,000 copies of *Nongch'on t'ongsin* and distributed them to peasants enrolled in its education programs. Over 10,000 copies of the first issue of *Chosŏn nongmin* were distributed to subscribers for a fee and to peasants. In 1927, Chosŏn nongminsa printed over 18,000 copies of its journal. The YMCA published only 1,800 copies of *Ch'ŏngnyŏn* each month, but it published far more issues of *Nongch'on ch'ŏngnyŏn* because it expected peasants to use the journal as part of their education in YMCA programs; for each month's issue, the YMCA published close to 35,000 copies.

   From articles on religion, modernity, and economics to stories on culture and history, the journals of all three movements helped peasants learn how to read and write through the study of diverse subjects. To the movements, acquiring literacy skills through reading and analyzing these journals served the practical function of giving peasants new means to obtain knowledge and communicate, but it also was expected to help peasants develop new forms of consciousness and undergo diverse experiences. Presbyterian rural leaders, for example, framed the importance of being literate as an issue of spiritual experience through textual analysis. From the start of their educational programs, Presbyterian leaders found it necessary for peasants to acquire literacy skills in order to access and comprehend the latest scientific and economic information.[28] In particular, however, they considered literacy a requirement for discovering new forms of religious experience. According to Yi Hun-gu, illiteracy prevented men and women from reading the Bible and therefore coming into direct contact with words that expressed and embodied God's truth, goodness, and beauty. Unable to read religious texts and connect with a sacred world, people would experience difficulties transitioning from a "dark" to a "bright" spiritual life.[29] Framing illiteracy as a problem that limited both material and spiritual growth, Yi theorized that the inability to read and write constituted a serious obstacle to developing a dynamic relationship with the material and spiritual worlds. Yi and Presbyterian rural leaders understood that without the ability to read, peasants would be unable to connect to the written word, foster a critical consciousness, and undergo transformative experiences.

Alongside opening peasants up to new forms of consciousness and experiences, the process of becoming literate through these journals and other programs gave peasants the opportunity to develop a new national community. As forms of literature shared among peasants in all three movements' educational programs, the journals made peasants aware of the world outside their local area and brought them together at a national level to form a collective consciousness. Reading the same articles and using the same charts to learn how to read, write, and do math, peasants from one part of the country were in a position to know that peasants in other local places were simultaneously duplicating their actions. Through their interactions with texts, peasants had the opportunity to be part of what Benedict Anderson calls an "imagined community."[30] Communal ties that transcended the boundaries of local spaces presumably developed through peasants reading about the activities of peasants in other villages in articles and the "Peasant Newspaper" sections of most of the journals. Through these journals, individual peasants were able to discover and experience a larger community that shared the same temporality and space of the spiritual Korean nation.

Short-Term Programs

The Presbyterian, YMCA, and Chosŏn nongminsa leaders set up programs—training programs (*suryŏn*, Presbyterian), winter lectures (Chosŏn nongminsa), and farm schools (YMCA)—that specifically introduced peasants to the latest information on farming and exposed them to various issues and developments in economics, culture, and religion. Instead of setting up a program in a village that was open only to its inhabitants, these new programs held a large session in a single area and invited peasants from surrounding villages to attend. In effect, they were short-term programs that gave peasants comprehensive technical and spiritual training on how to modernize their pastoral lives.

To support the work of peasant schools, Chosŏn nongminsa rural leaders used winter lectures in villages as a method to continually shape and influence peasant actions and thoughts. Beginning in 1928, rural leaders held winter lectures during January and February when they visited local villages for about three days and talked about a wide range of subjects, from economics to Korean history. In particular, lectures stressed the importance of the peasants in Korea's past, present, and future and pointed out the issues peasants faced and how to overcome them. This was quite apparent in the titles of certain lectures: "The Problem of Korea's Peasants," "Confronting Problems of the Peasants," "The History of Peasants," and "The Coming World Is of the Peasant." Chosŏn nongminsa leaders presented peasants as valuable components of the nation and the current nationalist movement in Korea by simultaneously lecturing on the topics "The Historical Mission of Korean Peasants" and "The Trends of the Nationalist Movement" during a single lecture session.[31] Because leaders stayed only for a short time in the villages, it is hard to measure the effectiveness of these lectures, but we may assume that by lecturing to peasants, rural leaders had an easier time communicating their ideas and influencing peasants because peasants only had to listen to the leaders instead of struggling to read the presented information.

For its local educational program, the Presbyterian rural movement focused on its training program. Started in 1933 after Pae became the leader of the movement, the training program called for rural leaders to offer a comprehensive set of classes in villages throughout the peninsula, especially around P'yŏngyang and in parts of Manchuria, where many Korean peasants had emigrated for better farming opportunities. From 1933 to 1937, Presbyterian rural leaders held sixteen training programs. These programs were open to all and attracted large crowds, with an average of 100 to 400 peasants attending at least one of the training programs.[32]

Running from November to March, a typical training program lasted five days.[33] In that short time, peasants learned about a wide range of subjects, from the most efficient ways of farming to the dangers of superstitions.[34] Because Presbyterian leaders thought that learning scientific knowledge was an important step to help peasants revitalize their economic livelihoods, training programs taught peasants extensive information on modern farming.[35] Kim

Sŏng-wŏn, an expert on modern agricultural skills, for example, showed peasants how to improve their farming production capacities by introducing information on seeds, fertilizers, different types of fruits and vegetables, and new farming tools. In order for peasants to deliver and market their goods efficiently as well as pool their resources and manpower to compete effectively in the market, Yu Chae-gi taught peasants about cooperatives, especially the philosophies behind cooperatives and how to construct a cooperative.[36] What Kim and Yu sought to give to peasants was the concrete tools to move from a feudal economic livelihood to a new, secure economic existence under capitalism.

While Kim and Yu reshaped the material bodies of peasants, Pae assumed the role of disciplining the "spiritual soul" of peasants. To Pae, aligning people's lifestyles toward experiencing the divine involved more than just reforming economic and social practices. It also required stripping away destructive cultural and spiritual customs and practices that were considered barriers between God and humanity. With this mind-set, Pae first introduced his form of Christian theology in a typical training program. In his lectures on Christian theology, he conveyed the importance of practically realizing God's love.[37] Judging from his theology, we can conclude that Pae also lectured about the importance of harmonious relations between individuals and people loving one another in order to experience God's ultimate love in their daily lives. Pae combined his lectures on Christian theology with discussions on why people should quit performing other religious customs, such as ancestor worship and shaman rituals.[38] He also exhorted peasants to stop all destructive habits, such as drinking, smoking, gambling, and infidelity.[39] Finally, he told peasants to curb their consumption habits, especially in holding weddings and funerals. According to Pae, it was the mundane practices in the everyday that contributed to an alienated spiritual state. Correcting and reforming daily practices were therefore essential to ensure that peasants would enjoy God's love and presence in the modern world.

Although the training program was open to all individuals, Presbyterian rural leaders offered a special educational class for women. Yi, in particular, supported the education of women since they had long been considered unequal to men and held a lower social position than males did. Because of the way society figured the female in traditional Korean society, Yi believed that social movements ignored women and configured a woman's role in society only from a male's point of view.[40] Aside from historical reasons, Presbyterian leaders also thought that education of women was important for strategic reasons. Because women represented half the population, giving women a modern education and making them active participants in the rural movement were important steps to building an ideal agrarian nation.

In a typical training program, classes for women taught them how to become efficient domestic workers. The Presbyterian rural movement figured that women should occupy and work only within the home instead of freely working outside it. The movement imagined women as the disciplinarians of the home who made sure that home life was stable and that family members carried out the modern practices and ideas that rural leaders had taught them. Without domesticated women, it was believed that the home would collapse, which would tear the fabric of society. Considering that the Korean Presbyterian Church connected women to the home on the basis of biblical texts, it is no surprise that Presbyterian rural leaders strictly followed this line of thought. At the same time at which the rural movement worked feverishly to overturn feudal practices and thoughts held by peasants, Presbyterian rural leaders refused to break free from traditional images of women and to introduce new thoughts and arrangements that would promote equality between the sexes. Instead, through its courses for female students, the rural movement perpetuated the belief that women naturally inhabited only the home instead of examining the history of this belief and truly preparing women for a lifestyle outside the home and the overall domestic sphere.

From Presbyterian leaders' standpoint, giving women a modern education was less about leveling the ground between males and females than about introducing women to contemporary techniques and thoughts that would make them efficient wives and daughters who could maintain structure and control in the home in order for the family to live a lifestyle without preventable flaws. In the training program, then, women attended sessions on domestic affairs that were usually led by Pae Min-su's wife, Sun Ok. For example, women learned about food preparation, how to cook different types of food, and how to make different types of clothing. These sessions taught women, who were to control the finances of the home, better consumption skills, which was an important task because rural leaders believed that peasant consumption habits contributed greatly to their overall state of poverty.[41] In addition to sessions on consumption, women also learned how to raise children properly and how to maintain hygienic and sanitary conditions in the home. Rural people, according to Pae, knew very little about sanitation.[42] To prevent illnesses and deaths, Pae and his wife decided that it was necessary to give women the modern information to maintain a clean way of living.

The efforts and purposes behind YMCA-led farm schools were the same as those of Chosŏn nongminsa winter lectures and Presbyterian training programs; only their governing structure differed. Farm schools operated under the direction of the Rural Committee of the National Christian Council in Korea, an ecumenical organization consisting of the YMCA, the Young Women's Christian Association (YWCA), Methodists, and Presbyterians. Yet despite the shared governance structure, the YMCA controlled the everyday affairs and direction of the farm schools. The leadership structure of the rural committee showed how great an influence the YMCA had over the organization. YMCA leaders, such as Hong Pyŏng-sŏn, Sin Hŭng-u, and F. O. Clark, were the primary leaders in the rural committee and the lead teachers at farm schools. Therefore, instead of setting up an independent short-term training program, the YMCA conducted its training program though farm schools.

First started in 1925, the schools operated in large villages or cities throughout the provinces with the expectation that peasants and independent farmers would travel to these areas to attend programs. Farm-school programs lasted about a week to ten days during the winter, although the YMCA held one program for six weeks.[43] On average, 80 to 300 peasants attended either a day or a night session and learned new farming information related to "crops, soil rotation, fertilizers, seed, fruit and animal husbandry."[44] Teachers also introduced new strains of seeds and new types of livestock. In one year, for example, farm schools gave away over 1,100 leghorn and Rhode Island Red chickens. The YMCA had a similar plan for distributing Holstein bull calves and Berkshire pigs, which A. C. Bunce had already introduced through his model-village program. YMCA rural leaders, such as Sin, Hong, and Clark, also taught participants how to build cooperatives and construct simple farm machinery and about the latest farming machinery used in other countries. They even showed peasants examples of successful farming projects through the screening of films that featured the farming methods of Western countries and successful farming enterprises in Korea.[45]

Even after YMCA leaders ended a session, they checked on their former students by visiting them and making sure that they were applying what they had learned to their daily lives. From these visits, the YMCA leaders often selected the finest produce and raised livestock to feature them in agricultural fairs at the YMCA headquarters in Seoul. Far from being simple venues where peasants displayed various fruits and vegetables and demonstrated to the public the use of the newest farming machinery, agricultural fairs became ideological mechanisms to show urban residents both the transformed nature of peasant life and that modernity was also spatially located in rural areas. At the fairs, the YMCA showed modernity as based on agriculture, with peasants whose lives were rooted in the present and incorporated contemporary and traditional elements to become richer in meaning and value. After attending a fair in November 1931, an editor of a newspaper in Seoul appeared to be impressed with these modern peasants:

> The editor had an unusual experience. He went to the farm exhibit at the Y.M.C.A. It is a western style building but inside was

the Korean atmosphere of the farm. When we came in the door the roosters were crowing. We caught the smell of our native earth. We saw the products of our soil. Our own farmers, in their good Korean dress, were thronging the place. We saw our farm implements used for many generations, and near them some light and strong machinery from the west that may help us. The phonograph was playing our own Korean music which is better for us than Wagner or Beethoven. Some people say the revolutionist is the hope of our country; but we think the farmer is our hope.[46]

Wanting the entire urban masses to feel what the editor felt, the YMCA relied on the farm schools and agricultural fairs to capture people's minds and condition them to believe that the present and the future of the modern nation-state lay in the countryside.

For YMCA officials, farm schools were sites of experimentation where teachers tried out and demonstrated various farming techniques and altered local ecosystems by introducing seeds and livestock from the United States; peasants were also able to reflect on and discuss how their learned training could be applied to a particular situation to transform it. As a large and comprehensive program, however, the farm schools faced certain problems that at times lessened their effectiveness. YMCA leaders cited high costs and location as some of the obstacles that prevented the programs from becoming fully successful.[47] Despite the various problems, however, the schools attracted a fair number of people at various programs that were held every year from 1929 to 1933.[48] From the school sessions, the YMCA was able to select a handful of peasants and independent farmers to become teachers in the programs. Given the YMCA's inability to go to every local village on the peninsula, the ability to send peasants as teachers most certainly gave YMCA officials the assurance that its influence in the countryside would be maintained.[49] In a sense, by using ordinary older peasants to teach classes, the farm schools worked as an institution to turn peasants into leaders.

All the short-term programs of the three movements provided the means for all participants to develop a consciousness from which they could create a new outlook on and a relationship with the overall environment, both built and natural. The programs encouraged peasants to use what they had learned in order to construct a new built environment from which "nature may adapt new natural processes that emerge from the conditions of the new place."[50] By teaching peasants a system on how to cultivate soil, determine what types of seeds and fertilizers worked best, and raise livestock properly, the training programs showed peasants that they could manipulate the way their crops and livestock grew and could therefore control the process of farming to produce

favorable results. Moreover, by teaching peasants how to construct and operate cooperatives, the training programs supplied the means through which
peasants could collectively streamline their operations and maximize financial
returns and thus create stable social conditions and overcome poverty. The
short-term programs taught peasants that they held the power and contemporary knowledge to construct a new built environment that could manipulate
the natural environment in ways that would improve their production of agricultural goods and lessen their chances of total financial ruin.

Conditioning and Disciplining the Minds of Rural Youth

All three rural movements opened their educational programs to all peasants,
but they also recognized the necessity of designing programs that specifically
catered to the energy and talents of the very volatile Korean youth. Especially
during the Chosŏn period, a Confucian-based social hierarchy system had
already determined the roles and responsibilities of young men and women
and expected them to pattern their lives after their ancestors. After the collapse of the Confucian system and the rise of colonialism, however, the youth
population underwent significant transformation in the way its members
thought about things and expressed themselves. During the 1920s, in particular, the combination of a changing capitalist economy, growing urbanization,
and the influx of cultural ideas and products from outside Korea turned
Korean cities into places where young people indulged in new desires as they
came into contact with diverse forms of consumption and entertainment.
Through shopping for foreign goods at Western-style department stores, watching Western films at movie theaters, reading and talking about romance novels while drinking coffee at cafés, listening to jazz at music clubs, and enjoying
a life powered by electricity, young people underwent a process of crafting new
identities that led them to doubt traditions. Arriving in cities either to find
work or to attend school, a youth became a "modern girl" or "modern boy"
who welcomed anything that was new while abandoning anything that was
considered traditional because it prevented the creation of a new life that was
appropriate for the present. The following description of Korean youth in the
1920s well encapsulates their dynamic nature:

> Korean youth, like the youth of other nations, began to throw off
> the inhibitions of the past. They ignored the old social order based
> on the Confucian system. As already mentioned, they incurred
> the wrath of their elders by refusing to perform the age-old cus-
> tom of "kow-tow." New customs and new words, already common
> in Japan, began to appear. "Mobo" (modern boy) and "Moga"

(modern girl) were introduced, along with Western dress and Western hairstyles. Strictures on the relationship between the sexes, which old Korea had so jealously guarded, began to break down. It was not uncommon for young couples to walk hand in hand in the streets, and the subject of love, which had been taboo in polite circles, became common talk. Modern novels, either original works or translations from abroad, were eagerly read. The love story was all the rage.[51]

Although a vast number of youths expressed new identities and forms of individualism through consumption and leisure, other young men and women pursued the development of new subjectivities through the rejection of traditional worldviews in favor of new ideologies, such as Marxism, social Darwinism, and fascism. They turned to these ideologies out of a need to interpret mass material and ideological changes and negotiate Japanese imperialism. Highly motivated to solve the most pressing political, economic, and social concerns facing the nation, these young men and women were often the same individuals who were organizing and participating in antireligion campaigns because they interpreted religion as a tradition that limited individual and social growth. Because of the changing political, economic, and social environment in the 1920s and 1930s, Korean youth pursued a process of constructing new identities and subjectivities that weakened what was considered stable and long lasting and questioned the power of traditions to reproduce the past in the present.

Concentrated in cities, this new youth culture established a spectacle of the urban that drew the hearts, minds, and bodies of rural youth. The YMCA, the Presbyterian Church, and Chosŏn nongminsa noticed that the rural youth longed to leave the countryside for what appeared to be a better and more exciting life in the city; they rejected a pastoral life that they considered filled with poverty and lacking any prospects and moved to cities in Korea and throughout the Japanese empire. Yi Hun-gu pointed out that many of the rural youths saw farming as a waste of time and became enamored with traveling to cities and experiencing the new.[52] Yi Sŏng-hwan wrote that because of the development of the capitalist economy, rural youth flocked to cities. Korean rural youths turned their backs on a traditional way of life that had no attraction or future and longed to become city youths.[53] Overall, Sin Hŭng-u had pointed out that the youth population in the 1920s, including those in the rural areas, lived in a restless state in which they sought direction and guidance during a period of massive economic, political, social, and cultural changes.[54] Along with his colleagues, Sin feared that this restlessness not only would lead to a mass exodus of youth from the country to the city but also would drive them to leftist organizations. Unsurprisingly, their concerns over youth leaving the countryside originated from the fear that heavy migration of the future generation of farmers would cause the evaporation of the backbone or nucleus of farming communities.[55] Leaders of the movements saw rural discontent as a threat to the future viability and preservation of rural communities because youths were needed to continue the work and practices that would eventually be vacated by older adults. In short, the youths' desire for an alternative urban lifestyle threatened the movements' plans to create a spiritual-agrarian nation-state. This potential ideological and material disaster in the countryside forced the three movements to establish specific measures and programs that would provide youths with a new education that would tie them to rural life.

This turn to control the present and future course of rural youth in Korea was part of a worldwide trend that had started in the beginning of the twentieth century. The Nazi Party created the Hitler Youth in the early 1920s and ideologically trained youths to become faithful followers of the party who would carry out its mission of National Socialism and carve a living space for the German nation. The Fascist Party under Mussolini established the Balilla in 1926, which was compulsory for all Italian youths and served as an institution to indoctrinate them with fascist messages. By the 1920s, the Boy Scouts movement had already been well under way in the United Kingdom through the efforts of its founder, General Robert Baden-Powell, who sought to improve the military fitness of young men because he believed that the British had suffered huge casualties in the Boer War as a result of poor training and preparation of soldiers. In 1910, after meeting Baden-Powell, W. D. Boyce started the Boy Scouts of America with the intention of training young men in character development and self-reliance in order for them to become devoted citizens. Finally, the Nationalist Party in China organized the Three People's Principle Youth Corps in 1937 as a revolutionary party that would bring new life to the nation and support national interests. Although these movements were far from all being the same, they still shared a similar purpose of controlling and shaping the desires and identities of youth out of fears that the activities of young men and women, which were mostly shaped by capitalism, threatened to erode traditions and therefore the stability, continuity, and power of the nation. Youth movements and parties were these organizations' ways of managing the changes caused by modernization and ensuring a present and future that would embody their nationalistic goals.

The YMCA and Presbyterian rural leaders set up new programs for rural youth, but Chosŏn nongminsa decided against specifically starting a youth program. In all likelihood, this decision resulted from its leaders' belief that a youth program was unnecessary because their parent organization, the Ch'ŏndogyo Youth Party, already had a mission of indoctrinating and influ-

encing the youth with Ch'ŏndogyo messages. While Chosŏn nongminsa carried out many of its programs with the help of urban and rural youth, the
YMCA and Presbyterian rural movements specifically established leadership
programs for rural youth to cultivate a corps of leaders who could guide peasants toward building a new paradise and become the vanguard of rural reconstruction. Presbyterian leaders, in particular, saw a great need to create new
leaders for this movement. Yi Hun-gu pointed out that choosing and cultivating peasants to become leaders was imperative because Koreans, who had always lived, worked, and moved as a single group, required efficient leaders to
guide them.[56] Yi's concept of leadership, of course, contradicted his claims of
fostering a society of equals. However, he stated that all societies had leaders
and those who followed.[57] Pae Min-su agreed with Yi and argued that these
new leaders would possess the local knowledge and relationships that would
help reform village life.[58] Pae realized that peasant leaders who already knew
the small details of their home villages and their neighbors would be more effective in implementing appropriate projects to build Jesus villages than rural
leaders, like himself, whom local villagers considered outsiders.

To help transform rural youth into ideal leaders, the Presbyterian rural
movement organized agricultural practical cultivation schools (nongŏp silsu
hakkyo), which were located in local villages so they would be easily accessible
to the many young men and women who lived in isolated villages. By the end
of 1936, three schools were operating and actively working to attract youths to
their rural programs. From the beginning, Presbyterian leaders envisioned
the schools having a socioeconomic and religious purpose in that they sought
to produce model rural leaders who possessed not only sufficient farming
skills but also the desire to spread God's love in the countryside.[59] To form the
ideal rural youth, the schools constructed programs that would implant the
following three ideals in the minds and bodies of rural youth: love of spirit,
love of neighbor, and love of land.[60] Taken directly from Denmark, the three
principles represented what were considered the most important ways of
thinking and living in a reconstructed rural society.

Agricultural practical cultivation schools offered a comprehensive education that cultivated the cooperative and spiritual sides as well as the farming
abilities of youth. Students, most of whom were male, lived together in dorms.
Cohabiting as one group, according to one report, promoted a communal lifestyle among students.[61] This form of communal relations among students extended beyond the dorms because students studied and worked together all
day. In the morning, they started with a daily worship service.[62] In these services, partaking in Christian rituals and practices presumably became methods through which Christian ideals and beliefs were reinforced in the minds
of students. Next, students together attended classes where they studied issues

concerning religion, society, and the economy, including the teachings of Christ, rural economics, and cooperative theories.[63] Finally, students practiced their newly learned skills by working together on farms. Agricultural practical cultivation schools strove to spark students' interest in rural affairs and prepare them to be leaders in their local communities.

Alongside agricultural practical cultivation schools, Denmark-style folk schools played a vital role of not only properly educating rural youths about rural economics and farming but also raising the next generation of local and national leaders. In Denmark, the purpose behind the folk school was not only to supply technical skills but also to mold young people into ethical and moral subjects who would become the vanguard force in rural society.[64] To develop an all-around character, folk schools had a comprehensive curriculum that emphasized Nikolai Frederik Severin Grundtvig's three principles for revitalizing Danish life: (1) love God; (2) love land; and (3) love family.[65] The curriculum specifically sought to build personalities based on love, cooperation, and trust.[66] Creating a strong character was vital, for it would be the basis from which to motivate people to develop their own lives and work to make a better society.[67] Alongside strong character, folk schools sought to strengthen people's national consciousness through the study of history. Grudtvig and folk-school organizers believed that exposing Danes to their "heroic past" would "awaken" the national spirit that had enabled the various successes in the past.[68] To this end, Danish folk schools carried out their mission not only through classroom work and lectures but also by forcing students to live, work, and study together. In this arrangement, students formed a community where they depended on and helped one another and, in doing so, materially actualized the principles that constituted a national consciousness and strong character.

The Presbyterian Folk School carefully selected the most outstanding twenty- to forty-year-old students from local areas who had the most potential to be revolutionary leaders. Presbyterian rural leaders based their selection of future leaders on five qualities. First, potential candidates needed to espouse high ideals. Second, they must carry a strong faith or conviction in religion. Third, rural leaders sought out those peasants who were forward thinking. Fourth, potential leaders needed to display a superior consciousness and a skillful nature. Finally, they must possess a spirit of sacrifice and service.[69] Presbyterian leaders searched for potential leaders who embodied a high moral and ethical stature. Selecting individuals who personified this type of personality was more important than picking individuals who could easily learn new things because fostering a strong character was far more difficult than teaching someone a new set of skills. Using this logic, rural leaders thought that teaching peasants who already displayed an ethical and moral way of life modern information and techniques would turn them into all-around leaders who could effectively motivate and guide their fellow villagers toward material and spiritual regeneration. The Presbyterian rural movement hoped to produce young peasant intellectuals, as defined by Antonio Gramsci, who had greater abilities than others to interpret the changes in society and organize people in a fashion that would lead to a thriving society.[70]

After being selected, students traveled to Sungsil University, where the folk-school programs were held. As a private school and seminary in P'yŏngyang, Sungsil University had served as the center of Presbyterian education since being founded by Western missionaries in 1897. Although the university taught mostly college students, it also offered specialized classes to teach young men how to farm, especially classes that enabled students to practice what they had learned on farms located on the university campus.[71] Because Sungsil was an influential Presbyterian institute, the majority of its faculty members came from the Presbyterian Church, including Yi Hun-gu and Cho Man-sik. Considering its resources and background, Sungsil University naturally served as the location to operate the folk school.

Starting in 1932, the first students, all of them males, underwent a rigorous and comprehensive program that ran from June to August. Living, learning, and working together for three months, folk school students daily experienced a constant disciplining of their consciousness and lifestyle. From 7 a.m. to 9:30 p.m., students took classes that taught topics such as modern farming techniques and skills, household economics, and cooperatives and also conducted experiments on farms.[72] Guided by teachers such as Yi Hun-gu and Yu Chae-gi, students practiced their farming skills on practice farms located at the university. Although it was imperative to reconstitute their social and economic abilities, the folk school also made a strong effort to make students into culturally and spiritually rich individuals since students were expected to help people develop all aspects of their personality and become spiritually whole. Consequently, alongside the economic and social programs, folk school students also took cultural classes, such as workshops on music, and attended lectures where teachers such as Pae emphasized the need to love and taught how to realize love practically and concretely. In these lectures, Pae most likely used these opportunities to expose students to his theological beliefs and to motivate young men from the rural areas to live for agriculture and God.

After students finished three successive sessions of the program, they were eligible to graduate from the school. In 1935, the first set of folk school students graduated. Alongside students from the agricultural practical cultivation schools, folk school students, in the minds of rural leaders, were expected to shoulder enormous responsibilities to revive agricultural life economically and spiritually in the present and also to pass on knowledge and information to future rural leaders. By continually educating and molding young students and older adults, rural leaders hoped that rural society would flourish and become a spiritual kingdom rather than collapse and be absorbed by the city and industrialization.

The YMCA also started its own folk school program, which was unsurprising because all its leaders were strong advocates of adopting Danish reforms. Perceiving the Danish Folk School as a very successful mechanism to educate and spiritually cultivate young men and women, Korean YMCA leaders constructed their own program based on the exact model operated by the Danes.[73] The philosophy and objectives behind the YMCA Folk School, in fact, were almost identical to the ones found in Denmark. The YMCA program promoted four goals: (1) to disregard the useless and by substitution and study find the necessary things of life; (2) to develop a definite hope and expectancy in the present and for the future; (3) to develop a determination to return home and put into practice what had been learned and to continue the learning process; and (4) to develop a Christlike attitude of thinking and mode of action for oneself and to become an advocate of these ideals in one's own neighborhood.[74] These four goals showed that the YMCA Folk School was determined to indoctrinate students with new values and make them into conduits who would spread YMCA beliefs, spark rural regeneration in local areas, and create new economic, social, and cultural paths in the present.

To ensure the overall success of the program, the YMCA paid careful attention to every small detail, from choosing the location of the folk school to picking the right type of students. As part of its national program, the YMCA built the folk school in Seoul on a ten-acre farm located next to Chosen Christian College. The YMCA strategically picked this site for the folk school because Chosen Christian College permitted the YMCA to use the land for free and the folk school was in a position to access valuable resources at the college. In fact, the college, which had a strong agricultural program, allowed some of its teachers to participate in the YMCA program.[75] Normally running from November to February, the school required potential students to be between the ages of eighteen and twenty-five, to hold a middle-school education, and to own some land. More important than age and how much land they owned, however, were leadership qualities, interests, and the ability to learn quickly.[76] In particular, the YMCA wanted students who had strong desires to make changes and showed enthusiasm about the project of rural reconstruction.

Nominated by local pastors, church officials, or missionaries, the young men who were selected to attend the school were required to pay only living expenses, since they would be living and studying together for four months. From its start in 1932 and in every subsequent year, the program was extremely popular. In the school's first year, over fifty young men from all over the peninsula applied for the thirteen openings. At the school, students took part in a comprehensive and rigorous program consisting of attending classes all day and sharpening their farming skills on experimental farms. Students attended the following twelve classes taught by YMCA members and agricultural experts from Chosen Christian College:

1. Lectures on Ideals—Sin Hŭng-u
2. Farm Economics—C. H. Lee
3. Adapted Singing—Rody Hyun
4. Sanitation
5. Cooperatives and Renewed Life—Hong Pyŏng-sŏn
6. Bookkeeping—I. H. Yi
7. Vegetable Raising—C. W. Sim
8. Fertilizers and Their Use—U. M. Kim
9. Common Farming and Sericulture—K. T. Yi
10. Animal Husbandry—P. H. Kay, G. W. Avison, B. P. Barnhart
11. Home Industries—Y. S. Whang
12. Danish Exercise—D. W. Hyun[77]

Although each class taught subjects in different areas, they all shared the common trait of teaching modern ideas and practices that would help students live disciplined and structured lives. The class on farm economics taught students about capitalism and the commercialization of agriculture. In classes on cooperatives, vegetable raising, and fertilizers, students learned how to organize themselves collectively to strengthen their economic power and how to grow crops efficiently. From the class on ideals, the young men learned about modernity, morals, and religion. Finally, sanitation and Danish exercise classes educated students on the importance of maintaining a healthy body.

To supplement the students' technical training and make them into well-rounded leaders, the folk school also gave lectures on Korean history and culture and on Christianity. In the evenings, students attended lectures where teachers talked about "great events in the lives of great historical characters."[78] Since *Nongch'on ch'ŏngnyŏn* published rural folktales and stories about events and key figures in Korean history, the evening history sessions presumably used the magazine to teach history. It can be argued that telling stories about Korea's past, including its rich agricultural history, was an attempt by leaders to convince students that their work was important because it preserved Korea's historical identity and ensured its survival in the future.

After the history classes, YMCA leaders held a devotional hour that involved reading the Bible, discussing issues related to Christianity, especially social gospel theology, and praying. To help students experience God through different means, folk school teachers led students in singing both religious and folk songs during the devotional hour. By teaching students Korean history alongside Christian principles, leaders hoped that students would realize that a connection existed between Christianity and Korea. They wanted students to see that Christianity was an important, if not essential, part of Korean history and culture. They wished students to understand that building a Christian country would enable the continual development of the Korean nation. YMCA rural leaders clearly held this intention when they taught the course titled "Spiritual Resources for National Prosperity."[79]

The YMCA's Folk School worked hard to turn young men into leaders, but the YMCA also helped develop a new core of female leaders for rural reconstruction. However, instead of running its own leadership programs, the YMCA collaborated with the Young Women's Christian Association (YWCA) to form and operate a folk school for women.[80] In both organizations, leaders strongly supported a plan to train women to become effective and productive rural leaders through a comprehensive educational program, such as the folk school program. As citizens of the Korean nation, women, according to leaders, held just as much responsibility as men to ensure that the Korean nation progressed smoothly under modernity. Depicting women as equal partners with men, the YMCA and the YWCA considered Korea's entrance into the modern world an event that demanded that women be taught contemporary skills and knowledge in order to help Korean society adjust to the transforming environment.[81] In fact, leaders in both organizations believed that providing a modern education to women was even more necessary than doing so for men because the development of women's character and skills had long been ignored and deemphasized within the patriarchal Confucian society.[82] Protestant Christian leaders recognized that Confucianism gave unequal status to women, which consequently caused them to be mistreated and to be given few opportunities to gain a formal education and advance in society. Moreover, Christian leaders acknowledged that women experienced further hardships because their husbands controlled their lives.[83]

The YWCA Folk School program represented an intensive and wide-ranging institution that would take young Korean females and mold them into modern women. But what YWCA and YMCA leaders conceptualized as a modern woman was far from the belief that women should have the freedom to pursue any occupation and to do anything they wanted. Instead, the leaders maintained the conservative belief that a woman's role in building a spiritual nation rested in supervising, controlling, and occupying the family sphere. Although they acknowledged women as equal partners to men, YMCA and YWCA leaders, influenced by traditional Christian theology, considered that the primary role of women in society was to maintain the health and hygiene of those in the home. Leaders also expected women to raise children, which was an important job since producing healthy children was the key component of maintaining a thriving rural society. Like Confucianism, YMCA and YWCA leaders taught that men held responsibilities in the space outside the home, while women worked inside the home.

The inability of YWCA and YMCA leaders to break free from traditional categories for women became clear through the stated purpose of the YWCA Folk School, which started in March 1933. The YWCA declared that the folk school sought to improve the spiritual, mental, and physical conditions of women in order for them to "broaden the outlook of their village home" and "uplift . . . spiritual, mental and physical welfare of village life."[84] Firmly believing that women's responsibilities lay in the home, the YWCA selected primarily young married women between the ages of eighteen and forty to participate in the folk school, located in the building used by the YMCA Folk School and held from the end of February to the end of April. Like the YMCA Folk School, the YWCA Folk School required students to pay only for living expenses and to live and work together.[85] Teachers from the YWCA (such as Helen Kim), the YMCA (including Hong and Sin), and Chosen Christian College lectured on the following subjects related to home and family life:

1. Cultivation of the mind
2. Household management
3. Commonsense ways of improving living conditions
4. Sewing
5. Cooking
6. Laundry
7. Dyeing
8. Household hygiene
9. Child welfare
10. Elementary history and geography
11. Games
12. Stories and songs for children.[86]

Just like the young men in the YMCA Folk School, young women attended classes on how to conduct everyday activities in modern ways. Unlike men, however, women learned only skills and knowledge that pertained to the domestic sphere because of the expectation that they would be the mental and physical disciplinarians in the home. Through the type of classes they taught, the YMCA and YWCA reaffirmed to female students a gendered form of modernity in which they would assume the responsibility of being the stabilizers of the home while men worked in society.

Students of the YMCA and YWCA Folk Schools learned modern ideals and were groomed to become future leaders. The YMCA also established a Farmers' Practice School based on the folk-school model in 1934 as a way for young men to refine their skills learned in classes through operating a farm and visiting villages to help peasants. Located on a farm in Kwangju, each session of the Farmers' Practice School lasted two years, during which twenty young men lived and worked together. The Farmers' Practice School resembled the folk school in that it had strict qualifications for enrollment, such as a strong evaluation of character from a pastor, a primary-school education, signs of leadership qualities, being from the country, and passing an examination that tested mental capacities.[87] Moreover, like the folk school, the Farmers' Practice School offered a wide-ranging curriculum. Students, for example, took classes with titles such as Theory of Agriculture, Animal Husbandry, Farm Economics, Health and Hygiene, Carpentry and Masonry, Home Economics, Food Preparation, First-Aid, Teaching the Bible, Cooperatives and Marketing, Singing, Village Athletics, and Letter Writing.[88] Judging from the types of classes the school offered, one can assume that teachers at the Farmers' Practice School pushed hard to turn students into yeoman farmers who could be self-sufficient and become independent, well-rounded leaders and model citizens for peasants.

Although the folk school and the Farmers' Practice School shared a similar educational program, the Practice School distinguished itself from the folk school by incorporating an intense hands-on training session where students translated their knowledge into actual practice by being given the responsibility to operate and upkeep a working farm. Farming on fields located next to the school, students had the opportunity to practice how to raise properly all types of crops, especially fruit and vegetable crops that were popular in the area.[89] By directly cultivating crops and performing other jobs on the farm, students not only had the chance to refine their farming skills but also learned how to run an entire farm, an invaluable experience that could help them when they ran their own farms in the future. More important, however, by raising, harvesting, and selling crops and working on the farm collectively, students were able to live out the principles of cooperation and develop a deeper understanding of how to create and maintain a strong community.

Alongside farm work, the school sent students to visit and work in surrounding villages to help peasants and to develop the students' leadership skills. The school expected students to "uplift" villages during their visits.[90] Uplifting villages presumably involved talking to peasants about their problems, setting up economic, social, and cultural programs to alleviate poverty, and making sure that peasants carried out plans by personally observing their activities. Forcing students to work directly with peasants while attending classes, the Farmers' Practice School wanted its students to understand that learning was a comprehensive process that took place in the classroom and in everyday life.

YMCA and YWCA leaders heavily relied on their folk schools to turn out young, capable leaders. They feared that modernization would not only ruin the countryside but also leave it without any future as rural youth flocked to cities to escape farming. Changes in colonial Korea continuously threatened to derail their drives to reconstruct rural Korea, so the leaders tried to control and shape the bodies and minds of rural youth. The YMCA and Presbyterian folk schools, therefore, were more than structures that simply prepared students to live in the new modern world; they were also institutions, or ideological state apparatuses, that indoctrinated youth with correct thoughts and inscribed a proper vision of the nation that the schools hoped would continuously materialize. Educational programs were the machineries of truth that sought to wipe out what was wrong and institute what was right. Particularly, they taught the rural youth that becoming modern required only developing a new attitude of being creative and innovative in the present instead of moving to the city in order to experience the new. These schools were institutions of hegemony that attempted to control youths and harness their raw energy to accomplish the goals of their rural movements.

The educational programs of the three rural movements positioned peasants to receive practical knowledge and skills that led to a reformed life that could effectively take on the newest problems that capitalism posed in the countryside. Acquiring literacy skills presented the opportunity both to access knowledge from a wide range of categories that would allow appropriate interpretations of the world and to imagine and develop new forms of community through which peasants could form collective power. The short-term training programs of each of the movements offered contemporary ideas and practices that could be employed to enhance agricultural productivity, streamline and maximize agricultural production, and safeguard peasants' physical health— all in a cooperative way. Finally, youth programs gave young men and women a diverse array of knowledge and the opportunity to practice what they learned so that they could become leaders in the drive for rural reconstruction and for strengthening and protecting the nation. Through these programs, leaders from the three movements expected peasants to control and manage the vast changes surrounding them in ways that would lead to the construction of a new society modeled after Denmark.

The process of providing this practical education involved questionable practices. The Presbyterian and YMCA / YWCA educational campaigns perpetuated gender hierarchy and stereotypes. Both groups spoke highly of equality, especially regarding access to education, but were unwilling and unable to break from traditional ways of thinking about the public and private roles of men and women that led to discriminatory practices in their educational campaigns. Progressive in many ways, both groups were nevertheless deeply swayed by conservative Confucian and Christian ideas on women, which showed that despite Koreans advocating progressive reforms in other areas of society and culture, breaking down gender norms and discriminatory ideas on women was one of the most difficult processes in colonial Korea. Alongside discrimination against women, the Presbyterian and YMCA youth programs, in particular, were problematic in the way they sought hegemonic control over youths. These youth programs emphasized control and discipline in order to force youths to believe in certain ways that were favorable to rural reconstruction and prevented changes from further ruining rural life. Although they did not employ physical punishment and extreme forms of discipline, the youth programs still set up a learning environment that clearly demarcated right from wrong for the sake of controlling change and thus refused to allow certain differences, such as permitting students even to think about living a life outside rural areas.

Leaders of the three movements made certain that educational programs indoctrinated peasants with their respective visions of the nation. Teaching messages on the value of religion, agriculture, farming, and peasants alongside introducing the latest innovations in farming, social organization, and practical living, the YMCA, Presbyterian, and Chosŏn nongminsa educational programs constructed an agrarian modernism for peasants. This vision of agrarian modernism allowed for the preservation of key aspects of the peasants' agrarian heritage, a valuable place for spirituality in peasant lives, and the incorporation of contemporary knowledge, practices, and institutions into a pastoral life. It emphasized that in materializing this form of modernism, the present would be far from a destabilizing moment in which peasants were required to shed their existing identity and heritage in their entirety. Instead, the present would be a moment full of value and stability where the old and the new joined to construct new possibilities for living and thought. As literacy classes, journals, training sessions, and folk schools as a whole presented the three movements' vision for agrarian modernism, the movements' educational programs gave peasants the opportunity to see and believe consciously that a successful model of modernity anchored in religion and a pastoral life was appropriate and possible in present-day colonial Korea. The educational programs wanted peasants, especially youths, not only to think critically about how to make changes and how agrarian reforms would turn out for the Korean nation, but also to confidently anticipate how their activities could lead to the birth of a heavenly kingdom and a powerful new nation.

Conclusion

L asting a little over a decade (1925–1937), the YMCA, Presbyterian, and Ch'ŏndogyo rural movements were collectively one of the largest rural movements in colonial Korea that furnished Koreans with an alternative vision of modernity that featured religion, agriculture, and pastoral living. As this book has shown, these three movements carried out reconstruction campaigns with the purpose of building a heavenly kingdom on earth where Korean peasants could find relief from the ideological and material upheavals caused by modernization. The movements pursued a path of reform centered on the reclamation of Korea's agrarian heritage. That is, by incorporating contemporary ideas, practices, and systems, particularly those found in Denmark's model of agrarian development, into the everyday lives of peasants, the movements believed that peasants could forge holistic, sacred lives that effectively negotiated economic, social, and cultural forces, especially capitalism. What underlay and grounded these faith-based rural movements was the religious belief that people's lives should be rooted in the present and that the present should be valued as a temporality open to the possibility of creating new political, economic, social, and cultural structures and environments. This conception of the present constituted a form of modernity that all three movements hoped would be embodied in the lives of Koreans. For the three rural movements and their leaders, being modern was not the achievement of a stage of history that featured normative values and systems, especially rationalization, industrialization, and urbanization. Rather, being modern meant the pursuit of creating new religious, economic, social, and cultural paths for Koreans in the present. This conception of modernity freed the leaders of the three movements to highlight religion, agriculture, and pastoral living in their rural reconstruction campaigns—despite the fact that standard definitions of the modern characterized these elements as antimodern—and allowed them to pursue a path of development that stood apart from several Korean nationalist movements and movements by the colonial state.

The reconstruction campaigns also served as vehicles to strengthen rural infrastructure and enhance farming life in order to stem the mass migration of peasants to urban centers and curtail the growing dominance of the city over the country. Although the leaders of the three movements were highly critical of urban life and believed that modernity should evolve and be cultivated in rural Korea, they found value in cities. In particular, Ch'ŏndogyo leaders, especially Yi Ton-hwa, acknowledged that valuable, contemporary ideas, practices, and systems were being developed in cities that should be spread to and applied by people in other parts of Korea to enhance their environments.[1] In fact, the various journals published by the Ch'ŏndogyo Youth Party that featured articles on urban life and developments, such as *Kaebyŏk* and *Sinin'gan,* served as important means to diffuse information from the city to the country. Realistically, the leaders also understood that Korea was a long way from becoming an industrial, urban-based society and that their country, still made up primarily of farmers, would not shed its identity as an agriculture-based society. They expected their campaigns to foster a harmonious and balanced relationship between the country and the city.

Still, by the middle of the 1930s, an increasing number of peasants were leaving the country for cities throughout the peninsula and in Japan and Manchukuo, which contributed to the urbanization of Korea. In many ways, the exodus of peasants from the countryside was a result of the new demands of the Japanese empire's political economy that encouraged industrialization in Korea and the immigration of Koreans to other parts of the empire to fulfill labor needs. Policies that contributed to urbanization and industrialization in Korea that were formulated by the colonial state, whose authorities remained in Tokyo, served as a reminder that the three rural movements did not have total control over their efforts to realize their respective visions of the Korean nation-state. The YMCA, Presbyterian, and Ch'ŏndogyo rural movements, however, escaped the strict colonial surveillance and policing that leftist movements experienced because the colonial authorities saw the rural movements as capable of pacifying peasant unrest. But the colonial state also recognized that the ideas the three rural movements conveyed to peasants could influence them to question and organize against colonial rule; thus the government-general's office closely watched the three movements. The YMCA, Presbyterian, and Ch'ŏndogyo rural movements also closely monitored their own programs because they were aware that the state would curtail or shut down those activities that appeared to threaten its authority.

After 1937, when Japan invaded China and sought to mobilize the Korean population for the war effort, colonial authorities exercised their powers by clamping down on all social activities and movements that had been permitted after the 1919 March First Movement, including the YMCA, Presbyterian, and Ch'ŏndogyo rural campaigns. The demise of the Ch'ŏndogyo rural movement had its roots in 1934 when the colonial state arrested and jailed members of the Ch'ŏndogyo Youth Party, the parent organization of Chosŏn nongminsa, for plotting to organize a second March First Movement. After these arrests, the state began regularly harassing the Youth Party. Persecution by the state became so intense that the party was forced underground after 1937, and Chosŏn nongminsa ceased operations and disbanded.

In many ways, the Presbyterian Church's rural movement ended in the same way as Chosŏn nongminsa's movement. Beginning in 1937, tensions grew between the colonial state and the Presbyterian Church over the state's requirement that all Koreans worship at Shinto shrines and perform Shinto ceremonies. Presbyterian leaders, particularly fundamentalists, strongly opposed this new requirement because of their belief that Christians could not follow or practice any other religion. As a result of their opposition, numerous followers were arrested for refusing to carry out the command of the state, Presbyterian missionaries were expelled from Korea, and the church closed down several Presbyterian schools in protest, including Sungsil University, which was a key institution where rural leaders carried out educational programs and crafted policies. Recognizing how difficult it would be to do their work, rural leaders started to wind down the activities of the movement in July 1937. Some leaders, such as Yu Chae-gi, went on to carry out small-scale rural reforms; others, like Pae Min-su, left Korea to study in the United States. This intimidating environment for Christians contributed to the end of the YMCA rural movement in 1938. In order to protect itself from the growing persecution of Christian institutions and organizations, the Korean YMCA merged with the Japanese YMCA.[2] Soon after merging, the organization ceased most rural movement activities, and key leaders, like Hong Pyŏng-sŏn, left the organization.[3] By the start of the Pacific War in 1941, all nationalist movements were strictly curtailed and every religious organization fell under the control of the state. In 1945, the colonial state forced the dissolution of all Protestant denominations and forced Christians to belong to the Kyodan, a government-operated denomination.

Although pressures from the colonial state were primarily responsible for the decline of the rural movements, internal developments within the Protestant Church during the 1930s also contributed to the weakening of the YMCA and Presbyterian rural movements. Even before the Shinto shrine crisis, fundamentalists in the Protestant Church attacked liberal forms of theologies held by people like Sin, Hong, and Pae. In 1934, Presbyterian fundamentalists censured Reverend Kim Ch'un-pae and Kim Yŏng-ju and relieved them of their duties because they had suggested that Christians interpret the Bible through scientific and historical methodologies instead of understanding the

Bible as a literal text. Fundamentalists waged a further battle against liberal theologies when they censured a handful of Presbyterian theologians who had helped translate the *Abingdon Bible Commentary,* which was based on liberal theology.[4]

To fundamentalists, liberal theologies that advocated criticism of sacred Christian texts and emphasized social activism not only diminished the value and truth of God but also drew attention and resources away from evangelical campaigns that promoted conversion, which was considered the only way for people to experience God. In this environment, more liberal YMCA and Presbyterian leaders faced ferocious criticism and attacks from fundamentalist Christian leaders who were successful in forcing out certain leaders from the two organizations and limiting their influence in Protestant Christian circles.[5] Strains between fundamentalist leaders and former leaders of the YMCA rural movement widened when some former rural movement leaders wrote articles during the war that voiced support for Japanese imperialism. Sin Hung-u, Hong Pyŏng-sŏn, and Helen Kim, for example, collaborated with the Japanese in publications that stressed the obligation of Koreans to aid the war effort as citizens of Japan. Among other things, they urged Koreans to enlist in the Japanese army or volunteer in Japanese organizations.[6] Although one could argue that Hong, Sin, and Kim collaborated with the Japanese for the larger purpose of overthrowing Western imperialism and as a way to reject Western-based modernization, explicating the precise reason for their actions is beyond the scope of this study.

The conflicts and controversies surrounding the Presbyterian and YMCA rural movements may explain why there are so few studies of these two movements, their leaders, and their views on religion, agriculture, and modernity. In South Korea during the Cold War, scant attention was paid to the colonial legacy, particularly because so many officials were former Japanese collaborators. Since the end of the Cold War and military dictatorship, however, there have been more attempts to address the issue of collaboration, especially through the 2005 Truth and Reconciliation Committee. But discussing collaboration is still difficult because it brings up many unresolved issues concerning national identity and the division of the peninsula. Telling the story of Christian collaborators is unsettling for the Christian community because it not only reminds it of the agonizing past but also reveals the deep schism that existed between conservative and liberal Christians during the colonial period. In particular, for fundamentalist Christian leaders in South Korea today, the story of Christians in the colonial period challenging seemingly immutable ideas about God and promoting social activism is threatening because it reveals diversity within Christian theology and demonstrates that change was an integral aspect of the Christian church. Moreover, criticisms of capitalism disrupt the standard narrative upheld by Protestant Christians in Korea who have insisted that their country has experienced development without any conflict. According to this narrative, Christians have enjoyed both spiritual prosperity and material wealth. Many Korean missionaries today recount this uncomplicated narrative about Korea's development in parts of Africa in order to convince Africans that Christianity is spiritually and materially beneficial.[7]

The small number of studies of the Ch'ŏndogyo rural movement can be explained by that religion's connection to the North Korean regime in the postliberation period. In October 1945, the Ch'ŏndogyo Youth Party reemerged and later set up branches in Seoul and P'yŏngyang. The northern branch broke off from the southern branch and established the North Korean Ch'ŏndogyo Youth Party on February 8, 1946. By the middle of 1947, this branch claimed to have over 1.6 million followers. As Charles Armstrong has pointed out, leaders in the party were active in North Korean politics, and the activities and ideas of Ch'ŏndogyo followers in North Korea showed that the organization's "line was generally in sync with the regime's domestic politics" by the late 1940s.[8] The alignment between North Korean and Ch'ŏndogyo politics was unsurprising since the North Korean state carried out reforms and programs for peasants that had been implemented or had long been advocated by Chosŏn nongminsa before 1945, for example, comprehensive land reforms, the education of peasants, and construction of cooperatives.[9] Considering the extent to which North Korean officials paid attention to and addressed rural needs, Ch'ŏndogyo leaders most certainly interpreted North Korean efforts as an extension of Chosŏn nongminsa's campaign to enhance and strengthen peasant lives. In fact, North Korean political philosophy and language mirrored and embodied many Ch'ŏndogyo principles, such as a heaven on earth (chisang ch'ŏn'guk) and the collective life (tonggwi ilch'e).[10] To this day, the Ch'ŏndogyo Youth Party is a junior member of the Korean Workers' Party.[11] Bringing to light and analyzing the efforts of Ch'ŏndogyo and Chosŏn nongminsa to build an agrarian paradise during the colonial period reminds Koreans not only of Ch'ŏndogyo's connection to North Korea but also of the politics of division between North and South Korea. Speaking about how Ch'ŏndogyo, a revered nationalist organization since its days as Tonghak, has had a strong presence and role in North Korea is a painful reminder for many South Koreans of the complicated and conflicted nature of Korean nationalism and postcolonial politics.

One primary goal of Building a Heaven on Earth has been to examine a little-known history of institutionally led faith-based social activism in Korea by looking back further than scholars have typically done. As a result, this book argues that the origins of such movements lie in the 1920s and 1930s colonial period when Koreans experienced the wide-ranging effects of modernization. This analysis of the YMCA, Presbyterian, and Ch'ŏndogyo rural movements from 1925 to 1937 has demonstrated that there were drives by religious institutions to combat poverty, social inequality, and cultural dislocation while building a new heaven on earth where Koreans could experience material stability and spiritual enlightenment. These movements introduced new religious ideas that emphasized the value of everyday life and the creation of a safe and just world in which people could discover peace and prosperity; they also taught Koreans how to build such a world. This book not only recovers a forgotten history but also highlights the need to reconceptualize and interpret religious events and developments during the colonial period. Specifically, a thorough examination of the relationship between religious ideas, practices, and movements and social processes and developments, particularly the development of capitalism, may help increase understanding of the religious dimension of colonial society.

The stories told here about the three rural movements help unpack the connection between religion, particularly Protestant Christianity, and social movements in postwar South Korea. Although these movements ended in 1937, their language and practices continued to circulate throughout South Korea when Pae Min-su and Hong Pyŏng-sŏn started new rural campaigns after the Korean War. With some support from the Presbyterian Church, Pae organized rural reconstruction campaigns after 1954 that succeeded in carrying out numerous programs that he had first designed in the 1930s and that embodied the principles found in the first Presbyterian rural movement.[12] His influence in the rural areas spread through Christian rural academies that he founded, including the Christian Farmers' Academy, the Christian Women Farmers' School, and the Samae (Three Loves) Agricultural Technology Institute. Hong also started a rural campaign after the war but then decided to focus on teaching and writing about rural development. While teaching rural and cooperative economics at several schools, including Chungang Seminary, he also published books on cooperative economics and on Denmark with the hope that South Korea would become an agrarian paradise.

Both Pae and Hong influenced not only young students from the countryside but also numerous Christian social reformers in postwar South Korea. For example, Kim Yong-gi, the founder of the Canaan Farming School, wrote that he learned about the value of cooperative economics and its relationship to Christianity by reading Hong's books on Denmark. Kim even hoped to follow in Hong's footsteps in pursuing a Danish-style revival in the Korean countryside.[13] Pae's and Hong's activities after 1953 and the YMCA, Presbyterian, and Ch'ŏndogyo rural movements during the colonial period show that religious concepts of social justice, economic equality, and social activism appeared well before the 1970s and 1980s, when liberal religious ideas such as Minjung theology (people's theology) were formulated and to which scholars typically point as the beginning of religion-based social activism.[14] Indeed, several ideas in social salvation theology, which grew in popularity during the late 1970s because it called for Christians to protest against the consequences of fast-paced industrial capitalism, such as social inequality and poverty, had already been well developed and articulated during the colonial period by leaders in the YMCA, Presbyterian, and Ch'ŏndogyo rural movements. But scholars today still give little credit to indigenous forces or factors in helping shape Minjung theology, which many believe was shaped by Western theology, especially liberation theology from Latin America.[15] Paying careful attention to faith-based social language, practices, and movements during the colonial period thus opens up ways of connecting the histories between the colonial and the postcolonial period and providing a comprehensive portrait of religious history in modern Korea.

The history of the YMCA, Presbyterian, and Ch'ŏndogyo rural movements also highlights the importance of religion for Koreans seeking ways to foster a meaningful, enriching, and secure life in the present. This history in particular shows the role religion plays in constructing alternative paths to modernity. As Koreans during the colonial period faced ideological and material upheavals, the three movements and their leaders provided a new way of viewing and comprehending the world and a new way of establishing a society in which individuals could experience sound and holistic development through reforms that emphasized communal relations and the value of place. Many of the beliefs and practices of these movements are embodied in the vibrant cooperative movement that exists in South Korea today. Many present-day studies of cooperative movements in Korea dismiss this fact, however, and tend to deny any connections between colonial and postcolonial South Korean society.[16]

The vision statements of two of the largest cooperatives in South Korea, Hansalim (1986) and Ture (2003), use the language of the YMCA, Presbyterian, and Ch'ŏndogyo rural movements that heavily criticized industrialization, especially its harmful impact on the built and natural environments, and sought to construct an alternative modern society that "places great emphasis on the community of solidarity."[17] Hansalim, in particular, not only "aims to create alternative life forms and values based on this solidarity" but also is deeply influenced by Tonghak / Ch'ŏndogyo philosophy.[18] Cooperatives like Ture and Hansalim continue the YMCA, Presbyterian, and Ch'ŏndogyo mission of stabilizing and enhancing the life of farmers today through marketing and consumer cooperatives that organize direct trade between farmers and consumers and strengthen the rights of both consumers and producers. During the past decade, when farmers saw their economic rights and opportunities diminish as a result of trade policies based on neoliberal philosophies, like the Free Trade Agreement with the United States (2011), and the loss of fertile land to urbanization, these cooperatives have helped protect farmers through the construction of agricultural and food systems based on the principle of food sovereignty. Moreover, they have created comprehensive economic, social, and cultural systems that have connected urban consumers with rural farmers in order to foster a united front that works to improve nutrition and food security through organic farming, overcome ecological devastation due to industrialization, protect the environment, and cultivate a holistic life that integrates humanity with the natural world. Like the YMCA, Presbyterian, and Ch'ŏndogyo rural movements, these cooperative movements seek to reclaim agriculture not simply to return to some romantic and simpler past but to create new ways of living through the adoption of contemporary reforms that value and enhance people's experiences in the present.

These ideas and practices of religion and agrarian life that influenced developments in South Korea resulted from the three organizations simultaneously carrying out a process of valuation through reclamation in the face of modernization. Despite their different backgrounds and traditions, each of the three organizations promoted similar values of religion, agriculture, and rural life because they recognized the necessity of developing fresh and alternative concepts and tools that would appropriately engage and overcome the violent forces of modernization. In colonial Korea, the process of valuation through reclamation, in particular, allowed religion to transform and acquire a new value that enabled it to continue as a source of new possibilities of thought, agency, and living. *Building a Heaven on Earth* shows that religion gains new value under modernization and has been and continues to be about transformation and adaptation in order to continue feeding the human imagination, cooperative social development, and the diversity of social living.

NOTES

Introduction

1. John H. Reisner, letter to Mr. Y. Mitsui, Bureau of Industry, Government of Chosen (May 25, 1926) (YMCA Archives, University of Minnesota, Minneapolis, photocopy), 1; and Reisner, "Survey by John H. Reisner of the College of Agriculture and Forestry of Nanking University [April 1926]" (YMCA Archives, University of Minnesota, Minneapolis, photocopy), 4.

2. Ibid.

3. "Panchonggyo undong e taehan naŭi saenggak," *Sinin'gan* (July 1926): 13.

4. Quoted in James Earnest Fisher, "Democracy and Mission Education in Korea" (PhD diss., Teachers College, Columbia University, 1928), 162.

5. Kim Kwangshik, "Buddhist Perspectives on the Anti-religious Movements in the 1930s," *Review of Korean Studies* 3, no. 1 (July 2000): 62.

6. "Agency" refers to being "capable of exerting some degree of control over the social relations in which one is enmeshed, which in turn implies the ability to transform those social relations to some degree." Being an agent means being capable of acting creatively to make social changes. For an exact definition of "agency," see William H. Sewell Jr., *Logics of History: Social Theory and Social Transformation* (Chicago: University of Chicago Press, 2005), 143–145.

7. See Michael D. Shin, "T'ukjip Miguk ŭi Han'guksa yon'gu: Miguk nae Han'gukhak ŭi kyebo," *Yŏksa pip'yŏng* 59 (Summer 2002): 76–98.

8. See Andrei Lankov, introduction to *The Dawn of Modern Korea* (Seoul: Eun-Haeng NaMu, 2007); Carter Eckert, *Offspring of Empire* (Seattle: University of Washington Press, 1991); and Soon-Won Park, *Colonial Industrialization and Labor in Korea* (Cambridge, MA: Harvard University Asia Center, 1999).

9. See Yi Tae-jin, *The Dynamics of Confucianism and Modernization in Korean History* (Ithaca, NY: Cornell East Asia Program, 2007).

10. Raymond Williams, *The Politics of Modernism* (London: Verso Press, 2007), 31.

11. Kim Dong-no, "National Identity and Class Interest in Peasant Movements during the Colonial Period" (working paper, Department of Sociology, Yonsei University, Seoul, photocopy), 5–7; Dilip Parameshwar Gaonkar, "On Alternative Modernities," in *Alternative Modernities,* ed. Dilip Parameshwar Gaonkar

(Durham, NC: Duke University Press, 2001), 1–9; and Marshall Berman, *All That Is Solid Melts into Air* (New York: Penguin Books, 1988), pts. 3 and 4.

12. See Prasenjit Duara, *Rescuing History from the Nation* (Chicago: University of Chicago Press, 1995), introduction and chap. 1.

13. Mitchell argues that the modern was imagined as originating in the West and that historical scholarship played a fundamental role in "staging" the West as the sole origin of and force behind the "modern." Timothy Mitchell, "The Stage of Modernity," in *Questions of Modernity,* ed. Timothy Mitchell (Minneapolis: University of Minnesota Press, 2000), 24.

14. Ibid., 15.

15. Stefan Tanaka, *Japan's Orient* (Berkeley: University of California Press, 1995).

16. James Ketelaar, *Of Heretics and Martyrs in Meiji Japan* (Princeton, NJ: Princeton University Press, 1990), chap. 2.

17. Duara, *Rescuing History from the Nation,* chap. 3.

18. Harry Harootunian, *Overcome by Modernity* (Princeton, NJ: Princeton University Press, 2000).

19. Civilization and Enlightenment discourse also included Christianity because it was seen as a powerful force that helped modernize the West. See Andre Schmid, *Korea between Empires* (New York: Columbia University Press, 2002), chap. 1.

20. The 1919 March 1st Movement was the first popular protest against Japanese colonial rule in which Koreans declared their independence from colonial rule. See Bruce Cumings, *Korea's Place in the Sun* (New York: W. W. Norton, 2005), 154–155.

21. According to Janice Kim, "The total value of production in mining and manufacturing skyrocketed from approximately thirty to five hundred million yen from 1910 to 1940." See Kim, *To Live to Work: Factory Women in Colonial Korea, 1910–1945* (Stanford, CA: Stanford University Press, 2009), 1.

22. See Se-Mi Oh, "Consuming the Modern" (PhD diss., Columbia University, 2008), 28, 51, 57.

23. The number of Koreans who lived in cities jumped from 3 to 14 percent of the population from 1910–1945. Janice Kim, *To Live to Work,* 1.

24. The type of reforms undertaken by the Japanese colonial government mirrored the kinds of modernization programs that governments and groups carried out in many noncolonized and colonized regions. See Timothy Mitchell, *Colonizing Egypt* (Berkeley: University of California Press, 1988), ix; Harootunian, *Overcome by Modernity;* Jean Comaroff and John L. Comaroff, *Of Revelation and Revolution,* vol. 1 (Chicago: University of Chicago Press, 1991); and Timothy Mitchell, *Rule of Experts* (Berkeley: University of California Press, 2002), chap. 2.

25. Berman, *All That Is Solid Melts into Air,* 16.

26. Anthony Giddens, *The Consequences of Modernity* (Stanford, CA: Stanford University Press, 1990), 139.

27. Ibid.
28. Sewell argues that the dynamics of capitalism, which he characterizes as "the relentless accumulation of capital through the pursuit of profit for profit's sake," causes this outcome of modernization. See Sewell, *Logics of History*, 277.
29. Mitchell, *Colonizing Egypt*, ix.
30. Studies of religion during the colonial period have tended to neglect any discussion of the rise of socially oriented systems of belief and religious movements between 1920 and 1945 in relation to modernization. The absence of monographs in English that socially contextualize Ch'ŏndogyo ideas during the 1920s and 1930s is due to there being only one book on the history of Tonghak and Ch'ŏndogyo. In addition, the majority of articles on Ch'ŏndogyo mostly cover its origins in Tonghak and its early years between 1905 and 1919. Most studies of Protestant Christianity during the 1920s and 1930s focus only on the efforts of Western missionaries to spread Christianity and the development of evangelicalism and theologies that emphasized personal salvation over social salvation and movements. On Protestant Christianity, see James H. Grayson, *Korea—A Religious History* (London: RoutledgeCurzon, 2002), pt. 4; Robert E. Buswell, ed., *Religions of Korea in Practice* (Princeton, NJ: Princeton University Press, 2007); Chong Bum Kim, "Preaching the Apocalypse in Colonial Korea," in *Christianity in Korea,* ed. Robert Buswell and Timothy Lee (Honolulu: University of Hawai'i Press, 2006), 149–166; Donald Clark, *Living Dangerously in Korea* (Norwalk, CT: Eastbridge, 2003); and Timothy S. Lee, *Born Again* (Honolulu: University of Hawai'i Press, 2010). See also Benjamin B. Weems, *Reform, Rebellion, and the Heavenly Way* (Tucson: University of Arizona Press, 1964). Weems's book provides few details on Ch'ŏndogyo social movements and supplies an incomplete picture of Ch'ŏndogyo because the majority of chapters are devoted to the history of Tonghak. Recent studies that effectively cover Tonghak history and the early years of Ch'ŏndogyo include George Kallander, *Salvation through Dissent: Tonghak Heterodoxy and Early Modern Korea* (Honolulu: Univ. of Hawai'i Press, 2013); and Carl Young, "Embracing Modernity: Organizational and Ritual Reform in Ch'ŏndogyo, 1905–1910," *Asian Studies Review* 29 (March 2005): 47–59.
31. These Korean Christian nationalists never questioned capitalism's impact on society and instead had a "rosy view of capitalism." See Kenneth Wells, *New God, New Nation* (Honolulu: University of Hawai'i Press, 1990), 61–63.
32. A few studies have analyzed the connection between larger trends in society and faith-based social activism immediately before and during the colonial period. However, they not only point out how religious followers, instead of formal religious organizations, exclusively started certain types of movements in society but also discuss and analyze only those movements that directly protested against colonial rule. For these studies, the criterion for a faith-based social movement is religious followers organizing and demonstrating

against Japanese imperialism. For examples, see Buswell and Lee, *Christianity in Korea*, pt. 3; Pori Park, *Trial and Error in Modernist Reforms: Korean Buddhism under Colonial Rule* (Berkeley: Institute of East Asian Studies, University of California, Berkeley, 2009); and Yun Kyŏng-no, *Han'guk kŭndaesa ŭi kidokkyosajŏk ihae* (Seoul: Yokminsa, 1992) (the exception to this is Chang Kyu-sik's *Ilche ha Han'guk kidokkyo minjokjuŭi yŏn'gu* [Seoul: Hyean, 2001]). Representative of these studies is Chung-shin Park, *Protestantism and Politics in Korea* (Seattle: University of Washington Press, 2003). Park argues that the Protestant Church retreated from social and political activities because of the growing institutionalization of the church and "otherworldly" Christian theologies or beliefs that pushed the Protestant Church to "devot[e] itself solely to religious activities and spiritual preparation for salvation in the afterlife." Thus Christians totally retreated from society, "did not show any interest in nationalist politics and social reform," and even "condemn[ed] social and political activity" during the 1920s and 1930s. What results from studies like Park's is the argument that no religious groups had an interest in or organized movements to combat economic and social problems between 1919 and 1937 and the perception that socially oriented theologies and movements that addressed the consequences of modernization first originated in the 1970s when religious figures developed new religious ideas such as Minjung theology in order to deal with political authoritarianism and fast-paced industrial capitalist development. See Park, *Protestantism and Politics in Korea*, 152 and 156.

33. The purpose of a cognitive map "is to enable a situational representation on the part of the individual subject to that vaster and properly unrepresentable totality which is the ensemble of society's structure as a whole." See Fredric Jameson, *Postmodernism; or, The Cultural Logic of Late Capitalism* (Durham, NC: Duke University Press, 1991), 52.

34. See the introduction to *Colonial Modernity in Korea*, ed. Gi-Wook Shin and Michael Robinson (Cambridge, MA: Harvard University Asia Center, 1999), 1–20.

35. Michael E. Robinson, *Korea's Twentieth-Century Odyssey* (Honolulu: University of Hawai'i Press, 2007), 78.

36. See representative works on colonial modernity, such as Robinson, *Korea's Twentieth-Century Odyssey*, chaps. 1–4; essays in *Colonial Modernity in Korea*; Janice Kim, *To Live to Work*; and Oh, "Consuming the Modern."

37. Cha Seung Ki, "The Colonial-Imperial Regime and Its Effects: Writer Kim Sa-ryang as an Exception," *Korea Journal* 50, no. 4 (Winter 2010): 107. See also Ch'a Sŭng-ki, *Pan kŭndaejŏk sangsangnyŏk ŭi imgyedŭl* (Seoul: P'urun yŏksa, 2009), introduction and chap. 1.

38. For a criticism of colonial modernity, see Shin, "T'ŭkjip Miguk ŭi Han'guksa yŏn'gu: Miguk nae Han'gukhak ŭi kyebo."

39. "Colonial modernity" for Asian studies was defined as a "speculative frame for investigating the infinitely pervasive discursive powers that increasingly con-

nect at key points to the globalizing impulses of capitalism." See Tani Barlow, "Introduction: On 'Colonial Modernity,'" in *Formations of Colonial Modernity in East Asia*, ed. Tani Barlow (Durham, NC: Duke University Press, 1997), 6.

40. The only two articles on agrarianism in colonial Korea are Gi-Wook Shin and Do-hyun Han, "Colonial Corporatism," in Shin and Robinson, *Colonial Modernity in Korea*, 70–96; and Gi-Wook Shin, "Agrarianism: A Critique of Colonial Modernity," *Comparative Studies in Society and History* 41, no. 4 (October 1999): 784–804.

41. Gaonkar, "On Alternative Modernities," 4–6.

42. Ibid., 4.

43. Charles Baudelaire, *Selected Writings on Art and Literature*, trans. P. E. Charvet (New York: Penguin Books, 1972), 403–406; Gaonkar, "On Alternative Modernities," 4–6; and Harootunian, *Overcome by Modernity*, chap. 3.

44. Jameson, *Postmodernism*, 310.

45. Ibid.

46. Alan Berger, a landscape architect, writes that reclaiming involves taking what exists already, integrating it with contemporary technology and means, and thus making something new or of "richer value and meaning," while restoration demands a return to a site's original conditions and therefore aims to move the present back into the past. Berger argues that restoring landscapes to their original condition is impossible because the site's origins have lost "significance and coherence over time," and "when humans attempt to reproduce a natural system, they are constrained to transfigure nature through the unavoidable contribution of their own devices and prejudices." According to Berger, however, "Reclamation (especially at larger scales) attempts to set up a new or modified framework from which nature may adapt new natural processes that emerge from the conditions of the new place." Thus "Reclaimed landscapes never re-create the old or represent it. They construct or assemble artificial conditions that accept alteration as the genesis of a new landscape structure. This results in the formation of a new ontological value from altered conditions." Berger's views articulate the thoughts and beliefs of YMCA, Presbyterian, and Ch'ŏndogyo rural leaders about reconstructing rural life because the leaders never sought to restore past conditions in the present as a way to manage modernization but instead envisioned combining the preexisting with the contemporary to achieve new opportunities for living and working. See Alan Berger, *Reclaiming the American West* (New York: Princeton Architectural Press, 2002), 61–71.

47. James C. Scott, *Seeing Like a State* (New Haven, CT: Yale University Press, 1998), pts. 2 and 3.

48. Harootunian, *Overcome by Modernity*, xvii.

49. See Harry Harootunian, *History's Disquiet* (New York: Columbia University Press, 2000), 62–63 and chap. 2, n. 4.

50. Craig Calhoun, Mark Juergensmeyer, and Jonathan VanAntwerpen, introduction to *Rethinking Secularism*, ed. Craig Calhoun, Mark Juergensmeyer, and Jonathan VanAntwerpen (New York: Oxford University Press, 2011), 6–11.
51. Ibid., 7 and 11.
52. David Scott, "Appendix: The Trouble of Thinking; An Interview with Talal Asad," in *Powers of the Secular Modern*, ed. David Scott and Charles Hirschkind (Stanford, CA: Stanford University Press, 2006), 298.
53. See Talal Asad, *Genealogies of Religion: Discipline and Reasons of Power in Christianity and Islam* (Baltimore: John Hopkins University Press, 1993), chap. 1.
54. John D. Boy, "Thinking about Revolution, Religion and Egypt with Talal Asad," *The Immanent Frame*, SSRC, February 23, 2011, accessed November 2012, http://blogs.ssrc.org/tif/2011/02/23/thinking-about-revolution-religion-and-egypt-with-talal-asad/.
55. See the various chapters in Calhoun, Juergensmeyer, and VanAntwerpen, *Rethinking Secularism*; and Courtney Bender and Ann Taves, eds. *What Matters? Ethnographies of Value in a Not So Secular Age* (New York: Columbia University Press, 2012).
56. "Value" means "the claims that people make regarding the importance of something (anything), regardless of whether the importance carries a positive or negative valence." See Bender and Taves, *What Matters?*, 10.
57. Ibid., 9.
58. See ibid., 61–85 and 86–118.
59. On the basis of YMCA, Presbyterian, and Ch'ŏndogyo writings, this book defines a peasant as a type of rural cultivator who mostly farms for self-subsistence and rents farming land. All three movements sought to transform peasants into farmers who were self-subsistence landowners who also grew agricultural goods for the market.

Chapter 1: Origins of Protestantism and Tonghak in Late Chosŏn Korea

1. Ch'oe Che-u, "Nonhakmun," in *Ch'ŏndogyo kyŏngjŏn haeŭi*, ed. Paek Se-myŏng (Seoul: Ch'ŏndogyo chungang ch'ongbu, 1963), 57.
2. See Jun Seong Ho, James B. Lewis, and Kang Han Rog, "Korean Expansion and Decline from the Seventeenth to the Nineteenth Century: A View Suggested by Adam Smith," *Journal of Economic History* 68, no. 1 (March 2008): 244–282.
3. Anders Karlsson points out that the "agricultural years of most widespread and severe crop failure were 1778 / 79, 1783 / 84, 1786 / 87, 1792 / 93 and 1794 / 95." See Anders Karlsson, "Famine, Finance and Political Power: Crop Failure and Land-Tax Exemptions in Late Eighteenth-Century Chosŏn Korea," *Journal of Economic and Social History of the Orient* 48, no. 4 (2005): 570.

4. Ibid., 555.

5. Outbreaks occurred in 1821, 1833, 1862, 1867, 1879, and 1895. See Ho, Lewis, and Kang, "Korean Expansion and Decline," 263; and Kim Hong-ch'ŏl, "Kaehanggi ŭi minjok chonggyo undong," in Han'guk minjok chonggyo undongsa, ed. No Kil-myŏng, Kim Hong-ch'ŏl, Yun I-hŭm, and Hwang Sŏn-myŏng (Seoul: Han'guk minjok chonggyo hyŏpŭihoe, 2003), 103.

6. Sun Joo Kim, Marginality and Subversion in Korea (Seattle: University of Washington Press, 2007), 6.

7. Ro Kil-myŏng, Han'guk sinhŭng chonggyo yŏn'gu (Seoul: Kyŏngsewŏn, 1996), 135–168.

8. Ro Kil-myung, "New Religions and Social Change in Modern Korean History," Review of Korean Studies 5, no. 1 (June 2002): 35–36.

9. For a list of the reforms, see "Kabo Reforms," in Sources of Korean Tradition, ed. Yŏng-ho Ch'oe, Peter H. Lee, and Wm. Theodore de Bary, vol. 2 (New York: Columbia University Press, 2000), 273–276.

10. I take "Tonghak Revolution" directly from the term scholars in Korea use for the Tonghak uprising: "Tonghak Hyŏngmyŏng" (Revolution).

11. Ch'oe Che-u, "Sudŏkmun," in Paek, Ch'ŏndogyo kyŏngjŏn haeŭi, 111–112.

12. See George Kallander, Salvation through Dissent: Tonghak Heterodoxy and Early Modern Korea (Honolulu: University of Hawai'i Press, 2013), 49–52.

13. Ch'oe Che-u, "P'odŏkmun," in Paek, Ch'ŏndogyo kyŏngjŏn haeŭi, 8–9.

14. Ibid., 10–11.

15. Ibid., 12–14.

16. Ch'oe wrote that he was able to overcome confusion and anxiety through this religious process. Ch'oe, "Sudŏkmun," 11.

17. Oh Ji-yŏng, Tonghaksa (Seoul: Yŏngch'ang sukwan, 1940), 26.

18. Kim Dong-no, "Peasants, State, and Landlords: National Crisis and the Transformation of Agrarian Society in Pre-colonial Korea," 2 vols. (PhD diss., University of Chicago, 1994), 1:155.

19. Claude Lévi-Strauss, The Savage Mind (Chicago: University of Chicago Press, 1966), 16–33.

20. Ro, Han'guk sinhŭng chonggyo yŏn'gu, 18.

21. Don Baker, "Hananim, Hanŭnim, Hanullim, and Hanŏllim: The Construction of Terminology for Korean Monotheism," Review of Korean Studies 5, no. 1 (June 2002): 127.

22. Ro, Han'guk sinhŭng chonggyo yŏn'gu, 82.

23. Ch'oe, "Nonhakmun," 77–78.

24. Ro, Han'guk sinhŭng chonggyo yŏn'gu, 84.

25. Ch'oe, "Nonhakmun," 77–78.

26. David Tracy, Plurality and Ambiguity: Hermeneutics, Religion, Hope (Chicago: University of Chicago Press, 1994), 89.

27. Ch'oe, "Nonhakmun," 67.

28. Robert C. Fuller, *Religious Revolutionaries: The Rebels Who Reshaped American Religion* (New York: Palgrave Macmillan, 2004), 93.

29. Ch'oe, "Nonhakmun," 88.

30. Kim Hong-ch'ŏl, "Kaehanggi ŭi minjok chonggyo undong," 110–111.

31. Ch'oe, "Sudŏkmun," 127.

32. Ibid., 127.

33. Joachim Wach, *Types of Religious Experience: Christian and Non-Christian* (Chicago: University of Chicago Press, 1951), 41–42.

34. Susan S. Shin, "The Tonghak Movement: From Enlightenment to Revolution," *Korean Studies Forum* 5 (1978–1979): 19.

35. Ch'oe, "Nonhakmun," 76.

36. According to George Kallander, the "talismans, in the shape of the Grand Ultimate (*t'aegŭk*), and the characters *kung*, were to be written on paper, burned, dissolved in cold water, and drunk as spiritual and physical remedies; the concoction would refresh the body and dispel illness." The sword dance was a shamanistic practice that involved dancing with a sword and singing songs." See Kallander, *Salvation through Dissent*, 65 and 84–86.

37. Ch'oe, "Nonhakmun," 88.

38. This type of experience is similar to Georges Bataille's ideas of inner experience in that individuals in this space would overcome discontinuity and be connected to the whole. See Georges Bataille, *Inner Experience*, trans. Leslie Anne Boldt (Albany: State University of New York Press, 1988).

39. Yi Ton-hwa, *Ch'ŏndogyo ch'anggŏnsa* (Seoul: Taedong Press, 1933), pt. 2, 37–38.

40. Ibid., pt. 2, 7.

41. Ro, *Han'guk sinhŭng chonggyo yŏn'gu*, 124–125.

42. Yi, *Ch'ŏndogyo ch'anggŏnsa*, pt. 2, 18.

43. Stanley Jeyaraja Tambiah, *Magic, Science, and the Scope of Rationality* (New York: Cambridge University Press, 1990), 109.

44. Mircea Eliade, *The Sacred and the Profane: The Nature of Religion* (New York: Harcourt, 1959), 62–65.

45. Kallander, *Salvation through Dissent*, 53–54 and 81–89.

46. Ibid., 81–89.

47. Ibid., 95–100.

48. Wach, *Types of Religious Experience*, 38–47.

49. Yi, *Ch'ŏndogyo ch'anggŏnsa*, pt. 2, 36.

50. Kallander, *Salvation through Dissent*, 95.

51. According to Emile Durkheim, sacred ideas and practices are those that are "set apart and forbidden." See Emile Durkheim, *The Elementary Forms of Religious Life*, trans. Karen E. Fields (New York: Free Press, 1995), 44.

52. Georges Bataille, *Theory of Religion*, trans. Robert Hurley (New York: Zone Books, 1992), 35.

53. Eliade, *Sacred and the Profane,* 179-201.

54. William H. Sewell Jr., "Historical Events as Transformations of Structures: Inventing Revolution at the Bastille," *Theory and Society* 25, no. 6 (December 1996): 869.

55. Charles Allen Clark, *Religions of Old Korea* (New York: F. H. Revell, 1932), 156.

56. Yi, *Ch'ŏndogyo ch'anggŏnsa,* pt. 2, 24 and 30.

57. Ibid., pt. 2, 7.

58. Kim Hong-ch'ŏl, "Kaehanggi ŭi minjok chonggyo undong," 119.

59. Yi, *Ch'ŏndogyo ch'anggŏnsa,* pt. 2, 40-41.

60. "Translator's Introduction," in Durkheim, *Elementary Forms of Religious Life,* xlvi.

61. Ibid., xlvii.

62. The spelling of *jup* is taken from Kim Dong-no, "Peasants, State, and Landlords," 1:160.

63. Yi, *Ch'ŏndogyo ch'anggŏnsa,* pt. 2, 34; and Benjamin Weems, *Reform, Rebellion, and the Heavenly Way* (Tucson: University of Arizona Press, 1964), 17.

64. There are few published figures on the number of Tonghak members in the 1890s. This figure is based on the number of participants in the Tonghak Revolution. Kim Hong-ch'ŏl, "Kaehanggi ŭi minjok chonggyo undong," 124.

65. Yi, *Ch'ŏndogyo ch'anggŏnsa,* pt. 2, 53-54.

66. Kim Jeong-in, "Ilche kangjŏmgi Ch'ŏndogyodan ŭi minjok undong yŏn'gu" (PhD diss., Seoul National University, 2002), 16-19.

67. They also demanded social equality in which slavery would be abolished and discrimination against outcasts would be forbidden. Kim Dong-no, "National Identity and Class Interest in Peasant Movements during the Colonial Period" (working paper, Department of Sociology, Yonsei University, Seoul, photocopy), 11.

68. See "Interrogation of Chŏn Pongjun, First Session," in *Sources of Korean Tradition,* ed. Yŏng-ho Ch'oe, Peter H. Lee, and Wm. Theodore de Bary, vol. 2 (New York: Columbia University Press, 2000), 267-272.

69. Jean Comaroff and John L. Comaroff, *Of Revelation and Revolution,* vol. 1 (Chicago: University of Chicago Press, 1991).

70. The following denominations came after the arrival of Allen, Underwood, and Appenzeller: the Presbyterian Church in the United States (PCUS) (1892), the Methodist Episcopalian South Church (1896), the Presbyterian Church of Victoria, Australia (1889), and the Canadian Presbyterian Church (1898).

71. Most of these discussions occurred through organizations established by the missionaries. In 1889, the PCUSA and the Australian Presbyterian Church first established the United Council of the Missions of the American and

Victorian Churches, which was renamed the Council of Missions when the PCUS joined in 1893. In 1905, the Presbyterian council was absorbed into a larger organization that included all the Protestant missionary groups in Korea and was renamed the Great Council of Evangelical Missions.

72. This plan was especially adopted by Presbyterians.

73. Charles Allen Clark, *The Korean Church and the Nevius Methods* (New York: Fleming H. Revell, 1930), 12.

74. J. L. Nevius, *The Methods of Mission Work* (Shanghai: Presbyterian Mission Press, 1886), 12–16.

75. C. C. Vinton, "Presbyterian Mission Work in Korea," *Missionary Review of the World* (September 1893): 671.

76. H. G. Underwood, "An Object Lesson in Self Support," *Chinese Recorder* 31 (August 1900): 386; and Vinton, "Presbyterian Mission Work in Korea," 671.

77. Vinton, "Presbyterian Mission Work in Korea," 671.

78. Ibid.

79. Clark, *Korean Church and the Nevius Methods,* 100–107.

80. Ibid., 106.

81. Horace G. Underwood, *Call of Korea* (New York: Fleming H. Revell, 1908), 146–148.

82. The Korean government designated Sungsil as a university in 1907, but the colonial government redesignated it as a four-year technical school. Today, in South Korea, it is a university. Throughout this book, I refer to Sungsil as a university because it carried out its mission and activities like any university at the time. Sungsil taehakyo, *Sungsil taehakgyo 100-yŏnsa I* (Seoul: Sungsil taehakgyo ch'ulp'anbu, 1997), 131.

83. For a description of the overall educational system, see Horace H. Underwood, *Modern Education in Korea* (New York: International Press, 1926).

84. William Scott, "Canadians in Korea: A Brief Historical Sketch of Canadian Mission Work in Korea" (typescript, 1975), 63.

85. Arthur Judson Brown, *The Mastery of the Far East: The Story of Korea's Transformation and Japan's Rise to Supremacy in the Orient* (New York: Charles Scribner's Sons, 1919), 507–508.

86. My ideas on trauma are taken from Dominick LaCapra. See Dominick LaCapra, *History in Transit* (Ithaca, NY: Cornell University Press, 2004), 45.

87. Robert E. Speer, *Reports on the Mission in Korea of the Presbyterian Board of Foreign Missions* (New York: Board of Foreign Missions of the Presbyterian Church in the USA, 1897), 6.

88. Arthur Judson Brown, *Report of a Visitation of the Korean Mission of Presbyterian Board of Foreign Missions* (New York: Board of Foreign Missions of the Presbyterian Church, USA, 1902), 12.

89. "The Time Opportune," *Korea Mission Field* (December 1905): 29.

90. King Kojong's Fourteen-Article Oath in 1895 further severed Korea from its Confucian heritage through proclamations, such as rejecting Korea's traditional ties with China and calling on all individuals to increase their wealth for the sake of the nation.

91. Clifford Geertz, *The Interpretation of Cultures* (New York: Basic Books, 1973), 108.

92. See "A Call to Special Effort," *Korea Mission Field* (December 1905): 29; "Time Opportune," 30; and W. G. Cram, "Revival Fires," *Korea Mission Field* (December 1905): 33.

93. W. N. Blair, quoted in George Paik, *The History of Protestant Missions in Korea 1832–1910* (Seoul: Yonsei University Press, 1970), 369.

94. G. Lee, "How the Spirit Came to Pyengyang [*sic*]," *Korea Mission Field* (March 1907): 33.

95. Ibid., 34.

96. Paik, *History of Protestant Missions in Korea*, 373–378.

97. W. M. Baird, "The Spirit among Pyengyang [*sic*] Students," *Korea Mission Field* (May 1907): 65.

98. James Gale, *Korea in Transition* (New York: Young People's Missionary Movement of the United States and Canada, 1909), 207–208.

99. G. Lee, "How the Spirit Came to Pyengyang," 36; and George Thrumbull Ladd, *In Korea with Marquis Ito* (New York: Charles Scribner's Sons, 1908), 107–109.

100. Ladd, *In Korea with Marquis Ito*, 107–109.

101. Paik, *History of Protestant Missions in Korea*, 370–371.

102. Gale, *Korea in Transition*, 209–210.

103. "Editorial," *Korea Mission Field* (May 1908): 70.

104. Geertz, *Interpretation of Cultures*, 105.

105. Dominick LaCapra believes that working through trauma "involves gaining critical distance on those experiences and recontextualizing them in ways that permit a reengagement with ongoing concerns and future possibilities." See LaCapra, *History in Transit*, 45.

106. From 1905 to 1907, the church's population increased from 25,000 believers to 118,000, and the number of churches doubled from 321 to 642. Underwood, *Call of Korea*, 146–148.

107. "Editorial," *Korea Mission Field* (March 1908): 33; and J. Z. Moore, "The Great Revival Year," *Korea Mission Field* (August 1908): 119.

108. Han'guk kyohoe paekjunyŏn chunbi wiwŏnhoe saryo punkwa wiwŏnhoe, ed., *Taehan yesugyo changnohoe paekyŏnsa* (Seoul: Taehan Yesugyo changnohoe ch'onghoe, 1984), 238–239; and Charles Allen Clark, *Digest of the Presbyterian Church of Korea* (Seoul: Korean Religious Book and Tract Society, 1918), 30–31.

109. Fuller, *Religious Revolutionaries*, 66.

110. David Tracy, *Blessed Rage for Order: The New Pluralism in Theology* (Chicago: University of Chicago Press, 1996), 24–25.

111. Jerald C. Brauer, *Protestantism in America: A Narrative History* (Philadelphia: Westminster Press, 1965), 61.

112. Ibid., 114.

113. Daniel T. Rodgers, *The Work Ethic in Industrial America, 1850–1920* (Chicago: University of Chicago Press, 1978), 7–27.

114. Rationalization of economic life entailed the "drive for maximization of profits through the adoption of the most efficient forms of organization." Jackson Lears, *No Place for Grace* (Chicago: University of Chicago Press, 1981), 9.

115. Ibid., 4–5.

116. Ibid., 57.

117. For an analysis of Revivalism in Korea, see Timothy S. Lee, "Born-Again in Korea: The Rise and Character of Revivalism in (South) Korea, 1885–1988" (PhD diss., University of Chicago, 1996).

118. Brown, *Mastery of the Far East*, 540.

119. Samuel A. Moffett, "Policy and Methods for the Evangelization of Korea," *Chinese Recorder* 37 (May 1906): 235.

120. Ibid., 237.

121. Ibid., 239.

122. T. S. Lee, "Born-Again in Korea," 60.

123. Moore, "Great Revival Year," 116.

124. Clark, *Korean Church and the Nevius Methods*, 113–114.

125. T. S. Lee, "Born-Again in Korea," 58.

126. George Heber Jones, "The Korean Passion for Souls," *Korea Mission Field* (January 1909): 10.

127. Clark, *Korean Church and the Nevius Methods*, 103.

128. See A. E. Lucas, "Industrial Work," *Korea Mission Field* (October 1918): 205–207; and *The Korea Mission Field* (January 1918).

129. Albert L. Park, "Christianity under Colonialism" (Master's Thesis, Columbia University, 1998), 42–50.

130. See Horace G. Underwood, "Korea's Crisis Hour," *Korea Mission Field* (August 1908): 132; George S. McCune, "Hand Training Necessary as Well as That of Head and Heart," *Korea Mission Field* (January 1918): 7; and Park, "Christianity under Colonialism."

131. Albert L. Park, "A Sacred Economy of Value and Production," in *Encountering Modernity*, ed. Albert L. Park and David Yoo (Honolulu: University of Hawai'i Press, 2014), 16–17.

132. Underwood, *Modern Education in Korea*, 115.

133. Horace H. Underwood, "Industrial Training in the Far East," *Missionary Review of the World* (September 1918): 679–680.

134. Frank M. Brockman, "Some of the Problems of Industrial Education in Korea," *Korea Mission Field* (July 1910): 173.

135. Mrs. Swinehart, "What Are You Doing in Your Station for the Help of Mothers?," *Korea Mission Field* (April 1916): 113, and W. N. Blair, "The Care of Babies and Children," *Korea Mission Field* (April 1918): 79–80.

136. Hyaeweol Choi, *Gender and Mission Encounters in Korea: New Women, Old Ways* (Berkeley: University of California Press, 2009), explores the complex relationship between Korean women and missionaries.

137. Timothy Mitchell, *Colonizing Egypt* (Berkeley: University of California Press, 1988), ix.

138. See Moffett, "Policy and Methods for the Evangelization of Korea," 235–248.

139. Brown, *Mastery of the Far East,* 541.

140. See Kim Sang-t'ae, "P'yŏng'ando kidokkyo seryŏk kwa ch'inmi ellit'ŭ ŭi hyŏngsŏng," *Yŏksa pip'yŏng* 45 (Winter 1998): 171–207.

141. Timothy S. Lee, "A Political Factor in the Rise of Protestantism in Korea: Protestantism and the 1919 March First Movement," *Church History* 69, no. 1 (March 2000): 127.

142. Ibid., 128.

143. For example, conservative missionaries complained that Severance Hospital focused too much of its activities on educational and medical work instead of directly evangelizing Koreans. See Yunjae Park, "Between Mission and Medicine: The Early History of Severance Hospital," in Park and Yoo, *Encountering Modernity.*

144. Kenneth Wells' book *New God, New Nation* (Honolulu: University of Hawai'i Press, 1990) provides an excellent analysis of the relationship between Christianity and nationalism in Korea. See *New God, New Nation,* chap. 2.

145. Formed in 1906, the Sinminhoe was a leading nationalist organization that focused on establishing a strong and healthy national body. Ahn Chang-ho became the chief leader of the organization.

146. Michael D. Shin, "The Specter of Yi Gwang-su: The March 1st Movement and the Nation in Colonial Korea" (unpublished manuscript), chap. 2, 13.

147. Yun promoted industrialization through several projects, especially through his directorship of the Southern Methodist–led Songdo School. See T.-H. Yun, "What Shall We Eat," *Korea Mission Field* (January 1918): 11–12.

148. Some Christian leaders even opposed land reform because it would "remove the only rural component—the landlord class—that could provide the wanted capital" and encouraged capitalist competition because it was the "source of prosperity and happiness." See Wells, *New God, New Nation,* 63.

149. Kil Sŏn-ju, "Malsehak," in *Yŏnggye Kil Sŏnju moksa chŏjakjip* (Seoul: Taehan kidokkyo sŏhoe, 1968), 27–28.

150. Chung-shin Park, *Protestantism and Politics in Korea* (Seattle: University of Washington Press, 2003), 60–66.

Chapter 2: Economic and Social Change under Japanese Colonialism

1. For a concise debate on the origins of capitalism in Korea, see Michael D. Shin, introduction to *Landlords, Peasants, and Intellectuals in Modern Korea*, ed. Pang Kie-chung and Michael D. Shin (Ithaca, NY: Cornell East Asia Program, 2005).

2. At that time, agricultural productivity increased through technological innovations and new farming techniques. These developments resulted in surplus crops that were sold in markets, which grew as important sites of vibrant commercial activity. According to Yi Tae-jin, "Markets in rural villages became more rooted and began to become visible in some local areas, leading to a wide distribution of goods." At these markets, new forms of currency, such as silver and cloth, aided the process of selling and exchanging agricultural goods. By the beginning of the nineteenth century, the countryside showed signs of a growing agricultural market in that some rural cultivators were moving away from self-subsistence farming. See Yi Tae-jin, *The Dynamics of Confucianism and Modernization in Korean History* (Ithaca, NY: Cornell East Asia Program, 2007), 97–98; Kim Yong-sŏp, "The Two Courses of Agrarian Reforms in Korea's Modernization," in Pang and Shin, *Landlords, Peasants, and Intellectuals in Modern Korea*, 25; and Kim Yong-sŏp, *Han'guk kŭnhyŏndae nongŏpsa yŏn'gu* (Seoul: Iljogak, 1992), pts. 1 and 2.

3. See Barrington Moore, *Social Origins of Dictatorship and Democracy* (Boston: Beacon Press, 1966); and Robert Brenner, "Agrarian Class Structure and Economic Development in Pre-industrial Europe," *Past and Present* 70 (February 1976): 30–75.

4. Kim Yong-sŏp's work has been instrumental in countering arguments made by historians of Korea who see industrialization as a necessity for capitalist development and thus argue that capitalism began only when the colonial government started industrial programs.

5. See Kim Yong-sŏp, "Two Courses of Agrarian Reforms in Korea's Modernization," 35.

6. Ibid., 1–40.

7. Informally, private landownership by members of the royal family, religious institutions, and members of the *yangban* class existed before 1910. For example, there had been a considerable class of landowners since the Koryŏ period (935–1392). See John B. Duncan, *The Origins of the Chosŏn Dynasty* (Seattle: University of Washington Press, 2000).

8. See Hoon Koo Lee (Yi Hun-gu), "A History of Land Systems and Policies in Korea" (PhD diss., University of Wisconsin, 1929).

9. Ch'in Yŏng-ch'ŏl, "Oerae chabonjuŭi ŭi Chosŏn anaesŏ ŭi paldal," *Hyesŏng* (May 1931): 15.

10. Yong-Ha Shin, "Landlordism in the Late Yi Dynasty (II)," *Korea Journal* 18, no. 7 (July 1978): 24.

11. Government-General of Chosen, *Thriving Chosen* (Keijo: Government-General of Chosen, 1935), 28–30.

12. Using this new elaborate transportation system, merchants dispatched goods to port cities where trading and selling occurred daily. See Hur Young-ran, "Colonial Modernity and Rural Markets during the Japanese Colonial Period," *International Journal of Korean History* 15, no. 2 (August 2010): 74–75.

13. The port cities were Chinnamp'o, Ch'ŏngjin, Inch'ŏn, Kunsan, Mok'po, Najin, Pusan, Shinŭiju. Sŏngjin, Unggi, Wŏnsan, and Yong-amp'o.

14. Government-General of Chosen, *Thriving Chosen*, 36.

15. Pang Ki-chung, *Han'guk kŭnhyŏndae sasangsa yŏn'gu* (Seoul: Yŏksa pip'yŏngsa, 1992), 37–44.

16. The main agricultural items for export were rice, soybeans, raw silk, cotton, and cattle. Most of these items were exported to Japan, the United States, China, and Manchukuo. See Government-General of Chosen, *Thriving Chosen*, 44 and 47.

17. Sin Il-yong, "Nongch'on munje yŏn'gu," *Kaebyŏk* (August 1925): 47.

18. Yi Sŏng-hwan, "Mŏnjŏ nongmin put'ŏ haebang haja," *Kaebyŏk* (January 1923): 33–41.

19. Yi Sun-t'ak, "Chosŏnin musanhwa ŭi t'ŭkching," *Sinmin* (August 1926): 7–14.

20. Ch'oe Chin-wŏn, "Nongch'on munje pip'an t'ŭkchip nan," *Pip'an* (October 1932): 18–23; Pak Man-ch'un, "Nongch'on kyŏngje e daehan ili ŭi hakjŏk koch'al," *Pip'an* (October 1932): 29–33; Yi Ch'ŏng-won, "Chosŏn nongŏp ŭi sangsankyu," *Pip'an* (April 1936): 100–110.

21. "Nongch'on munje t'ŭkchip," *Tonggwang* (April 1931): 18–21.

22. Ibid.; and Pak Tŏk-u, "Nongch'on pip'ye ŭi wŏnin," *Sinmin* (May 1929): 19.

23. Yi Sun-t'ak, "Chosŏnin musanhwa ŭi t'ŭkching," 7–14.

24. Helen Kiteuk Kim, "Rural Education for the Regeneration of Korea" (PhD diss., Columbia University, 1931), 8.

25. Hoon Koo Lee (Yi Hun-gu), *Land Utilization and Rural Economy in Korea* (Chicago: University of Chicago Press, 1936), 262.

26. Chung Seung-mo, *Markets: Traditional Korean Society*, trans. Cho Yoon-jung and Min Eun-young (Seoul: Ewha University Press, 2006), 49.

27. Hur, "Colonial Modernity and Rural Markets during the Japanese Colonial Period," 80.

28. Anthony Giddens, *The Consequences of Modernity* (Stanford, CA: Stanford University Press, 1990), 19–21.

29. Gi-Wook Shin, *Peasant Protest and Social Change in Colonial Korea* (Seattle: University of Washington Press, 1996), 51.

30. See Edmund de Schweinitz Brunner, "Rural Korea: A Preliminary Survey of Economic, Social and Religious Conditions," in *The Jerusalem Meeting of the International Council, March 24–April 8, 1928*, vol. 6, *The Christian Mission in Relation to Rural Problems* (New York: International Missionary Council,

1928), 84–172; and John H. Reisner, "Survey by John H. Reisner of the College of Agriculture and Forestry of Nanking University [April 1926]" (YMCA Archives, University of Minnesota, Minneapolis, photocopy), 4.

31. The number of pure tenants jumped to 1,546,456 in 1932 and 1,583,358 in 1939, while a large number of tenants, semitenants, and independent farmers became slash-and-burn farmers and agricultural laborers. See Kim Yong-sop, "The Landlord System and the Agricultural Economy during the Japanese Occupation Period," in Pang and Shin, *Landlords, Peasants, and Intellectuals in Modern Korea*, 169, table 3.

32. Chŏng Jin-yŏng, *Chosŏn sidae hyangch'on sahoesa* (Seoul: Han'gilsa, 1999), 234–245; and Hoon Koo Lee, *Land Utilization and Rural Economy in Korea*, 250–251.

33. Yi Hun-gu, *Chosŏn nongŏpnon* (Seoul: Hansŏng, 1935), 323.

34. Yi Sŏng-hwan, "Chosŏn ŭi nongmin i yŏ," *Sinmin* (June 1929): 36.

35. Although some landlords surveyed the first yields of the crop and then determined how much rent should be paid (*t'oji* rent), the majority of landlords demanded half of the crops (*t'ajak* rent). Hoon Koo Lee, *Land Utilization and Rural Economy in Korea*, 163.

36. Sin, "Nongch'on munje yŏn'gu," 47.

37. Yi Kak-chŏng, "Sojak munje e ch'uihaya," *Sinmin* (December 1925): 51–52; Yi Hun-gu, *Chosŏn nongŏpnon*, 323; Ch'oe Man-tal, "Nongch'on ŭi changnae wa oin ŭi kago," *Sinmin* (July 1925): 13; Sin, "Nongch'on munje yŏn'gu," 47.

38. Yi Kak-chŏng, "Sojak munje e ch'uihaya," 51–52; and Yi Hun-gu, *Chosŏn nongŏpnon*, 323.

39. In-Geol Kim, "Confucian Tradition in Rural Society during the Late Chosŏn Dynasty: Changing Elite Perceptions of Community Administration," *Seoul Journal of Korean Studies* 16 (2003): 122–133.

40. Hoon Koo Lee, *Land Utilization and Rural Economy in Korea*, 173.

41. Yi Kak-chŏng, "Sojak munje e ch'uihaya," 51–52; and Ch'oe Man-tal, "Nongch'on ŭi changnae wa oin ŭi kago," 13.

42. Yi Hun-gu, *Chosŏn nongŏpnon*, 323.

43. There were also Japanese land corporations, including the Oriental Development Company and Sŏngŏpsa, a land-managing company established by the Industrial Bank of Chosen. See Hong Song-chan, "The Emergence of New Types of Landlords in the Occupation Period," in Pang and Shin, *Landlords, Peasants, and Intellectuals in Modern Korea*, 185–196.

44. According to Government-General records and Gi-Wook Shin, "The Type B landlord was three to five times more common than Type A and ascended substantially in number, from 50,312 in 1916 to 83,520 in 1924." See Gi-Wook Shin, *Peasant Protest and Social Change in Colonial Korea*, 47; and Chōsen sōtokufu, *Chōsen no kosaku kanshū* (Keijo: Chōsen sōtokufu, 1929), 28–29.

45. Hong Sŏng-ch'an. "Nongji kaehyŏk chŏnhu ŭi taejiju tonghyang," in *Nongji kaehyŏk yŏn'gu*, ed. Hong Sŏng-ch'an (Seoul: Yonsei University Press, 2001), 165–224.

46. Hong Sŏng-ch'an, "Emergence of New Types of Landlords in the Occupation Period," 186.

47. Ibid., 187.

48. James Dale Van Buskirk, *Korea: Land of the Dawn* (New York: Missionary Education Movement of the United States and Canada, 1931), 77.

49. Editorial, "Nongch'on munje t'ŭkjip," *Tonggwang* (April 1931): 554; and Kim Hyŏng-uk, "Chapter Five," in *Nongmin ŭi hwallo*, ed. R. A. Hardie (Kyŏngsŏng: Chŏson kidokkyo ch'angmunsa, 1930), 37.

50. John H. Reisner, "Letter to Mr. Y Mitsui, Bureau of Industry, Government of Chosen [May 25, 1926]" (YMCA Archives, University of Minnesota, Minneapolis, photocopy), 1; and Reisner, "Survey by John H. Reisner," 4.

51. Hoon Koo Lee, *Land Utilization and Rural Economy in Korea*, 163.

52. Kim Dong-no, "National Identity and Class Interest in Peasant Movements during the Colonial Period" (working paper, Department of Sociology, Yonsei University, Seoul, photocopy), 25–27.

53. Yi Kak-chŏng, "Sojak munje e ch'uihaya," 51–52; and Kim Cha-p'yŏng, "Nongch'on kuje taech'aek ilban," *Sinmin* (May 1929): 42.

54. Yi Hun-gu, *Chosŏn nongŏpnon*, 323.

55. Youn-tae Chung, "The Spread of Peasant Movements and Changes in the Tenant Policy in the 1920's Colonial Korea," *International Journal of Korean History* 2 (December 2001): 163.

56. Lee Yong-ki, "The Study of Korean Villages during the Japanese Colonial Period and Colonial Modernity," *International Journal of Korean History* 15, no. 2 (August 2010): 35.

57. Within a locality, knowledge and ideas held by individuals inform material practices, such as rituals, rites, and the construction of homes and buildings, which in turn reinforce the organizing ideas and concepts within individuals. This interrelationship between ideas and material practices forms the fundamental basis of a locality. Through a locality, relationships, communities, institutions, activities, and experiences are formed and gain meaning and value. Arjun Appadurai, *Modernity at Large* (Minneapolis: University of Minnesota Press, 1996), 178–188.

58. Yi Hun-gu, *Chosŏn nongŏpnon*, 104–110; and Lee Yong-ki, "Study of Korean Villages during the Japanese Colonial Period and Colonial Modernity," 55.

59. Helen Kim, "Rural Education for the Regeneration of Korea," 18.

60. Martina Deuchler, *The Confucian Transformation of Korea* (Cambridge, MA: Harvard Council on East Asian Studies, 1992), 175.

61. Ibid., 178.

62. Seong Ho Jun and James B. Lewis, "Accounting Techniques in Korea: 18th Century Archival Samples from a Non-profit Association in the Sinitic World," *Accounting Historians Journal* 68, no. 1 (June 2006): 59.

63. "The Village Gilds [*sic*] of Korea," *Transactions of the Korea Branch of the Royal Asiatic Society* 4, pt. 2 (1913): 14 and 17.

64. Seong Ho Jun and Lewis, "Accounting Techniques in Korea," 62.

65. Appadurai, *Modernity at Large*, 180–181.

66. As quoted in Yi Kyŏng-ran, "1930-yŏndae nongmin sosŏl tonghae pon 'singminji kŭndaehwa' wa nongmin saenghwal," in *Ilcheha ŭi singmin chibae wa ilsangsaenghwal*, ed. Kim Dong-no (Seoul: Hyean, 2004), 391.

67. Helen Kim, "Rural Education for the Regeneration of Korea," 18.

68. Hong Pyŏng-sŏn, "Chojik kwa hapryŏk kwa chohap," *Nongch'on ch'ŏngnyŏn* (October 1929): 1.

69. Lee Sangoon, "The Rural Control Policy and Peasant Ruling Strategy of the Government-General of Chosŏn in the 1930–1940s," *International Journal of Korean History* 15, no. 2 (August 2010): 12–13.

70. The colonial government dismantled the corporate taxation system, which had fostered solidarity among village members. See Kim Dong-no, "National Identity and Class Interest in Peasant Movements," 22–23.

71. Cho Min-hyŏng, *Chosŏn nongch'on ku kujech'aek* (Kyŏngsong: Sinhak saekyesa, 1929), 8. [0]

72. For a chart showing debt problems, see Yi Kyŏng-chun, "Chapter 6," in Hardie, *Nongmin ŭi hwallo*, 39–49.

73. Brunner, "Rural Korea," 109.

74. Hoon Koo Lee, *Land Utilization and Rural Economy in Korea*, 272.

75. Kim Dong-no, "Peasants, State, and Landlords: National Crisis and the Transformation of Agrarian Society in Pre-colonial Korea," 2 vols. (PhD diss., University of Chicago, 1994), 2:298.

76. See Helen Kim, "Rural Education for the Regeneration of Korea," 6.

77. The colonial government supervised recruitment campaigns by Japanese companies to hire peasants to work in Japan. See Ken Kawashima, *The Proletarian Gamble* (Durham, NC: Duke University Press, 2009), 32–43.

78. The number of Koreans in Japan jumped from 40,755 in 1920 to over 1 million residents by 1940. The population of Koreans in Manchuria grew to 1 million by 1944. See Andrew J. Grajdanzev, *Modern Korea* (New York: Institute of Pacific Relations, 1944), 81–82.

79. Sakai Toshio, quoted in Kawashima, *Proletarian Gamble*, 47.

80. Bruce Cumings, *The Origins of the Korean War*, vol. 1 (Princeton, NJ: Princeton University Press, 1981), 54.

81. Se-Mi Oh, "Consuming the Modern" (PhD diss., Columbia University, 2008), chap. 2.

82. Yi Hun-gu, "Nongch'on ch'ŏngnyŏn kwa hyangt'o chungsin," *Nongmin saenghwal* (April 1932): 5–6; and Yi Hun-gu, "Nongch'on ch'ŏngnyŏn ege ponaenŭn ŭi hŭimang," *Nongmin saenghwal* (May 1936): 265–268.

83. Kim Bŏm-chin, "Nongch'on ch'ŏngnyŏn a nongch'on chikk'ira," *Nongmin saenghwal* (January 1933); and Yi Hun-gu, "Nongch'on ch'ŏngnyŏn kwa hyangt'o chungsin."

84. See Kim Pyŏng-ch'an, "Chapter 2," in Hardie, *Nongmin ŭi hwallo*, 9–12.

85. Yi Hun-gu, quoted in Hoon Koo Lee, *Land Utilization and Rural Economy in Korea*, 172.

86. R. A. Hardie, "The Church's Responsibility in the Present Economic Situation," *Korea Mission Field* (December 1928): 259.

87. Hoon Koo Lee, *Land Utilization and Rural Economy in Korea*, 172.

88. Frank T. Boreland, "The Rural Problem in Korea and Some Ways in Which It Is Being Faced," *Korea Mission Field* (July 1933): 133.

89. Brunner, "Rural Korea," 129.

90. Yu Ch'i-jin, *The Ox*, in *Korean Drama under Japanese Occupation*, trans. Jinhee Kim (Dumont, NJ: Homa Sekey Books, 2004), 65.

91. Pak Dal-sŏng, "Sigŭp'i haegyŏl hal Chosŏn ŭi idae munje," *Kaebyŏk* (June 1920): 29.

92. Kim Pyŏng-ch'an, "Chapter 2," 9–12.

93. See Gi-Wook Shin, *Peasant Protest*, 54–74; and Kim Dong-no, "National Identity and Class Interest in Peasant Movements," 16.

94. Chi Su-gŏl, *Ilche ha nongmin chohap undong yŏn'gu* (Seoul: Yŏksa pip'yŏng, 1993), 54–55; Cho Tong-gŏl, *Ilche ha Han'guk nongmin undongsa* (Seoul: Han'gilsa, 1979), 199–200; Gi-wook Shin and Do-hyun Han, "Colonial Corporatism," in *Colonial Modernity in Korea*, ed. Gi-Wook Shin and Michael Robinson (Cambridge, MA: Harvard University Asia Center, 1999), 86–88.

95. Governor-General Ugaki, *Chosen and among Its People* (Keijo: Foreign Affairs Section, 1933), 5.

96. See Yi Jun-sik, "Hyŏngmyŏngjŏk nongminchohap undong kwa Ilche ŭi nongch'on chaejŏngch'aek: Hamgyŏng-bukdo ŭl kwangbok hyangyak ŭl chungsim ŭro," in *Ilche singminji sigi ŭi t'ongch'i ch'ejae hyŏngsŏng*, ed. Kim Dong-no (Seoul: Hyean, 2006), 226–268.

97. See Hyun Ok Park, *Two Dreams in One Bed: Empire, Social Life, and the Origins of the North Korean Revolution in Manchuria* (Durham, NC: Duke University Press, 2005).

98. Pang, *Han'guk kŭnhyŏndae sasangsa yŏn'gu*, 65–226; and Pang Kie-Chung, "Paek Nam'un and Marxist Scholarship during the Colonial Period," in Pang and Shin, *Landlords, Peasants, and Intellectuals in Modern Korea*, 245–308.

99. See "Resolution of the E.C.C.I. on the Korean Question," in *Documents of Korean Communism*, ed. Dae-sook Suh (Princeton, NJ: Princeton University Press, 1970), 248.

100. Nearly 1,300 peasant associations were built by 1933. The number of members in associations ranged from 2,000 to 4,500 peasants in Hamgyŏng alone. See Chi, *Ilche ha nongmin chohap undong yŏn'gu*, 97; and Yi Jun-sik, "Hyŏngmyŏngjŏk nongminchohap undong kwa Ilche ŭi nongch'on chaejŏngch'aek," 226–268.

101. Sa Kong-pyo (An Kwang-ch'on), "Chosŏn ŭi chŏngse wa Chosŏn kongsan-juija ŭi tangmyŏn immu," in Pae Sŏng-chan, *Singminji sidae sahoe undong-non yŏn'gu* (Seoul: Tolpegae, 1987), 99.

102. Cumings, *Origins of the Korean War*, 63.

103. As quoted in Pae, *Singminji sidae sahoe undongnon yŏn'gu*, 216.

104. "Chosŏn ŭi sahoe kyegŭp ŭi chuŭi—chaesam kyegŭp ŭi yŏnghyang, I and II," *Tonga ilbo*, May 10 and 11, 1921.

105. Yi Sŭng-yŏl, *Cheguk kwa sangin* (Seoul: Yŏksa p'ip'yŏngsa, 2007), 314–316; and Pak Ch'an-sŭng, *Han'guk kŭndae chŏngch'i sasangsa yŏn'gu* (Seoul: Yŏksa p'ip'yŏngsa, 1992), 263.

106. Michael D. Shin, "Nationalist Discourse and Nationalist Institutions in Colonial Chosŏn" (PhD diss., University of Chicago, 2002), 163.

107. For a list of objectives of the society and its charter, see "Chosŏn mulsan changnyŏnhoe ch'wijisŏ," *Sanŏpgye* (December 1923): 55–56; and "Chosŏn mulsan changnyŏnhoe hŏnch'ik," *Sanŏpgye* (December 1923): 57–58.

108. See Oh, "Consuming the Modern," 143–146.

109. See Lee Ji-Won, "An Chaehong's Thought and the Politics of the United Front," in Pang and Shin, *Landlords, Peasants, and Intellectuals in Modern Korea*, 314–317.

110. *Chosŏn ilbo 50-yŏnsa* (Seoul: Chosŏn ilbosa, 1970), 350–351.

111. Anne Pedler, "Going to the People: The Russian Narodniki in 1874–75," *Slavonic Review* 6, no. 6 (June 1927): 130–141.

112. Gi-Wook Shin, "Agrarianism: A Critique of Colonial Modernity in Korea," *Comparative Studies in Society and History* 41, no. 4 (October 1999): 795.

113. Ibid., 798.

114. See the special issue of *Sinmin* (March 1929): 113–118 and 128–131.

115. Youngna Kim, *20th Century Korean Art* (London: Laurence King, 2005), 110.

116. Karl Polanyi, *The Great Transformation* (Boston: Beacon Press, 1944), 157–159.

117. James C. Scott, *Weapons of the Weak* (New Haven, CT: Yale University Press, 1985), 346.

118. Slavoj Žižek, *The Fragile Absolute—or, Why Is the Christian Legacy Worth Fighting For?* (New York: Verso Press, 2000), 40.

119. Byron P. Barnhart, "Athletics and the Rural Communities," *Korea Mission Field* (August 1928): 162.

Chapter 3: A Heavenly Kingdom on Earth

1. Fifteen were Ch'ŏndogyo leaders, sixteen were Protestant Christian leaders, and two were Buddhist monks.

2. Kenneth Wells' book *New God, New Nation* (Honolulu: University of Hawai'i Press, 1990) does discuss the rise of religious reconstruction movements, es-

pecially before 1919. However, the difference between religion-based social movements before and after 1919 was their approaches to modernity. As discussed earlier, reforms and campaigns carried out by religious figures before 1919 supported modernization and rarely questioned the norms of modernity, whereas movements after 1920 questioned and problematized the very nature of modernity and how it was evolving on the peninsula and fostered an alternative vision of modernity rooted in religion.

3. Michael D. Shin, "The Specter of Yi Gwangsu: The March 1st Movement and the Nation in Colonial Korea" (unpublished manuscript), chap. 5, 9.

4. Takashi Fujitani shows that colonial rule between 1937 and 1945 can also be characterized as a period of governmentality. See Takashi Fujitani, *Race for Empire: Koreans as Japanese and Japanese as Americans during World War II* (Berkeley: University of California Press, 2011), pt. 3.

5. Ro Kil-myung, "New Religions and Social Change in Modern Korean History," *Review of Korean Studies* 5, no. 1 (June 2002): 50.

6. "The church contained thousands of pastors and church workers who led some 200,000 adherents and more than 2,000 churches in the peninsula." Chung-shin Park, *Protestantism and Politics in Korea* (Seattle: University of Washington Press, 2003), 130.

7. Donald Clark, *Living Dangerously in Korea* (Norwalk, CT: Eastbridge, 2003), 44.

8. Between 1911 and 1918, the Congregational Church built over 149 churches with 13,631 members. See Shin, "Specter of Yi Gwangsu," chap. 5, 31.

9. Yang Ju-sam, "My Country—Korea," in *Sources of Korean Christianity*, ed. Sung-Deuk Oak (Seoul: Hanguk kidokkyo yŏksa yŏn'guso, 2004), 381.

10. Shin, "Specter of Yi Gwangsu," chap. 5, 29–30; and Yoshikawa Buntaro, *Chōsen no shukyō* (Keijo: Chōsen Insatsu, 1921), 5.

11. Yoshikawa, *Chōsen no shukyō*, 6.

12. Shin, "Specter of Yi Gwangsu," chap. 5, 29.

13. Ro, "New Religions and Social Change in Modern Korean History," 50.

14. Michael D. Shin, "Nationalist Discourse and Nationalist Institutions in Colonial Chosŏn, 1914–1926" (PhD diss., University of Chicago, 2002), 151.

15. Ibid.

16. David Harvey, *The Condition of Postmodernity* (Cambridge, MA: Blackwell, 1990), 260–283; Harry Harootunian, *Overcome by Modernity* (Princeton, NJ: Princeton University Press, 2000); and Max Horkheimer, "The State of Contemporary Social Philosophy and the Tasks of an Institute for Social Research," in *Critical Theory and Society*, ed. Stephen Eric Bonner and Douglas MacKay Kellner (New York: Routledge, 1989), 29–32.

17. Shin, "Nationalist Discourse and Nationalist Institutions in Colonial Chosŏn," 178.

18. Quoted in ibid., 152.

19. Editorial, "Kot haeyahal minjokjŏk chungsim seryŏk ŭi chaksŏng," *Kaebyŏk* (April 1923): 4–12.

20. See Robert T. Handy, "The American Religious Depression, 1925–1935," *Church History* 29, no. 1 (March 1960): 7.

21. Vladimir Tikhonov, "Han Yongun's Buddhist Socialism in the 1920s and 1930s," *International Journal of Buddhist Thought and Culture* 6 (February 2006): 210.

22. See Shin, "Nationalist Discourse and Nationalist Institutions in Colonial Chosŏn," 183.

23. See Kim Myŏng-sik, "Chosŏn chonggyoron," *Pip'an* (April 1934): 22; and Pak Sŭng-kŭk, "Pan chonggyoron," *Pip'an* (July / August 1931): 2–5.

24. Pae Sŏng-nyong, "Pan chonggyo undong ŭi ŭiŭi," *Kaebyŏk* (November 1925): 57.

25. Hyŏn In, "Chonggyo pip'an kwa pan chonggyo undong," *Pip'an* (September 1931): 46.

26. "Sasŏl," *Tonga ilbo*, January 7, 1922. See also "Sasŏl," *Tonga ilbo*, December 27, 1928.

27. "Kidokkyo chŏngnyŏnhoe ŭi kŭmil ŭi ch'ŏji," *Chosŏn ilbo*, January 17, 1926; and Sin Hŭng-u, "Chosŏn ilbo sasŏl ilko," *Chŏngnyŏn* (February 1926): 9–11.

28. Yi Kwang-su, "Kidokkyo sasang," *Sinsaenghwallon* (September 1918), reprinted in *Yi Kwang-su chŏnjip* (Seoul: Samchungtang, 1971), 10:345–351.

29. As quoted in Tikhonov, "Han Yongun's Buddhist Socialism in the 1920s and 1930s," 211.

30. Kim Kwon-jung, "1920-yŏndae kidokkyo seryŏk ŭi pankidokkyo undong taeŭng kwa minjok undong ŭi chŏngae," *Han'guk kidokkyo wa yŏksa* 14 (2001): 79–106.

31. See Kim Kwangshik, "Buddhist Perspectives on Anti-religious Movements in the 1930s," *Review of Korean Studies* 3, no. 1 (July 2000): 55–75.

32. "Christianity in Korea," *Korea Mission Field* (June 1926): 150–151.

33. "Questions from Korean Students," *Korea Mission Field* (November 1924): 226.

34. W. L. Nash, "Following the Example of Jesus at the Y.M.C.A. Student Conference, Kongju," *Korea Mission Field* (March 1926): 46–48.

35. W. L. Nash, "Student Conference of the Korean Y.M.C.A. National Council," *Korea Mission Field* (January 1927): 15.

36. "Report of the Australian Presbyterian Mission," in Oak, *Sources of Korean Christianity*, 422.

37. Kim San and Nym Wales, *Song of Ariran* (New York: John Day, 1941), 26.

38. "Cultural Distance" is a term coined by Paul Ricoeur. See Paul Ricoeur, "The Language of Faith," in *The Philosophy of Paul Ricoeur*, ed. Charles E. Reagan and David Steward (Boston: Beacon Press, 1978), 223–238.

39. Yi Yong-gu went on to start Sich'ŏn'gyo, a new religion. Yi has been vilified by Ch'ŏndogyo narratives "as a collaborator with the Japanese who betrayed not only Ch'ŏndogyo but also the Korean nation." George Kallander, *Salvation*

through Dissent: Tonghak Heterodoxy and Early Modern Korea (Honolulu: University of Hawai'i Press, 2013), 128.

40. Ibid., 209.

41. Carl Young, "Embracing Modernity: Organizational and Ritual Reform in Ch'ŏndogyo, 1905–1910," *Asian Studies Review* 29 (March 2005): 53.

42. Kallander, *Salvation through Dissent,* 128–146.

43. Young, "Embracing Modernity," 47–59.

44. See Hŏ Su, "1920-chŏnhu Yi Ton-hwa ŭi hyŏnsil insil kwa kŭndae ch'ŏrhak suyong," *Yŏksa munje yŏn'gu,* no. 9 (December 2002): 175–216.

45. The new faction and the Ch'ŏndogyo Youth Party will be discussed in more detail in Chapter 4.

46. Yi Ton-hwa, "Hondon ŭro put'ŏ t'ongil," *Kaebyŏk* (July 1921): 2–6.

47. Ibid., 2–4; and Yi Ton-hwa, "Innaech'ŏn ŭi yŏn'gu II," *Kaebyŏk* (July 1920): 65.

48. Yi Ton-hwa, *Innaech'ŏn youi* (Keijo: Kaebyŏksa, 1924), 202.

49. Ibid., 9.

50. Yi Ton-hwa, "Innaech'ŏn ŭi yŏn'gu II," 65; and Yi Ton-hwa, "Innaech'ŏn ŭi yŏn'gu I," *Kaebyŏk* (June 1920): 39.

51. Yi Ton-hwa, *Innaech'ŏn youi,* 8.

52. Yi Ton-hwa, "Innaech'ŏn ŭi yŏn'gu II," 66; and Hŏ, "1920-chŏnhu Yi Ton-hwa ŭi hyŏnsil insil kwa kŭndae ch'ŏrhak suyong," 192–194.

53. Yi Ton-hwa, "Innaech'ŏn ŭi yŏn'gu IV," *Kaebyŏk* (September 1920): 46.

54. Yi Ton-hwa, "Ch'ŏnguk haeng," *Kaebyŏk* (July 1924): 7.

55. Yi Ton-hwa, "Innaech'ŏn ŭi yŏn'gu IV," 46–50; and Yi Ton-hwa, *Sinin ch'ŏrhak* (Seoul: Ch'ŏndogyo chungang ch'ongbu, 1968), 10.

56. Yi wrote that Hanŭllim always raised and developed goodness (*sŏn*). See Yi Ton-hwa, *Innaech'ŏn youi,* 52, 61.

57. Yi Ton-hwa, "Ch'ŏnguk haeng," 5.

58. Yi Ton-hwa, *Innaech'ŏn youi,* 52.

59. Ibid., 91–101.

60. Ibid., 95–100.

61. Yi Ton-hwa, "Ch'ŏnguk haeng," 7.

62. Hŏ, "1920-chŏnhu Yi Ton-hwa ŭi hyŏnsil insil kwa kŭndae ch'ŏrhak suyong," 195.

63. Yi Ton-hwa, *Innaech'ŏn youi,* 60.

64. Yi Ton-hwa, "Ŭimisang kwanhan chaa ŭi kwanyŏm, innaech'ŏn yŏn'gu VII," *Kaebyŏk* (January 1921): 73–76.

65. Ibid.

66. Ibid., 75.

67. Yi wrote that "*hyŏnje* [the present] was reality." Since he believed that reality was Hanŭllim, he was pointing out that the present was the time when one experienced Hanŭllim. Yi Ton-hwa, *Innaech'ŏn youi,* 96–98.

68. Ibid., 98.
69. Ibid., 199–200.
70. Ibid., 199.
71. Ibid., 64–68.
72. Ibid., 200.
73. Yi Ton-hwa, "Saengmyŏng ŭi ŭisikhwa wa ŭisik ŭi inbonhwa," *Kaebyŏk* (May 1926): 8–9.
74. From Bertrand Russell's theories on the possessive and creative side of humanity, Yi took the idea that material conditions suppressed the divine nature of humanity. See Yi Ton-hwa, "Saramsŏng ŭi haebang kwa saramsŏng chayŏnjuŭi," *Kaebyŏk* (April 1921): 21.
75. Yi Ton-hwa, *Innaech'ŏn youi*, 74–79.
76. Ibid., 200–201.
77. Yi Ton-hwa, "Saenghwal ŭi chokŏn ŭl ponwi ro han Chosŏn ŭi kaejo saŏp," *Kaebyŏk* (September 1921): 2–13; and Yi Ton-hwa, "Saenghwal ŭi chokŏn ŭl ponwi ro han Chosŏn ŭi kaejo saŏp (2)," *Kaebyŏk* (October 1921): 18–27.
78. Yi Ton-hwa, "Munwajuŭi wa inkyŏksang p'yŏngdŭng," *Kaebyŏk* (November 1920): 10–13.
79. Yi Ton-hwa, "Saenghwal ŭi chokŏn ŭl ponwi ro han Chosŏn ŭi kaejo saŏp," 6.
80. Yi was influenced by Russell's book *Principles of Social Reconstruction*. See Bertrand Russell, *Principles of Social Reconstruction* (London: George Allen and Unwin, 1916).
81. Yi Ton-hwa, "Saramsŏng ŭi haebang kwa saramsŏng chayŏnjuŭi," 21.
82. Yi Ton-hwa, *Innaech'ŏn youi*, 202.
83. Ibid., 64–67.
84. Yi Ton-hwa," Tanch'e saenghwal kwa ŭijiyŏk," *Kaebyŏk* (April 1931): 27.
85. Quoted in Se-Mi Oh, "Consuming the Modern" (PhD diss., Columbia University, 2008), 110–111.
86. Dilip Parameshwar Gaonkar, "On Alternative Modernities," in *Alternative Modernities*, ed. Dilip Parameshwar Gaonkar (Durham, NC: Duke University Press, 2001), 13.
87. Yi Ton-hwa, *Innaech'ŏn youi*, 77.
88. See Kim Dong-No, "Peasants, State, and Landlords: National Crisis and the Transformation of Agrarian Society in Pre-colonial Korea," 2 vols. (PhD diss., University of Chicago, 1994), 1:156–159.
89. Yi Ton-hwa, *Innaech'ŏn youi*, 203–206.
90. Yi Ton-hwa, *Sinin ch'ŏrhak*, 147–161.
91. Quoted in Wells, *New God, New Nation*, 107.
92. See Pak Hŭi-do, "Sahoe saenghwal kwa chonggyo munje," *Sinsaenghwal* (September 1922): 2–6.
93. Chang Kyu-sik, "1920-yŏndae kaejoron ŭi hwaksan kwa kidokkyo sahoejuŭi ŭi suyong chŏngch'ak," *Yŏksa munje yŏn'guso*, no. 21 (April 2009): 121–122.

94. John N. Mills, "The Cause of Changes in Korea," *Missionary Review of the World* (February 1922): 115–116.

95. See International Missionary Council, *The Jerusalem Meeting of the International Missionary Council, March 24–April 8, 1928*, vol. 5, *The Christian Mission in Relation to Industrial Problems*, and vol. 6, *The Christian Mission in Relation to Rural Problems* (New York: International Missionary Council, 1928).

96. Edmund de Schweinitz Brunner, "Rural Korea: A Preliminary Survey of Economic, Social and Religious Conditions," in International Missionary Council, *Christian Mission in Relation to Rural Problems*, 147–149.

97. See International Missionary Council, *Christian Mission in Relation to Industrial Problems*, 141–151; and International Missionary Council, *Christian Mission in Relation to Rural Problems*, 245–255.

98. W. A. Nobel, Samuel A. Moffett, Chŏng In-kwa, Sin Hŭng-u, Helen Kim (Kim Hwal-lan), and J. S. Ryang (Yang Ju-sam) attended the meeting.

99. Kim Hwal-lan, "Jerusalem taehoe wa kumhu kidokkyo," *Ch'ŏngnyŏn* (November 1928): 2–5.

100. Min Kyŏng-bae, *Han'guk kidokkyohoesa* (Seoul: Yonsei University Press, 2002), 100.

101. Robert Handy defines "social gospel" as the movement in the United States among liberal-minded Protestant evangelicals to rally Christians to deal with the problems of society that were intensifying in the early twentieth century. Social gospel advocates believed that Christianity would be best spread and realized by addressing social issues, especially the difficulties arising from industrialization and urbanization. Many social gospel movements in the United States concentrated on combating urban slums and addressing the condition of labor. See Robert T. Handy, *A Christian America* (New York: Oxford University Press, 1984), 134–151.

102. "Kidok sinuhoe ch'angnip," *Kidok sinbo*, June 5, 1929.

103. Ibid.

104. Paul Tillich, *Systematic Theology*, vol. 1 (Chicago: University of Chicago Press, 1951), 3.

105. Hong Pyŏng-sŏn, "Hyŏndae saenghwal ŭi kyŏnghyang kwa oin ŭi t'aedo," *Ch'ŏngnyŏn* (November 1926): 9–12.

106. Ibid., 10.

107. Hong Pyŏng-sŏn, "Hyŏndae saenghwal ŭi kach'i," *Ch'ŏngnyŏn* (June 1930): 5; and Hong Pyŏng-sŏn, "Hyŏndaein ŭi komin kwa haegyŏl," *Ch'ŏngnyŏn* (February 1925): 6.

108. Hong, "Hyŏndaein ŭi komin kwa haegyŏl," 6.

109. Hong, "Hyŏndae saenghwal ŭi kach'i," 4.

110. Hong Pyŏng-sŏn, "Inch'ungsimjuŭi," *Sŏkwang* (March 1920): 28; and Hong, "Hyŏndaein ŭi komin kwa haegyŏl," 6.

111. Hong, "Inch'ungsimjuŭi," 28.

112. Hong, "Hyŏndae saenghwal ŭi kyŏnghyang kwa oin ŭi t'aedo," 11–12.

113. Hong Pyŏng-sŏn, "Sasang kwa silsaenghwal," *Ch'ŏngnyŏn* (April 1931): 10.

114. Hong Pyŏng-sŏn, "Sangt'u tasi hongpŏn chalŭch'a," *Ch'ŏngnyŏn* (March 1926): 20; and Hong Pyŏng-sŏn, *Nongch'on hyŏpdong chohap kwa chojikpŏp* (Kyŏngsŏng: Ch'ŏngnyŏnhoe yŏnhap'oe, 1930), 4–6.

115. Hong, "Hyŏndaein ŭi komin kwa haegyŏl," 6.

116. Ibid.

117. Hong, "Hyŏndae saenghwal ŭi kyŏnghyang kwa oin ŭi t'aedo," 11.

118. Hong, "Hyŏndaein ŭi komin kwa haegyŏl," 6; and Hong, "Hyŏndae saenghwal ŭi kyŏnghyang kwa oin ŭi t'aedo," 11.

119. Hong, "Hyŏndae saenghwal ŭi kyŏnghyang kwa oin ŭi t'aedo," 9.

120. Hong Pyŏng-sŏn, "Sidae ŭi kwajŏng," *Kidok sinbo* (February 1922).

121. Ibid.

122. Hong, "Sasang kwa silsaenghwal," 10.

123. Hong Pyŏng-sŏn, "Hyŏpdong ," *Ch'ŏngnyŏn* (May 1925): 6.

124. Hong, "Hyŏndae saenghwal ŭi kyŏnghyang kwa oin ŭi t'aedo," 10–12.

125. Ibid., 7.

126. Hong Pyŏng-sŏn, "Saenghwal ŭi saenghwal," *Ch'ŏngnyŏn* (October 1926): 17.

127. Hong criticized Christians who believed that Christianity was only about evangelizing, reading the Bible, and worshipping God in church. See Hong Pyŏng-sŏn, "Sahoe saenghwal kwa chonggyo," *Ch'ŏngnyŏn* (September 1925): 6.

128. At times, Hong referred to God as truth. See Hong Pyŏng-sŏn, "Yuil ŭi hyangro," *Ch'ŏngnyŏn* (July 1925): 4; and Hong Pyŏng-sŏn, "Hananim ŭi silun," *Ch'ŏngnyŏn* (October 1925): 17.

129. Hong, "Saenghwal ŭi saenghwal," 18; and Hong Pyŏng-sŏn, "Saenghwalsŏn e iphan oin," *Ch'ŏngnyŏn* (January 1928): 11–13.

130. Hong Pyŏng-sŏn, "Sim ŭi kuwŏn kwa yuk ŭi kuwŏn," *Ch'ŏngnyŏn* (April 1925): 5.

131. Hong, "Sahoe saenghwal kwa chonggyo," 5.

132. Barth was considered a leading theologian who revolutionized the categories of understanding God. Hong admired Barth and wanted him to come and lecture in Korea. See "Segyejŏk chŏngch'i ka sasang ka munho kwahakcha," *Samch'ŏlli* (December 1935): 31.

133. Karl Barth, "Creation as Benefit," in *Karl Barth: Theologian of Freedom*, ed. Clifford Green (Minneapolis: Fortress Press, 1991), 192–193.

134. Emily Anderson, "Christianity in the Japanese Empire" (PhD diss., University of California, Los Angeles, 2010), 46.

135. Other Japanese Christians shared Tsuneyoshi's conception of God. Ebina Danjo (1856–1937), for example, argued that Christianity was the ultimate realization of religious consciousness that therefore connected it to Confucianism and Shintoism. Danjo was Tsuneyoshi's mentor and later became the chancellor of Doshisha University (1920–1928), where Hong received his theological education.

136. Hong Pyŏng-sŏn, "Ch'oedae manjok," *Ch'ŏngnyŏn* (March 1925): 7.
137. Ibid.
138. Ibid.
139. Hong, "Sahoe saenghwal kwa chonggyo," 6.
140. Hong, "Saenghwal ŭi saenghwal," 16–18.
141. Hong, "Inch'ungsimjuŭi," 28; and Hong, "Hyŏndae saenghwal ŭi kach'i," 4–5.
142. Hong Pyŏng-sŏn, "Kaejoron ŭi jinŭi," *Sŏkwang* (June 1920): 23–29.
143. Hong, "Saenghwal ŭi saenghwal," 18.
144. Ibid.
145. Hong, "Sim ŭi kuwŏn kwa yuk ŭi kuwŏn," *Ch'ŏngnyŏn* (April 1925): 5.
146. Hong believed that a relationship existed between the mind / spiritual and the body / material. See ibid.
147. Hong, "Hyŏndae saenghwal ŭi kach'i," 4; and Hong, "Inch'ungsimjuŭi," 28.
148. Hong Pyŏng-sŏn, "Munje wa in'gansŏng," *Ch'ŏngnyŏn* (February 1927): 49.
149. See Paul Tillich, "Estrangement and Sin," in *Paul Tillich: Theologian of the Boundaries,* ed. Mark Kline Taylor (Minneapolis: Fortress Press, 1991): 198–204.
150. Hong, "Hyŏndaein ŭi komin kwa haegyŏl," 7; and Hong, "Inch'ungsimjuŭi," 29.
151. Hong, "Hyŏndae saenghwal ŭi kyŏnghyang kwa oin ŭi t'aedo," 11.
152. Hong, "Hyŏndae saenghwal ŭi kachi," 5.
153. Hong, "Hyŏndaein ŭi komin kwa haegyŏl," 7.
154. Hong, "Inch'ungsimjuŭi," 29.
155. Hong, "Hyŏndae saenghwal ŭi kyŏnghyang kwa oin ŭi t'aedo," 12.
156. To Hong, the present was a time when people could be with God and discover the everlasting forces that would supply meaning, value, and order to lives. Hong called the present an "eternal moment of nothingness." See Hong Pyŏng-sŏn, "Chosŏn kyohoe ŭi changrae wa kyohoe ŭi kako," *Chinsaeng* (September 1925): 31.
157. Cho Man-sik (1883–1950) was a well-known Korean nationalist who was active in the Presbyterian Church. He organized many nationalist campaigns and worked with Pae on agrarian issues. His progressive Christian views on social reforms distinguished him from the conservative majority in the Presbyterian Church. See Wells, *New God, New Nation,* ch.7.
158. Pae Min-su, "Pogŭmjuŭi wa kidokkyo nongch'on undong (1)," in *Pogŭmjuŭi wa kidokkyo nongch'on undong,* ed. Pang Ki-chung (Seoul: Yonsei University Press, 2000), 31–33; Pae Min-su, "Pogŭmjuŭi wa kidokkyo nongch'on undong (III)," ibid., 38; and Minsoo Pai (Pae Min-su), "The Rural Evangelistic Movement," *Korea Mission Field* (July 1935): 148.
159. Pae Min-su, "Pogŭmjuŭi wa kidokkyo nongch'on undong (1)," 31–33.
160. Paul Tillich, *Systematic Theology,* vol. 3 (Chicago: University of Chicago Press, 1963), 134.
161. Pae Min-su, "Kidokkyo nongch'ŏn undong ŭi chidoron (1)," in Pang, *Pogŭmjuŭi wa kidokkyo nongch'on undong,* 49.

162. Pae took this idea of love as a transformative force from Henry T. Hodgkin's *The Way of Jesus* (New York: George H. Doran, 1923).
163. Hodgkin, *Way of Jesus,* 84.
164. Pai, "Rural Evangelistic Movement," 148.
165. Pang Ki-chung, *Pae Min-su ŭi nongch'on undong kwa kidokkyo sasang* (Seoul: Yonsei University Press, 1999), 135–196.
166. Pae Min-su, "Pogŭmjuŭi wa kidokkyo nongch'on undong (1)," 32; and Pai, "Rural Evangelistic Movement," 148.
167. Pae Min-su, *Who Shall Enter the Kingdom of Heaven: Pae Min-su chasŏjŏn* (Seoul: Yonsei University Press, 1999), 224–228.
168. Pai, "Rural Evangelistic Movement," 148.
169. Ibid.
170. Ibid., 149.
171. Pae Min-su, "Pogŭmjuŭi wa kidokkyo nongch'on undong (2)," in Pang, *Pogŭmjuŭi wa kidokkyo nongch'on undong,* 34.
172. Ibid., 34.
173. Pai, "Rural Evangelistic Movement," 149.
174. Although this quote is from a document that Pae issued in 1954, he believed that Koreans at that time were the same as they had been in the colonial period in terms of becoming dominated by materialism. In fact, the contents of this document are nearly identical to the contents of his various writings during the 1920s and 1930s. See Minsoo Pai, "How to Evangelize Post-war Korea" (Princeton Theological Seminary, Princeton, NJ, photocopy, 1954), 6.
175. Pai, "Rural Evangelistic Movement," 148.
176. Pae wrote that material concerns and pursuits led to people committing "all kinds of inhuman deeds." See Pai, "How to Evangelize Post-war Korea," 6.
177. Pae Min-su, "Pogŭmjuŭi wa kidokkyo nongch'on undong (3)," in Pang, *Pogŭmjuŭi wa kidokkyo nongch'on undong,* 38–39.
178. Pai, "Rural Evangelistic Movement," 150.
179. Pae Min-su, "Hyŏpdong," in Pang, *Pogŭmjuŭi wa kidokkyo nongch'on undong,* 41.
180. Pae Min-su, "Kidokkyo nongch'ŏn undong ŭi chidoron (1)," 51.
181. Pae Min-su, "Hyŏpdong," 41.
182. See Sherwood Eddy, *Religion and Social Justice* (New York City: George H. Doran, 1927).
183. Pae Min-su, "Hyŏpdong," 40–42.
184. Pae Min-su, "Pogŭmjuŭi wa kidokkyo nongch'on undong (1)," 32–33.
185. Pai Min-su, "Rural Evangelistic Movement," 149.
186. Ibid., 148.
187. Pae Min-su, "Pogŭmjuŭi wa kidokkyo nongch'on undong (2)," 35.
188. Pai, "Rural Evangelistic Movement," 149.
189. Ibid., 148–149.

190. Raymond Williams, *Marxism and Literature* (New York: Oxford University Press, 1977), 130.

191. William H. Sewell Jr., *Logics of History: Social Theory and Social Transformation* (Chicago: University of Chicago Press, 2005), 143–144.

192. See Ricoeur, "Language of Faith," 223–238.

Chapter 4: The Path to the Sacred

1. Sa Kong-pyo (An Kwang-ch'on), "Chosŏn ŭi chŏngse wa Chosŏn kongsanjuŭicha ŭi dangmyŏn immu," in Pae Sŏng-chan, *Singminji sidae sahoe undongnon yŏn'gu* (Seoul: Tolpegae, 1987), 109.

2. Ji-Won Lee, "An Chaehong's Thought and the Politics of the United Front," in *Landlords, Peasants, and Intellectuals in Modern Korea*, ed. Pang-Kie Chung and Michael D. Shin (Ithaca, NY: Cornell East Asia Program, 2005), 309–350.

3. Raymond Williams, *The Country and the City* (New York: Oxford University Press, 1973); and Leo Marx, *The Machine in the Garden* (New York: Oxford University Press, 1964).

4. Williams, *Country and the City*, 232.

5. See Harry Harootunian, *Overcome by Modernity* (Princeton, NJ: Princeton University Press, 2000), chap. 1; and Leo Ou-fan Lee, "Shanghai Modern: Reflections on Urban Culture in China in the 1930s," in *Alternative Modernities*, ed. Dilip Parameshwar Gaonkar (Durham, NC: Duke University Press, 2001), 86–122.

6. See Williams, *Country and the City*.

7. See Michael J. Sandel, *Democracy's Discontent* (Cambridge, MA: Harvard University Press, 1996), 142–160.

8. See Barrington Moore, *Social Origins of Dictatorship and Democracy* (Boston: Beacon Press, 1966), 492.

9. Gavin Lewis, "The Peasantry, Rural Change and Conservative Agrarianism: Lower Austria at the Turn of the Century," *Past and Present* 81 (November 1978): 119–143; Margherita Zansai, *Saving the Nation: Economic Modernity in Republican China* (Chicago: University of Chicago Press, 2006), 60–61; and Stephen Vlastos, "Agrarianism without Tradition," in *Mirror of Modernity*, ed. Stephen Vlastos (Berkeley: University of California Press, 1998), 79–94.

10. Terry Eagleton, *Ideology: An Introduction* (London: Verso Press, 1991), 115.

11. Sin had established deep ties with the Methodist Church, first through his enrollment at Paejae Hakdang and later through teaching there after he received a master's degree from the University of Southern California in 1911. For a good biography of Sin, see Kim Sang-tae, "Ilche ha Sin Hŭng-u ŭi 'sahoe pogŭmjuŭi' wa minjokundongnon," *Yŏksa munje yŏn'gu*, no. 1 (December 1996): 163–170.

12. Sin Hŭng-u, "A Declaration of Positive Faith [1932]" (YMCA Archives, University of Minnesota, Minneapolis, photocopy), 1.

13. See Sin Hŭng-u, "Chosŏn ilbo sasŏl ilgo," *Ch'ŏngnyŏn* (February 1926): 2.

14. Sin, "Declaration of Positive Faith," 1.

15. Korean Young Men's Christian Association (KYMCA), *The Rural Program of the Young Men's Christian Association* (Seoul: National Council of the Korean Young Men's Christian Association, 1932), 4.

16. Ibid., 1–5; and Hong Pyŏng-sŏn, "Nongch'on saŏp ŭi chinŭi II," *Kidok sinbo*, November 20, 1929.

17. KYMCA, *Rural Program of the Young Men's Christian Association*, 4.

18. Hong, "Nongch'on saŏp ŭi chinŭi II."

19. John H. Reisner, "Report on Study of Certain Agricultural and Rural Projects in Korea, February to July 1931" (YMCA Archives, University of Minnesota, Minneapolis, photocopy), 2.

20. Hugh Cynn (Sin Hŭng-u), "Laymen and the Church: Hugh Heung-wu Cynn," in *Within the Gate,* ed. Charles Sauer (Seoul: Korea Methodist News Service, 1934), 122–123.

21. Mott served as the general secretary of the International Committee of the YMCA (ICYMCA), and Brockman was the associate general secretary of the ICYMCA.

22. See Sherwood Eddy, *Religion and Social Justice* (New York: George H. Doran, 1927), 9.

23. KYMCA, *Rural Program of the Young Men's Christian Association*, 5.

24. The ICYMCA sent five secretaries to Korea from 1925 to 1932: Gordon Avison, A. C. Bunce, F. O. Clark, F. T. Shipp, and H. A. Wilber. B. P. Barnhart had arrived before 1925.

25. Sin Hŭng-u, "Nongch'on kaepal chillyŏk," *Tonga ilbo*, January 1, 1925.

26. Hong, Sin, and leaders from the Seoul YMCA served as national secretaries. In this position, they traveled to the various branches and associations to offer assistance.

27. Only the P'yŏngyang branch operated autonomously from the national headquarters in Seoul because the head of the P'yŏngyang YMCA was Cho Mansik, who was more aligned with the PCRM.

28. Local branches and associations were expected to raise their own donations that were separate from donations to the national headquarters in Seoul.

29. In 1930, nearly 80 percent of the budget ($6,433) was supported by "North American contributions." In 1931, contributions from North America slightly decreased to $4,500. See "Statistics and Information for the Calendar Year 1931" (YMCA Archives, University of Minnesota, Minneapolis, photocopy), 3.

30. Letter to B. P. Barnhart from Frank V. Slack, April 23, 1935 (YMCA Archives, University of Minnesota, Minneapolis, photocopy), 1.

31. The Hŭngŏp kurakbu was founded in March 1925 and was closely aligned with Syngman Rhee's Tongjihoe, which was founded in 1923 with the mission to promote cultural activities for the creation of a new nation.

32. Frank M. Brockman, "Projected Policy for Rural Work of the Young Men's Christian Association of Korea" (YMCA Archives, University of Minnesota, Minneapolis, photocopy), 2.

33. Ibid.

34. Hong Pyŏng-sŏn, *Nongch'on hyŏpdong chohap kwa chojikpŏp* (Kyŏngsŏng: Ch'ŏngnyŏnhoe yŏnhaphoe, 1930), 4.

35. Hong shared Karl Marx's belief that the creation and circulation of money, or surplus capital, served as the sole purpose of production, exchange, and consumption under capitalism.

36. Hong Pyŏng-sŏn, "Saram kwa kigye," *Nongch'on ch'ŏngnyŏn* (February 1930): 1; and Sin Hŭng-u, "Hyŏndae ŏdaero?," *Ch'ŏngnyŏn* (January 1928): 2.

37. Sin, "Hyŏndae ŏdaero?," 2.

38. Hong Pyŏng-sŏn, "Inch'ungsimjuŭi," *Sŏkwang* (March 1920): 28.

39. Anthony Giddens, *The Consequences of Modernity* (Stanford, CA: Stanford University Press, 1990), 11–12.

40. Hong, *Nongch'on hyŏpdong chohap kwa chojikpŏp,* 5.

41. Ibid., 5–6; and Sin Hŭng-u,"Muljŏk saenghwal uri yogu II," *Ch'ŏngnyŏn* (November 1926): 7–8.

42. Hong, *Nongch'on hyŏpdong chohap kwa chojikpŏp,* 5.

43. Ibid.; and Hong Pyŏng-sŏn, "Tohoe saenghwal kwa nongch'on saenghwal," *Chinsaeng* (July 1930): 17.

44. The use of "proletariat" is based on the definition given by Ken Kawashima, *The Proletarian Gamble* (Durham, NC: Duke University Press, 2009), 12.

45. Hong, *Nongch'on hyŏpdong chohap kwa chojikpŏp,* 6.

46. Ibid., 7.

47. Sin Hŭng-u, "Pyŏnch'ŏn sidae e kyoyuk pasŭn saram ŭi saenghwal," *Ch'ŏngnyŏn* (March 1927): 100–106.

48. Ibid., 101–102.

49. Karl Marx, *Capital,* vol. 1, trans. by Ben Fowkes (London: Penguin Books, 1976), 538.

50. Hong, "Tohoe saenghwal kwa nongch'on saenghwal," 19.

51. Hong, "Saram kwa kigye," 1.

52. Hong, "Tohoe saenghwal kwa nongch'on saenghwal," 17.

53. Ibid., 18.

54. Hong, *Nongch'on hyŏpdong chohap kwa chojikpŏp,* 7.

55. Ibid.; and Sin Hŭng-u, "Mulchil saenghwal uri yogu II," *Chŏngnyŏn* (November 1926) 8.

56. Hong, *Nongch'on hyŏpdong chohap kwa chojikpŏp,* 7.

57. Sin, "Mulchil saenghwal uri yogu II," 8.

58. Ibid., 7–9.

59. Hong associated "simple life" with an agriculture-based life. See Hong, "Tohoe saenghwal kwa nongch'on saenghwal," 19.

60. Se-Mi Oh, "Consuming the Modern" (PhD diss., Columbia University, 2008), 137–147; and Pak Ch'an-sŭng, *Han'guk kŭndae chŏngch'i sasangsa yŏn'gu* (Seoul: Yŏksa pip'yŏngsa, 1992), 266–267.

61. Hong, *Nongch'on hyŏpdong chohap kwa chojikpŏp*, 3.

62. Ibid.

63. Hong Pyŏng-sŏn, *Chŏngmal nongmin kwa Chosŏn* (Seoul: Kwangmun, 1949), 62.

64. Ibid., 62.

65. Hong, *Nongch'on hyŏpdong chohap kwa chojikpŏp*, 3.

66. Hong pointed out that the loss of a life based on *chajak chagŭp* increased poverty in rural Korea because peasants purchased goods made in cities at high prices. By not practicing *chajak chagŭp*, peasants bought more "useless goods" from cities that led them to financial ruin. Hong argued that cities now had control over the lives of peasants because of the erosion of a *chajak chagŭp* life. See Hong Pyŏng-sŏn, "Chosŏn ŭi nongch'on hyŏnsang e taehaya," *Chungmyŏng* (February 1933): 51–52.

67. Sin, "Pyŏnch'ŏn sidae e kyoyuk pasŭn saram ŭi saenghwal," 100–106.

68. For a description of Jefferson's views on agriculture and farmers, see Sandel, *Democracy's Discontent*, 123–150.

69. International Missionary Council, *The Jerusalem Meeting of the International Missionary Council, March 24–April 8, 1928*, vol. 6, *The Christian Mission in Relation to Rural Problems* (New York: International Missionary Council, 1928), 239.

70. Harry A. Rhodes, ed., *History of the Korean Mission Presbyterian Church U.S.A.*, vol. 1, *1884–1934* (Seoul: Presbyterian Church of Korea Department of Education, 1934), 541–555.

71. International Missionary Council, *Christian Mission in Relation to Rural Problems*, 247–248.

72. Pak Hak-chŏn, "Changrokyo chonghoe nongch'onbu," *Sindong'a* (February 1935): 85.

73. "Mŏrimal," *Nongmin saenghwal* (June 1929): 1.

74. Yun Chŏng-ho, "P'ip'ye hayŏ kananuri nongch'on kyŏngje," *Nongmin saenghwal* (June 1929): 11–13.

75. Cho was known as the "Gandhi of Korea" because he believed in a gradualist, nonviolent approach to the struggle against the Japanese. After liberation, the Soviet Union placed him at the head of a transitional government, but he was soon forced out. For a description of his nationalist activities, see Kenneth Wells, *New God, New Nation* (Honolulu: University of Hawai'i Press, 1990), chaps. 6 and 7.

76. Yu took many of Kagawa's ideas and applied them to rural work, which he began in 1924. See Chang Kyu-sik, "1920-yŏndae kaejoron ŭi hwaksan kwa kidokkyo sahoejuŭi suyong chŏngch'ak," *Yŏksa munje yŏn'guso*, no. 21 (April 2009): 111–136.

77. Yu Chae-gi, "Yesuch'on kŏnsŏl ŭi samdae iron," *Nongmin saenghwal* (September 1931): 32; and Chang, "1920-yŏndae kaejoron ŭi hwaksan kwa kidokkyo sahoejuŭi suyong chŏngch'ak," 119–126.

78. For a list of members of this organization, see the section "Nongch'on undong," *Nongmin saenghwal* (November 1929): 26.

79. Yu, "Yesuch'on kŏnsŏl ŭi samdae iron," 32.

80. Ibid.

81. "Nongch'on yŏn'gu hoe kyuyak," *Nongmin saenghwal* (November 1929): 27.

82. Yu, "Yesuch'on kŏnsŏl ŭi samdae iron," 32.

83. Yu agreed with Pae that mutual assistance produced human love, which in turn became a way for people to experience God's love. Yu wrote, "People are a conduit for God's love." See Yu Chae-gi, "Kidokkyo wa hyŏpdong chohap," *Nongch'on t'ongsin* (July 1935): 4.

84. "Ch'onghoe nongch'onbu sangsŏl kigwan sŏlch'i je haya," *Chonggyo sibo* (November 1933): 16.

85. David Harvey, *The Condition of Postmodernity* (Cambridge, MA: Blackwell, 1990), 272–283.

86. Various organizational problems prevented the start of a major movement. See Pang Ki-chung, *Pae Min-su ŭi nongch'on undong kwa kidokkyo sasang* (Seoul: Yonsei University Press, 1999), 135–204.

87. "Ch'onghoe nongch'onbu sangsŏl kigwan sŏlch'i je haya," 16.

88. As a theologian, Ch'ae Pil-gŭn taught at Sungsil University in P'yŏngyang. He contributed articles to PCRM journals that gave theological justification for PCRM activities.

89. For a biography of Yi Hun-gu, see Pang Ki-chung, "Ilche ha Yi Hun-gu ŭi nongŏpnon kwa kyŏngje sasang," *Yŏksa munje yŏn'gu*, no. 1 (December 1996): 113–162.

90. Pang Kie-chung, "Yi Hun-gu's Agricultural Reform Theory and Nationalist Economic Thought" (paper presented at the conference "Between Colonialism and Nationalism: Power and Subjectivity in Korea, 1931–1950," University of Michigan, Ann Arbor, May 2001), 19.

91. Ch'ae Pil-gŭn, "Kidokkyo nongch'on undong ŭi chillo," *Nongch'on t'ongsin* (July 1935): 1.

92. Yi Hun-gu, "Sŏnggyŏng e nat'anan chungnongjuŭi sasang," *Chonggyo sibo* (January 1935): 10–11.

93. Ch'ae, "Kidokkyo nongch'on undong ŭi chillo," 1.

94. Yi Hun-gu, "Sŏnggyŏng e nat'anan chungnongjuŭi sasang," 10–11.

95. Ibid., 11.

96. Yi Hun-gu, "Chosŏn yesugyo wa nongch'on," *Chonggyo sibo* (March 1933): 13.

97. Ibid.

98. Pak Hyŏng-yong, "Nongch'on kasa sŏnjicha pullŏra," *Nongch'on t'ongsin* (September 1935): 1.

99. Kim Sŏng-wŏn, "Nongŏp ŭi ponjil kwa nongŏpcha ŭi t'aedo," *Nongch'on t'ongsin* (August 1935): 2.

100. Yi Hun-gu, "Sŏnggyŏng e nat'anan chungnongjuŭi sasang," 11.

101. Ibid.

102. "Nongch'on kwa tosi," *Nongch'on t'ongsin* (May 1935): 1.

103. Yi Hun-gu, "Nongch'on ch'ŏngnyŏn ponunka ŭi hŭimang," *Nongmin saeng-hwal* (May 1936): 265–268.

104. "Nongch'on kwa tosi,"1.

105. Yi Hun-gu, "Chosŏn yesugyo wa nongch'on," 13.

106. Yi Hun-gu, "Chosŏn nongch'on p'ip'ye ŭi wŏnin kwa kidaech'aek (1)," *Nong-min saenghwal* (May 1935): 295–297.

107. Pang, "Yi Hun-gu's Agricultural Reform Theory and Nationalist Economic Thought," 21.

108. Yi Hun-gu, *Chosŏn nongŏpnon* (Seoul: Hansŏng Publishing, 1935), 1–5.

109. Pae Min-su, *Who Shall Enter the Kingdom of Heaven: Pae Min-su chasŏjŏn* (Seoul: Yonsei University Press, 1999), 226.

110. Minsoo Pai (Pae Min-su), "The Rural Evangelistic Movement," *Korea Mission Field* (July 1935): 149; and Pae, *Who Shall Enter the Kingdom of Heaven*, 224.

111. Chŏng Yong-sŏ, "Ilche ha haebang hu Ch'ŏndogyo seryŏk ŭi chŏngch'i un-dong" (PhD diss., Yonsei University, 2010), 19.

112. Benjamin Weems, *Reform, Rebellion, and the Heavenly Way* (Tucson: Univer-sity of Arizona Press, 1964), 68.

113. Membership in the church declined from 177,692 in 1910 to 175,780 in 1919. See Timothy S. Lee, *Born Again* (Honolulu: University of Hawai'i Press, 2010), 32.

114. Chŏng, "Ilche ha haebang hu Ch'ŏndogyo seryŏk ŭi chŏngch'i undong," 19.

115. Beginning in the 1920s, Ch'ŏndogyo faced internal divisions over several is-sues, including how to deal with Japanese colonialism and leadership ques-tions. By the middle of the 1920s, the organization had split along the lines of the traditional (Ku) and new (Sin) factions. The new faction, which held most of the power in the organization, planned to be a key player in the Culture Movement and therefore started various organizations, including the Ch'ŏndogyo Youth Party and Chosŏn nongminsa. The traditional faction set up rival organizations, including its own youth party. Throughout the 1920s and early 1930s, both groups tried to reconcile their differences and to unite both factions. These attempts to unite failed, however. Throughout the re-peated efforts to overcome divisions and during the short times in which the factions united, the two groups still operated autonomously under different organizing structures. Consequently, the Ch'ŏndogyo Youth Party rarely ex-perienced interference from the traditional faction. See Chŏng, "Ilche ha haebang hu Ch'ŏndogyo seryŏk ŭi chŏngch'i undong," 97–99.

116. Yi Ton-hwa, *Ch'ŏndogyo ch'anggŏnsa* (Seoul: Taedong Press, 1933), pt. 4, 5.

117. P'yo Yŏng-sam, *Ch'ŏndogyo ch'ŏngnyŏnhoe p'alsipsa*, compiled by Ch'ŏndogyo Ch'ŏngnyŏnhoe Chungang Ponbu (Seoul: Kŭl Namu, 2000), 113–114.

118. Michael D. Shin, "The Specter of Yi Gwangsu: The March 1st Movement and the Nation in Colonial Korea" (unpublished manuscript), ch. 6, 8.

119. "Ch'ŏngnyŏnhoe ch'ŏngnyŏndang ŭro kyoch'ijanun Ch'ŏndogyo ch'ŏngnyŏnhoe," *Tonga ilbo*, September 2, 1923.

120. P'yo, *Ch'ŏndogyo ch'ŏngnyŏnhoe p'alsipsa*, 113–114; and Yi Ton-hwa, *Ch'ŏndogyo ch'anggŏnsa*, pt. 4, 5.

121. P'yo, *Ch'ŏndogyo ch'ŏngnyŏnhoe p'alsipsa*, 275.

122. Sin Il-yong, "Nongch'on munje yŏn'gu," *Kaebyŏk* (August 1925): 42–51.

123. Providing a modern education became a favored solution of peasant problems. See Han Wŏn-bin, "Sojakjaeng ŭi wŏnin kwa taech'aek," *Nongmin* (June 1930): 20–23; Ilkicha, "Nongch'on kujech'aek e taehaya nongch'on pamul ŭi wŏnin," *Tangsŏng* (August 1932): 2; and Kim Pyŏng-sun, "Nongmin undong ŭi pŏmju," *Nongmin* (November 1933): 3–8.

124. The organization instituted a decentralized system in 1928.

125. See "Chosŏn nongminsa ŭi yŏnhyŏk," *Chosŏn nongmin* (June 1930): 29.

126. Ibid.

127. This journal was renamed *Nongmin* (Peasant) when Chosŏn nongminsa reorganized in 1930.

128. Yi Sŏng-hwan, "Chosŏn nongmin ŭi samdae chech'ang," *Chosŏn nongmin* (December 1925): 2.

129. Clark Sorenson argues that Chosŏn nongminsa recognized the *nongmin* as "no longer the rocks on which society are built, but rather the very body of the nation." Clark Sorenson, "National Identity and the Category 'Peasant' in Colonial Korea," in *Colonial Modernity in Korea*, ed. Gi-Wook Shin and Michael Robinson (Cambridge, MA: Harvard University Asia Center, 1999), 305.

130. Yi Sŏng-hwan, "Chosŏn nongmin ŭi samdae chech'ang," 2–5.

131. See Yi Sŏng-hwan, "Karoro nongcha chŏnha chidaebon ilka?," *Chosŏn nongmin* (May 1926): 2–5.

132. Sorenson, "National Identity and the Category 'Peasant' in Colonial Korea," 303.

133. Yi Ton-hwa, "Nongsa chinŭn nongbunim e," *Chosŏn nongmin* (December 1925): 9.

134. Yi Sŏng-hwan, "Chosŏn nongmin ŭi samdae chech'ang," 4.

135. Yi Ton-hwa, "Nongsa chinŭn nongbunim e," 8.

136. Ibid., 8–9.

137. Yi Sŏng-hwan, "Chosŏn nongmin ŭi samdae chech'ang"; Yi Sŏng-hwan, "Karoro nongcha chŏnha chidaebon ilka?," 2–5; Kim Pyŏng-hyang, "Nongŏp illyŏng saenghwal ŭi kich'o sanŏp," *Nongmin* (January 1932): 2–3.

138. Kim Pyŏng-hyang, "Nongŏp illyŏng saenghwal ŭi kich'o sanŏp," 2–3.

139. Yi Ton-hwa, "Nongsa chinŭn nongbunim e," 7.

140. Kim Kyŏng-chae, "Nongŏp in'gan saenghwal ŭi kibon," *Chosŏn nongmin* (January 1926): 7.

141. Kim Pyŏng-hyang, "Nongŏp illyŏng saenghwal ŭi kich'o sanŏp," 3.

142. Ibid., 4.

143. Stephen Gudeman, *Economics as Culture* (London: Routledge, 1986), 72.

144. Ibid.

145. Charles Gide and Charles Rist, *A History of Economic Doctrines* (London: George C. Harrap, 1915), 12.

146. "Chungnongjuŭi," *Nongmin* (July 1933): 28.

147. Yi Ton-hwa, "Nongsa chinŭn nongbunim e," 7–10.

148. Yi Sŏng-hwan, "Chosŏn nongmin ŭi samdae chech'ang," 3. Sŏk is a traditional unit of measure. One sŏk of rice is approximately equal to five bushels.

149. Yi Ton-hwa, "Nongsa chinŭn nongbunim e," 9.

150. For Yi Sŏng-hwan and Chosŏn nongminsa leaders, being independent was important because people could do anything without restrictions. See Yi Sŏng-hwan, "Chosŏn nongmin nun ttŏda," *Chosŏn nongmin* (January 1926): 19–23.

151. Yi Sŏng-hwan, "Karoro nongcha chŏnha chidaebon ilka?," 2–5 ; and Kim Pyŏng-hyang, "Nongŏp illyŏng saenghwal ŭi kich'o sanŏp."

152. Yi wrote that nature was alive and a living force. See Yi Ton-hwa, "Saram ŭi chinjŏnghan haengpok ŭn tosi e innun'ga? Chŏnwŏn e innun'ga," *Chosŏn nongmin* (June 1926): 4–6.

153. "Sin Chosŏn ŭi unmyŏng kwa nongmin ŭi chiwi," *Kaebyŏk* (November 1923): 3–6. For this translation, see Gi-Wook Shin, "Agrarianism: A Critique of Colonial Modernity in Korea," *Comparative Studies in Society and History* 41, no. 4 (October 1999): 795–796.

154. See Kim Il-tae, "Chosŏn nongmin sayaksa," *Nongmin* (October 1930): 14–15.

155. Oh, "Consuming the Modern," 250.

156. Partha Chatterjee, *The Nation and Its Fragments* (Princeton, NJ: Princeton University Press, 1993), 200–239.

157. Leo Marx, *Machine in the Garden*, 101–103.

158. Ibid.

Chapter 5: Spiritualizing the National Body

1. For the difference between changes in the 1920s and the 1930s, see Edwin Gragert, *Landownership under Colonial Rule: Korea's Japanese Experience, 1900–1935* (Honolulu: University of Hawai'i Press, 1994), chap. 6.

2. This was especially the case for *kadenmin,* who were "those roaming dispossessed peasants who try to wrest a living from half-cleared patches in the forests." See Andrew J. Grajdanzev, *Modern Korea* (New York: Institute of Pacific Relations, 1944), 109.

3. See Ken Kawashima, *The Proletarian Gamble* (Durham, NC: Duke University Press, 2009), 45–66.

4. Grajdanzev, *Modern Korea*, 110.

5. Karl Marx, quoted in Shlomo Avineri, *The Social and Political Thought of Karl Marx* (Cambridge: Cambridge University Press, 1968), 107.

6. Karl Polanyi, *The Great Transformation* (Boston: Beacon Press, 1944), 239.

7. Jackson Lears, *No Place of Grace* (Chicago: University of Chicago Press, 1981), 61–73.

8. Daniel Rodgers, *Atlantic Crossings: Social Politics in a Progressive* Age (Cambridge, MA: Harvard University Press, 1998), 326.

9. They also established consumer and marketing cooperatives. See Martin Buber, *Paths in Utopia*, trans. R. F. C. Hull (London: Routledge and Kegan Paul, 1949), 62–63.

10. See Tetsuo Najita, *Ordinary Economics in Japan* (Berkeley: University of California Press, 2009), 142–143.

11. Chan Han-seng, "Cooperatives as a Panacea for China's Ills," *Far Eastern Survey* 6, no. 7 (March 31, 1937): 71–77.

12. Tetsuo Najita, "Traditional Co-operatives in Modern Japan: Rethinking Alternatives to Cosmopolitanism and Nativism," in *Social Futures, Global Visions*, ed. Cynthia Hewitt de Alcántara (Cambridge, MA: Blackwell, 1996), 148.

13. Frederic C. Howe, *Denmark: A Cooperative Commonwealth* (New York: Harcourt, Brace, 1921), 11–14.

14. See Steven Borish, *The Land of the Living* (Nevada City, CA: Blue Dolphin, 1991), 125; Rodgers, *Atlantic Crossings,* 356.

15. See Jarka Chloupkova, Gunnar Lind Hasse Svendsen, and Gert Tinggaard Svendsen, "Building and Destroying Social Capital: The Case of Cooperative Movements in Denmark and Poland," *Agriculture and Human Values* 20 (2003): 243.

16. E. C. Branson quoted in Rodgers, *Atlantic Crossings,* 355.

17. Frederic C. Howe, *Denmark,* 17–18.

18. According to the Institute of Korean History's database on colonial-era newspapers, *Tonga ilbo* published more than three hundred articles about Denmark. For articles on Denmark, see Pang T'ae-yŏng, "Chŏngmal nongmin kŭp kyoyuk," *Tonggwang* (November 1926): 28–32; Ch'oe Hŏn-sik, "Tangmyŏn han modŭn chujang-Chŏngmal ŭi nongmin chŏngsin ŭl," *Sinmin* (January 1928): 96–96; Pang T'ae-yŏng, "Nagwŏn ŭi Chŏngmal," *Sinmin* (June 1929): 108–118; Kim Po-yŏng, "Chŏngmal ŭi kungmin cheyuk," *Samch'ŏlli* (February 1933): 34–37; and Yang Ju-sam, "Nongmin ŭi nagwŏnin Chŏngmal," *Kamri hoebo* (January 1929): 11–22. See also Helen Kiteuk Kim, "Rural Education for the Regeneration of Korea" (PhD diss., Columbia University, 1931); and Kim Hwallan (Helen Kim), *Chŏngmalin ŭi kyŏngje puhŭngron* (Kyŏngsŏng: Han'guk kidokkyo ch'ŏngnyŏnhoe yŏnhaphoe, 1931).

19. Induk Park, "Work among Rural Women," *Korea Mission Field* (July 1933): 137.

20. Hong traveled around Denmark with Sin Hŭng-u and Helen Kim, the head of the YWCA, from February 26 to March 11, 1928.

21. Some of his articles on Denmark include Hong Pyŏng-sŏn, "Chŏngmal kachŏng ŭi aoŭmtaoun chŏm," *Sinsaenghwal* (May 1932); and Hong Pyŏng-sŏn, "Chŏngmal ŭl hyanghamyŏnsŏ," *Ch'ŏngnyŏn* (July–August 1928). As for books, before 1945, Hong wrote *Chŏngmal kwa Chŏngmal nongmin* (Kyŏngsang: Han'guk kidokkyo ch'ŏngnyŏn hoeryon haphoe, 1929); and *Nongch'on hyŏpdong chohap kwa chojikpŏp* (Kyŏngsŏng: Ch'ŏngnyŏnhoe yŏnhaphoe, 1930). After liberation, Hong wrote four more books on Denmark and cooperatives: *Chŏngmal nongmin kwa Chosŏn* (Seoul: Kwangmun, 1949); *Chŏngmal nongmin kwa nongch'on ŭi chaegŏn* (Seoul: Kwangmun, 1951); *Nongŏp hyŏpdong chohap kanghwa* (Seoul: Sŏngmunsa, 1958); and *Sobi chohap ŭi wŏlli wa silje* (Seoul: Sŏngmunsa, 1960).

22. Kim Yong-gi and Yŏ Oun-hyŏk, the founders of the Christian utopian village Bonganisangch'on in 1935 and the influential Canaan Farming School in the postliberation era, learned about Denmark through Hong's publications. See Im Yŏng-ch'ŏl, *Kanaan isangch'on undong* (Seoul: Chaedanpŏpin ilgachaedan, 2009), 178.

23. Hong Pyŏng-sŏn, "Kyohoe wa nongch'on saŏp," *Nongmin saenghwal* (July 1929): 5–6. For the advertisements, see 23–24 of the same issue.

24. *Nongmin* was named *Chosŏn nongmin* before 1930. See Hong Pyŏng-sŏn, "Chŏngmal ŭi Nongmin saenghwal," *Chosŏn nongmin* (August 1929); "Chosŏn nongmin yŏrŏpun ae," *Nongmin* (May 1930): 23; and "Hyŏnsang Chosŏn nongch'on kuje ŭi samdae kin'gŭp ch'aek," *Nongmin* (June 1930): 15–16.

25. Hong Pyŏng-sŏn, "Chŏngmal ŭl hyanghamyŏnsŏ," *Ch'ŏngnyŏn* (July–August 1927): 3–4.

26. Hong, *Chŏngmal kwa Chŏngmal nongmin*, 188 and 1.

27. Ibid., 122–130.

28. Ibid., 122, 162–164; and Hong, *Nongch'on hyŏpdong chohap kwa chojikpŏp*, 15–16.

29. Hong, *Chŏngmal kwa Chŏngmal nongmin*, 122–158.

30. Ibid., 168–170.

31. Hong Pyŏng-sŏn, "Nongch'on saŏp ŭi chinŭi 15," *Kidok sinbo*, April 2, 1930.

32. Hong Pyŏng-sŏn, "Sanŏp sinyong chohap e taehaya," *Ch'ŏngnyŏn* (May 1927): 15.

33. Hong wrote that love developed through cooperatives. See Hong Pyŏng-sŏn, "Nongch'on saŏp ŭi chinŭi 5," *Kidok sinbo*, December 18, 1929.

34. Hong, *Chŏngmal kwa Chŏngmal nongmin*, 126.

35. Anthony Giddens, *The Consequences of Modernity* (Stanford, CA: Stanford University Press, 1990), 34.

36. Hong Pyŏng-sŏn, "Sinyong chohap," *Nongch'on ch'ŏngnyŏn* (November 1929): 1.

37. Hong realized that class differences and social hierarchy had long existed in Korea and caused social divisions. However, he believed that money under a capitalist economy only exacerbated social division in the modern period. Hong Pyŏng-sŏn, "Kyohoe wa sajo 13," *Kidok sinbo,* October 24, 1923.

38. Hong Pyŏng-sŏn, "Kyohoe wa sajo 12," *Kidok sinbo,* October 17, 1923.

39. Yu Chae-gi, "Kidokkyo wa hyŏpdong chohap," *Nongch'on t'ongsin* (July 1935): 4.

40. Yi Hun-gu, "Chosŏn nongch'on p'ip'ye ŭi wŏnin kwa kudaech'aek (5)," *Nongmin saenghwal* (July / August 1935): 474–475.

41. Yi Ton-hwa, "Saengmyŏng ŭi ŭisikhwa wa ŭisik ŭi inbonhwa," *Kaebyŏk* (May 1926): 9.

42. See Yi Hun-gu, "Ŭipong ŭi ch'ŏrhak (2)," *Nongmin saenghwal* (October 1933): 6; and Sin Hŭng-u, "Chŏngmal ŭi hyŏpdong chohap," *Ch'ŏngnyŏn* (December 1928): 13–15.

43. Hong, *Chŏngmal kwa Chŏngmal nongmin,* 205–217.

44. Paek Min, "Chŏngmal ŭl paeuja," *Nongmin* (January 1932): 14–15.

45. Hong, *Chŏngmal kwa Chŏngmal nongmin,* 125.

46. Ibid., 126; Paek, "Chŏngmal ŭl paeuja," 22.

47. Yi Hun-gu, "Chosŏn nongch'on p'ip'ye ŭi wŏnin kwa kudaech'aek (5)," 476.

48. James C. Scott, *The Moral Economy of the Peasant* (New Haven, CT: Yale University Press, 1976).

49. Paek, "Chŏngmal ŭl paeuja," 15, 21.

50. Han Tong-wu, "Chŏngmal nongch'on sanghwang," *Nongmin* (September 1930): 36. He also wrote an additional article about Denmark. See "Chŏngmal nongch'on sanghwang (II)," *Nongmin* (November 1930).

51. Yu Chai-gi, "Hyŏpdong chohap ŭi iyagi," *Nongmin saenghwal* (August 1934): 505–506; Yi Hun-gu, "Ŭibong ŭi ch'ŏrhak (2)," *Nongmin Saenghwal* (October 1933): 6.

52. Hong, *Chŏngmal kwa Chŏngmal nongmin,* 185–195.

53. Ibid., 185.

54. Moreover, because Denmark's rural revitalization program started with religious intentions to revive Danes spiritually, each movement most certainly believed that the Danish example was most appropriate for its own religion-based movement. For a description of other cooperative movements, see Brett Fairbairn, "History from the Ecological Perspective: Gaia Theory and the Problem of Cooperatives in Turn-of-the-Century Germany," *American Historical Review* 99, no. 4 (October 1994): 1215–1221; Najita, *Ordinary Economics in Japan;* and Kenneth Scott Latourette, *World Service: A History of the Foreign Work and World Service of the Young Men's Christian Associations of the United States and Canada* (New York: Association Press, 1957), 136–137.

55. Hong, *Nongch'on hyŏpdong chohap kwa chojikpŏp.*

56. John H. Reisner, "Report on Study of Certain Agricultural and Rural Projects in Korea, February to July 1931" (YMCA Archives, University of Minnesota, Minneapolis, photocopy), 71.

57. The Rural Credit Society was first started in 1907. By 1934, there were close to 692 rural credit societies with more than 1.1 million members. See Government-General of Chosen, *Thriving Chosen* (Keijo: Government-General of Chosen, 1935), 28–29.

58. See Sin, "Chŏngmal ŭi hyŏpdong chohap"; and Sin Hŭng-u, "Mulchŏk saeng-hwal uri yogu III," *Ch'ŏngnyŏn* (December 1926): 7–10.

59. Ibid.

60. J. C. Penney, the founder of the line of department stores that bear his name, founded Penney Farms. Clark and the Penney Farms "endeavored to do for their farms what the Danish Government had done for the farmers of that country." See F. S. Brockman, letter to W. W. Lockwood (January 30, 1929) (YMCA Archives, University of Minnesota, Minneapolis, photocopy).

61. Bunce left Korea in the 1930s but later returned as an adviser for the U.S. Army after 1945.

62. A. C. Bunce, letter to Mr. Herschleb (April 14, 1929) (YMCA Archives, University of Minnesota, Minneapolis, photocopy).

63. Hugh Heung-woo Cynn (Sin Hŭng-u), "What May Be Learned from Other Countries," *Korea Mission Field* (December 1928): 246.

64. In an official study of Christian rural movements, John Reisner acknowledged Hong as the primary force behind the YMCA cooperative movement. See Reisner, "Report on Study of Certain Agricultural and Rural Projects in Korea," 81.

65. Hong presumably advocated that local villagers should use their own capital for cooperatives because of the power of outside capital to transform local relations and activities. See Hong, *Nongch'on hyŏpdong chohap kwa chojikpŏp*, 12–13; and; Hong Pyŏng-sŏn, "Nongch'on saŏp ŭi chinŭi 14," *Kidok sinbo*, March 26, 1930.

66. Hong Pyŏng-sŏn, "Sanŏp sinyong chohap e taehaya," *Ch'ŏngnyŏn* (May 1927): 15.

67. Hong Pyŏng-sŏn, "Nongch'on saŏp ŭi chinŭi 16," *Kidok sinbo*, April 9, 1930.

68. According to Hong, in the 1920s, many *kyes* collapsed because of "harmful" factors and "wicked" and "evil" leaders. See Hong Pyŏng-sŏn, "Chojik kwa hapryŏk kwa chohap," *Nongch'on ch'ŏngnyŏn* (October 1929): 1; and Hong, *Nongch'on hyŏpdong chohap kwa chojikpŏp*, 15.

69. YMCA, "Statistics and Information for the Calendar Year 1930" (YMCA Archives, University of Minnesota, Minneapolis, photocopy), 3; Korean Young Men's Christian Association (KYMCA), *The Rural Program of the Young Men's Christian Association in Korea* (Seoul: National Council of the Young Men's Christian Association in Korea, 1932), 9.

70. Reisner, "Report on Study of Certain Agricultural and Rural Projects in Korea," 81–82.

71. Ibid.

72. The YMCA noted that the loan and interest were paid back at the time of harvest, and therefore the principal amount of the cooperative fund increased. See KYMCA, *Rural Program of the Young Men's Christian Association in Korea*, 15.

73. Reisner, "Report on Study of Certain Agricultural and Rural Projects in Korea," 81–82.

74. Ibid., 82.

75. Ibid.

76. KYMCA, *Rural Program of the Young Men's Christian Association in Korea*, 15.

77. Hugh H. Cynn (Sin Hŭng-u), "The Second Stage in Rural Work," *Korea Mission Field* (August 1933): 163.

78. Reisner, "Report on Study of Certain Agricultural and Rural Projects in Korea," 82.

79. KYMCA, *Rural Program of the Young Men's Christian Association in Korea*, 6.

80. Ibid., 7.

81. Cynn, "Second Stage in Rural Work," 163.

82. See KYMCA, *Rural Program of the Young Men's Christian Association in Korea*, 9; and Reisner, "Report on Study of Certain Agricultural and Rural Projects in Korea," 79–80.

83. James C. Scott, *Seeing Like a State* (New Haven, CT: Yale University Press, 1998), 257–258.

84. A. C. Bunce, letter to Charles Herschleb (March 6, 1931) (YMCA Archives, University of Minnesota, Minneapolis, photocopy), 1.

85. A. C. Bunce, letter to Charles A. Herschleb (September 7, 1931) (YMCA Archives, University of Minnesota, Minneapolis, photocopy), 1.

86. A. C. Bunce, letter to Charles Herschleb (March 6, 1931), 1.

87. Ibid.; A. C. Bunce, letter to Charles A. Herschleb (September 7, 1931), 1.

88. A. C. Bunce, letter to Charles Herschleb (March 6, 1931), 1; A. C. Bunce, "Some Rural Observations," *Korea Mission Field* (May 1931): 95.

89. A. C. Bunce, letter to Mr. Herschleb (November 4, 1929) (YMCA Archives, University of Minnesota, Minneapolis, photocopy), 4.

90. A. C. Bunce, letter to unnamed addressee (November 28, 1931) (YMCA Archives, University of Minnesota, Minneapolis, photocopy).

91. Ibid.

92. Among the three types of apples marketed by the cooperative, the *hongok* apple garnered the most profits: 122.80 yen (grade 1), 102.80 yen (grade 2), and 82.80 yen (grade 3). See A. C. Bunce, "Comparative Receipts from Apples Sold

Locally and from Apples Sold Cooperatively in Japan (December 28, 1931)" (YMCA Archives, University of Minnesota, Minneapolis, photocopy).

93. Bunce, letter to unnamed addressee (November 28, 1931).

94. Ibid., 1.

95. A. C. Bunce, letter to Charles A. Herschleb (December 22, 1933) (YMCA Archives, University of Minnesota, Minneapolis, photocopy).

96. Yi Hun-gu, "Nongch'on ŭi pudam kyŏnggamk'e haja," *Nongmin saenghwal* (5 Year Anniversary, 1934): 350.

97. Ibid., Yi Hun-gu, "Chosŏn nongch'on p'ip'ye ŭi wŏnin kwa kidae ch'aek," *Nongmin saenghwal* (May 1935): 296.

98. For his definition of wealth, see Yi Hun-gu, "Nongch'on ŭi pudam kyŏnggamk'e haja," 347.

99. Yi Hun-gu, "Chosŏn nongch'on ŭi p'ip'ye wŏnin kwa kidae ch'aek," 296.

100. Yi Hun-gu, "Chosŏn nongch'on ŭi p'ip'ye wŏnin kwa kidae ch'aek (V cont.)," *Nongmin saenghwal* (October 1935): 708–711; Yi Hun-gu, "Toji poyu haja," *Nongmin saenghwal* (January 1935): 5–8.

101. Yi Hun-gu, "Chosŏn nongch'on ŭi p'ip'ye wŏnin kwa kidae ch'aek (V cont.)," 710.

102. Ibid., 708–711; Yi Hun-gu, "Toji poyuhaja," *Nongmin saenghwal* (January 1935): 5–8.

103. Yi Hun-gu, "Toji poyuhaja," 8.

104. Ibid., 7.

105. Edwin Gragert's study of changing landholding patterns during the 1920s and 1930s confirms Yi's observation on the growing number of absentee landowners and the increasing number of foreigners owning land in Korea. See Gragert, *Landownership under Colonial Rule*, 120, 148–149.

106. Yi Hun-gu, "Nongch'on ŭi pudam kyŏnggamk'e haja," 347–48; Yi Hun-gu, "Chosŏn nongch'on ŭi p'ip'ye wŏnin kwa kidae ch'aek," 295.

107. Yi Hun-gu, "Chosŏn nongch'on ŭi p'ip'ye wŏnin kwa kidae ch'aek," 296.

108. Ibid., 297.

109. Hoon Koo Lee, *Land Utilization and Rural Economy in Korea* (Chicago: University of Chicago Press, 1936), 241–251.

110. Ibid., 245.

111. Ibid., 241–242; Gragert, *Landownership under Colonial Rule*, 128.

112. Yi Hun-gu, "Nongga puch'ae rŭl ŏttŏke hamyŏn jŏngni halsu issŭlkka?," *Nongmin saenghwal* (March 1934): 135–138.

113. Andrew Grajdanzev pointed out that interest rates were dependent on the nationality of the borrower, with "Koreans paying as a rule 25 percent more than Japanese." See Grajdanzev, *Modern Korea*, 207; and Lee, *Land Utilization and Rural Economy in Korea*, 238.

114. Lee, *Land Utilization and Rural Economy in Korea*, 251.

115. This figure includes tenants and cultivators who owned the land. See ibid., 234.

116. Yi Hun-gu, "Chosŏn nongch'on ŭi p'ip'ye wŏnin kwa kidae ch'aek (II)," *Nongmin saenghwal* (June 1935): 375.

117. The Industrial Bank of Chosen was a quasi-public institution since the colonial government established it to carry out the economic policies of the government, and individuals invested in the bank through stocks and bonds.

118. Lee, *Land Utilization and Rural Economy in Korea*, 243.

119. Ibid., 375.

120. Ibid.

121. Yi Hun-gu, "Nongch'on ŭi pudam kyŏnggamk'e haja," 347.

122. Yi certainly developed this concern under the influence of Richard Ely, who taught at the University of Wisconsin, where Yi received his doctorate in agricultural economics. A critic of industrial capitalism, Ely argued that owners of large capital promoted a form of monopoly capitalism in which they controlled production and prices and stifled any form of competition. This form of economic control led to an imbalanced society in which a few people with large capital controlled the majority who "lack[ed] the opportunities for a full and harmonious development of their faculties." See Richard Ely, "The Nature and Significance of Monopolies and Trust," *International Journal of Ethics* (April 1900): 281.

123. Yi Hun-gu, "Chosŏn nongch'on ŭi p'ip'ye wŏnin kwa kidae ch'aek (V cont.)," 708; Yi Hun-gu, "Chosŏn nongch'on ŭi p'ip'ye wŏnin kwa kidae ch'aek (V)," *Nongmin saenghwal* (July 1935): 475.

124. Yi Hun-gu, "Chosŏn nongch'on ŭi p'ip'ye wŏnin kwa kidae ch'aek (V)," 474.

125. Yi Hun-gu, "Nongch'on ŭi pudam kyŏnggamk'e haja," 347.

126. Yi Hun-gu, "Toji poyuhaja," 7.

127. PCRM leaders' deep concern over capital's power to transform areas strongly suggests that they valued the credit cooperative's power to control the direction of capital and its overall movement in a local area.

128. Yu Chae-gi, "Sobi chohap muŏt in'ga?," *Nongmin saenghwal* (November 1929): 6–8; and Yi Hun-gu, "Chosŏn nongch'on ŭi p'ip'ye wŏnin kwa kidae ch'aek (VI)," *Nongmin saenghwal* (November 1935): 798–800.

129. Yi Hun-gu, "Chosŏn nongch'on ŭi p'ip'ye wŏnin kwa kidae ch'aek (VI)," 800.

130. For a list of these cooperatives, see Han Kyu-mu, *Ilche ha Han'guk kidokkyo nongch'on undong, 1925–1937* (Seoul: Han'guk kidokkyo yŏksa yŏn'guso, 1997), 161.

131. "Chungang sinyong chohap," *Kidok sinbo*, July 16, 1930.

132. Han Kyu-mu, *Ilche ha Han'guk kidokkyo nongch'on undong*, 161–162.

133. Yu Chae-gi wrote about the success of some cooperatives during his visits to the countryside in 1935. See Yu Chae-gi, "Nongch'on sunhoe ŭi sa ch'ŏlli," *Nongch'on t'ongsin* (March 1935): 3; Yu Chae-gi, "Nongch'on sunhoe ŭi ilmalli II," *Nongch'on t'ongsin* (April 1935): 3; Yu Chae-gi, "Nongch'on sunhoe ŭi ilmalli III," *Nongch'on t'ongsin* (May 1935): 4; and Yu Chae-gi, "Nongch'on sunhoe ŭi ilmalli IV," *Nongch'on t'ongsin* (June 1935): 4.

134. "Hyŏpdong chohap sullye III," *Nongmin saenghwal* (July 1934): 441–444.

135. Although leaders spoke of talking about cooperatives, there are no records that show exactly what was said about cooperatives in classes or lectures. However, because *Nongmin saenghwal* and *Nongch'on t'ongsin* served as the official "textbooks" for the movement, it can be strongly presumed that the ideas that appeared in the journal were introduced in the classes and lectures.

136. Yi Hun-gu, "Chosŏn nongch'on ŭi p'ip'ye wŏnin kwa kudaech'aek (V cont.)," 708–709.

137. Ibid.

138. Ibid., 709.

139. Yi Hun-gu, "Ŭipong ŭi ch'ŏrhak," *Nongmin saenghwal* (August 1933): 6–7.

140. See Minsoo Pai, "The Rural Evangelistic Movement," *Korea Mission Field* (July 1935): 150; Pae Min-su, "Hyŏpdong," in *Pogumjuŭi wa kidokkyo nongch'on undong*, ed. Pang Ki-chung (Seoul: Yonsei University Press, 2000), 3; and Yu Chae-gi, "Kidokkyo wa hyŏpdong chohap," 4.

141. Yu Chae-gi, "Kidokkyo wa hyŏpdong chohap," 4; Yu Chae-gi, "Sobi chohap muŏt in'ga?," 6–9.

142. Yu Chae-gi, "Kidokkyo wa hyŏpdong chohap," 4; Yu Chae-gi, "Sanŏp chohap iyagi I," *Kidok sinbo*, January 1, 1935; Yu Chae-gi, "Sanŏp chohap iyagi II," *Kidok sinbo*, January 16, 1935; Yu Chae-gi, "Sanŏp chohap iyagi II," *Kidok sinbo*, January 30, 1935.

143. Yu Chae-gi, "Kidokkyo wa hyŏpdong chohap," 4.

144. Pae, "Hyŏpdong," 3.

145. Gragert, *Landownership under Colonial Rule*, 141.

146. Grajdanzev, *Modern Korea*, 110.

147. Discussions started around 1927–1928. See "Huch'ŏn saenghwal ŭi mulchŏk kich'o nŭn kongjakkye," *Sinin'gan* (May 1934): 354.

148. Kim Hwal-lan, "Chipdan nongjang kwa sojak hamnihwa," *Nongmin* (August 1931): 31–32; Chŏng Yong-sŏ, "1930-yŏndae Ch'ŏndogyo seryŏk ŭi nongŏp munje insik kwa nongŏp kaehyŏkron," *Tongbang hakji* 117 (September 2002): 60–61.

149. Kim Hwal-lan, "Chipdan nongjang kwa sojak hamnihwa," 32.

150. Kim Byŏng-soon, "Tangmyŏn munje ABC," *Nongmin* (February 1932): 6–8; Kim Hwal-lan, "Chipdan nongchang kwa sojak hamnihwa," 30.

151. P'yo Yŏng-sam, *Ch'ŏndogyo ch'ŏngnyŏnhoe p'alsipsa*, compiled by Ch'ŏndogyo Ch'ŏngnyŏnhoe Chungang Ponbu (Seoul: Kŭl Namu, 2000), 294.

152. Chŏng, "1930-yŏndae Ch'ŏndogyo seryŏk ŭi nongŏp munje insik kwa nongŏp kaehyŏkron," 71.

153. "Huch'ŏn saenghwal ŭi mulchŏk kich'o nŭn kongjakkye," 355.

154. Yu Ho, "Kongjakkye sŏlch'i ŭi silje," *Sinin'gan* (March 1933): 22.

155. Ibid., 23.

156. "Huch'ŏn saenghwal ŭi mulchŏk kich'o nŭn kongjakkye," 354.

157. "Kongjakkye kyuyak," *Sinin'gan* (April 1933): 28.

158. See Im Yŏn, "Hyŏpdong chohap chaeil," *Nongmin* (October 1930): 26–28; Han Wŏn-bin, "Chohap undong ŭi chaemunje," *Nongmin* (July 1932): 22–24; Han Wŏn-bin, "Chohap undong ŭi chaemunje II," *Nongmin* (November 1932): 26–29; Han Wŏn-bin, "Kongsaeng chohap iran muŏt inya?," *Sinin'gan* (May 1932): 47–48; and "Kongsaeng chohap e taehan munje," *Tangsŏng* (August 1932): 3.

159. P'yo, *Ch'ŏndogyo ch'ŏngnyŏnhoe p'alsipsa*, 291.

160. Sŭng Kwan-ha, "Kongjakkye wa kongsaeng chohap kwa ŭi ch'aichŏm e taehaya," *Sinin'gan* (September 1933): 32.

161. Chŏng, "1930-yŏndae Ch'ŏndogyo seryŏk ŭi nongŏp munje insik kwa nongŏp kaehyŏkron," 73–75.

162. Ch'ŏndogyo leaders seemed to fear that peasants could not recognize the difference between the two systems and therefore would not be motivated to create a CCA, especially if they were already part of a cooperative. Ch'ŏndogyo leaders therefore publicly talked about the difference between the systems. See Sŭng, "Kongjakkye wa kongsaeng chohap kwa ŭi ch'aichŏm e taehaya," 32.

163. For a description of the democratic governing structure of a cooperative, see Han Wŏn-bin, "Chohap undong ŭi chaemunje," 22–24; Han Wŏn-bin, "Chohap undong ŭi chaemunje II," 26–29; Han Wŏn-bin, "Kongsaeng chohap iran muŏt inya?," 47–48; "Kongsaeng chohap e taehan munje," 3; and "Nongmin sinmun," *Nongmin* (August 1933): 53.

164. "Kongjakkye kyuyak," 28.

165. Ibid.

166. "Huch'ŏn saenghwal ŭi mulchŏk kich'o nŭn kongjakkye," 354.

167. See Moshe Lewin, *Russian Peasants and Soviet Power: A Study of Collectivization*, trans. Irene Nove (New York: W. W. Norton, 1968).

168. See ibid., 391; and Scott, *Seeing Like a State*, 202.

169. Ch'ŏndogyo leaders certainly had direct knowledge of Soviet collectivization because many leaders studied in the Soviet Union, such as Ch'oe Rin.

170. P'yo, *Ch'ŏndogyo ch'ŏngnyŏnhoe p'alsipsa*, 297.

171. Pak Mun-ho, "Chosŏn nongminsa ŭi kŭmhu chusik hoesa ro pyŏngyŏng hamyŏnsŏ," *Sinin'gan* (November 1936): 416.

172. Pang Kie-chung, "Ideological Roots of the South Korean Land Reform" (paper presented at the annual meeting of the Association for Asian Studies, Chicago, March 2001), 5–6.

173. P'yo, *Ch'ŏndogyo ch'ŏngnyŏnhoe p'alsipsa*, 295–296.

174. Ibid., 297–298.

175. "Nongmin sinmun," 53.

176. Ibid.; "Anchangsa ŭi kongdong kyŏngjak pangsik," *Nongmin* (April 1933): 40–41.

177. "Nongmin sinmun," 53.

178. Ibid.

179. A *ture* promoted collective labor based on the principle of mutual support. Unlike the *kye*, a *ture* was not an administrative organization; it served as an organization through which peasants in a village volunteered to help their neighbors cultivate and harvest agricultural goods. *Ture* activities included physical labor and various communal recreational activities; normally there was a festive atmosphere during planting and harvest season.

180. "Nongmin sinmun," 51.

181. P'yo, *Ch'ŏndogyo ch'ŏngnyŏnhoe p'alsipsa*, 294.

182. "Kongsaeng chohap sŏlch'i e taehaya," *Tangsŏng* (August 1931): 6; "Kongsaeng chohap e taehan munje," 3.

183. Yu Ho, "Kongjakkye sŏlch'i ŭi silje," 22; "Kongjakkye kyuyak," 28; Sŭng, "Kongjakkye wa kongsaeng chohap kwa ŭi ch'aichŏm e taehaya," 31.

184. Han Wŏn-bin, "Chohap undong ŭi chaemunje," 22–24; Han Wŏn-bin, "Kongsaeng chohap iran muŏt inya?," 47–48; Sŭng, "Kongjakkye wa kongsaeng chohap kwa ŭi ch'aichŏm e taehaya," 32; Sŭng Kwan-ha, "Kongsaeng chohap paljŏngi esŏ," *Nongmin* (December 1932): 30–33; "Kongsaeng chohap e taehan munje," 3.

185. Yu Ho, "Kongjakkye sŏlch'i ŭi silje," 23.

186. Kim explained how under cooperative cultivation, peasants should raise agricultural products that would be of superior quality in order to obtain the best prices when they were sold in Korea and abroad. See Kim Hwal-san, "Chipdan nongjang kwa sojak hamnihwa," 33.

Chapter 6: Constructing National Consciousness

1. See James Earnest Fisher, "Democracy and Mission Education in Korea" (PhD diss., Teachers College, Columbia University, 1928), 67.

2. See Andrew J. Grajdanzev, *Modern Korea* (New York: Institute of Pacific Relations, 1944), 263.

3. Fisher, "Democracy and Mission Education in Korea," 65–68.

4. Ibid., 127.

5. Franco Moretti, *The Way of the World* (London: Verso, 1987), 4–5.

6. Frank Brockman, letter to Fletcher Brockman (1926) (YMCA Archives, University of Minnesota, Minneapolis, photocopy), 1.

7. H. Heung-Wu Cynn (Sin Hŭng-u), "The Young Men's Christian Association," *Korea Mission Field* (January 1929): 15.

8. Yi Sŏng-hwan, "Chosŏn nongmin kyoyuk ŭi isang kwa pangbŏp," *Chosŏn nongmin* (November 1926): 2–16.

9. P'yo Yŏng-sam, *Ch'ŏndogyo ch'ŏngnyŏnhoe p'alsipsa*, compiled by Ch'ŏndogyo Ch'ŏngnyŏnhoe Chungang Ponbu (Seoul: Kŭl Namu, 2000), 285.

10. G. W. Avison, "Annual Report of G. W. Avison, May 1928, Kwangju, Korea" (YMCA Archives, University of Minnesota, Minneapolis, photocopy), 2; Kim

Hak-san, "Nongch'on put'ŏ yahak," *Nongch'on ch'ŏngnyŏn* (October 1926): 12–13; and Korean Young Men's Christian Association (KYMCA), *Rural Program of the Young Men's Christian Association in Korea* (Seoul: National Council of the Korean Young Men's Christian Association, 1932), 8.

11. Avison, "Annual Report of G. W. Avison, May 1928, Kwangju, Korea," 2.

12. Kim Hak-san, "Nongch'on put'ŏ yahak," 12–13.

13. Koen De Ceuster, "The YMCA's Rural Development Program in Colonial Korea, 1925–1935: Doctrines and Objectives," *Review of Korean Studies* 3, no. 1 (July 2000): 15.

14. "Nongch'on pogosŏ," *Ch'ŏngnyon* (February 1925): 16.

15. Hong Pyŏng-sŏn, "Nongch'on saŏp ŭi chinŭi," *Kidok sinbo,* February 26, 1930.

16. Ibid.

17. Hong Pyŏng-sŏn, "Nongch'on saŏp ŭi chinŭi 15," *Kidok sinbo,* March 5, 1930.

18. Ibid.

19. Ibid.

20. V. N. Volosinov, *Marxism and the Philosophy of Language,* trans. Ladislav Matejka and I. R. Titunik (Cambridge, MA: Harvard University Press, 1973), 13.

21. The YMCA printed close to 1,800 copies of *Ch'ŏngnyŏn* a month. See "Statistics and Information for the Calendar Year 1930" (YMCA Archives, University of Minnesota, Minneapolis, photocopy), 2.

22. See *Nongch'on ch'ŏngnyŏn* (August 1928): 1–9; *Nongch'on ch'ŏngnyŏn* (October 1929): 1–16; *Nongch'on ch'ŏngnyŏn* (November 1929): 1–16; and *Nongch'on ch'ŏngnyŏn* (December 1929): 12.

23. Pyŏn Jip-sil, "Nongŏp sajŏn," *Nongch'on ch'ŏngnyŏn* (November 1929): 15.

24. Hong Pyŏng-sŏn, "Saram kwa kigye," *Nongch'on ch'ŏngnyŏn* (February 1930): 1; and Hong Pyŏng-sŏn, "Isang kwa hwanggyŏng," *Nongch'on ch'ŏngnyŏn* (January 1931): 2.

25. "Chosŏn yŏksa," *Nongch'on ch'ŏngnyŏn* (February 1930): 3–5; and "Nongch'on yahwa," *Nongch'on ch'ŏngnyŏn* (February 1930): 12–14.

26. P'yo, *Ch'ŏndogyo ch'ŏngnyŏnhoe p'alsipsa,* 286.

27. *Chosŏn nongmin* became *Nongmin* in 1930 after a transition in leadership in the Ch'ŏndogyo rural movement.

28. Yi Hun-gu, "Mŏnjŏ kyemong undonghaja," *Nongmin saenghwal* (January 1934): 3–4.

29. Ibid., 3.

30. Benedict Anderson, *Imagined Communities* (London: Verso Press, 1983), 34–36.

31. See P'yo, *Ch'ŏndogyo ch'ŏngnyŏnhoe p'alsipsa,* 285; and "Sinnyŏn kwa nongmin kangjwa," *Chosŏn nongmin* (January 1929): 25.

32. See Pae Min-su, *Who Shall Enter the Kingdom of Heaven: Pae Min-su chasŏjŏn* (Seoul: Yonsei University Press, 1999), 258.

33. Ibid., 258.
34. In the literacy programs, peasants learned Korean and also read texts from the Bible. See Pak Hak-chŏn, "Changrokyo ch'onghoe nongch'onbu saŏp ŭi hyŏnsang kwa kigyehoek," *Sindong'a* (February 1935): 88.
35. See editorial, "Kwahakchŏk nongŏp haja," *Nongmin saenghwal* (July 1933): 1.
36. Pae, *Who Shall Enter the Kingdom of Heaven*, 258.
37. Ibid., 258–259.
38. Ibid.
39. Ibid.
40. Yi Hun-gu, "Chosŏn nongch'on ŭi kaengsaeng kwa yŏsŏng immu," *Nongmin saenghwal* (March 1933): 7–8.
41. Yi believed that under the new market economy, peasant women had begun to buy more products rather than make their own products, which caused them to spend more money and increase their debts. Because peasants were consuming like capitalists, Yi said that they should be taught how to spend more wisely and to make their own products. See ibid., 8.
42. Pae, *Who Shall Enter the Kingdom of Heaven*, 260.
43. B. P. Barnhart, "Training for Rural Leadership in Korea (1934)" (YMCA Archives, University of Minnesota, Minneapolis, photocopy), 3.
44. "Rural Reconstruction Work in Korea (1935)" (YMCA Archives, University of Minnesota, Minneapolis, photocopy), 3.
45. KYMCA, *Rural Program of the Young Men's Christian Association in Korea*, 10.
46. "A Rural Project in Seoul (1931)" (YMCA Archives, University of Minnesota, Minneapolis, photocopy), 1.
47. Barnhart, "Training for Rural Leadership in Korea," 3.
48. By the end of 1933, a total of 7,200 people had taken part in the programs that Farm Schools offered. See "Rural Reconstruction Work in Korea," 3.
49. YMCA officials asked peasant teachers to continue their teaching duties at another institute. See Barnhart, "Training for Rural Leadership in Korea," 3.
50. Alan Berger, *Reclaiming the American West* (New York: Princeton Architectural Press, 2002), 61.
51. William Scott, "Canadians in Korea: A Brief Historical Sketch of Canadian Mission Work in Korea" (typescript, 1975), 115.
52. Yi Hun-gu, "Nongch'on ch'ŏngnyŏn kwa hyangdo chŏngsin," *Nongmin saenghwal* (April 1932): 5–6.
53. Yi Sŏng-hwan, "Chosŏn nongmin yoyuk ŭi isang kwa pangbŏp," *Nongmin saenghwal* (November 1926): 9–11.
54. Sin Hŭng-u, "Siljŏk saenghwal hyanghanŭn kumil ŭi ch'ŏngnyŏn," *Ch'ŏngnyŏn* (July–August 1927): 1–2.
55. Kim Bŏm-jin, "Nongch'on ch'ŏngnyŏn a nongch'on chk'ira," *Nongmin saenghwal* (January 1933): 17.
56. Yi Hun-gu, "Onŭl uri ga yoguhanun nongch'on chidoja ŭi yoŏn," *Nongmin saenghwal* (August 1934): 489–494.

57. Ibid., 489–491.

58. Pae, *Who Shall Enter the Kingdom of Heaven,* 257.

59. "Songsan kodŭng nongsa hakwŏn," *Nongmin saenghwal* (February 1936): 139.

60. Ibid.; and "Masan pokŭm nongŏp silhyang hakkyopyŏn," *Nongmin saenghwal* (January 1936): 61.

61. "Masan pokŭm nongŏp silhyang hakkyopyŏn," 62.

62. Ibid.

63. "Songsan kodŭng nongsa hakwŏn," 139.

64. For a description of Danish folk schools, see A. H. Hollman, "The Folk High School," in Josephine Goldmark, *Democracy in Denmark* (Washington, DC: National Home Library Foundation, 1936); and Kim Hwal-lan (Helen Kim), *Chŏngmalin ŭi kyŏngje puhŭngron* (Kyŏngsŏng: Han'guk kidokkyo ch'ŏngnyŏnhoe yŏnhaphoe, 1931), chap. 3.

65. Grundtvig was the main leader behind the rural revival movement in Denmark and the founder of the folk school program.

66. Hong Pyŏng-sŏn, *Chŏngmal kwa Chŏngmal nongmin* (Kyŏngsang: Han'guk kidokkyo ch'ŏngnyŏnhoe hoeryon haphoe, 1929), 55–56.

67. Helen Kim wrote that the purpose of education and folk schools was to develop a new spirit or new characteristics within students. See Helen Kiteuk Kim, "Rural Education for the Regeneration of Korea" (PhD diss., Columbia University, 1931), 64–71.

68. Ibid., 66.

69. Yi Hun-gu, "Onŭl uri ga yoguhanun nongch'on chidoja ŭi yoŏn," 489–494.

70. See Antonio Gramsci, *Selections from the Prison Notebooks,* ed. and trans. Quintin Hoare and Geoffrey Nowell Smith (New York: International Publishers, 1971), 5–23.

71. Sungsil taehakgyo, *Sungsil taehakgyo 100-yŏnsa* I (Seoul: Sungsil taehakgyo ch'ulp'anbu, 1997), 282–289.

72. Yi Hun-gu, "Kongdong nongŏp hagwŏn 2 chae iran saŏp," *Nongmin saenghwal* (September 1934): 552–556.

73. H. A. Wilbur, letter to Mr. F. S. Harmon (1933) (YMCA Archives, University of Minnesota, Minneapolis, photocopy), 2.

74. B. P. Barnhart, "Annual Report of B. P. Barnhart, 1934–1935, Exhibit C" (YMCA Archives, University of Minnesota, Minneapolis, photocopy), 1–2.

75. Wilbur, letter to Mr. F. S. Harmon (1933), 1.

76. Barnhart, "Annual Report of B. P. Barnhart, 1934–1935, Exhibit C," 1–2; Barnhart, "Training for Rural Leadership in Korea," 2; and Wilbur, letter to Mr. F. S. Harmon (1933), 1.

77. Barnhart, "Annual Report of B. P. Barnhart, 1934–1935, Exhibit C," 1–2.

78. Wilbur, letter to Mr. F. S. Harmon (1933), 1.

79. Ibid.

80. The Korean YWCA was established in 1922.

81. C. I. McLaren, "Rural Life in Korea," *Korea Mission Field* (March 1934): 47.

82. Ibid., 46–47.
83. Induk Park, "Work among Rural Women," *Korea Mission Field* (July 1933): 136.
84. "The Training Institute for Rural Leaders under the Auspices of the National YWCA of Korea," *Korea Mission Field* (February 1934): 42.
85. Ibid.
86. Ibid.
87. Barnhart, "Training for Rural Leadership in Korea," 1.
88. Ibid.; and G. W. Avison, "Kwangju Project (1937)" (YMCA Archives, University of Minnesota, Minneapolis, photocopy), 1.
89. Barnhart, "Training for Rural Leadership in Korea," 1.
90. Avison, "Kwangju Project," 1.

Conclusion

1. Yi Ton-hwa, "Chosŏn sinmunhwa kŏnsŏl e taehan t'oan," *Kaebyŏk* (October 1920): 13–14.
2. Smaller than the Korean YMCA, the Japanese YMCA in Seoul was staffed by Japanese Christians and offered programs only to Japanese citizens living in Korea.
3. A. C. Bunce and F. O. Clark had left Korea because of funding issues.
4. Chung-shin Park, *Protestantism and Politics in Korea* (Seattle: University of Washington Press, 2003), 80–81.
5. In 1935, Sin Hŭng-u created the Positive Faith Party, which issued an economic platform calling for the creation of moral and spiritual lives that would be protected from capitalism. Conservative Korean Christian leaders opposed the ideas in his platform, especially his belief that the group was more important than the individual, called him a fascist, and eventually forced him to resign from the YMCA.
6. See Kim Seung-tae, ed., *Han'guk kidokkyo ŭi yŏksajŏk pansŏng* (Seoul: Tasankŭl pang, 1994), 411–416.
7. See Ju Hui Judy Han, "The Intimacy of the Global: Contemporary Korean Mission Encounters" (paper presented at the conference "Negotiating the Global with the Local: Translating Christianity in Modern East Asia," Claremont, CA, February 2010), 1–22.
8. Charles Armstrong, *The North Korean Revolution, 1945–1950* (Ithaca, NY: Cornell University Press, 2003), 128.
9. A high number of cooperatives and cooperative farms constructed by Chosŏn nongminsa were located in areas around P'yŏngyang and other parts of what is North Korea today.
10. Armstrong, *North Korean Revolution*, 129.
11. Ibid., 133.

12. For the goals and principles of this movement, see Pai Minsoo, "How to Evangelize Post-war Korea" (Princeton Theological Seminary, Princeton, NJ, photocopy, 1954).

13. Im Yŏng-ch'ŏl, *Kanaan isangch'on undong* (Seoul: Chaedanpŏpin ilgachaedan, 2009), 178.

14. Park, *Protestantism and Politics in Korea,* chap. 7; and James Grayson, *Korea—A Religious History* (London: RoutledgeCurzon, 2002), pt. 4.

15. See Wonil Kim, "Minjung Theology's Biblical Hermeneutics," in *Christianity in Korea,* ed. Robert Buswell and Timothy Lee (Honolulu: University of Hawai'i Press, 2006), 226–232.

16. Some studies place the origins of the modern cooperative movement after the Korean War when the South Korean state established the Agricultural Bank (1956), the Agricultural Cooperative Law (1957), and the Agricultural Cooperative (Nonghyŏp) (1958). See Hyejin Choi, "Institutionalization of Trust as Response to Globalization: The Case of Consumer Cooperatives in South Korea," *Transition Studies Review* 16, no. 2 (May 2009): 457.

17. Ku Do-Wan, "The Emergence of Ecological Alternative Movement in Korea," *Korean Social Science Journal* 36, no. 2 (2009): 10.

18. Ibid., 9–10.

BIBLIOGRAPHY

Archival Materials and Government Records

Chōsen sōtokufu. *Chōsen no kosaku kanshū*. Keijo: Chōsen sōtokufu, 1929.

Government-General of Chosen. *Thriving Chosen*. Keijo: Government-General of Chosen, 1935.

Governor-General Ugaki. *Chosen and among Its People*. Keijo: Foreign Affairs Section, 1933.

Papers, letters, and official documents from the Young Men's Christian Association (YMCA) Archives, University of Minnesota, Minneapolis.

Journals and Newspapers from 1920s and 1930s Colonial Korea

Chinese Recorder

Chinsaeng (Truthful Life)

Chonggyo sibo (News of Religion)

Ch'ŏngnyŏn (The Young Korean)

Chosŏn ilbo (Chosŏn Daily)

Chosŏn nongmin (Chosŏn Peasant)

Hyesŏng (Comet)

Kaebyŏk (Creation)

Kamri hoebo (The Methodist Bulletin)

Kidok sinbo (The Christian Daily)

Korea Mission Field

Missionary Review of the World

Nongch'on ch'ŏngnyŏn (The Rural Youth)

Nongch'on t'ongsin (The Rural News)

Nongmin (Peasant)

Nongmin saenghwal (Farmer's Life)

Pip'an (Criticism)

Samch'ŏlli (Three Thousand Ri)

Sanŏpgye (Industrial World)

Silsaenghwal (Sincere Life)

Sindong'a (The New East)

Sinin'gan (New Human)

Sinmin (New People)

Sinsaenghwal (New Life)

Sinsaenghwallon (Theory of New Life)

Sŏkwang (Dawn)

Tangsŏng

Tonga ilbo (Eastern Daily)

Tonggwang (Eastern Light)

Books and Articles in Korean and Japanese

Ch'a Sŭng-ki. *Pan kŭndaejŏk sangsangnyŏk ŭi imgyedŭl.* Seoul: P'urun yŏksa, 2009.

Chang Kyu-sik. "1920-yŏndae kaejoron ŭi hwaksan kwa kidokkyo sahoejuŭi ŭi suyong chŏngch'ak." *Yŏksa munje yŏn'guso,* no. 21 (April 2009): 111–136.

———. *Ilche ha Han'guk kidokkyo minjokjuŭi yŏn'gu.* Seoul: Hyean, 2001.

Chi Su-gŏl. *Ilche ha nongmin chohap undong yŏn'gu.* Seoul: Yŏksa pip'yŏng, 1993.

Cho Min-hyŏng. *Chosŏn nongch'on kujech'aek.* Kyŏngsŏng: Sinhak saekyesa, 1929.

Cho Tong-gŏl. *Ilche ha Han'guk nongmin undongsa.* Seoul: Han'gilsa, 1979.

Chŏng Jin-yŏng. *Chosŏn sidae hyangch'on sahoesa.* Seoul: Han'gilsa, 1999.

Chŏng Yong-sŏ. "1930-yŏndae Ch'ŏndogyo seryŏk ŭi nongŏp munje insik kwa nongŏp kaehyŏkron." *Tongbang hakji* 117 (September 2002): 51–83.

———. "Ilche ha haebang hu Ch'ŏndogyo seryŏk ŭi chŏngch'i undong." PhD diss., Yonsei University, 2010.

Chosŏn ilbo 50-yŏnsa. Seoul: Chosŏn ilbosa, 1970.

Han Kyu-mu. *Ilche ha Han'guk kidokkyo nongch'on undong, 1925–1937.* Seoul: Han'guk kidokkyo yŏksa yŏn'guso, 1997.

Han'guk kyohoe paekjunyŏn chunbi wiwŏnhoe saryo punkwa wiwŏnhoe, ed. *Taehan yesugyo changnohoe paekyŏnsa.* Seoul: Taehan Yesugyo changnohoe ch'onghoe, 1984.

Hardie, R. A., ed. *Nongmin ŭi hwallo.* Kyŏngsŏng: Chŏson kidokkyo ch'angmunsa, 1930.

Hŏ Su. "1920-chŏnhu Yi Ton-hwa ŭi hyŏnsil insil kwa kŭndae ch'ŏrhak suyong." *Yŏksa munje yŏn'gu,* no. 9 (December 2002): 175–216.

Hong Pyŏng-sŏn. *Chŏngmal kwa Chŏngmal nongmin.* Kyŏngsang: Han'guk kidokkyo ch'ŏngnyŏnhoe hoeryon haphoe, 1929.

———. *Chŏngmal nongmin kwa Chosŏn.* Seoul: Kwangmun, 1949.

———. *Chŏngmal nongmin kwa nongch'on ŭi chaegŏn.* Seoul: Kwangmun, 1951.

———. *Nongch'on hyŏpdong chohap kwa chojikpŏp.* Kyŏngsŏng: Ch'ŏngnyŏnhoe yŏnhaphoe, 1930.

———. *Nongŏp hyŏpdong chohap kanghwa.* Seoul: Sŏngmunsa, 1958.

———. *Sobi chohap ŭi wŏlli wa silje.* Seoul: Sŏngmunsa, 1960.

Hong Sŏng-ch'an. "Nongji kaehyŏk chŏnhu ŭi taejiju tonghyang." In *Nongji kaehyŏk yŏn'gu,* edited by Hong Sŏng-ch'an, 165–224. Seoul: Yonsei University Press, 2001.

Im Yŏng-ch'ŏl. *Kanaan isangch'on undong.* Seoul: Chaedanpŏpin ilgachaedan, 2009.

Kil Sŏn-ju. "Malsehak." In *Yŏnggye Kil Sŏnju moksa chŏjakjip,* 23–172. Seoul: Taehan kidokkyo sŏhoe, 1968.

Kim Dong-no, ed. *Ilche singminji sigi ŭi t'ongch'i ch'ejae hyŏngsŏng.* Seoul: Hyean, 2006.

———, ed. *Ilcheha ŭi singmin chibae wa ilsangsaenghwal.* Seoul: Hyean, 2004.

Kim Hong-ch'ŏl. "Kaehanggi ŭi minjok chonggyo undong." In *Han'guk minjok chonggyo undongsa,* edited by No Kil-myŏng, Kim Hong-ch'ŏl, Yun I-hŭm, and Hwang Sŏn-myŏng, 99–164. Seoul: Han'guk minjok chonggyo hyŏpŭihoe, 2003.

Kim Hwal-lan (Helen Kim). *Chŏngmalin ŭi kyŏngje puhŭngron.* Kyŏngsŏng: Han'guk kidokkyo ch'ŏngnyŏnhoe yŏnhaphoe, 1931.

Kim, Jeong-in. "Ilche kangjŏmgi Ch'ŏndogyodan ŭi minjok undong yŏn'gu." PhD diss., Seoul National University, 2002.

Kim Kwon-jung. "1920-yŏndae kidokkyo seryŏk ŭi pankidokkyo undong taeŭng kwa minjok undong ŭi chŏngae." *Han'guk kidokkyo wa yŏksa* 14 (2001): 79–106.

Kim Sang-t'ae. "Ilche ha Sin Hŭng-u ŭi 'sahoe pogŭmjuŭi' wa minjokundongnon." *Yŏksa munje yŏn'gu,* no. 1 (December 1996): 163–208.

———. "P'yŏng'ando kidokkyo seryŏk kwa ch'inmi ellit'ŭ ŭi hyŏngsŏng." *Yŏksa pip'yŏng* 45 (Winter 1998): 171–207.

Kim Seung-tae, ed. *Han'guk kidokkyo ŭi yŏksajŏk pansŏng.* Seoul: Tasankŭl pang, 1994.

Kim Yong-sŏp. *Han'guk kŭnhyŏndae nongŏpsa yŏn'gu.* Seoul: Iljogak, 1992.

Min Kyŏng-bae. *Han'guk kidokkyohoesa.* Seoul: Yonsei University Press, 2002.

Oh Ji-yŏng. *Tonghaksa.* Seoul: Yŏngch'ang sukwan, 1940.

Pae Min-su. *Who Shall Enter the Kingdom of Heaven: Pae Min-su chasŏjŏn.* Seoul: Yonsei University Press, 1999.

Pae Sŏng-chan. *Singminji sidae sahoe undongnon yŏn'gu.* Seoul: Tolpegae, 1987.

Paek Se-myŏng, ed. *Ch'ŏndogyo kyŏngjŏn haeŭi.* Seoul: Ch'ŏndogyo chungang ch'ongbu, 1963.

Pak Ch'an-sŭng. *Han'guk kŭndae chŏngch'i sasangsa yŏn'gu.* Seoul: Yŏksa pip'yŏngsa, 1992.

Pang Ki-chung. *Han'guk kŭnhyŏndae sasangsa yŏn'gu.* Seoul: Yŏksa pip'yŏngsa, 1992.

———. "Ilche ha Yi Hun-gu ŭi nongŏpnon kwa kyŏngje sasang." *Yŏksa munje yŏn'gu,* no. 1 (December 1996): 113–162.

———. *Pae Min-su ŭi nongch'on undong kwa kidokkyo sasang.* Seoul: Yonsei University Press, 1999.

———, ed. *Pogumjuŭi wa kidokkyo nongch'on undong.* Seoul: Yonsei University Press, 2000.

P'yo Yŏng-sam. *Ch'ŏndogyo ch'ŏngnyŏnhoe p'alsipsa.* Compiled by Ch'ŏndogyo Ch'ŏngnyŏnhoe Chungang Ponbu (Seoul: Kŭl Namu, 2000)

Ro Kil-myŏng. *Han'guk sinhŭng chonggyo yŏn'gu.* Seoul: Kyŏngsewŏn, 1996.

Shin, Maik'ŭl D. (Michael D. Shin). "T'ŭkjip Miguk ŭi Han'guksa yŏn'gu: Miguk nae Han'gukhak ŭi kyebo." *Yŏksa pip'yŏng* 59 (Summer 2002): 76–98.

Sungsil taehakgyo. *Sungsil taehakgyo 100-yŏnsa I.* Seoul: Sungsil taehakgyo ch'ulp'anbu, 1997.

Yi Hun-gu. *Chosŏn nongŏpnon.* Seoul: Hansŏng, 1935.

Yi Jun-sik. "Hyŏngmyŏngjŏk nongminchohap undong kwa Ilche ŭi nongch'on chaejŏngch'aek: Hamgyŏng-bukdo ŭl kwangbok hyangyak ŭl chungsim ŭro." In *Ilche singminji sigi ŭi t'ongch'i ch'ejae hyŏngsŏng,* edited by Kim Dong-no, 223–268. Seoul: Hyean, 2006.

Yi Kwang-su. *Yi Kwang-su chŏnjip.* Seoul: Samchungtang, 1971.

Yi Kyŏng-ran. "1930-yŏndae nongmin sosŏl tonghae pon 'singminji kŭndaehwa' wa nongmin saenghwal." In *Ilcheha ŭi singmin chibae wa ilsangsaenghwal,* edited by Kim Dong-no, 387–444. Seoul: Hyean, 2004.

Yi Sŭng-yŏl. *Cheguk kwa sangin.* Seoul: Yŏksa pip'yŏngsa, 2007.

Yi Ton-hwa. *Ch'ŏndogyo ch'anggŏnsa.* Seoul: Taedong Press, 1933.

———. *Innaech'ŏn youi.* Keijo: Kaebyŏksa, 1924.

———. *Sinin ch'ŏrhak.* Seoul: Ch'ŏndogyo chungang ch'ongbu, 1968.

Yoshikawa Buntaro. *Chōsen no shukyō.* Keijo: Chōsen Insatsu, 1921.

Yun Kyŏng-no. *Han'guk kŭndaesa ŭi kidokkyosajŏk ihae.* Seoul: Yokminsa, 1992.

Books and Articles in English

Anderson, Benedict. *Imagined Communities.* London: Verso Press, 1983.

Anderson, Emily. "Christianity in the Japanese Empire." PhD diss., University of California, Los Angeles, 2010.

Appadurai, Arjun. *Modernity at Large.* Minneapolis: University of Minnesota Press, 1996.

Armstrong, Charles. *The North Korean Revolution, 1945–1950.* Ithaca, NY: Cornell University Press, 2003.

Asad, Talal. *Genealogies of Religion: Discipline and Reasons of Power in Christianity and Islam.* Baltimore: John Hopkins University Press, 1993.

Avineri, Shlomo. *The Social and Political Thought of Karl Marx.* Cambridge: Cambridge University Press, 1968.

Baker, Don. "Hananim, Hanŭnim, Hanullim, and Hanŏllim: The Construction of Terminology for Korean Monotheism." *Review of Korean Studies* 5, no. 1 (June 2002): 105–131.

Barlow, Tani. "Introduction: On Colonial Modernity." In *Formations of Colonial Modernity in East Asia,* edited by Tani Barlow, 1–20. Durham, NC: Duke University Press, 1997.

Barth, Karl. "Creation as Benefit." In *Karl Barth: Theologian of Freedom,* edited by Clifford Green, 191–194. Minneapolis: Fortress Press, 1991.

Bataille, Georges. *Inner Experience.* Translated by Leslie Anne Boldt. Albany: State University of New York Press, 1988.

———. *Theory of Religion.* Translated by Robert Hurley. New York: Zone Books, 1992.

Baudelaire, Charles. *Selected Writings on Art and Literature.* Translated by P. E. Charvet. New York: Penguin Books, 1972.

Bender, Courtney, and Ann Taves. "Introduction: Things of Value." In *What Matters? Ethnographies of Value in a Not So Secular Age,* edited by Courtney Bender and Ann Taves, 1–33. New York: Columbia University Press, 2012.

Berger, Alan. *Reclaiming the American West.* New York: Princeton Architectural Press, 2002.

Berman, Marshall. *All That Is Solid Melts into Air.* New York: Penguin Press, 1988.

Borish, Steven. *The Land of the Living.* Nevada City, CA: Blue Dolphin, 1991.

Boy, John D. "Thinking about Revolution, Religion and Egypt with Talal Asad." *The Immanent Frame,* SSRC, February 23, 2011, accessed November 2012, http://blogs.ssrc.org/tif/2011/02/23/thinking-about-revolution-religion-and-egypt-with-talal-asad/.

Brauer, Jerald C. *Protestantism in America: A Narrative History.* Philadelphia: Westminster Press, 1965.

Brenner, Robert. "Agrarian Class Structure and Economic Development in Pre-industrial Europe." *Past and Present* 70 (February 1976): 30–75.

Brown, Arthur Judson. *The Mastery of the Far East: The Story of Korea's Transformation and Japan's Rise to Supremacy in the Orient.* New York: Charles Scribner's Sons, 1919.

———. *Report of a Visitation of the Korean Mission of Presbyterian Board of Foreign Missions.* New York: Board of Foreign Missions of the Presbyterian Church, USA, 1902.

Brunner, Edmund de Schweinitz. "Rural Korea: A Preliminary Survey of Economic, Social and Religious Conditions." In *The Jerusalem Meeting of the International Missionary Council, March 24–April 8, 1928,* vol. 6, *The Christian Mission in Relation to Rural Problems,* 84–172. New York: International Missionary Council, 1928.

Buber, Martin. *Paths in Utopia.* Translated by R. F. C. Hull. London: Routledge and Kegan Paul, 1949.

Buswell, Robert E., ed. *Religions of Korea in Practice.* Princeton, NJ: Princeton University Press, 2007.

Buswell, Robert and Timothy Lee, eds. *Christianity in Korea.* Honolulu: University of Hawai'i Press, 2010.

Calhoun, Craig, Mark Juergensmeyer, and Jonathan VanAntwerpen. Introduction to *Rethinking Secularism,* edited by Craig Calhoun, Mark Juergensmeyer, and Jonathan VanAntwerpen, 3–30. New York: Oxford University Press, 2011.

Cha Seung Ki. "The Colonial-Imperial Regime and Its Effects: Writer Kim Saryang as an Exception." *Korea Journal* 50, no. 4 (Winter 2010): 99–126.

Chan Han-seng. "Cooperatives as a Panacea for China's Ills." *Far Eastern Survey* 6 no. 7 (March 31, 1937): 71–77.

Chatterjee, Partha. *The Nation and Its Fragments.* Princeton, NJ: Princeton University Press, 1993.

Chloupkova, Jarka, Gunnar Lind Hasse Svendsen, and Gert Tinggaard Svendsen. "Building and Destroying Social Capital: The Case of Cooperative Movements in Denmark and Poland." *Agriculture and Human Values* 20 (2003): 241–252.

Ch'oe, Yŏng-ho, Peter H. Lee, and Wm. Theodore de Bary, eds. *Sources of Korean Tradition.* Vol. 2. New York: Columbia University Press, 2000.

Choi, Hyaeweol. *Gender and Mission Encounters in Korea: New Women, Old Ways.* Berkeley: University of California Press, 2009.

Choi, Hyejin. "Institutionalization of Trust as Response to Globalization: The Case of Consumer Cooperatives in South Korea." *Transition Studies Review* 16, no. 2 (May 2009): 450–461.

Chung Seung-mo, *Markets: Traditional Korean Society.* Translated by Cho Yoon-jung and Min Eun-young. Seoul: Ewha University Press, 2006.

Chung, Youn-tae, "The Spread of Peasant Movement and Changes in the Tenant Policy in the 1920's Colonial Korea." *International Journal of Korean History* 2 (December 2001): 157–192.

Clark, Charles Allen. *Digest of the Presbyterian Church of Korea.* Seoul: Korean Religious Book and Tract Society, 1918.

———. *The Korean Church and the Nevius Methods.* New York: Fleming H. Revell, 1930.

———. *Religions of Old Korea.* New York: F. H. Revell, 1932.

Clark, Donald. *Living Dangerously in Korea.* Norwalk, CT: Eastbridge, 2003.

Comaroff, Jean, and John L. Comaroff. *Of Revelation and Revolution: Christianity, Colonialism, and Consciousness in South Africa.* Chicago: University of Chicago Press, 1991.

Cumings, Bruce. *Korea's Place in the Sun.* New York: W. W. Norton, 2005.

———. *The Origins of the Korean War.* Vol. 1. Princeton, NJ: Princeton University Press, 1981.

De Ceuster, Koen. "The YMCA's Rural Development Program in Colonial Korea, 1925–1935: Doctrine and Objectives." *Review of Korean Studies* 3, no. 1 (July 2000): 5–33.

Deuchler, Martina. *The Confucian Transformation of Korea.* Cambridge, MA: Harvard Council on East Asian Studies, 1992.

Duara, Prasenjit. *Rescuing History from the Nation.* Chicago: University of Chicago Press, 1995.

Duncan, John B. *The Origins of the Chosŏn Dynasty.* Seattle: University of Washington Press, 2000.

Durkheim, Emile. *The Elementary Forms of Religious Life.* Translated by Karen E. Fields. New York: Free Press, 1995.

Eagleton, Terry. *Ideology: An Introduction.* London: Verso Press, 1991.

Eckert, Carter. *Offspring of Empire.* Seattle: University of Washington Press, 1991.

Eddy, Sherwood. *Religion and Social Justice.* New York City: George H. Doran, 1927.

Eliade, Mircea. *The Sacred and the Profane: The Nature of Religion.* New York: Harcourt, 1959.

Ely, Richard T. "The Nature and Significance of Monopolies and Trust." *International Journal of Ethics* 10, no. 3 (April 1900).

Fairbairn, Brett. "History from the Ecological Perspective: Gaia Theory and the Problem of Cooperatives in Turn-of-the-Century Germany." *American Historical Review* 99, no. 4 (October 1994): 1203–1239.

Fisher, James Earnest. "Democracy and Mission Education in Korea." PhD diss., Teachers College, Columbia University, 1928.

Fujitani, Takashi. *Race for Empire: Koreans as Japanese and Japanese as Americans during World War II*. Berkeley: University of California Press, 2011.

Fuller, Robert C. *Religious Revolutionaries: The Rebels Who Reshaped American Religion*. New York: Palgrave Macmillan, 2004.

Gale, James S. *Korea in Transition*. New York: Young People's Missionary Movement of the United States and Canada, 1909.

Gaonkar, Dilip Parameshwar, ed. *Alternative Modernities*. Durham, NC: Duke University Press, 2001.

———. "On Alternative Modernities." In *Alternative Modernities,* edited by Dilip Parameshwar Gaonkar, 1–23. Durham, NC: Duke University Press, 2001.

Geertz, Clifford. *The Interpretation of Cultures*. New York: Basic Books, 1973.

Giddens, Anthony. *The Consequences of Modernity*. Stanford, CA: Stanford University Press, 1990.

Gide, Charles, and Charles Rist. *A History of Economic Doctrines*. London: George C. Harrap, 1915.

Goldmark, Josephine. *Democracy in Denmark*. Washington, DC: National Home Library Foundation, 1936.

Gragert, Edwin H. *Landownership under Colonial Rule: Korea's Japanese Experience, 1900–1935*. Honolulu: University of Hawai'i Press, 1994.

Grajdanzev, Andrew J. *Modern Korea*. New York: Institute of Pacific Relations, 1944.

Gramsci, Antonio. *Selections from the Prison Notebooks*. Edited and translated by Quintin Hoare and Geoffrey Nowell Smith. New York: International Publishers, 1971.

Grayson, James H. *Korea—A Religious History*. London: RoutledgeCurzon, 2002.

Gudeman, Stephen. *Economics as Culture*. London: Routledge, 1986.

Han, Do-Hyung. "Shamanism, Superstition, and the Colonial Government." *Review of Korean Studies* 3, no. 1 (July 2000): 34–54.

Han, Ju Hui Judy. "The Intimacy of the Global: Contemporary Korean Mission Encounters." Paper presented at the conference "Negotiating the Global with the Local: Translating Christianity in Modern East Asia," Claremont, CA, February 2010.

Handy, Robert T. "The American Religious Depression, 1925–1935." *Church History* 29, no. 1 (March 1960): 3–16.

———. *A Christian America.* New York: Oxford University Press, 1984.

Harootunian, Harry. *History's Disquiet.* New York: Columbia University Press, 2000.

———. *Overcome by Modernity.* Princeton, NJ: Princeton University Press, 2000.

Harvey, David. *The Condition of Postmodernity.* Cambridge, MA: Blackwell, 1990.

Hodgkin, Henry T. *The Way of Jesus.* New York: George H. Doran, 1923.

Hollman, A. H. "The Folk High School." In *Democracy in Denmark.* Washington, DC: National Home Library Foundation, 1936.

Horkheimer, Max. "The State of Contemporary Social Philosophy and the Tasks of an Institute for Social Research." In *Critical Theory and Society,* edited by Stephen Eric Bonner and Douglas MacKay Kellner, 25–36. New York: Routledge, 1989.

Howe, Frederic C. *Denmark: A Cooperative Commonwealth.* New York: Harcourt, Brace, 1921.

Hur Young-ran. "Colonial Modernity and Rural Markets during the Japanese Colonial Period." *International Journal of Korean History* 15, no. 2 (August 2010): 69–96.

International Missionary Council. *The Jerusalem Meeting of the International Missionary Council, March 24–April 8, 1928.* Vol. 5, *The Christian Mission in Relation to Industrial Problems.* Vol. 6, *The Christian Mission in Relation to Rural Problems.* New York: International Missionary Council, 1928.

Jameson, Fredric. *Postmodernism, or, The Cultural Logic of Late Capitalism.* Durham, NC: Duke University Press, 1991.

Jun Seong Ho, James B. Lewis, and Kang Han Rog. "Korean Expansion and Decline from the Seventeenth to the Nineteenth Century: A View Suggested by Adam Smith." *Journal of Economic History* 68, no. 1 (March 2008): 244–282.

Kallander, George. *Salvation through Dissent: Tonghak Heterodoxy and Early Modern Korea.* Honolulu: University of Hawai'i Press, 2013.

Karlsson, Anders. "Famine, Finance and Political Power: Crop Failure and Land-Tax Exemptions in Late Eighteenth-Century Chosŏn Korea." *Journal of Economic and Social History of the Orient* 48, no. 4 (2005): 552–592.

Kawashima, Ken. *The Proletarian Gamble.* Durham, NC: Duke University Press, 2009.

Ketelaar, James. *Of Heretics and Martyrs in Meiji Japan.* Princeton, NJ: Princeton University Press, 1990.

Kim, Chong Bum. "Preaching the Apocalypse in Colonial Korea." In *Christianity in Korea*, edited by Robert Buswell and Timothy Lee, 149–166. Honolulu: University of Hawai'i Press, 2006.

Kim Dong-no. "National Identity and Class Interest in Peasant Movements during the Colonial Period." Working Paper, Department of Sociology, Yonsei University, Seoul, photocopy.

———. "Peasants, State, and Landlords: National Crisis and the Transformation of Agrarian Society in Pre-colonial Korea." 2 vols. PhD diss., University of Chicago, 1994.

Kim, Helen Kiteuk. "Rural Education for the Regeneration of Korea." PhD diss., Columbia University, 1931.

Kim, In-Geol. "Confucian Tradition in Rural Society during the Late Chosŏn Dynasty: Changing Elite Perceptions of Community Administration." *Seoul Journal of Korean Studies* 16 (2003): 113–134.

Kim, Janice. *To Live to Work: Factory Women in Colonial Korea, 1910–1945*. Stanford, CA: Stanford University Press, 2009.

Kim Kwangshik. "Buddhist Perspectives on Anti-religious Movements in the 1930s." *Review of Korean Studies* 3, no. 1 (July 2000): 55–75.

Kim San and Nym Wales. *Song of Ariran*. New York: John Day, 1941.

Kim, Sun Joo. *Marginality and Subversion in Korea*. Seattle: University of Washington Press, 2007.

Kim, Wonil. "Minjung Theology's Biblical Hermeneutics." In *Christianity in Korea*, edited by Robert Buswell and Timothy Lee, 221–237. Honolulu: University of Hawai'i Press, 2006.

Kim, Youngna. *20th Century Korean Art*. London: Laurence King, 2005.

Korean Young Men's Christian Association. *The Rural Program of the Young Men's Christian Association*. Seoul: National Council of the Korean Young Men's Christian Association, 1932.

Ku Do-Wan. "The Emergence of Ecological Alternative Movement in Korea." *Korean Social Science Journal* 36, no. 2 (2009): 1–32.

LaCapra, Dominick. *History in Transit: Experience, Identity, Critical Theory*. Ithaca, NY: Cornell University Press, 2004.

Ladd, George Thrumbull. *In Korea with Marquis Ito*. New York: Charles Scribner's Sons, 1908.

Lankov, Andrei. *The Dawn of Modern Korea*. Seoul: EunHaeng NaMu, 2007.

Latourette, Kenneth Scott. *World Service: A History of the Foreign Work and World Service of the Young Men's Christian Associations of the United States and Canada*. New York: Association Press, 1957.

Lears, Jackson. *No Place for Grace.* Chicago: University of Chicago Press, 1981.

Lee, Hoon Koo. "A History of Land Systems and Policies in Korea." PhD diss., University of Wisconsin, 1929.

———. *Land Utilization and Rural Economy in Korea.* Chicago: University of Chicago Press, 1936.

Lee Ji-Won. "An Chaehong's Thought and the Politics of the United Front." In *Landlords, Peasants, and Intellectuals in Modern Korea,* edited by Pang-Kie Chung and Michael D. Shin, 309–352. Ithaca, NY: Cornell East Asia Program, 2005.

Lee, Leo Ou-fan. "Shanghai Modern: Reflections on Urban Culture in the 1930s." In *Alternative Modernities,* edited by Dilip Parameshwar Gaonkar, 86–122. Durham, NC: Duke University Press, 2001.

Lee Sangoon. "The Rural Control Policy and Peasant Ruling Strategy of the Government-General of Chosŏn in the 1930–1940s." *International Journal of Korean History* 15, no. 2 (August 2010): 1–33.

Lee, Timothy S. *Born Again.* Honolulu: University of Hawai'i Press, 2010.

———. "Born-Again in Korea: The Rise and Character of Revivalism in (South) Korea, 1885–1988." PhD diss., University of Chicago, 1996.

———. "A Political Factor in the Rise of Protestantism in Korea: Protestantism and the 1919 March First Movement." *Church History* 69, no. 1 (March 2000): 116–142.

Lee Yong-ki. "The Study of Korean Villages during the Japanese Colonial Period and Colonial Modernity." *International Journal of Korean History* 15, no. 2 (August 2010): 35–67.

Lévi-Strauss, Claude. *The Savage Mind.* Chicago: University of Chicago Press, 1966.

Lewin, Moshe. *Russian Peasants and Soviet Power: A Study of Collectivization.* Translated by Irene Nove. New York: W. W. Norton, 1968.

Lewis, Gavin. "The Peasantry, Rural Change and Conservative Agrarianism: Lower Austria at the Turn of the Century." *Past and Present* 81 (November 1978): 119–143.

Marx, Karl. *Capital.* Vol. 1. Translated by Ben Fowkes. London: Penguin Books, 1976.

Marx, Leo. *The Machine in the Garden.* New York: Oxford University Press, 1964.

Mitchell, Timothy. *Colonizing Egypt.* Berkeley: University of California Press, 1988.

———, ed. *Questions of Modernity.* Minneapolis: University of Minnesota Press, 2000.

———. *Rule of Experts.* Berkeley: University of California Press, 2002.

Moore, Barrington. *Social Origins of Dictatorship and Democracy.* Boston: Beacon Press, 1966.

Moretti, Franco. *The Way of the World: The Bildungsroman in European Culture.* London: Verso, 1987.

Najita, Tetsuo. *Ordinary Economics in Japan.* Berkeley: University of California Press, 2009.

———. "Traditional Co-operatives in Modern Japan: Rethinking Alternatives to Cosmopolitanism and Nativism." In *Social Futures, Global Visions,* edited by Cynthia Hewitt de Alcántara, 141–150. Cambridge, MA: Blackwell, 1996.

Nevius, J. L. *The Methods of Mission Work.* Shanghai: Presbyterian Mission Press, 1886.

Oak, Sung-Deuk, ed, *Sources of Korean Christianity.* Seoul: Hanguk kidokkyo yŏksa yŏn'guso, 2004.

Oh, Se-Mi. "Consuming the Modern." PhD diss., Columbia University, 2008.

Pai Minsoo. "How to Evangelize Post-war Korea." Princeton Theological Seminary, Princeton, NJ, photocopy, 1954.

Paik, George. *The History of Protestant Missions in Korea, 1832–1910.* Seoul: Yonsei University Press, 1970.

Pang Kie-chung. "Ideological Roots of the South Korean Land Reform." Paper presented at the annual meeting of the Association for Asian Studies, Chicago, March 2001.

———. "Paek Namun and Marxist Scholarship during the Colonial Period." In *Landlords, Peasants, and Intellectuals in Modern Korea,* edited by Pang Kie-chung and Michael Shin, 245–308. Ithaca, NY: Cornell East Asia Program, 2005.

———. "Yi Hun-gu's Agricultural Reform Theory and Nationalist Economic Thought." Paper presented at the conference "Between Colonialism and Nationalism: Power and Subjectivity in Korea, 1931–1950," University of Michigan, Ann Arbor, May 2001.

Pang Kie-chung and Michael D. Shin, eds. *Landlords, Peasants, and Intellectuals in Modern Korea.* Ithaca, NY: Cornell East Asia Program, 2005.

Park, Albert L. "Christianity under Colonialism: A Study of the Creation of 'Work Ethic' and 'Motherhood' by the Presbyterian Church USA and the Young Men's Christian Association in Colonial Korea, 1910–1919." Master's Thesis, Columbia University, 1998.

———. "A Sacred Economy of Value and Production." In *Encountering Modernity,* edited by Albert L. Park and David Yoo, 19–46. Honolulu: University of Hawai'i Press, 2014.

Park, Chung-shin. *Protestantism and Politics in Korea.* Seattle: University of Washington Press, 2003.

Park, Hyun Ok. *Two Dreams in One Bed: Empire, Social Life, and the Origins of the North Korean Revolution in Manchuria.* Durham, NC: Duke University Press, 2005.

Park, Pori. *Trial and Error in Modernist Reforms: Korean Buddhism under Colonial Rule.* Berkeley: Institute of East Asian Studies, University of California, Berkeley, 2009.

Park, Soon-Won. *Colonial Industrialization and Labor in Korea.* Cambridge, MA: Harvard University Asia Center, 1999.

Park, Yun-jae. "Between Mission and Medicine: The Early History of Severance Hospital." In *Encountering Modernity,* edited by Albert L. Park and David Yoo. Honolulu: University of Hawai'i Press, 2014.

Pedler, Anne. "Going to the People: The Russian Narodniki in 1874–75." *Slavonic Review* 6, no. 6 (June 1927): 130–141.

Polanyi, Karl. *The Great Transformation.* Boston: Beacon Press, 1944.

Rhodes, Harry A. ed. *History of the Korean Mission Presbyterian Church U.S.A.,* vol. 1, *1884–1934.* Seoul: Presbyterian Church of Korea Department of Education, 1934.

Ricoeur, Paul. "The Language of Faith." In *The Philosophy of Paul Ricoeur,* edited by Charles E. Reagan and David Steward, 223–238. Boston: Beacon Press, 1978.

Ro Kil-myung. "New Religions and Social Change in Modern Korean History." *Review of Korean Studies* 5, no. 1 (June 2002): 31–62.

Robinson, Michael E. *Korea's Twentieth-Century Odyssey.* Honolulu: University of Hawai'i Press, 2007.

Rodgers, Daniel T. *Atlantic Crossings: Social Politics in a Progressive Age.* Cambridge, MA: Belknap Press of Harvard University Press, 1998.

———. *The Work Ethic in Industrial America, 1850–1920.* Chicago: University of Chicago Press, 1978.

Russell, Bertrand. *Principles of Social Reconstruction.* London: George Allen and Unwin, 1916.

Sandel, Michael J. *Democracy's Discontent.* Cambridge, MA: Harvard University Press, 1996.

Sauer, Charles, ed. *Within the Gate.* Seoul: Korea Methodist News Service, 1934.

Schmid, Andre. *Korea between Empires.* New York: Columbia University Press, 2002.

Scott, David. "Appendix: The Trouble of Thinking; An Interview with Talal Asad." In *Powers of the Secular Modern,* edited by David Scott and Charles Hirschkind, 243–304. Stanford, CA: Stanford University Press, 2006.

Scott, James C. *The Moral Economy of the Peasant.* New Haven, CT: Yale University Press, 1976.

———. *Seeing Like a State.* New Haven, CT: Yale University Press, 1998.

———. *Weapons of the Weak.* New Haven, CT: Yale University Press, 1985.

Scott, William. "Canadians in Korea: A Brief Historical Sketch of Canadian Mission Work in Korea." Typescript, 1975.

Seong Ho Jun and James B. Lewis. "Accounting Techniques in Korea: 18th Century Archival Samples from a Non-profit Association in the Sinitic World." *Accounting Historians Journal* 68, no. 1 (June 2006): 53–88.

Sewell, William H., Jr. "Historical Events as Transformations of Structures: Inventing Revolution at the Bastille." *Theory and Society* 25, no. 6 (December 1996): 841–881.

———. *Logics of History: Social Theory and Social Transformation.* Chicago: University of Chicago Press, 2005.

Shin, Gi-Wook. "Agrarianism: A Critique of Colonial Modernity in Korea." *Comparative Studies in Society and History* 41, no. 4 (October 1999): 784–804.

———. *Peasant Protest and Social Change in Colonial Korea.* Seattle: University of Washington Press, 1996.

Shin, Gi-wook, and Do-hyun Han. "Colonial Corporatism." In *Colonial Modernity in Korea,* edited by Gi-Wook Shin and Michael Robinson, 70–96. Cambridge, MA: Harvard University Asia Center, 1999.

Shin, Michael D. "Nationalist Discourse and Nationalist Institutions in Colonial Chosŏn, 1914–1926." PhD diss., University of Chicago, 2002.

———. "The Specter of Yi Gwangsu: The March 1st Movement and the Nation in Colonial Korea." Unpublished manuscript.

Shin, Susan S. "The Tonghak Movement: From Enlightenment to Revolution." *Korean Studies Forum* 5 (1978–1979): 1–79.

Shin, Yong-Ha. "Landlordism in the Late Yi Dynasty (II)." *Korea Journal* 18, no. 7 (July 1978): 22–29.

Sorenson, Clark. "National Identity and the Category 'Peasant' in Colonial Korea." In *Colonial Modernity in Korea,* edited by Gi-Wook Shin and Michael Robinson, 288–310. Cambridge, MA: Harvard University Asia Center, 1999.

Speer, Robert E. *Report on the Mission in Korea of the Presbyterian Board of Foreign Missions.* New York: Board of Foreign Missions of the Presbyterian Church, USA, 1897.

Suh, Dae-sook, ed. *Documents of Korean Communism.* Princeton, NJ: Princeton University Press, 1970.

Tambiah, Stanley Jeyaraja. *Magic, Science, and the Scope of Rationality.* New York: Cambridge University Press, 1990.

Tanaka, Stefan. *Japan's Orient.* Berkeley: University of California Press, 1995.

Tikhonov, Vladimir. "Han Yongun's Buddhist Socialism in the 1920s and 1930s." *International Journal of Buddhist Thought and Culture* 6 (February 2006): 207–228.

Tillich, Paul. "Estrangement and Sin." In *Paul Tillich: Theologian of the Boundaries,* edited by Mark Kline Taylor, 198–204. Minneapolis: Fortress Press, 1991.

———. *Systematic Theology.* Vol. 1. Chicago: University of Chicago Press, 1951.

———. *Systematic Theology.* Vol. 3. Chicago: University of Chicago Press, 1963.

Tracy, David. *Blessed Rage for Order: The New Pluralism in Theology.* Chicago: University of Chicago Press, 1996.

———. *Plurality and Ambiguity: Hermeneutics, Religion, Hope.* Chicago: University of Chicago Press, 1987.

Underwood, Horace H. *Call of Korea.* New York: Fleming H. Revell, 1908.

———. *Modern Education in Korea.* New York: International Press, 1926.

Van Buskirk, James Dale. *Korea: Land of the Dawn.* New York: Missionary Education Movement of the United States and Canada, 1931.

"The Village Gilds [*sic*] of Korea." *Transactions of the Korea Branch of the Royal Asiatic Society* 4, pt. 2 (1913): 13–44.

Vlastos, Stephen. "Agrarianism without Tradition." In *Mirror of Modernity,* edited by Stephen Vlastos, 74–94. Berkeley: University of California Press, 1998.

Volosinov, V. N. *Marxism and the Philosophy of Language.* Translated by Ladislav Matejka and I. R. Titunik. Cambridge, MA: Harvard University Press, 1973.

Wach, Joachim. *Types of Religious Experience: Christian and Non-Christian.* Chicago: University of Chicago Press, 1951.

Weems, Benjamin. *Reform, Rebellion, and the Heavenly Way.* Tucson: University of Arizona Press, 1964.

Wells, Kenneth. *New God, New Nation.* Honolulu: University of Hawai'i Press, 1990.

Williams, Raymond. *The Country and the City.* New York: Oxford University Press, 1973.

———. *Marxism and Literature.* Oxford: Oxford University Press, 1977.

———. *The Politics of Modernism.* London: Verso Press, 2007.

Yi Tae-jin. *The Dynamics of Confucianism and Modernization in Korean History.* Ithaca, NY: Cornell East Asia Program, 2007.

Young, Carl. "Embracing Modernity: Organizational and Ritual Reform in Ch'ŏndogyo, 1905–1910." *Asian Studies Review* 29 (March 2005): 47–59.

Yu Ch'i-jin. *The Ox*. In *Korean Drama under Japanese Occupation*, translated by Jinhee Kim, 61–128. Dumont, NJ: Homa Sekey Books, 2004.

Zansai, Margherita. *Saving the Nation: Economic Modernity in Republican China*. Chicago: University of Chicago Press, 2006.

Žižek, Slavoj. *The Fragile Absolute—or, Why Is the Christian Legacy Worth Fighting For?* New York: Verso Press, 2000.

INDEX

❧

agrarianism (*nongbonjuui*), 74–75
agriculture: and agrarianism, 74, 117–118;
and agrarian movements outside
Korea, 119; in the Bible, 135–137; and
capitalism, 57, 59–60, 62, 74, 150, 160;
and Ch'ŏndogyo rural movement,
139, 141, 150, 188, 198–199, 218; and
Chosen Christian College, 212–213;
and Chŏson nongminsa (Korean
Peasant Society), 142–146, 180, 198;
commercialization of, 55–56, 58–60,
63, 70, 76, 213; and cooperatives, 166,
169, 180, 185–186, 188, 227; Denmark
as model, 12, 151, 154–156, 160–164,
188; and depression, 67; and
economy, 2, 56–57, 61, 64, 74, 119, 132,
135, 138, 147; and education, 59, 177,
192, 206, 216–218; and estates
(*nonjang*), 62–63; entrepreneurs, 62;
experts on, 1, 61, 63, 121, 135, 162, 171,
202, 213; fairs by YMCA, 204–205;
and five-day markets, 60; and folk
schools, 210, 212; and food
sovereignty, 227; and global markets,
154; idealization of, 74–75, 138; and
Japanese colonial rule, 57, 59, 63,
147–148, 163; and Korean nation,
74–75, 118, 138, 142, 146, 148, 162, 188,
192–193, 213, 221; and March First
Movement of 1919, 117; and
modernity, 3, 13, 18, 147–148, 204, 220,
223; and physiocracy, 144–145; and
practical cultivation schools (*nongŏp
silsu hakkyo*) by Presbyterian Church

Rural Movement (PCRM), 209–210;
and Presbyterian Church Rural
Movement (PCRM), 132–133, 135,
137–138, 150, 177, 188, 196, 202, 218;
production of, 1, 206; and religion,
3, 11–13, 18, 118, 120, 135–137, 193, 211,
220, 223, 227; and Rural Revitalization
Campaign, 59; tariffs on, 58; and
Thirty-Year Plan, 1; and working
class, 150; and Triangular Clubs,
195; and YMCA, 122–123, 128, 150,
161, 163–164, 166–168, 188, 197, 218.
See also cadastral land survey;
Samae (Three Loves) Agricultural
Technology Institute
An Chae-hong, 72–73, 117
An Ch'ang-ho, 52, 73
Anna Davis School, 49
anthropology, 17, 24
Anti-Christian Student Federation, 85
antireligion movements, 2, 80, 89, 140,
207; and Buddhism, 2, 87; in China,
6, 85; and Japanese colonialism, 88;
and Kim San, 88; and bourgeois
nationalists, 10, 86; and leftists, 10,
84–88; and March First Movement,
85, 88; and missionaries, 88; and
National Chŏson People's Movement
Convention, 87; and National Chŏson
Youth Party, 87; at National Youth
Party Convention (1923), 87;
responses to, 10, 19, 79, 98; in the
Soviet Union, 85; in the United
States, 85; and YMCA, 87–88

297

Production Notes for Park / *Building a Heaven on Earth*
Jacket design by Mardee Melton
Text design by Erika Arroyo
   with display type in Warnock Pro and text in Minion Pro
Composition by Westchester Publishing Services
Printing and binding by Sheridan Books, Inc.
Printed on 60 lb. House White Opaque, 466 ppi.